Optimally Irrational

For a long time, economists have assumed that we were cold, self-centred, rational decision makers – so-called *Homo economicus*; the last few decades have shattered this view. The world we live in and the situations we face are of course rich and complex, revealing puzzling aspects of our behaviour. *Optimally Irrational* argues that our improved understanding of human behaviour shows that apparent 'biases' are good solutions to practical problems – that many of the 'flaws' identified by behavioural economics are actually adaptive solutions.

Page delivers an ambitious overview of the literature in behavioural economics and, through the exposition of these flaws and their meaning, presents a sort of unified theory of behaviouralism, cognitive psychology and evolutionary biology. He gathers theoretical and empirical evidence about the causes of behavioural 'biases' and proposes a big picture of what the discipline means for economics.

LIONEL PAGE is a professor of economics and the Director of the Behavioural and Economic Science Cluster at the University of Queensland. He has worked on a wide range of topics in behavioural economics, such as risk preferences, social preferences and strategic behaviour.

D1738710

Optimally Irrational

The Good Reasons We Behave the Way We Do

LIONEL PAGE
University of Queensland

Shaftesbury Road, Cambridge CB2 8EA, United Kingdom

One Liberty Plaza, 20th Floor, New York, NY 10006, USA

477 Williamstown Road, Port Melbourne, VIC 3207, Australia

314–321, 3rd Floor, Plot 3, Splendor Forum, Jasola District Centre,
New Delhi – 110025, India

103 Penang Road, #05–06/07, Visioncrest Commercial, Singapore 238467

Cambridge University Press is part of Cambridge University Press & Assessment,
a department of the University of Cambridge.

We share the University's mission to contribute to society through the pursuit of
education, learning and research at the highest international levels of excellence.

www.cambridge.org
Information on this title: www.cambridge.org/9781009209199

DOI: 10.1017/9781009209175

First published 2023

A catalogue record for this publication is available from the British Library.

ISBN 978-1-009-20919-9   Hardback
ISBN 978-1-009-20920-5   Paperback

Contents

Tables

Figures

Preface

There is something oddly satisfying, and mysterious, in the emergence of mathematical patterns in nature. The geometric patterns made by flowers offer vivid examples of this. Flowers have, in particular, one puzzling characteristic: their number of petals tend to land on the *Fibonacci sequence*. Named after an Italian mathematician from the twelfth century, this sequence starts with the following numbers: 0, 1, 1, 2, 3, 5, 8, 13, 21. In this sequence, each number is the sum of the two previous numbers: $0 + 1 = 1$, $1 + 1 = 2$, $1 + 2 = 3$ .... A study looking at 650 species of plants found that the Fibonacci numbers were present in more than 92% of them (Jean 2009). For example, lily and iris have 3 petals; columbine, delphinium and gilliflower, 5; buttercup and delphinium, 8; garden mum, 13; astra, 21; daisy, 34, 55, 89. How could such patterns emerge in organisms a priori unable to engage in fancy mathematical calculations? The seemingly impossible emergence of mathematical regularities such as the Fibonacci sequence in the random natural world is fascinating and puzzling. It is easy to understand that it has fostered many theories on divine or magic meanings.

To try to understand how such a pattern can emerge, let's imagine for a minute that you are a flower. You have to decide where to place the petals growing around your centre (pistil). For your first petal, it is an easy job. Any location around the centre will do. Let's consider the clock position and let's say that you place your petal at 3. If you want to add more petals, the problem becomes a bit more difficult. Where should you put each additional petal relative to the position of the previous ones? Suppose you opt for a simple solution: to rotate around your pistil with a given angle and place a new petal. Then you can repeat this action once more, using the same angle and place another petal, and so on. In other words, you are considering a simple rule to place your petals: repeatedly rotate around the flower's centre with the same angle and place a new petal each time. Once you have adopted such a rule, your

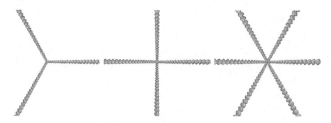

FIGURE P.1. Hypothetical flowers with petals progressively added following rotations of 1/3 circle (right), 1/4 circle (centre) and 1/8 circle (left).

problem is now quite simple: to grow petals, you need to find a good angle, or even better the *best angle* to determine the location of new petals.

What should this angle be? If the angle is half a circle, the second petal is on the other side of the centre. That is good, but the third petal goes on top of the first one, and the fourth petal goes on top of the second, and so on. This rule would not create a balanced flower, but a flower with two "arms", one at the clock position 3 and one at the clock position 9. If the angle is a third of a circle, you will have three "arms" of petals instead of two. The first petal is again on clock position 3, the second is on clock position 7, the third is on clock position 11 and the fourth falls back on position 3, restarting the cycle. Indeed, for any rational number (a number that is the ratio of two natural numbers, e.g., 1/4 or 3/8) the petals will grow in a limited number of arms. Figure P.1 illustrates this fact for rotations of 1/3, 1/4 and 1/8 of a circle.

For irrational numbers (numbers that cannot be written as the ratio of two natural numbers), something interesting happens. The petals grow in arms that are not straight, but form spirals. Intuitively, the number of arms depends on the rational number that best approximates this irrational number.

Let's then ask our question: Among all the possible angles, what is the one that would optimise the location of your petals? Suppose that you want to leave the least space as possible between petals. In other words, you want to pack as many petals as possible in a given amount of space. What rotation should you follow to achieve this goal? Given that rational numbers and approximations of rational numbers create arms, what about a number that is not easily approximated by a rational number, or perhaps even the number that is the *least easily approximated by a rational number*? One such number exists, it is the *Golden ratio*, which is approximately equal to 0.618. This number has been dubbed "the most irrational of the irrational numbers" (Tung 2007, p. 9). Being the hardest to approximate with a rational number, the Golden ratio allows an *optimal* spread of petals around the flower's circle.[1] Figure P.2

---

[1] The optimality of the Golden ratio to pack petals was demonstrated by Ridley (1982).

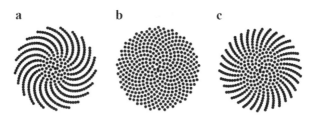

FIGURE P.2. Flower patterns for different rotations close to the golden ratio (0.61803 ≈ 137.5078°): a) 137.3° (left), b) 137.5° (centre), c) 137.6° (right).

illustrates this fact. It shows a sunflower packed with petals through rotations slightly different or equal to 137.5° (0.618 ratio).[2]

There is a deep connection between the Golden ratio and the Fibonacci sequence: the ratio between two consecutive numbers in the Fibonacci sequence is roughly equal to this ratio: 2/3 ≈ 5/8 ≈ 8/13 and this approximation grows closer as we go higher in the sequence. As a consequence, a plant's approximation of the Golden ratio angle will determine the number of arms of petals its flower has and leads this number to be one of the numbers of the Fibonacci sequence (Okabe et al. 2019). The beautiful geometric patterns of flowers that follow the Fibonacci sequence are therefore *optimally irrational*. Flowers are the way they are for a good reason: the rule they follow, even though puzzling, at first sight, is a good answer to the problem they face in nature. Aeons of evolution have found a way for flowers to approximate this optimal solution, to our amazement (Okabe 2015).

The optimal irrationality of flowers is a great metaphor for this book. I will look here at many quirky patterns in human behaviour that may seem mysterious and have often been dubbed "irrational" because it seems hard to find good reasons to explain them. This word does not refer to the same thing for numbers and behaviour. But, in each case, the irrationality sounds like an oddity. The fact that an irrational number like the Golden ratio is found frequently in the natural world seems, at first sight, intriguing and mysterious. In the same way, irrationalities found in human behaviour can seem puzzling and unexplainable. In both cases, though, there is generally a good explanation: plants and humans are the product of evolution. When they do something systematically, the reason is usually that it made them more efficient at solving the problems they faced in their environment.

This is, in a nutshell, the story of this book. I present both a broad overview of the widely discussed "irrational patterns" in human behaviour and how they exist for a good reason. Many economists and psychologists cited in this book have made a similar argument. This book integrates their insights and the work of many other behavioural scientists.

---

[2] This figure is reproduced from Prusinkiewicz and Lindenmayer (2012).

The intended audience is anyone with a deep interest in understanding human behaviour. This book should be easy to read for economists. I hope it will be of interest to them by bringing a rich set of empirical and theoretical works together with a different perspective than what is usually presented in texts on *behavioural economics* (the study of human behaviour using insights from economics and psychology). This book should also be accessible to any social scientist interested in thinking about the deep roots of human behaviour. Finally, this book should be of interest to any person (scientist or not) interested in deciphering the puzzling aspects of human behaviour. I have kept the technicality of the discussions to a minimum.

The literature I cover in this book is vast. My intention is in no way to give an exhaustive presentation of each topic I discuss. Instead, for readers unfamiliar with some of the topics, this book can serve as an introduction, with a specific angle: discussing how we can make sense of the main findings about human decision-making, with an evolutionary perspective. Each chapter contains references to go further into the specific topics. For readers well versed in the topics covered, I hope that I have done justice to the subtlety of the research findings, while at the same time often providing novel insights about the reasons people behave the way they do.

In the process of writing this book, I have benefitted from discussions with many people. Particular thanks go to Jason Collins, David Hirshleifer, Joshua Miller, Moshe Hoffman, Peter Wakker, Itzhak Gilboa, Ken Binmore, Peter Bossaerts, Luis Rayo, two different reading groups at the University of Queensland and at the University of Technology Sydney gathering Vera te Velde, Alice Solda, Matt Peddie, Alex Karakostas, David Smerdon, Bill von Hippel, Changxia Ke, Greg Kubitz, Zachary Breig, Xiqian, Stephanie Tobin, David Butler, Kenan Kaylaci, Ozan, David Goldbaum, Jingjing Zhang, Elif Incekara-Hafalir, Hanlin Lou, Adrian Camilleri, Ben Young, Alexander Caminer and Stephen Cheung. The book is much clearer and richer thanks to their suggestions and comments. Finally, I thank my wife Katie for her understanding, support and encouragements throughout the process of writing this book.

I start the book, in Part I, with a broad introduction on how economists and psychologists have looked at the rationality of human behaviour. After this introduction, I review a broad range of behaviours that have been cast as puzzling or irrational. I gather types of behaviour in two broad categories. In Part II, I look at situations where decisions are made in isolation (e.g., taking a risky gamble). In Part III, I look at situations where decisions involve interactions with other people (e.g., cooperation). I cover a wide range of behaviours throughout. My aim is to get you to see the underlying meaning to the often mysterious ways we seem to live our lives.

PART I

SETTING THE SCENE

I

The Homo Economicus Model

Political economy ... does not treat the whole of man's nature as modified by the social state, nor of the whole conduct of man in society. It is concerned with him solely as a being who desires to possess wealth, and who is capable of judging the comparative efficacy of means for obtaining that end.

—Mill (1836)

Traditionally, economic theory has been based on an assumption that behavior is "rational," ... whereas most psychological and sociological theory insists that behavior is, at least largely, "irrational".

—Rose (1957)

The starting point in economic theory is that the individual or the firm is maximizing something, usually utility or profit. Economists, almost without exception, make constrained maximization the basic building block of any theory.... Few economists are willing to concede that individuals simply do not know what they are doing.

—Lazear (2000)

Summary: Economists have been very successful using a simplified model of human behaviour, the homo economicus model. This model is typically understood as explaining behaviour by the ability and desire to maximise material personal well-being.

In many aspects, economics has been one of the most successful disciplines in the social sciences. Analyses of citation flows show that economists export their results to other social sciences more than they import from them (Fourcade et al. 2015). Economics has greatly influenced other disciplines, such as sociology, political science, law, psychology and even biology, with its tools, results and ways of thinking. This influence, sometimes described as "economic imperialism", is a reflection of the success of its "standard model" of human behaviour, the *homo economicus* (Lazear 2000).

But in spite of its success, this model has been the target of much scorn and rejection in social sciences. Inside the economic discipline, a new field of research, behavioural economics, has grown primarily as a criticism of the homo economicus model. Behavioural economics has enriched economics' understanding of human behaviour by bringing new ideas from psychology into the discipline. However, we should not merely dismiss the standard economic approach, and we should understand its strength, before we look into the insights from behavioural economics.

Imagine yourself as a social scientist trying to understand how and why people do what they do. How easy would it be for you to make sense of the behaviour you observe in society? This task quickly appears daunting. People do a wide range of things. Some things may seem trivial, like deciding what to buy for dinner. But many things look quite complicated, such as political demonstrations or religious rituals. The drivers of human behaviours seem innumerable, from basic desires (e.g., hunger, thirst) to more complex ones (e.g., ambitions, moral feelings). Among the complex drivers of behaviour are those social in nature: people engage in many actions influenced by norms, cultures and traditions. You may be tempted to catalogue the wide range of possible drivers of behaviour to explain what you observe. It would be studying social behaviour like early biologists studied wildlife: simply observing it and labelling it. Your study of behaviour could conclude that: "People follow a norm of honesty in situations A, they express national pride in situations B, they care about their social status in situations C, they have friendship norms in situation D, etc." Such an approach is not useless, but we do not gain an understanding of *why* people act in the way they act. The strength and appeal of the homo economicus model are that, instead, it relies on minimal behavioural assumptions.

In their quest to understand the world, scientists build models that are simplified versions of reality. For example, objects in space are three-dimensional, but physicists often represented them as points (with zero dimension) to study their motions. In the same way, economists and other social scientists build simplified versions of people and societies to study them. How simplified these models should be is an important and non-trivial question. Make a model too simple and it doesn't look enough like reality to help us understand it. Make a model too complex and it is hard to get insights from it. An excellent way to think about models is to compare them to maps: a map should not be too simple in order to help you find your route, but it should also not be overly crammed with details cluttering it.

A key scientific principle to determine how simple a model should be is Occam's razor. This principle states that scientific models should be *as simple as possible* to explain the phenomenon they purport to represent. Isaac

Newton rephrased this principle, saying, "We are to admit no more causes of natural things than such as are both true and sufficient to explain their appearances" (Newton 1687/1999). In that regard, one of the strengths of the homo economicus model is its simplicity: it relies on only a small number of assumptions. And still, in spite of this simplicity, it has proven useful to understand a wide range of behaviour.

To start with, economists make two assumptions about behaviour that are so simple they almost seem innocuous. Think about an agent facing different options to choose from. The first assumption is that the agent knows what he wants (*completeness of preferences*). The second one is that the agent does not have incoherent/conflicting preferences (*transitivity*). For economists, these two assumptions are what characterise "rational" preferences in consumer theory (Mas-Colell et al. 1995). The notion of *rationality* is an important one in economics. In everyday use, it typically means that somebody is sensible/reasonable. Economists define rationality according to a few principles of behaviour, like completeness and transitivity.[1]

Beyond these two core principles, more demanding ones have also been used to characterise a rational agent. Economists, for instance, commonly assume that a rational agent would form beliefs that reflect the strength of the available information using *Bayesian updating*, which specifies how prior beliefs should be updated after the observation of new evidence. When agents use Bayesian updating, their subjective beliefs about the probability of different possible events respect the rules of consistency imposed on measures of probability.[2] In practice, this extended notion of rationality corresponds to the assumption that people know what they want, have internally consistent preferences and beliefs, and adequately use the means available to reach the best option available among the set of possible options.

Note that, defined in that way, "rationality" is not about the kind of things that people want. For instance, this definition of rationality does not say that some things *should* be more desirable for people and some other things *should not*. It only means that people should not be inconsistent in their preferences, whatever these preferences are. In other words, rationality is not about the content of preferences; it is about their coherence. If John decides to go on a cruise with spa and massages while Jane chooses to go on a retreat in the jungle with minimal living standards, neither of them is more or less rational. They just have different preferences.

This definition of rationality can, however, be a bit problematic for the applied economist trying to understand human behaviour in the real world. Any

---

[1] I discuss this notion in length in the Epilogue of the book.

[2] The probability of an event is a measure of its plausibility. Kolmogorov and Bharucha-Reid (1933/2018) defined a set of principles that a probability needs to respect to be a measure in the same way as measures of length, area or volume. These principles imply Bayesian updating.

difference in behaviour observed between people could easily be "explained" as reflecting differences in their inner preferences. For example, if John sacrifices his private life to climb the social ladder and make a lot of money, we could explain his behaviour as being driven by "his preferences". If Jane works on a low salary in an NGO to reduce world poverty, we could also explain her behaviour as being driven by "her preferences". Furthermore, any change in behaviour over time could also be explained by changes in preferences: if Jane quits her NGO job to work in a hedge fund, we could simply say that it is because her preferences have changed. Talking of "preferences" in that way, we have not explained anything. Preferences are, in that sense, a *tautology*: people's preferences are what they choose to do, and they choose to do it because it is their preference.

For the notion of preferences to have some bite when studying behaviour, economists usually impose some restrictions on the likely content of these preferences. Classical economists like John Stuart Mill had assumed that, when studying economic activities, we could consider people's goals as being restricted to increasing their wealth and material well-being. In their famous article "De gustibus non est disputendum" Nobel Prize–winners George Stigler and Gary Becker rephrased this principle with specific types of restrictions on people's preferences. Their first restriction is that preferences are stable over time: "one does not argue over tastes for the same reason that one does not argue over the Rocky Mountains – both are there, will be there next year, too, and are the same to all men". Their second restriction is that people follow their material interest, and behaviour can for this reason mostly be explained by prices and income: "the economist continues to search for differences in prices or incomes to explain any differences or changes in behavior" (Stigler and Becker 1977). These restrictions consist in looking for explanations of human behaviour that rely on the pursuit of material self-interest.

Stigler and Becker acknowledged in their initial article that these restrictions are not necessarily the only valid way to investigate human behaviour. They likely proposed to restrict the possible explanations of human behaviour primarily for methodological reasons. Even if humans do not have stable preferences and even if they do not care only about money, it may be useful for economists to make these simplifying assumptions. The reason is that a scientific approach is stronger when it can explain a lot of facts with only a few clear assumptions, rather than with a lot of different assumptions. In the case of human behaviour, it is more appealing to explain a wide range of observed behaviour with one single motive, material self-interest, rather than to use different types of preferences for the different types of behaviour observed.

The distinction between a methodological assumption (about how the world should be studied) and a substantive assumption (about how the world is) can, however, be blurry. Economists have often taken the selfish assumption as true in practice. This "self-interest theory" has been one of the tenets of the homo economicus model.[3] Behaviours that violate self-interest have, as a consequence, frequently been labelled "irrational".[4]

One of the noticeable benefits of the economists' assumptions about rationality is that they make it possible to model human behaviour formally (i.e., using mathematical models). Under these assumptions, we can characterise how individuals will choose between different options: they will choose the option bringing the highest material benefits among all the possible options available. Modelling behaviour that way makes it possible to make predictions. These predictions can then be tested using observed behaviour.

The selfishness hypothesis is convenient as a methodological approach because it reduces the dimensions the agent cares about when making choices (e.g., agents just care about money). Other secondary hypotheses[5] about the homo economicus have also been very convenient to model people's decisions formally. One of the most important of such hypotheses is that the homo economicus is really good at maths.

To see how an economist would use the good-at-math homo economicus model to represent a human decision process, let's take a simple life situation. Suppose John is looking for a restaurant in an unknown city. He stumbles upon a first restaurant and observes its menu and prices. Should he stop there, or look for another restaurant?

The homo economicus model gives us a well-defined conceptual framework to think about this problem. First, it would depend on John's existing preferences: how hungry he is, how tired of walking he is, what his preferences are for the type of food in this restaurant versus other types of food likely available in the neighbourhood, and how much he is willing to pay for better food. The assumption of completeness of preferences means that, when considering other potential restaurants characterised by distance, price, and type of food, John would be able to determine whether he prefers another restaurant to the one he is facing now. In other words, John is able to make trade-offs between all the different restaurants' characteristics. For example, he knows how much he is willing to walk to save a few dollars off his dinner price and he knows how much he is willing to pay for better quality food. To choose whether

---

[3] It is the case, even though theoretical economists working on the foundations of the discipline in the twentieth century were usually agnostic about the content of preferences (see Chapter 10).

[4] For instance, in early economic experiments, participants were observed acting in ways not always maximising the monetary gains at stake in small games. Instead, many participants seemed to care about other participants' payoffs (see Chapter 10). These findings, replicated in many cultural contexts, have been branded as invalidating the "selfishness axiom" at the heart of the homo economicus model (Henrich et al. 2005).

[5] I use here the term "secondary hypothesis" to emphasise that these are not canonical hypotheses laid out in the core of the homo economicus model. The core hypotheses are easy to find in textbooks and often labelled "axioms". Instead, secondary hypotheses are additional hypotheses that are de facto made by economists without being necessarily laid out explicitly in the textbook descriptions of the homo economicus.

to stop or not John would then use his knowledge about the likely presence and characteristics of other restaurants in the neighbourhood and his decision would simply be the one with the *highest expected subjective satisfaction*: if he is more likely to be satisfied with the present restaurant, he'll go in; if he is more likely to be satisfied with another one, he'll try his luck elsewhere. In the latter case, John may end up being unsuccessful. Having failed to find another restaurant, he may have to come back to the first restaurant. But if he is likely enough to find a good restaurant, the risk will be worth it. The advantage of this economic model is that it will allow the economist to predict how John would make decisions given his utility for food, time and money. Once this solution is determined the economist can then investigate *how this choice is likely to change* if some of these variables change themselves: if the restaurant's food quality is lower, if the price is higher, if the nearest alternative option is closer. Being able to predict how people would make choices given some assumptions on their utility is very appealing compared to the inability to make specific predictions. These predictions can then be investigated with empirical observations. With this approach relying on making predictions and investigating them empirically, economics seems to adopt the scientific approach from natural sciences.

Another convenient hypothesis is to assume that the decision maker's beliefs are correct. Here again, this assumption has some methodological benefits, like the assumptions about stable and selfish preferences. Accurate beliefs constrain the economists' ability to explain any behaviour with just-so stories. If any belief could be assumed, any behaviour could be explained as maximising self interest for some peculiar belief. For instance, suppose you observe that John prefers butter to margarine; you could assume that it is because he believes it is better for his health. If Jane prefers margarine to butter, you may just assume that it is because she has the opposite belief and think that margarine is better for her health.

In that light, assuming that agents have accurate beliefs is a useful methodological constraint. But it can also become an implausible hypothesis when it leads economists to assume that people never have wrong prior beliefs and that they can perfectly aggregate complex and diffuse elements of information to form accurate beliefs. Going back to our restaurant search example, the assumption of correct beliefs would imply that if John believes there is a 50% chance of finding a better restaurant, in 50% of the cases where he looks for a restaurant elsewhere, he will indeed find a better one.

These different hypotheses do not form a strict and unified definition of rationality, and the word "rationality" has had different meanings in economics, depending on the hypotheses it represented. In some cases, it refers only to an individual having complete and coherent preferences. In other cases, it stands for much stronger assumptions about the content of preferences, the accuracy of beliefs and the ability to solve problems. The precise meaning of rationality varies depending on the research area in economics.[6] In its stronger version, the homo economicus is a decision maker who has consistent preferences, is self-interested, is good at maths and has accurate beliefs.

The homo economicus is not the type of human you and I encounter in our daily lives. And many critiques have simply rejected this model as ill-conceived and deeply flawed. They consistently pointed out that economists made unrealistic assumptions about the cognitive ability of individuals. To appreciate this critique, let's consider again the example of John having to choose whether to stop at a given restaurant or to look for another one. Economists using the homo economicus model would study human behaviour assuming that people can find the best approach to solve this problem. Specifically, a homo economicus would find the optimal stopping strategy that sets a rule about when to stop looking for another restaurant and enter into the one they currently face. To find this rule, an economist would spend hours solving complex equations where the best decision depends on the beliefs of the agent about the possibility of finding a better restaurant elsewhere (using some probability distribution), on the cost of searching for another option, and on a utility function that converts menu quality, search time and food price into one single dimension of satisfaction for the agent. Having found the solution for these equations (a stopping rule that maximises the utility of the agent), the economist would write a computer program that runs calculations to find what the agent would do in practice, given the parameters of the situation considered (e.g., search costs, utility for food quality). Depending on the complexity of the problem, the program could take minutes or hours to find the solution. The economist would then use this solution to describe how John would quickly choose whether to stop at a restaurant or not. It is not unreasonable to question the validity of his approach.

Nonetheless, we should not reject the old homo economicus approach offhandedly. This model has been a very successful research program that has led to many great insights about human behaviour and society. The reductionism of the homo economicus model proposes to look for a unifying explanation behind all these different behaviours: people are reasonable and follow their self-interest. Reductionism, explaining many different things with a few principles, is one of the most effective scientific principles. A demonstration of the strength of the homo economicus model is the insights it can give from rejecting the conventional explanations provided by people for their behaviour. People may have interests to put forward some of their motives and to hide others. Politicians are more likely to be elected if they present their motives as "defending the national interest", rather than enjoying the prestige of high

---

[6] I delve into an in-depth discussion of the economic notion of rationality at the end of this book.

office. Pop stars are more likely to be likeable if they claim to sing because they enjoy making their public happy, rather than to make money.[7]

Beyond individual agents, social organisations also build narratives that buttress justifications for their existence. The government "represents the interest of citizens", the police force "protects citizens and decrease crime", and the Church "helps guide believers through their lives". These narratives purposely ignore the possible existence of other motives from the agents within these organisations: politicians can favour making decisions against the national interest to increase their chance of being elected; the police force may sometimes prefer covering up a mistake, even if a crime is left unresolved, or even if it is uncertain whether the person put in prison is actually guilty; some religious representatives may engage in criminal behaviour and be protected by their church.

In their famous book *Freakonomics*, Levitt and Dubner (2005) describe the two Japanese words that reflect this dual reality in society: *honne* (people's true feelings and desires) and *tatemae* (the behaviours and opinions people display in public). By rejecting the official narratives given by society about human behaviour (*tatemae*), the economic approach has been subversive. It has allowed in many instances to get a glance at the real motives of observed behaviour (*honne*). And this has been a major source of insights that has made economics very successful.

Levitt and Dubner give a striking illustration of this fact through the investigation of corruption in the world of sumo wrestling. Sumo is a discipline firmly embedded in a culture of honour and the respect of old traditions. If there is a domain where you would expect economic incentives to be left at the door, it is this one. But winning fights provide prestige and material rewards. Equipped only with his homo economicus model, Levitt asked a simple question, a question that would normally be dismissed in the world of sumo wrestling: Do wrestlers react to material incentives even when these conflict with the traditional norms of the game?

The answer was a resounding "yes". The statistical evidence pointed out the fact that, once sumo wrestlers were already qualified to move up in rank, they sometimes threw away matches they didn't need to win. These matches were frequently lost against opponents who needed to win the match in order to move up in ranks. Noticeably, the result tended to be reversed the next time the same two wrestlers met. It suggested that the wrestler who dearly needed

---

[7] The best illustration of such incentives was given by Paul McCartney recalling sitting down with John Lennon in 1964 to write a new song. "John would be getting an extension on his house or something, and the joke used to be, 'Okay! Today let's write a swimming pool.' It was great motivation. Then in the next three hours, 'Help!' appears from nowhere, you'd suddenly get the idea, this'll be a hit, this is a good one. You become aware what you were doing was making money. Making good money" (Roller 2012).

to win was offered an easy win in the first encounter and repaid the favour in the second encounter. The pattern in the data was not leaving much doubt to it being anything else than a cheating system whereby wrestlers exchange victories for their own benefit. Shortly after the result was made public, it surfaced that exchanges of monetary bribes could also take place around these arranged results. In brief, economists had been able to unveil hidden behaviour in conflict with the official narrative of the sumo wrestling community *because* they had not taken at face value this official narrative. Instead, they had applied their reductionist approach, assuming that material incentives are likely to matter.

Historically, this incisive approach used by economists in the study of human behaviour has been coupled with a rigorous mathematical theoretical framework able to make predictions, and empirical analysis tools that were possibly the best in the social sciences. During the time where the homo economicus model was predominant, the economic methodology and principles influenced and sometimes converted other social sciences.

$$\therefore$$

Whenever we criticise the homo economicus, we should not ignore all the contributions of this "standard model" to economics and other social sciences. I will argue in this book that the way beyond the homo economicus is not to throw away the past insights and just state that people are "irrational". On the contrary, it is the enrichment of this model that often offers the best insights into the rich and complicated patterns of human behaviour.

2

The Psychology of Biases in Human Behaviour

The foundation of political economy and, in general, of every social science, is evidently psychology. A day may come when we shall be able to deduce the laws of social science from the principles of psychology.

—Pareto (1906/2014)

It has been said that man is a rational animal. All my life I have been searching for evidence which could support this.

—Bertrand Russell

The problem is with the model being used by economists, a model that replaces homo sapiens with a fictional creature called homo economicus.

—Thaler (2015)

Summary: When psychologists looked at the assumptions of the homo economicus model, they did not find evidence supporting them. For a while, economists did not pay too much attention. But over the last thirty years, the insights from psychologists have progressively had a profound impact in economics.

Whilst economists were invading other social sciences with their model of rational decision-making, one discipline was resisting. Not just that, it was fighting back. The opposition was coming from psychology. Among social sciences, psychology had some specific advantages, which made it a tougher contender than others. First, it was, besides economics, one of the social sciences with the best set of formal tools to study human behaviour. While economics had developed statistical techniques to study real-world data, psychologists had mastered the methodology of behavioural experiments and the required statistical methods to study experimental data. Psychologists had a very good understanding of the fact that correlation does not mean causation. They were aware that whenever behaviour is observed in a given situation, one needs to be careful not to conclude that the situation caused the behaviour. Indeed, the individual with the observed behaviour could have chosen the situation, or another factor could cause both the situation and the observed behaviour. Many confounding variables can hide behind correlations. Psychologists had, accordingly, developed rigorous methods to identify the factors that influence human behaviour.

When economists claimed to have a theory of human behaviour, psychologists just did what they were good at: they investigated the economic ideas with their experimental methods. This investigation was not initially necessarily driven by disapproval. Indeed, one of the psychologist pioneers to study decision-making, Ward Edwards, was the son of an economist himself. He started by trying to introduce the economic theory of decision-making to psychologists for them to engage with it constructively:[1]

It is easy for a psychologist to point out that an economic man who has the properties discussed above is very unlike a real man. In fact, it is so easy to point this out that psychologists have tended to reject out of hand the theories that result from these assumptions. This isn't fair.... The most useful thing to do with a theory is not to criticize its assumptions but rather to test its theorems. If the theorems fit the data, then the theory has at least heuristic merit. (Edwards 1954)

Psychologists working with and around Ward Edwards started to investigate in depth the behavioural assumptions posed by "armchair economists".[2] What they found surprised them. Economic assumptions about behaviour were not just occasionally violated; they tended to be *systematically* violated, and in specific ways. Such systematic and specific violations suggested that economic assumptions were not good approximations. Instead, people looked to be simply following different behavioural rules altogether (Lichtenstein and Slovic 2006).

Psychologists slowly accumulated a mountain of evidence about human deviations from the rationality assumed by economists. These findings led to conflicts with economists. In 1979, Grether and Plott sounded the alarm about the incoming threat coming from psychology.

---

[1] Ward ended up being the mentor of many leading psychologists in this area, such as Paul Slovic, Sarah Lichtenstein and Amos Tversky, who would likely have received the Nobel Prize in economics with his co-author Daniel Kahneman in 2002 if he had not died early in 1996. See Phillips and von Winterfeldt (2007) for a presentation of Ward Edwards' seminal contribution.

[2] Expression used by the economist and Nobel Prize winner Herbert Simon to describe economists who simply use introspection from the depth of their armchair to design models of human behaviour.

A body of data and theory has been developing within psychology which should be of interest to economists. Taken at face value the data are simply inconsistent with preference theory and have broad implications about research priorities within economics. The inconsistency is deeper than the mere lack of transitivity or even stochastic transitivity. It suggests that no optimization principles of any sort lie behind even the simplest of human choices and that the uniformities in human choice behavior which lie behind market behavior may result from principles which are of a completely different sort from those generally accepted. This paper reports the results of a series of experiments designed to discredit the psychologists' works as applied to economics (Grether and Plott 1979).

Now it was economics that was on the defensive, and it started a required work of fortification. Economists looked critically into the evidence coming from psychology. But this evidence proved more robust than they would have initially expected. Grether and Plott's article is a good case in point. The two economists studied a specific type of deviation called "preference reversal", the fact that people can change their preferences between two options when asked about their preference in different ways.[3] To their surprise, they found a confirmation of the existence of this phenomenon using different experimental approaches. They nonetheless maintained a defense of the economic approach: "The fact that preference theory and related theories of optimization are subject to exception does not mean that they should be discarded." Like them, most economists initially clung to the homo economicus assumptions.

The tide of evidence coming from psychology was however eventually going to break the dam and lead to the emergence of new theories. The same year, in 1979, Kahneman and Tversky published in *Econometrica* what is now the second most cited economic article of all time. In this article, they presented the evidence for a number of systematic deviations to the standard economic theory of decision and proposed an alternative model, "prospect theory", which explains many deviations with a few principles (e.g., loss aversion, distortion of subjective probabilities). It was the start of what would become the "behavioural revolution" in economics.

Over the years, the literature in the economics and psychology of decision-making – now known as "behavioural economics" – has become very large. The list of deviations from the homo economicus has grown with it. A long list of "biases" and puzzling behavioural patterns has progressively been identified and labelled by behavioural economists. In this book, I will give an overview of a wide range of such behavioural patterns. The following is a short description of the topics I will cover in the different chapters. They cover the main themes

---

[3] A body of research initiated by Lichtenstein and Slovic (1971) has found that people can often switch their preferences between two simple gambles such as 10% chance of winning $20 versus 50% chance of winning $4. People tend to prefer the gamble with the highest probability when asked the one they prefer, but they are willing to pay more to play the one with the highest reward.

from the behavioural economic literature and go a bit beyond in some cases, such as in Chapters 12 and 13.

Rules of thumb and gut feeling (Chapter 5). The homo economicus model assumed that people find the best solution to their problems. But it seems that people often follow rules of thumb – also called heuristics – when making decisions instead of calculating the costs and benefits of every option. It can lead them to make mistakes, and it is seen as one of the typical examples of deviation from economic rationality.

Reference-dependence and loss aversion (Chapter 6). People's subjective satisfaction is not a reflection of the absolute level of the desirable things they have (e.g., income, wealth). Instead, people's satisfaction tends to be *relative* to a reference level they seem to compare their outcome to. For instance, people tend to perceive their given level of income as satisfying if it is above a *reference point* they compare it to, and they would find this same level of income as frustrating if their reference point was much higher. This reference-dependence has been found to play a very substantial role in how people value the options they face when making decisions. In particular, people tend to avoid "losses" relative to their reference points more than they appreciate "gains".

Overweighting of the probabilities of extreme outcomes (Chapter 7). When making decisions between risky prospects, people seem to overweight the probabilities of extreme outcomes. They behave as if these events are more likely than they actually are.

Randomness of choices (Chapter 8). People frequently make different decisions when they are asked to choose between the same options several times. Their preferences seem in part random. It suggests that they either make mistakes or don't know exactly what they want.

Present bias (Chapter 9). When making choices that will impact their future, people tend to overly favour their present satisfaction. They adopt behaviour today that will come at a cost tomorrow (e.g., eating unhealthily, smoking). Individuals themselves seem to disapprove this present bias even though they often struggle to eliminate it. As a result, they display inconsistencies in preferences about how to allocate personal costs and benefits over time. These situations have provided some of the most discussed examples of failures of the homo economicus.

Kindness and social preferences (Chapter 10). Unlike what the selfishness assumption suggests, people have been found to be willing to sacrifice their own well-being for others. People also seem to care about other intentions and about principles of good behaviour in a way that is quite foreign to the standard homo economicus model.

Emotions and losing one's control (Chapter 11). Unlike the cold, rational person assumed by economists, people often lose their self-control in situations where they are overwhelmed by emotions. It is the case when people are under the influence either of anger or love. Since antiquity, thinkers have characterised these losses of self-control as a failure of reason to rein in irrational passions.

Social identity (Chapter 12). In many situations people seem to experience strong feelings of a shared purpose with members of a common group. In some cases they can also feel strong antagonistic feelings towards members of other groups. Such feelings play an important role in groups as different as national populations, political parties, religious groups, and sport clubs supporters. These group feelings and their influence on behaviour is not explained by the standard homo economicus model.

Indirect speech, ambiguity and innuendos (Chapter 13). Even though language can be used to convey information and beliefs in elaborate ways, people frequently opt to communicate in ambiguous ways. They do not say exactly what they want or what they think. And they often prefer to suggest it to others using veiled messages and innuendos. It is one of the most puzzling aspects of human communication.

Overconfidence and self-deception (Chapter 14). One of the most well-known deviations from having accurate beliefs on reality is that people tend to think that they are better than they are. These misbeliefs lead to costly mistakes, and *overconfidence* is regularly cited as one of the classical failures of the homo economicus model to reflect actual human behaviour.

∴

The idea that individuals are poor decision makers has progressively undermined the homo economicus model as a credible model to understand and predict human behaviour. The criticism of economic assumptions had initially started from outside by psychologists. Economists ignored them first, then they fought them back, but, in the end, this strand of research led to a profound change in how economics studies human behaviour.

3

The Logic of a Scientific Revolution in Economics

Scientific revolutions are inaugurated by a growing sense ... that an existing paradigm has ceased to function adequately in the exploration of an aspect of nature to which that paradigm itself had previously led the way.
—Kuhn (1962/2012, p. ix)

For years, many economists strongly resisted the call to base their models on more accurate characterizations of human behavior. But thanks to an influx of creative young economists who have been willing take some risks and break with the traditional ways of doing economics, the dream of an enriched version of economic theory is being realized. The field has become known as "behavioral economics."
—Thaler (2015)

Summary: The way science works differs slightly from the ideal view of a succession of Eureka moments. Big changes in scientific theories are rare. When changes happen, it takes some time to replace old ideas with a consistent set of new ideas. With the behavioural revolution, the old homo economicus model has largely been abandoned, but we do not have a clear replacement yet.

For non-scientists, science is often seen as an enterprise to find the *truth*. In the course of history, scientists have discovered many things that were previously ignored such as the place of Earth in the universe or the DNA molecule that is present in all living organisms we know of. But defining science that way is somewhat problematic. The new discoveries of today disconfirm the scientific views from yesterday. By extension, the scientific views from today may be disconfirmed by scientists from tomorrow. There is no guarantee that scientific ideas held today are the truth. Even if they are, we may never know for sure that they won't be disproven later.

The philosopher Karl Popper resolved this problem with his influential definition of science: it is a set of assertions that are falsifiable (can be proven wrong) but that have not been proven wrong yet (Popper 1945/2005). In that view, the criticism of existing theories with evidence is central to how science works. Science is required to be open to debates, to be a forum where ideas are compared and tested. It should be a challenging public arena where the prevailing rule is the "survival of the fittest": good ideas survive, and bad ideas are replaced by better ones (Popper 1948).

Unfortunately, this view of science may be a bit too optimistic. Scientists are humans and humans are not impartial judges of the ideas they hold. They can become besotted with some of their ideas. They can have conflicts of interest, in particular, when their social status depends on ideas they have defended in the past.[1]

It may be too optimistic to hope that scientists will simply sit down and accept the best views around and not tend to unduly stick to their own ideas. Retelling a scientific debate he was part of, the physicist Max Planck famously described an alternative vision of how science really works: "A new scientific truth does not triumph by convincing its opponents and making them see the light, but rather because its opponents eventually die, and a new generation grows up that is familiar with it" (Planck 1950, pp. 33–34).

Planck's vision is certainly too pessimistic, but his cynicism certainly has some truth in it. Science is not just a pure affair of ideas; it is also a human affair. New ideas may fail to win over a field when a generation of scientists has built their convictions and careers on old theories. It is, however, not just a matter of power and politics. Understanding how science works and how scientific knowledge progresses requires us to understand how these human realities interplay with the relative strengths of ideas.

In his book *The Structure of Scientific Revolution*, Kuhn (1962/2012) proposes another insightful vision of how science works in practice. Popular representations often depict scientists with a figure like Albert Einstein, peering thoughtfully into a complex problem until the occurrence of a Eureka moment,[2] when clarity is suddenly reached and new knowledge is generated. But Kuhn explains that the reality of scientific research is actually more mundane and underwhelming. Most of the time, scientists resolve only small problems. If scientific research was compared to the activity of solving a jigsaw puzzle with thousands of pieces, the activity of a scientist would not be to masterfully guess

[1] The social status of scientists is often associated with the ideas they have put forward in the past. If such ideas are proven invalid, it would impact negatively the recognition they receive.

[2] It is said that the Greek expression "Eureka," "I have found it," was stated loudly by mathematician Archimedes when, while taking a bath, he understood that a body submerged displaces a volume of water equivalent to its own.

the big picture of the puzzle, but rather it would be to solve how to put one specific piece in a tiny little corner of the puzzle.

Kuhn calls this way of doing science the *normal science*. When science is normal, the activity of a scientist is heavily determined by the whole jigsaw puzzle, which prescribes the little corners left to solve and the method to investigate whether a piece fits there. Researchers do not spend most of their time thinking about big and fundamental questions. Rather, they focus on finding precise answers to specific issues. Their activity is heavily constrained by what other scientists think about the questions that should be investigated and the valid methods to do so. The set of accepted problems and methods constitutes what Kuhn calls a *paradigm*.

Kuhn's big insight is that science is fundamentally a social activity. Researchers do not build knowledge in a vacuum. Instead, they work within the framework of what other scientists believe at a time. This framework, or paradigm, faces, at any moment in time, many unanswered questions. Scientists' daily job consists primarily in closing these questions by showing that the paradigm works in this particular case. The main activity of a scientist is not to test whether the paradigm is the right way to answer a question. Instead, it is to find how it is possible to answer the question within the paradigm. In Kuhn's world, you can have as many Eureka moments as you want, but if you are not solving a problem other scientists consider important, you'll just be considered a strange fellow by other scientists.

This "normal" state of science does not cover, however, all scientific activity for Kuhn. The history of scientific fields typically features a time in the past when separate schools of thoughts produced different and incompatible visions of the world. These visions were often partly overlapping, partly inconsistent, and there was no cumulative progress of knowledge as seen in modern science.[3] At some point, though, one way of explaining the world overtook the others and united the field of research around common ideas. That is when science started its normal state.

The typical example of this process is how Newtonian principles came to become the foundation of classical mechanics. After Newton's discoveries, the diverse schools of thought trying to explain the movements of bodies on Earth and in the sky progressively disappeared. In their place a unified field of physics emerged. With Newtonian physics, scientists started to look for the

---

[3] Discussing the example of physical optics, Kuhn writes: "Those men were scientists. Yet anyone examining a survey of physical optics before Newton may well conclude that … the net result of their activity was something less than science. Being able to take no common body of belief for granted, each writer on physical optics felt forced to build his field anew from its foundations. In doing so, his choice of supporting observation and experiment was relatively free, for there was no standard set of methods or of phenomena that every optical writer felt forced to employ and explain" (Kuhn 1962/2012, p. 13).

specific questions laid out by their theoretical framework; they entered normal scientific activity. In normal science, knowledge becomes cumulative because new scientists do not try to rebuild knowledge from first principles. Instead, they take for granted the results and methods of other scientists in the field and aim to contribute small pieces of knowledge within this shared paradigm.

Normal science is the usual state of modern science. It is what most young scientists nowadays experience when entering doctoral studies. However, science does not stay normal forever. Over time, a paradigm can start being questioned. In fact, there are always unresolved tensions during a normal phase of science: some questions that are being investigated and are still unanswered. As long as these questions find answers within a reasonable amount of time, leaving the place to new questions, scientists can be confident in their paradigm. They can assume that whenever a new question arises, it is only a matter of time before it is answered. But sometimes, some questions resist investigation longer than expected; they become *anomalies*. This situation is not necessarily a problem in and of itself. Scientific fields can happily live with a few resisting anomalies. Scientists regularly assume that these are just difficult problems that will, eventually, be resolved at some point. But sometimes, a problem not only resists but grows as researchers try to chip at it. Multiple explanations are proposed that are found to fail, one by one, at answering the question. Then this question can point to other related questions that are unresolved, and so on. In that case, the tension created by these anomalies can grow to the point where doubts may arise about the ability of the paradigm to answer them.

It is in such situations that something dramatic can happen: the shared faith in the scientific paradigm can shatter. Kuhn famously called the process that then unfolds a *scientific revolution*: "scientific revolutions are ... those non-cumulative developmental episodes in which an older paradigm is replaced in whole or in part by an incompatible new one" (Kuhn 1962/2012, p. 92). Bold scientists start proposing new radical theories, turning previous ones on their heads. Instead of staying on the fringes of the scientific discussions, these radical ideas become commonplace in the main scientific journals and conferences. They lead to new empirical tests to investigate novel predictions that would support alternative theories to the prevailing, but ailing, paradigm. Different schools of thought start competing for their conceptual frameworks to become the new paradigm in the discipline. Eventually, one school triumphs and lays the new foundations of the field.

The best way to describe this phenomenon is, once again, to look back at the example of physics. Armed with Newtonian laws of physics, classical mechanics became a tremendously successful paradigm, able to explain and predict celestial bodies' trajectories as well as terrestrial objects' movements. One can easily imagine the mindset of a physicist towards the end of the nineteenth century: confidently chipping away at the universe's mysteries with a simple and elegant theoretical framework and rigorous empirical methods.

A tension, though, was still there. Many questions were left unanswered. One of them, in particular, was resisting investigation. While Newtonian mechanics was able to predict the motions of most planets very precisely, Mercury was exhibiting unexplained anomalies in its orbit around the Sun. As scientists commonly do when faced with unresolved questions, they initially did not question their paradigm. They assumed that an answer would naturally be found using the laws of Newtonian mechanics. Perhaps some calculations were wrong and there was actually no real anomaly in the first place. Perhaps there was a hidden celestial body, yet to be found, that was exerting a gravitational pull on Mercury. These alternative explanations were carefully investigated. But, over time, the anomalies in Mercury's orbit resisted the attempts to find a conventional explanation within the prevailing paradigm.

In short, Newtonian physics was being tested, and it was failing the test. The solution was going to come with the most famous of all scientific revolutions: the advent of the theory of general relativity proposed by Albert Einstein, a German clerk in the Swiss Patent Office. Einstein proposed a radically different view of the universe than Newtonian physics. In the process, he showed that Newton's equations are an approximation of the "true" equations (those equations that this new theoretical framework posits as being the true equations required to understand motion in space and time). Most of the time, the differences in predictions between Newton's and Einstein's equations are so small that they are unnoticeable. But, in some cases, Newton's and Einstein's theories lead to observable and predictable differences. It is the case for Mercury's orbit. The planet's proximity to the Sun was leading to gravitational effects slightly different from those predicted by Newtonian mechanics.

Kuhn's vision of how scientists change their mind offers a compromise between the optimist vision of Popper and the ironical cynicism of Planck: "Because scientists are reasonable men, one or another argument will ultimately persuade many of them. But there is no single argument that can or should persuade them all. Rather than a single group conversion, what occurs is an increasing shift in the distribution of professional allegiances" (Kuhn 1962/2012, p. 158).

Kuhn's model of science and how it changes helps us understand the history of the scientific debate in the economics and psychology of decision-making. For decades, the homo economicus model provided a paradigm for economics to investigate human behaviour. With a few behavioural principles and a mathematical approach to the study of human decisions, it was able to explain a wide range of individual and social behaviour. True, some patterns of behaviour were left unexplained, but they were just seen as residual issues, left to be resolved at a later point in time.

These residual issues were, for instance, the existence of altruistic and reciprocal behaviour, or the fact that people make mistakes in their decisions in some predictable ways. But like the orbit of Mercury, these issues did not go away over time. Evidence about the existence of *anomalies* accumulated, led from outside by psychologists and from inside by experimental economists. Progressively, a behavioural revolution took place: new theories of behaviour abandoning the homo economicus principles appeared. These new theories assumed that people care about others, that they can be unsure about what they want, that they can make poor decisions in the present and regret them in the future, and so on.

After two decades of resistance, the revolution swept quickly through economics. In 2002, Daniel Kahneman, a psychologist, received the Nobel Prize in economics for his work on decision-making. Since then, three more behavioural economists have earned this distinction: Alvin Roth (2012), Robert Shiller (2013) and Richard Thaler (2017). These three recipients have all been presidents of the American Economic Association. Behavioural economists are now commonly hired by governments and private firms to solve problems using their understanding of how people really behave.

Forty years after the now classical paper by Kahneman and Tversky in *Econometrica*, the changes it initiated have led to an overhaul of how economists understand and study human behaviour. Twenty years ago, the label "behavioural economist" referred to rebels in strife with their mainstream colleagues. Today, in younger cohorts of economists, it is hard to identify who is a "behavioural economist". Economists now seamlessly blend insights from behavioural economics in their different fields such as labour economics, development economics and industrial organisation. Behavioural ideas are endorsed to such an extent that it can be said that economics has entered a behavioural synthesis (Angner 2019).[4]

This short history is what a scientific success story looks like. As a researcher in behavioural economics who started in the early 2000s, I have witnessed the last phase of this revolution when behavioural economics quickly changed its status from a critical sub-field on the fringes of economics to a leading field of research at the centre of the discipline. For the behavioural economists involved in this evolution it has definitely been an exciting experience.

However, science does not stop. Behavioural economics has transformed economics; it is now time to ask, "What next?" The behavioural revolution has taken the form described by Kuhn: a burgeoning of new theories, while the old paradigm progressively faded away. We now have new theories about social preferences, risk preferences, time preferences, strategic thinking, and so on. The excitement of a scientific revolution is, however, not the normal way science works. Eventually, economics has to go back to working with a new paradigm and solve small problems. The multitude of theories, often unrelated to each other, has to be replaced or underpinned by a unifying

---

[4] As a reflection of this success, Thaler (2016) predicts that the term "behavioural economics" may eventually disappear as all economics becomes behavioural.

theoretical framework that will become the new scientific paradigm within which economists can work.

There is a growing feeling in economics that a unifying theoretical framework is missing. Behavioural economics is not constituted of a set of ideas coherently inserted in an overarching framework. It is rather a collection of piecewise theories explaining different parts of human behaviour. For some behaviour, it is not even clear that behavioural economics has theories; rather, it has labels such as "biases" or "effects" that are used to describe a deviation from the homo economicus model without giving insights into why and how this deviation occurs. This "atheoretical style" does not allow behavioural economics to transform its revolution into a shift to a new paradigm (Spiegler 2019). After having subverted the old order, it is time for economists to build again an understanding of human behaviour based on a unified framework.

It is the central theme of this book that evolutionary theory naturally provides this unifying framework. Humans are the product of aeons of evolution. Therefore, it makes sense to look at evolutionary mechanisms to build a unifying theory of human behaviour. Whenever a consistent pattern is observed in human behaviour, it is reasonable to think that there are good reasons for it and that it may have been selected by evolution. Noticeably, given that both economics and evolutionary theory have been shaped as a study of optimal choices, the building of such an evolutionary foundation can easily be done while keeping many of the current tools and insights from economics.

∴

In this book, I will review a wide range of behaviour that has defied the predictions of the homo economicus model and how evolutionary theory can explain these behaviours in a unified theoretical framework. Before I do so, the next section will present the broad principles of such a framework.

4

Evolution and the Logic of Optimisation

Nothing in biology makes sense except in the light of evolution
—Dobzhansky (1973)

In the case of wing form, then, we want to understand why selection has favoured particular phenotypes. The appropriate mathematical tool is optimisation theory. We are faced with the problem of deciding what particular features (e.g. a high lift: drag ratio, a small turning circle) contribute to fitness, but not with the special difficulties which arise when success depends on what others are doing. It is in the latter context that game theory becomes relevant.
—Maynard Smith (1982, p. 1)

The evolutionary high ground cannot be approached hastily. Even the most difficult problems can be solved, and even the most precipitous heights can be scaled, if only a slow, gradual, step-by-step pathway can be found.
—Dawkins (1997)

Summary: An evolutionary perspective should help us understand why people behave the way they do. To a great extent, evolutionary theory and economics address similar problems and use similar conceptual tools. The search for a unified approach to explain human behaviour needs to rely on an understanding of its evolutionary roots.

Behavioural economics has first been hugely successful as a sub-discipline in economics. Beyond economics, it has then become a recognised name in the public sphere: bestsellers sold in airports, policy units created by government agencies and even movie appearances.[1] When presented to the public,

---

[1] See Richard Thaler's cameo appearance as himself in the movie *The Big Short*, which was dedicated to the explanation of the causes of the 2008 financial crisis.

behavioural economics is most often described as being the part of economics that studies how people make decisions, showing that they tend to make *mistakes*. This is sometimes summarised as saying that behavioural economics finds that people are "predictably irrational".[2]

4.1 IF WE ARE SO DUMB, HOW DID WE MAKE IT HERE?

This characterisation of the progress of our understanding of human behaviour is somewhat unsatisfying. Saying that behavioural economists have shown that people are "irrational" cannot be accepted as the end of a scientific road. It is, in short, saying that people's actions do not make sense. The purpose of scientists is to make sense of what they study. When economists study human behaviour, they cannot be satisfied with a description of it as nonsensical (even if in some predictable ways). As behavioural scientists, economists must aim to explain why people behave the way they do (rather than in one of the innumerable other ways we could imagine).

Besides, the idea that people behave largely in nonsensical ways is obviously wrong. If humans were very poor at making decisions, one would have to wonder how we can even be here to have this discussion. As Richard Dawkins pointed out, if we are here now, it is because we are the descendants of a long line of ancestors who were successful at surviving, finding a mate and producing offspring (2008).[3] To do so, they had to use resources to give the required energy to their body to survive; they had to come on top in contests that could be deadly; they had to find a mate; they had to produce offspring and provide the support for them to have the best chance of being successful in the next generation.

This line of ancestors successful at surviving and reproducing does not start with primates; in its broadest sense, it goes back to the single-cell organisms, which appeared 3 billion years ago. Due to genetic variations and mutations, new designs appeared in every generation and on average the best ones at solving the challenges described above were selected. This process is long and imperfect, but it produced the incredible complexity of the biological machinery that structures our bodies, starting from the simplest cells, which are marvellous biological machines in themselves, to our human brain, which is one of the most complex structures we know in the universe (Ransford 2015).

[2] This term, which was the title of a book by Dan Ariely, was also used to describe the award of the Nobel Prize to Richard Thaler for "his pioneering work in establishing that people are predictably irrational" (*New York Times*, 9 October 2017, "Nobel in economics is awarded to Richard Thaler").

[3] "Thousands of our ancestors' contemporaries failed in all these respects, but not a single solitary one of our ancestors failed in any of them" (Dawkins 2008).

The world out there is a tough place, and bad decisions are costly. It would be surprising if the long and unforgiving selection process of evolution produced people who make nonsensical decisions. A famous quip at financial analysts who sell their investment advice for a fee goes, "If you are so smart, why aren't you rich?" Similarly, one could answer to a behavioural economist: "If I am so dumb, why am I here"?

Behavioural economists have successfully shown that people do not behave in the way predicted by the old homo economicus model. But cataloguing the many ways in which people deviate from this model cannot be the ultimate aim of economics. We have to look for a better model of how people actually behave and for an understanding of why they behave this way. In this book, I show that there are good reasons behind many of our behaviours that may seem puzzling at first sight. These good reasons often come from evolutionary theory, which provides a natural framework to unify our understanding of behaviour.[4] I present in this chapter a short introduction to the key concepts of evolutionary theory. I also discuss how these can be relevant to understanding behaviour.

4.2 WHAT IS EVOLUTION?

The key insight from Charles Darwin (1859) in the *Origin of Species* was that the variety of organisms on Earth could be explained, without design, by a process of *natural selection*. Natural selection is often described as the "survival of the fittest", an expression coined by the sociologist Spencer (1864) after reading Darwin's work. This expression seems intuitive. It evokes the view of animals trying to escape predators, with only the healthiest, quickest, smartest ones to survive. As a definition of natural selection, it is, however, problematic. It does not define "fitness". If fitness is understood as the ability to survive in one's environment, then the definition is a tautology and says the same thing twice: natural selection is the survival of those who are able to survive.

In evolutionary theory, the term "fitness" actually does not refer to the ability of an organism to survive. It represents its *reproductive success*, or, to simplify, its number of offspring. If organisms have some characteristics leading them to leave more offspring, they have, on average, relatively more descendants. The characteristics of these organisms become progressively more prevalent in the population. From generation to generation, the characteristics of a population evolve. Natural selection tends to make organisms more efficient at surviving and reproducing.

---

4 This book is not the first one to make this suggestion. See the contributions by Anderson (1990), Jones (2000), Gintis (2007), Haselton et al. (2009), Okasha and Binmore (2012), Aumann (2019) and Lieder and Griffiths (2020).

Natural selection exerts pressure on the organism's *phenotype*. This term refers both to the physical aspect of the organism and to its behaviour.[5] To survive and reproduce, organisms need to find resources (food, shelter) and avoid becoming a resource for other organisms (predators, parasites and germs). This pressure explains the progressive *adaptation* of physical characteristics to the local environment. A good example is colour, which is key to minimise visibility both for predators (grizzly bears are brown, polar bears are white) and for prey (common hares are brown, arctic hares are white).[6]

In addition to natural selection, there is something else playing a role in the evolution process for organisms with sexual reproduction: producing offspring requires finding a mate. The characteristics of the chosen mate are important. They influence the characteristics of the offspring and thus the opportunity for these offspring to have offspring themselves.[7] Organisms increase their fitness when finding mates with more desirable characteristics. And, as consequence, the ability to find a mate with desirable characteristics becomes itself a desirable characteristic that is selected for. This *sexual selection* creates an evolutionary pressure on the ability of organisms to compete with other organisms from the same sex and convince organisms from the other sex to select them as mates.[8]

Due to natural and sexual selection, an evolutionary pressure exists on organisms' decision-making. Decision-making processes that are conducive to survival and reproduction tend to be selected positively. Decision-making processes that fail to be fitness-inducing tend to be selected negatively.

4.3 EVOLUTION AND THE MAXIMISATION OF FITNESS

I have just discussed the process of evolution as if it selects for organisms that maximise their *individual fitness*. Things are, however, a bit more complicated. The information about the organism's phenotype (such as the colour of its fur) is encoded in its genes. Through reproduction, an organism transmits these genes (or some of these genes) to the next generation. The genes that contribute to making an organism more successful at surviving and reproducing will tend

---

[5] The phenotype is largely determined by the organism's *genotype*, that is, its genes. The surrounding environment also plays a role: a given genotype can lead to different phenotypes in different environments.

[6] Natural selection can sometimes happen quickly when changes in the environment have large effects on organisms' chances of survival. Recent research, for instance, found that following hurricanes in the Caribbean, some species of lizards have developed larger toe pads that give them better grip to remain on trees in situations of high-speed winds (Donihue et al. 2020).

[7] While fitness is commonly discussed in terms of offspring in the next generation, it has to be conceived as the future offspring over many generations.

[8] Sexual selection can select for traits that have nothing to do the adaptation to a given environment. Strange traits and physiological features used in courting displays are a typical example (e.g., peacocks' tails). I'll discuss the reasons for such traits to be selected using *signalling theory* in Chapter 13.

to be selected. For that reason, the selection can be thought to be at the level of the genes, not at the level of the individual (Dawkins 1976).

You may wonder: if individuals are characterised by their genes, isn't it the same to say that evolution selects individuals who maximise their personal fitness, or genes that increase their chance of being reproduced? Actually, we have learned that it is not the same. A conflict between the organism's fitness and its genes' fitness can arise when an organism shares the same genes as other organisms. In that case, an individual-centred approach would require the organism to maximise its personal fitness. In comparison, a gene-centred approach can explain why the organism may accept to sacrifice some of its personal fitness to increase the fitness of other organisms with the same genes. This argument explains the existence of *altruism* towards close relatives.

A striking example is the case of eusocial insects like bees or ants. They live in colonies of sisters closely related genetically.[9] Individuals in these colonies are willing to sacrifice themselves for others. Most ants or bees are infertile and dedicate their life only to the development of the colony. In case of attack by other animals, the defence of the colony can rely on some members dying on purpose, like the bees who die after stinging their enemies.

This altruism towards kin is also observed in humans. The saying "blood is thicker than water" reflects the fact that members of a family are linked by special bonds that are stronger than typical relationships with non-family members. A parent may be willing to make great sacrifice for a child, and even a sibling may make large sacrifices for another sibling. People are much more likely to risk their lives for other members of their family than for people they are not related to. The notion of *inclusive fitness* proposed by Hamilton (1963) addresses this issue by adding to an organism's personal fitness, the indirect fitness it gets via the personal fitness of its close relatives like siblings and cousins. This notion aims to bridge the gap between the individual-centred and gene-centred approach.

These considerations show that the suggestion that evolution pushes towards fitness maximisation is not as simple as it is often described. The idea makes sense, but the unit to consider will not always be the organism. For most of the topics covered in this book, restricting the discussion to an individual-centred approach will be useful enough. Most of the topics in behavioural economics are (to the extent we understand them) primarily related not to relationships between kin but to individuals making decisions alone or individuals interacting with strangers. In such cases, we can assume that an individual-centred perspective is good enough. When I discuss evolutionary

---

[9] Ants are in a way "supersisters" (Hamilton 1964). They are haplodiploid, which means that only females develop from fertilised eggs, while males develop from unfertilised eggs. As a consequence, males have only half the number of chromosomes as females and they transmit all these chromosomes to their offspring. Females share all of their father's genes and 50% of their mother's genes. As a result, they share on average 75% of their genes and are relatively much more genetically related than sisters in most species.

explanations, I will focus on how evolution would select for behaviours that maximise the fitness of the individual.[10]

4.4 AN IMPERFECT OPTIMISATION PROCESS

Throughout this book, I will stress why seemingly puzzling patterns of behaviour likely exist for good reasons. I will often present explanations where such behaviour can be understood as approximating optimal solutions to the problems human face. I think it is a very fruitful perspective to understand behaviour, and I hope this book will make this point clear. I should, however, stress that evolution can only be, at best, an imperfect optimisation process. There are several reasons why we should not expect decision-making processes to be always perfectly adapted to the organism's environment. I give here a brief overview of them.

Biological Constraints
Evolution optimises decision-making processes *under biological constraints*. For instance, perceiving, processing and storing information is costly. These constraints mean that an ideal organism design is likely unreachable. It is illusory to expect organisms to solve problems as if they had access to the solution that would be reached by a supercomputer. The evolution process pushes towards optimal designs under these biological constraints. It can lead to second-best solutions that differ substantially from the ideally optimal solutions.

Incremental Steps
A fundamental characteristic of evolution is that it is an *incremental optimisation* process that can creep towards optimal designs only through small steps. It can therefore get stuck on local optima: designs that are the best among similar designs, but that are not the best overall. The specific course of history may push evolution on the road of some designs that will never be the best possible. Once on this road, it may be unlikely for evolution to lead to large jumps towards very different designs that are actually better. The classic metaphor here is to think of evolution as a climber trying to go up in a mountainous range. As a climber starts going up, they may end up climbing on a peak that is not the highest one. To find the right path to the highest peak may then require first a long detour back through a valley. As evolution can make only small steps upward, it can stay stuck on a small peak. This fact is illustrated by evolutionary

---

[10] The notion of inclusive fitness plays an important role in evolutionary biology to explain the emergence of altruism between kin. In Chapter 10, I look at altruistic and reciprocal behaviour. Since economists have primarily been puzzled by the existence of such behaviour between unrelated individuals, this chapter will also take an individual-centred perspective and leave aside the (important) considerations about altruism between kin.

FIGURE 4.1. "Kludged" flat fish.

kludges: situations where an evolutionary adaptation has taken the form of a clumsy tweak on an existing design, rather than a thoroughly new and perfect design (Marcus 2009; Ely 2011). Figure 4.1 gives an example of kludged design, a flatfish that visibly evolved from non-flat ancestors.[11]

Robustness versus Efficiency Trade-Off

Evolution is also imperfect because organisms may face different types of environments. An ideal design in one environment may be poorly adapted to other environments. Optimisation will thus require a *trade-off between efficiency* (how well an organism is adapted to a given environment) *and robustness* (how well an organism fares across different types of environments).

It is easy to explain this problem with a simple example. Imagine you have to build a racing car. Your car will have to take part in many future races. Races vary in characteristics. Some tracks have narrow bends, while others have mostly long stretches and broad turns. Some races tend to be in dry conditions, others during a rainy season. Let's assume you can build the car that would perform best overall on these different tracks. Given the differences between tracks, you face trade-offs: it is impossible to make a car that is best at everything. If you design a car that is best designed for rainy conditions, it will perform relatively less well on a dry track than a car specifically designed for dry conditions.

---

[11] This picture comes from a presentation from Jeffrey Ely. Richard Dawkins described the reason for the asymmetric shape of such fish (Dawkins 1997). Flatfish became so because their ancestors progressively spent more time hiding flat on the floor of the sea. While skates' and rays' ancestors were already somewhat flat and could lie on their belly, plaices' and soles' ancestors were deep-bodied blade-shaped fish that needed to lie on one side on the floor.

This simple fact explains why we should not expect an optimal design to work perfectly in all the situations it can face in the world. Evolution should push towards a design that is as good as possible, given the different environments it faces. It should be as close as possible to being the best in each environment (efficiency), given the constraints that it needs to also perform well under all the other environments that can be experienced (robustness).

A Slow Process

Evolution is a *very slow process*: it takes time to tailor the design of organisms to make them efficient in their environment. While evolution takes place over aeons, the environment faced by organism happens to change over time. Changes occur for many reasons, such as the evolution of climate or the appearance of new populations/species. When a big change in the environment happens suddenly, there may be a systematic *mismatch* between a design and its environment. Decision-making processes selected in a past environment can lead to systematic errors in the present environment. It is reasonable to expect some mismatch when considering how recent and unusual our modern urban lifestyle is relative to the lifestyle of our ancestors. Just 100 years ago, when our great-grandparents were alive, only a small minority of humanity lived in big cities. Even more striking, what seems to us like very ancient prehistory is still only a blip on the timescale of evolution. As pointed out by Seabright (2010), if you were to assemble together your mother, your grandmother, your great-grandmother and all your other female ancestors up to the dawn of agriculture, you would fit with them in a medium-sized lecture hall. It is not surprising that some of our evolved behaviours sometimes conflict with the novel aspects of modern life. The canonical example of a mismatch is our taste for high-energy food, which was scarce in ancestral times and therefore highly desirable. Such food is now easy to access, and our taste for it is one of the causes of the modern problem of obesity. Mismatches are the clearest examples of behavioural errors.[12]

Spandrels

Perhaps we should not expect every part of an organism's phenotype to be adaptive. In a famous article, biologists Stephen Jay Gould and Richard Lewontin laid out a critique of the method of trying to explain organisms'

---

[12] The field of evolutionary psychology has used the notion of cognitive "module" to describe a specialised cognitive process designed by evolution to make decisions in a specific context. Sperber (1994) distinguishes the proper domain of cognitive modules (the type of situations in which a module was selected to address to make the organism successful) and the actual domain (all the situations where the module may actually be activated). The actual domain can be larger than the proper domain and lead to situations in which a module is activated out of context. In that perspective, evolutionary mismatches can be seen as such situations where the environment we now face has led to a new range of situations falling in the actual domain of our cognitive modules where they lead to poor decisions.

phenotypes as the product of an optimisation process (Gould and Lewontin 1979). In their view, organisms' designs are so contrained by "pathways of development and general architecture" that focusing on these constraints is more useful than trying to look for explanations relying on optimisation. One of the concepts they introduced is the notion of *spandrel*. In architecture, a spandrel is the triangular spaces formed by the intersection of two rounded arches at right angles. Spandrels exist due to the constraints of architectural design. They are generally decorated, but they do not exist to be decorated. They exist because they come along as a byproduct of a desirable architectural feature (arches). Evolutionary spandrels are likely to exist as characteristics selected along useful traits but which, in themselves, do not have useful functions. There is a risk in always trying to look for the function of a trait. In some cases, it may be a spandrel.

Optimisation Is Not Necessarily Adaptation

Finally, we should be cautious not to conflate the idea that evolution pushes towards organisms maximising their inclusive fitness with the idea that organisms tend to progressively acquire traits optimised for the environment they populate.[13] As soon as interactions with other organisms play a significant role in the maximisation of fitness, the existence of other organisms changes the environment itself. As a consequence, while evolution pushes towards organism designs that are best responses to the environment, the best designs to interact with other organisms may not be the best ones to live in the original environment as such (Metz et al. 2008). If this statement seems a bit abstract, think of how some plants and animals have developed very elaborate shapes and colour to camouflage and hide from predators; some animals and plants have developed toxic substances not to be eaten; and some animals develop very energy-intensive displays to attract a mate or very efficient weaponry (e.g., horns, antlers) to defeat other specimens of the same sex. All these designs are useful only to the extent that they emerge as best responses to the presence and characteristics of other organisms when interacting with them.[14]

4.5 THE BRIDGES BETWEEN ECONOMICS AND EVOLUTIONARY THEORY

The imperfection of evolution as an optimisation process means that we cannot expect that evolution will always have produced the best designs. However, given that evolution pushes towards optimisation, it is reasonable to look for optimal designs as benchmarks. In this search, economics and evolutionary theory are approaches that can naturally be combined

---

[13] See, for instance, Anderson's (1990) influential hypothesis that "the cognitive system operates at all times to optimize the adaptation of the behavior of the organism."

[14] We'll see in Chapter 14 how such interactions can explain some of the biases in our beliefs.

Economics and evolutionary theory are conceptually closely related.[15] One of the classical definitions of economics is that it is the science of the allocation of scarce resources to satisfy the (unlimited) needs of the decision maker (Robbins 2007). Economics is the science of optimal behaviour. It studies the best choices decision makers should make in order to maximise their well-being over time. When considering decision makers interacting with each other, economics investigates the best strategies they should follow in order to get the best possible outcome.

Evolutionary theory studies organisms competing for scarce resources in their environment. From its origin, it has been influenced by economics. It is the reading of the economist Malthus that allowed Darwin to articulate clearly the idea of natural selection.[16] Like economics, evolutionary theory looks at optimal behaviour. The pressure of evolution towards the maximisation of inclusive fitness takes two forms, along the lines described in the quote from John Maynard Smith in the epigraph to this chapter. For a range of traits, like the shape of a wing for a bird, evolution will select more efficient designs given the natural environment. Similarly, it is reasonable to think that for some fundamental aspects of behaviour evolution operates a pressure towards optimisation. It is likely to be the case for our ability to perceive external stimuli (e.g., light, sound, heat) and to assess the relative value of the different choices we face. In support of this view, Glimcher (2011, p. 191) states in his discussion of the neural basis for decision making that "evolution pushes all animals towards the maximization of [fitness], and the evidence we have is that it pushes hard ... nervous systems are pushed to effectively maximize fitness with efficient neural circuitry." In that perspective, the mathematical tools of optimisation, widely used in economics to study behaviour, can be used to make sense of observed behaviour.

In many cases, however, the success of a trait depends on its strategic interactions with the traits of other organisms. These interactions can be with organisms of the same species (e.g., males competing against each other) or different species (e.g., parasites and their hosts or predators and their prey). When strategic interactions play an important role in success, economists and biologists both use the tools of *game theory* to study the strategies that are best responses to others' strategies.

[15] Hirshleifer (1977), Hirshleifer (1985), Gandolfi (2002/2018) and Hammerstein and Hagen (2005) present detailed discussions of the connections between economics and evolutionary theory.

[16] In a letter, Darwin writes: "In October 1838, that is, fifteen months after I had begun my systematic inquiry, I happened to read for amusement Malthus on *Population*, and being well prepared to appreciate the struggle for existence which everywhere goes on from long-continued observation of the habits of animals and plants, it at once struck me that under these circumstances favourable variations would tend to be preserved, and unfavourable ones to be destroyed. Here, then, I had at last got a theory by which to work. I came to the conclusion that selection was the principle of change from the study of domesticated productions; and then, reading Malthus, I saw at once how to apply this principle" (cited in Vorzimmer, 1969).

In economics, decision makers choose strategies. When each decision maker chooses the best response to the action of the other decision makers, they are locked in an *equilibrium*.[17] In biology, organisms' traits can be considered as strategies that evolve across time. Evolution pushes towards traits that are best responses to others' traits. Since other organisms evolve too, over time, evolution tends to push organisms interacting with each other towards strategies that are mutual best responses to each other. We call these traits *evolutionary stable strategies*. When organisms have adopted such traits, new variations in traits are unable to replace the existing ones. Any new trait would not be a best response to the existing traits in the population (they are already mutual best responses to each other).[18]

In summary, both evolutionary theory and economics look at optimal behaviour under constraints (the optimal use of resources) and at situations where strategic interactions (e.g., competition, cooperation) play a major role to determine individual success. As a consequence, evolutionary biologists and economists share many common formal tools, such as optimisation techniques and game theory.

4.6 MAKING SENSE OF BEHAVIOUR WITH AN EVOLUTIONARY PERSPECTIVE

Taking the point of view that we were shaped by evolution should lead us to be sceptical of simply labelling some puzzling human behaviour as "irrational". This label reflects a judgement from the economist (or psychologist) that the decision maker's behaviour deviates from the prescriptions of a rational model of behaviour in the situation studied. For this judgement to be relevant, we have to be confident that the model successfully integrates the key features of the decision situation. But there is no guarantee that it is the case. Models simplify reality, and, in the process, a model can become overly simplistic. It can miss critical aspects that are relevant for the decision maker. The model's prediction of what a "rational" behaviour is may then differ from observed behaviour, because people are actually facing a situation that differs in critical ways from the ones assumed by the model.

The following is a good metaphor. Imagine the situation where Jane, an expert in astrophysics, meets John, an astrophysics enthusiast. John is unaware that Jane is an expert on the topic. Confident that he knows a lot about the

---

[17] A familiar example of equilibrium is a "Mexican standoff" where two or more opponents have guns pointed at each other. In that situation, nobody has interest to change their behaviour by either firing or dropping the gun (both options are more dangerous than staying still). The notion of equilibrium is discussed more in Part III.

[18] This presentation is simplified. The selection of a trait also depends on how well it does against itself (when two individuals with this trait interact). See Huttegger and Zollman (2012) for a discussion.

topic, he may start explaining to Jane what she should know about it. If Jane makes a statement that seems odd, *because* of her deep understanding of this complex topic, John may start correcting her, explaining how she should be thinking about the problem instead. The possibility of such situations should prompt us to be cautious. When we tell people what they should do, we may risk making John's mistake. People may actually know much more about the problem they face than we do. The real world is rich in informational and strategic complexity. People who are used to making decisions in real life are likely to have some implicit expertise about what they are doing.

Many behaviours can seem puzzling at first sight. A social scientist armed with a simple model of the world should be careful before labelling these behaviours "irrational". Instead, we should ask: Why do people behave that way? We should try to ascertain whether there may be good reasons behind people's actions. To answer this question, we can engage in a *reverse engineering* approach and ask: What kind of problems would lead to such a behaviour as a good solution? If we can find that a given behaviour can be explained as a good solution to some problems, we can then investigate whether these problems are credibly those the decision maker faces in the real world.

For example, in several parts of this book, we will see that economists called "irrational" some observed behaviour after assuming that decision makers have access to all the relevant information without any cost to gather, process and store it. This assumption leads to models where decision makers have *complete information* about the risks and opportunities they face, and about the characteristics of the other people with whom they interact. In reality, an organism trying to assess the values of different options has to process a lot of information that is being gathered with sensory stimuli (vision, hearing) or stored in memory. It then has to process this information to consider the different possible choices it faces and the likelihood of each one of them to be the best. Finally, it has to decide which option to choose in the set of all possible options, given their expected rewards and risks. Evolution cannot design organisms able to process all this information at zero cost. Processing information is costly. We are all aware of it when we pay higher prices for faster computers. For humans, a simple fact demonstrates this cost: the brain represents only 2% of an average adult body's weight, but 20% of its consumed energy.

A reverse engineering approach often shows that the "irrational" behaviour can be explained as a good solution to situations where decision makers face costs to gather, process and store information. Such costs are a credible constraint that makes this new explanation credible as well.

When following this approach, we will frequently abandon many of the hypotheses associated with the homo economicus model. But the new explanations we will investigate retain key features of the economic way of thinking about decision making. Herbert Gintis (2007) has proposed a useful way to characterise this approach, unifying economics and evolutionary biology: the *beliefs, preferences and constraints (BPC) model*. With that term, Gintis describes the modelling of a decision maker "optimizing a preference function subject to informational and material constraints." Compared to the traditional homo economicus model, the BPC model retains the principle of optimisation under constraints. But it is not tied to specific hypotheses about the type of beliefs (e.g., they do not need to be accurate), the type of preferences (e.g., they do not need to be selfish) and the type of constraints or lack thereof (e.g., information acquisition and processing can be costly).

In some cases, this reverse engineering does not require venturing into considerations about evolution. It simply requires extending *the standard toolbox of economics* to study behaviour with less simplistic assumptions about the context people face. For example, by simply relaxing the assumption that information is free, we may understand better why people behave the way they do.

In some other cases, a proper evolutionary outlook helps us understand why people have the type of preferences they have. Standard economics was built on a rejection of psychology. It aimed to study human behaviour by only assuming coherent preferences. Such an approach somehow rests unsteadily on a vacuum. Where do preferences come from? Surely, not every type of preference had an equal chance of emerging from an evolutionary process. As an extreme example, an economist agnostic about the content of preferences would not say that jumping from cliffs is irrational. However, we would not expect a preference for such a practice to be selected by evolution. An evolutionary approach can help ascertain the types of preferences modern humans are likely to have given the problems humans face (or faced). If we observe some puzzling preferences, a reverse-engineering approach can help us find out what kind of problems/situations such preferences would have helped our ancestors navigate successfully. With such a perspective, we will see, for instance, that there are good reasons why people do not behave selfishly as often assumed by economists (Chapter 10).

I will argue that by asking, "What are the good reasons that could explain why people behave the way they do?," we can very often explain seemingly strange or misguided behaviours as good solutions to problems that people credibly face (or have faced in the past). Many explanations I give in this book explicitly use an evolutionary approach to explain observed human behaviour. But in many cases, I will simply show that richer models can explain apparently puzzling behaviour as good solutions to the complex situations we face.

Before proceeding further, I should stress that I do not claim that evolution has led us always to be perfect decision makers. The argument is, rather, that, given the aeons of evolution, it is reasonable to assume that key features of our decision-making processes approximate optimal solutions. As pointed out by Mobbs et al. (2018) in a discussion on economics and evolutionary theory: "approximation [of optimal behaviour] must be ubiquitous." In that perspective, looking for the optimal solutions to the problems people face can give us benchmarks that, in practice, people may approximate in the real world.

In Part II of this book, I discuss situations where decision makers make decisions on their own, such as making a risky decision or not, or eating something now or later. In such situations, it is reasonable to assume that social interactions are minimal. As a consequence, it is a type of situation where we can expect evolution to push towards efficient decision processes that make the decision maker more adapted to the external environment. In such situations, the tools of *optimisation theory* can be used to study how we make decisions.

In Part III, I discuss situations where decision makers interact with others in social situations. To study such situations, the tools of *game theory* are necessary. I will discuss how many social behaviours that may seem strange can actually be best responses to the games played in social contexts.

$$\therefore$$

Throughout this book, I will argue that evolution theory provides a framework to understand why people behave the way they do. When the right evolutionary perspective is taken, the human biases unveiled by psychologists and behavioural economists often do not appear as shortcomings. Instead, they are good solutions to the problems people face. Taking this perspective, we can look past the myriad of "biases" listed in behavioural economics and psychology textbooks to see that people are very well designed to navigate the complex world in which they live.

PART II

INDIVIDUAL DECISIONS

5

Rules of Thumb and Gut Feelings

Economic man has a complete and consistent system of preferences that allows him always to choose among the alternatives open to him; he is always completely aware of what these alternatives are; there are no limits to the complexity of the computations he can perform in order to determine which alternatives are best; probability calculations are neither frightening nor mysterious to him.

—Simon (1957, p. xvi)

When a man throws a ball high in the air and catches it again, he behaves as if he had solved a set of differential equations in predicting the trajectory of the ball. He may neither know nor care what a differential equation is, but this does not affect his skill with the ball. At some subconscious level, something functionally equivalent to the mathematical calculations is going on.

—Dawkins (1976)

We think of intelligence as a deliberate, conscious activity guided by the laws of logic. Yet much of our mental life is unconscious, based on processes alien to logic: gut feelings, or intuitions.

—Gigerenzer (2007, p. 3)

Summary: We face many complex problems in our daily life. It seems that, instead of calculating the solutions to these problems, we often use heuristics (rules of thumb) and gut feelings to make decisions. This way of making decisions is commonly presented as clear evidence of deviations from optimal behaviour. But this view is too pessimistic: heuristics are likely ways to approximate problems' solutions quickly using minimal information, and gut feelings can reflect pre-processed information helping us to make good decisions.

One of the assumptions from the homo economicus model is that individuals can effortlessly find the solutions to very complex quantitative problems. This assumption has been criticised as being highly unrealistic. I review these criticisms in this chapter and present several alternative assumptions about how human decision makers behave when faced with difficult decision problems.

5.1 BOUNDED RATIONALITY, HEURISTICS AND AUTOMATIC THINKING

Bounded Rationality and Heuristics

Herbert Simon received the Nobel Prize in 1978 for his work on *bounded rationality*, investigating the effect of cognitive limitations on human decisions. Instead of studying an abstract homo economicus, Simon proposed to study "a kind of rational behaviour that is compatible with the access to information and the computational capacities that are actually possessed by organisms, including man, in the kinds of environments in which such organisms exist" (Simon 1957, p. 240).

One of the most influential concepts Simon put forward is the idea that humans do not maximise but *satisfice*: "While economic man maximizes – selects the best alternative from among all those available to him; his cousin ... looks for a course of action that is satisfactory or 'good enough'" (Simon 1957, p. xxv).

Simon's contribution has been widely acknowledged, but his notion of satisficing has not been extensively adopted as a conceptual tool to model human behaviour in economics. Perhaps its shortcoming is that it does not lead to predictions that systematically deviate from those of the homo economicus model in a clear and predictable manner. To replace a dominating theory, an alternative theory generally needs to provide a way to make different predictions. The idea of bounded rationality does not give a strict framework constraining researchers into making specific predictions. It says that people opt for satisficing solutions without giving a clear rule to define the minimal level of satisfaction people are willing to accept. As a consequence, a satisficing model could potentially explain any decision by simply stating that the agent had reached their aspiration level when making a decision.

The psychologists Daniel Kahneman and Amos Tversky complemented Simon's criticism. They agreed that people use simple rules – so-called heuristics – to make complex decisions. These rules work most of the time, but they lead to errors in many situations. In their 1974 *Science* article, "Judgment under uncertainty: Heuristics and biases", Tversky and Kahneman explain that "people rely on a limited number of heuristic principles by which they reduce the complex tasks of assessing likelihoods and predicting values to simpler judgmental operations. In general, these heuristics are quite useful, but sometimes they lead to severe and systematic errors" (Tversky and Kahneman 1974).[1]

By carefully cataloguing errors in human decisions and associating them with heuristics, Kahneman, Tversky and the other psychologists involved in this field of research provided a set of predictions of how human behaviour can be expected to deviate from the homo economicus model in specific situations. In their *Science* article, Kahneman and Tversky listed three heuristics people used to decide between options whose outcomes are uncertain.

The *representativeness heuristic* is a rule used when trying to assess whether an object or event belongs to a larger category of possible objects or events. It implies that a decision maker will estimate these probabilities by assessing how the specific object/event is representative of (looks similar to) the category considered. Doing so, people may ignore other elements when making their choice. Consider the following description by Kahneman and Tversky: "Steve is very shy and withdrawn, invariably helpful, but with little interest in people, or in the world of reality. A meek and tidy soul, he has a need for order and structure, and a passion for detail." When people are asked whether Steve is a farmer or a librarian, they tend to say "librarian". Steve's description seems closer to the stereotype of somebody in this profession. But, by choosing "librarian", people may fail to take into account the proportion of farmers and librarians in the population. There are, in particular, many more farmers than librarians in the United States. This negligence (so-called *base rate neglect*) can lead to erroneous judgements.

The *availability heuristic* is the rule according to which people may form beliefs about the probability of an event by how easy instances of this event come to their mind. For example, people may overestimate the probability of air plane accidents because these accidents are widely reported in the media, making it easier to remember one or several of them. Similarly, they overestimate the risks of shark attacks, even though mosquitoes have been estimated to kill more people in one day than sharks in 100 years.

The *anchoring heuristic* is the rule according to which people will start estimating a quantity from a given point and adjust upward or downward. Doing so, their final estimate may be biased towards the initial value they started with. For instance, in an experiment, participants were asked to estimate the value of the product: $1 \times 2 \times 3 \times 4 \times 5 \times 6 \times 7 \times 8$. Another group was asked to estimate the value of the product $8 \times 7 \times 6 \times 5 \times 4 \times 3 \times 2 \times 1$. The median estimate for the first group was 512 and for the second group 2,250.

---

[1] The word *heuristic* comes from the Greek word *heuriskein*, to discover. It was used in 1954 by Stanford mathematician Polya to distinguish between intuition and analytic thinking. Polya introduced Herbert Simon to heuristics and the term was later used by Kahneman and Tversky (Gigerenzer 2007, pp. 233–234).

Such a difference can be explained if the participants in the first group started with low numbers as anchoring points and moved upward, while the second group started with high numbers (note that the actual value is 40,320).

With their work, Kahneman and Tversky opened a whole field of research in psychology. The evidence of deviations from the economic principles of rationality accumulated and the list of behavioural biases became very substantial over time. If you look at the Wikipedia page "List of cognitive biases", you will find around 200 of them. This proliferation of biases has contributed to foster the view that humans are fundamentally flawed decision makers.

Thinking Too Fast? The Influence of Gut Feelings

One of the factors that contributed to the rise in fame of behavioural economics in the broad public was the great success of Kahneman's book *Thinking, Fast and Slow* 2011. One year after its publication, it had sold over one million copies.

In that book, Kahneman presents an overview of the research on heuristics and biases, wrapped in an overall description of the human mind as composed of two types of cognitive systems, an idea initially suggested by Stanovich and West (2000). The first one, System 1, "operates automatically and quickly, with little or no effort and no sense of voluntary control." The second one, System 2, "allocates attention to the effortful mental activities that demand it, including complex computations."

Broadly speaking, System 2 represents conscious reasoning. It is the voice in our head when we are thinking about a problem. System 1, instead, represents all the unconscious cognitive processes that influence our decisions without us being fully aware of them. System 1 helps us make good decisions most of the time, but it is also impulsive and somewhat naive in many situations: in the words of Kahneman, System 1 "jumps to conclusions"; it is "gullible and biased to believe"; it is "not readily educable"; and it is "the origin of much that we do wrong". System 1 represents "a deep challenge to the rationality assumption favored in standard economics." It is the cause of our biases and limitations. It helps us think fast, but it also leads us to make mistakes. We need our slow and rational System 2 to correct these mistakes.

As System 2 is effortful, decisions will tend to be made by System 1 by default. Examine the following question: "A mobile phone and its case are worth $110. The phone is worth $100 more than its case. How much is the case?"

If you are not familiar with this question, give it a thought. It is adapted from a study by Frederick (2005) on how people make quick judgements. When asked this question, many people answer "$10". This answer seems intuitive, but it is wrong. If the case is $10, then the phone is $100, which means it is only $90 more expensive than the case. By using conscious calculation, you find that the answer has to be $5 for the case, with the phone costing $105.

This example illustrates how our intuitive judgements can play an oversized role in our decisions.[2] Psychologists who worked on the study of heuristics and intuitive judgements often shared the view that we act as *cognitive miser*. Since conscious reasoning is effortful, we "take shortcuts whenever [we] can", and, therefore, "errors and biases stem from inherent features of the cognitive system" (Fiske and Taylor 1991, p. 41).

5.2 THE ADAPTIVE NATURE OF HEURISTICS AND GUT FEELINGS

Heuristics: Simple Rules That Make Us Smart

The research initiated by Kahneman and Tversky has been tremendously successful, and it has substantially changed our view of human rationality with its critique of the homo economicus. However, in the process, this field of study has certainly led researchers to be overly focused on finding biases. Gerd Gigerenzer, a renowned German psychologist, has been very critical of this research program. In his words: "the heuristics-and-biases view of human irrationality would lead us to believe that humans are hopelessly lost in the face of real-world complexity, given their supposed inability to reason according to the canon of classical rationality, even in simple laboratory experiments" (Gigerenzer and Goldstein 1996). Gigerenzer labelled the tendency to see biases everywhere as the "bias bias" (Gigerenzer 2018).

In the highly influential edited book *Heuristic and Biases: Psychology of Intuitive Judgement*, Gilovich and Griffin (2002) admitted that "the heuristics and biases program has most often been seen through the cognitive miser lens". And even though this school has often stressed on how good our intuitions can be, the focus has been, rather, on identifying biases in decision-making. Instead of investigating how people make good decisions quickly, researchers have focused on how our quick rules of thumb lead us astray in many situations. This focus on mistakes was a natural consequence of how this field of research was constituted with the aim to test the validity of the homo economicus model.[3]

---

[2] The fact that the role of our conscious awareness is overestimated was one of the significant messages proposed by Freud, who argued that many of our decisions are guided by subconscious thoughts. For him, his work on the subconscious was a third outrage to humanity's self-esteem (Freud 1916–1917/1977). First, Copernicus had shown that humans were not located at the centre of the universe. Then Darwin had shown that humans had not been specially created outside the animal world. Finally, Freud was showing that humans were not even masters in their own mind. While Freud's approach is questionable from a scientific point of view (Eysenck 1985), this specific message is somewhat evocative of modern developments in psychology.

[3] While the psychological research on heuristic and biases has focused on deviations from rationality, it should be noted that Kahneman and Tversky always saw their findings compatible with an evolutionary approach. In a discussion of the criticisms faced by the heuristic and biases program, Gilovich and Griffin (2002) addressed directly the counter argument that "people are not that dumb": "This critique owes much of its pervasiveness and appeal to the fanfare that

Gigerenzer took a different view. He defended that heuristics are not as flawed as the "heuristic and biases" school suggested. Instead, they are adaptive rules that use a small amount of information to make good decisions in a given environment. To start, Gigerenzer rejects the homo economicus as a benchmark to assess the rationality of human behaviour. The perfect decisions of the homo economicus are just impossible: "Humans and animals make inferences about the world under limited time and knowledge. In contrast, many models of rational inference treat the mind as a Laplacean Demon, equipped with unlimited time, knowledge, and computational might" (Gigerenzer and Goldstein 1996). The homo economicus model is unrealistic: humans are not able to solve complex problems like a computer with infinite memory and computing capacity. However, rejecting the homo economicus as a benchmark is not saying that humans are poor decision makers. On the contrary, humans use decision rules that have been selected to be adaptive in their environment and allow them to make good decisions, most of the time. Gigerenzer calls this ability to make good decisions in one's environment *ecological rationality*: "how cognitive strategies exploit the representation and structure of information in the environment to make reasonable judgments and decisions" (Gigerenzer 2000, p. 57).

Heuristics typically use a selected slice of the available information to help people make a decision. There are at least two reasons why it may be a good idea to use limited information when making decisions. First, a decision maker may want to make quick decisions. Collecting and processing information to make the best decision possible may require expending too much time and effort. In that case, a heuristic may be the solution to an *effort-accuracy trade-off*.[4] Second, a decision maker having to make choices based on limited information may be wary of the uncertainty associated with drawing conclusions from this information. In that case, a heuristic using less information may be the solution to a *bias-variance trade-off*.

Heuristics as Solutions to the Effort-Accuracy Trade-Off

Making decisions involves processing information, a lot of information. It is easy for us to underappreciate the amount of information we process to

---

the negative message of the heuristics and biases program has generated at the expense of its positive counterpart.... There is, however, one version of this critique to which researchers in the heuristics and biases tradition must plead 'no contest' or even 'guilty'. This is the criticism that studies in this tradition have paid scant attention to assessing the overall ecological validity of heuristic processes.... It is ironic that the heuristics and biases approach would be criticized as inconsistent with the dictates of evolution because it is an evolutionary account.... there is no deep-rooted conflict between an evolutionary perspective on human cognition and the heuristics and biases approach." The compatibility between the evolutionary and heuristic and biases approaches was also stressed by Samuels et al. (2002) in their discussion of what they called the "rationality wars".

[4] Also called speed-accuracy trade-off given that the effort to process information takes time.

navigate some of the most mundane situations of our daily lives. Problems that look simple, such as grabbing a glass of water, riding a bike, or catching a ball thrown in the air, are actually extremely hard to solve. Contemplate the challenge of extending our arm to grab a glass of water resting on a table. We have to adjust our trajectory carefully not to miss the glass, our speed not to bump it, our grip not to let it fall. Our brain has to process the visual stimuli, make inferences about the best course of action and send accurate orders to our muscles for them to operate precisely for the task to be completed. Grabbing a glass of water comes so naturally to us that we would not think of it as a difficult task. However, it is an arduous task to do successfully. We had to learn, slowly and with effort, how to do it. You can see this difficulty when you observe toddlers trying to complete this task without dropping the glass. They look clumsy and uncertain about the best way to do it. Grabbing and carrying the glass successfully requires a lot of concentration for them.

Consider now the situation where you want to kick a football (soccer) ball. The first thing you have to do is to identify precisely the location of the ball in its surroundings. You have to discriminate the shape of the ball from other surrounding shapes. You have to estimate how far it is, and in which direction. If it is moving, you have to predict the evolution of its position to be able to intercept its trajectory and hit it. This task is incredibly hard and requires processing a large amount of information. Once again, looking at toddlers learning to play football helps us appreciate that it is not an easy problem. Even when they already know how to walk and run, they will often miss the ball altogether when attempting to kick it.

Another way to realise the difficulty of the task is to try to build a machine able to do it. In 2014, the Australian team of the University of New South Wales won the World Robocup football competition. This competition uses small humanoid-like robots on a small football pitch. The robots' hardware is the same, and the teams compete on building the best computer programs to animate the robots. These computer programs are designed for robots to make the best decisions on the pitch to increase their chances of winning the match.

Think a few seconds about the problems that such a program has to solve. If you had to guess, what would you think is the task consuming the most processing resources for these robots to play successfully? Is it finding the optimal strategy to position the team? Is it coordinating passes to score? Is it trying to understand the strategy of the opposition to defeat it? No, it is none of these tasks. Instead, the task consuming most processing resources is identifying where the ball is on the pitch, using the visual inputs from the robots' cameras (Ashar et al. 2015).

Given the complexity of this task and the quantity of information to process, the programmers opted to use a simple rule to identify the ball's location based on the contrast around the contour of the ball between the ball itself and the surrounding area (Figure 5.1). It is a perfect example of how solving complex problems can often be done with simple rules.

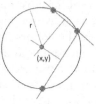

FIGURE 5.1. Ball detection by robots in the Robocup competition. Once a possible point of interest for the location of the ball is identified (left), colour classification allows fast identification of approximate areas of objects (middle), and edge detection using a gray-scale gradient allows the position of the object to be found very accurately (right).

When making decisions, a heuristic can use a subset of the information available with simple decision rules to approximate the best solution. It can be a very efficient way to resolve the problem by reducing the cost and time required. This solution will not always be the best, but it may be close enough to being the best when the cost of processing information is taken into account. While the cost of cognitive effort may be limited, the time it takes to make a decision may be significant. A timely response can make the difference between a safe escape and being the meal of a predator. Similarly, on the football pitch, it may be better to have a robot who hits the ball approximately right quickly than one who would hit the ball perfectly right later, when the ball is already gone. Heuristics, as fast approximations of the optimal solution to complex problems, can be particularly advantageous in competitions where time is of the essence.[5]

Let us consider a much more difficult problem: intercepting a plane in mid-air. In the 1930s, the British Royal Air Force was facing precisely this challenge, and they were looking for an algorithm to determine a trajectory for its fighter aircrafts to intercept possible bombers.[6] In spite of complex mathematical techniques, they could not reach their target rate of 90% successful interceptions. The problem was finally solved when a commander of the RAF, E. O. Greenfell, declared he could do a better job by eye. Greenfell was given the command of the operation table, and he successfully directed fighters to around 90% interceptions, without the help of any computer. What he had done, he explained, was use a simple rule about the angle between the chasing fighter and the target. Greenfell's approach was then slightly tweaked to a very simple rule: set an initial angle between the fighter, the bomber and the expected

---

5 Kahneman (2011) made the same argument in the case of the detection of dangers: "By shaving a few hundredths of a second from the time needed to detect a predator, this circuit improves the animal's odds of living long enough to reproduce. The automatic operations of System 1 reflect this evolutionary history."

6 The elements of this paragraph are described in the excellent paper on this issue by Hamlin (2017).

FIGURE 5.2. The gaze heuristic: keeping constant the angle of a gaze to a falling object is a simple rule that leads to the object's landing point.

interception point, given the planes' initial velocity, then maintain this angle even if the planes' velocity or their trajectory changed.

This technique became known as the "Tizzy angle" from the name of Sir Henry Tizard, who was leading this research and who made small changes to Greenfell's technique. It greatly increased the success rate of interception of the RAF, and it gave Britain a crucial advantage in the Battle of Britain, which took place in 1940 between the RAF and the Luftwaffe. After the war, this interception method was used to design the guiding system of autonomous air-to-air missiles able to track enemy planes. Modern missiles still use this heuristic to determine their trajectories.

The Tizzy angle is identical to what Gerd Gigerenzer has called the "gaze heuristic": when trying to catch a ball, keep constant the angle between the ground and the line connecting the ball to your eyes. If you adjust your position progressively to respect this rule, you will end up at the right location (Figure 5.2). This simple rule solves a complex problem. To catch a ball thrown in the air, you would have, in theory, to solve mathematical equations to estimate the landing point of the ball and move towards this point. These equations are not trivial. The trajectory of a ball in the air would follow a perfect parabola if there were no air friction. In the real world, air friction slows the ball, and this effect increases with the speed of the ball. The trajectory of a ball thrown in the air is therefore determined by differential equations.[7]

---

[7] Another great example of complex problem that may seem to use deceptively simple is the fact of riding a bike. To keep it balanced requires adjustments that depend on the speed and position of

If people were homo economicus, you would see them estimate the landing location and then run to this location to catch the ball.[8] Instead, you usually observe people keeping constant eye contact with the ball as they progressively adjust their position to reach the point where the ball lands. The gaze heuristic provides a straightforward way to solve this problem. Studies on baseball players (McBeath et al. 1995; Fink et al. 2009), dogs (Shaffer et al. 2004) and dragonflies (Olberg et al. 2000) have shown that they indeed use heuristics based on angles, similar to the gaze heuristic, to track and catch flying objects.

In summary, simple rules can be good solutions to the complex problems we face in our daily lives. In the examples above, a heuristic is used to make good decisions: use of contrast to identify shapes, use of one angle to track moving objects. These heuristics are *fast and frugal*: they allow the decision maker to make quick decisions at a small cost in terms of information processing (Gigerenzer and Goldstein 1996). If the cost of deviating from the fitness-maximisation decision is small or if the cost of taking time to reach this decision is high, fast and frugal rules can be the best solutions (Modelling Animal Decisions Group et al. 2014).

Heuristics as Solutions to the Bias-Variance Trade-Off
Gigerenzer and his colleagues have also put forward another argument in favour of heuristics. They argue that sometimes *less is more*: simple rules can be better to make decisions than trying to use all the information available.

One experiment, by Gerd Gigerenzer and Dan Goldstein, illustrates this idea. They compared the ability of different approaches to determine which of two German cities has a larger population. They used data on different cues such as whether the city has a team in the major football league or whether it is a regional capital. They then simulated respondents having access to some cues, not always the same across respondents. These pseudo-respondents made decisions using the data they had. Gigerenzer and Goldstein found that a simple rule that they named "take-the-best" was very effective at finding the most populous city. Surprisingly, it was even better than linear regression. This rule consists of ordering the cues available in order of validity and stopping as soon as one city beats the other on one cue. Formally, this is called a *lexicographic rule*. It is the same rule used to sort words in a dictionary: words are sorted on their first letter, if the first letter is the same, then they are sorted on their second letter, and so on. In the case of two cities, one may ask first whether

---

the bicycle. It means that, by riding a bicycle, you de facto solve differential equations (Meijaard et al. 2007). Millions of people cycle every day in the world, even though most likely none one of them attempts to solve consciously the underlying mathematical problem they face.

[8] Using this model, economists could assume that the agent has perfect information about the ball speed and direction and the ability to solve the corresponding mathematical problem. It would also be possible to relax the assumption of perfect information and model the agent as picking the location that maximises the expected chances of catching the ball.

the cities are regional capitals. If both are, one looks next at whether they have a top professional football team. If it is the case for one city and not the other, then we stop and choose the city with the football team as the likely largest city.

This idea that less can be more seems puzzling at first. How could it be better to use less information? Gigerenzer explained the success of simple rules by the fact that they can protect you against risky *extrapolations* when you try to draw a conclusion from limited data. The mapping between past observations and future predictions can be called a *model*. A good model should do two things. First, it should make sense of past observations. Second, it should make good predictions about future observations. Unfortunately, these two goals are somewhat in conflict. When you try to improve how well you can explain past observations, you may end up *overfitting* past data, that is, trying to explain the specific *quirks* of past observations, which are not going to be repeated in the future. One way to avoid overfitting is not to try for your model to perfectly explain past data. To do so, you can opt for a model *underfitting* the data (not capturing some of the features of past observation). Figure 5.3 shows examples of model overfitting or underfitting the available data.

In this choice of a model, you face a *bias-variance trade-off*. The prediction errors a model makes on future observations comes from its possible *bias* (a model may, in expectation, find an answer different from the right one) and its *variance* (the variability of its predictions). The bias-variance trade-off comes from the fact that, as you improve the fit of your model, you are likely to reduce the bias of its predictions, but you also run the risk of adopting a model that captures the quirks of past observations and that will give noisy predictions in the future. This noise increases the variance of your model. In short, a model overfitting the data will have low bias but high variance, and a model underfitting the data will have high bias and low variance.

To make this trade-off intuitive, let's consider the problem faced by Jane, who sells bagels in a food truck. Every morning she needs to assess the likely demand she will face on the day: the number of customers asking for bagels. She does not want to make too few bagels as she would lose out on possible sales. She also does not want to make too many bagels as she would then have to throw them away. Suppose she starts on Monday at a new location for which she has little knowledge about the demand to expect on each day of the week. On Monday, she receives 8 requests for bagels; on Tuesday, she receives 16 requests and on Wednesday, 32. On Thursday morning, Jane has to decide how many bagels to cook for the day. To do so, she needs to form a view on the likely demand on Thursday. To make a good prediction, Jane can use what she knows about the past observations of demand to make inferences about today's demand.

She notices that between Monday and Wednesday, the demand doubled every day. Jane could think of extending this pattern and plan for a demand of 64 bagels on Thursday. Intuitively, Jane may be wary of drawing such a confident conclusion. The doubling rule predicts perfectly past increases, but

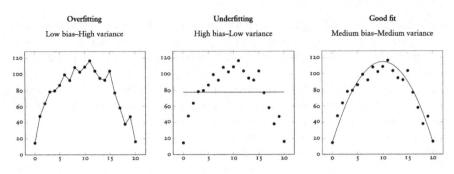

FIGURE 5.3. Examples of overfitting and underfitting.

what if the fact that demand doubled every day was just a fluke due to random daily variations in demand? Looking at the first three days, the demand has only been around 15 on average. The prediction of 64 bagels is more than four times this number. Producing such a large number of bagels may be risky and leave Jane with lots of them unsold at the end of the day.

Instead of extrapolating the growth in demand that way, Jane could use the average demand, 15, as a safe prediction. The average demand ignores information in the past observations, like the increase in demand over the last few days. It is most likely a biased estimate of the demand on Thursday. But it is less risky. Using a parsimonious model when trying to make predictions can make sense. Such a model can have a bias, but the model can be a good solution if this bias is small and the model's predictions have low enough variance.

Gigerenzer and Brighton (2009) point to this trade-off to justify that using less information can, in some cases, be a good strategy to make inferences. Heuristics make a conservative use of the available information and may protect the decision maker against wild extrapolations.[9]

---

[9] It should be noted that, for Gigerenzer, this argument is an indictment against optimisation. In his view, the complexity of many decision situations precludes living organisms from finding the optimal solution. Decision rules are just solutions that are good enough. Note, however, that finding good approximations that are the best solutions to an effort-accuracy trade-off or a bias-variance trade-off is still a process of optimisation. The issue of complexity is, however, worth addressing. As pointed out by Bossaerts and Murawski (2017), decisions that are computationally complex to solve may in many cases also be computationally complex to approximate. The evidence I present in this book suggests that assuming that people approximate optimality can be very effective to understand behaviour. However, the issue of complexity is an important one. It is likely to be important in future theoretical and empirical research in behavioural sciences.

Errors Are a Feature, Not a Bug

As heuristics use only limited information, they are bound to lead to mistakes. But natural selection should exert a pressure towards an *optimal amount of mistakes* by favouring rules that perform well in the type of situations that the individual tends to encounter.[10] Mistakes will likely arise in situations that are less common and for which heuristics are less well suited. As pointed out by Mobbs et al. (2018): "approximations [of optimality] are presumably tailored to work well in common and relevant environments at the expense of rare ones".

Great examples of such mistakes are optical illusions. They are situations where our senses give us a misleading impression from visual stimuli. It typically comes from the fact that brain processes are very good at interpreting visual information in standard situations, using shortcuts. Under rare and specific circumstances, these shortcuts do not work, and they fail to interpret the visual information appropriately. Describing our ability to perceive motion, Weiss et al. (2002) describe motion illusions as the result of an optimal design: "mistakes of human motion perception represent the best solution of a rational system designed to operate in the presence of uncertainty". Similarly, in a recent commentary of his research on visual perception, the neuroscientist Thomas Serre stated: "There is growing consensus that optical illusions are not a bug but a feature.... They may represent edge cases for our visual system, but our vision is so powerful in day-to-day life and in recognizing objects."[11]

Explaining Famous Heuristics

To illustrate how to make sense of heuristics, let's look again at the three heuristics listed by Kahneman and Tversky in their 1974 article.

First, there was the *representativeness heuristic*. In this case, it is possible that there was no bias to start with. Let's consider the example of Steve being either a librarian or a farmer. Saying that Steve is more representative of a librarian given Steve' characteristics (shy and withdrawn) can be interpreted as the fact that you observe more people with such characteristics among librarians than among farmers. This is relevant information. Looking at this problem from a Bayesian perspective,[12] Tenenbaum et al. (2001) propose to think of representativeness as the *ratio between the posterior and the prior probability after considering the weight of evidence* an observation provides between two

---

[10] For a discussion about how rules can be selected to be adapted to the structure of the environment, see Modelling Animal Decisions Group et al. (2014).

[11] Cited by sciencenode.org when discussing his research on the effect of context on visual perception (Mély et al. 2018).

[12] The Bayesian approach specifies how to update one's belief when faced with new evidence.

hypotheses. In that sense, Steve is representative of a librarian, if the probability that he is librarian, given that he is shy and withdrawn, is higher than the probability for a random person in the population to be a librarian.[13] In that sense, the representativeness of an observation is informative. It is not a mistake to take it into account when making a judgement. However, to make a good judgement, this informativeness should be associated with an accurate belief about the probability of observing a librarian or a farmer (before hearing about Steve).[14] Kahneman and Tversky have interpreted the result of their experiment as suggesting an over-reliance on representativeness and the neglect of the base rate probability. In the case of Steve, people may neglect the fact that there are many more farmers than librarians in the United States. Kahneman and Tversky also controlled for this base rate by describing hypothetical populations with specific proportions of the different professions.

However, this criticism works only if the participants believe the chances to be drawn from the sample are equal to the sample's proportions. What if the experimental participants considered instead the chance that the experimenter came up with an example of a librarian (or of a farmer)? Perhaps, as the experiment takes place on a university campus, they may find the idea that the person described is a librarian more likely.[15] This criticism was made by Hilton (1995): the answers of respondents may depend on how they interpret the situation presented by the experimenter. In a replication of Kahneman and Tversky's study of the representativeness heuristic, participants behaved as if they neglected the base rate when given the information by a psychologist, but they used the right base rate when the information was given by a computer. In the latter case, they had less reason to try to infer a motive in the computer's selection of examples (Schwarz et al. 1991).

---

[13] Think about the likelihood for somebody to be librarian if shy and withdrawn, $P(librarian|shy$ & $withdrawn)$ and the likelihood for somebody to be a librarian, $P(librarian)$. Then Tenenbaum et al. (2001) suggest that the representativeness of shy and withdrawn people to librarians can be represented by the log of the ratio: $ln\left(P(librarian|shy$ & $withdrawn)/P(librarian)\right)$. This assumption is supported by how this measure correlates with the perception of representativeness elicited from experimental participants. Before Tenenbaum, Gigerenzer and Hoffrage (1995) had proposed to define representativeness as the likelihood itself.

[14] This is the *base rate probability*, which acts as a prior belief.

[15] Note Tversky and Kahneman (1974) report results of this experiment where participants gave the right base rate when not provided with any information. To conclude that they overweight the description of the person relative to base rate requires assuming that the only information they take from the description is the description itself. Instead, they may be influenced by the fact that it is a description that the experimenter has chosen to give to them.

These results illustrate the risk of describing a type of behaviour as a "bias". When a behavioural scientist uses this term, it implies that this scientist has a model of what should be a good behaviour in the situation. The term "bias" reflects that the scientist has a better understanding than the individual about the right way to behave. But often it can be hard to assess whether it is the case. A type of behaviour can be called a bias while it is, in fact, the scientist's model of ideal behaviour that is wrong.[16]

The same concern affects another famous experiment, whose results have been interpreted to support the representativeness heuristics: the "Linda problem". Tversky and Kahneman (1982) presented participants in an experiment with the following description:

Linda is 31 years old, single, outspoken and very bright. She majored in philosophy. As a student, she was deeply concerned with issues of discrimination and social justice, and also participated in anti-nuclear demonstrations.

They were then asked to rank statements about Linda according to their probability. These statements included: "Linda is a bank teller" and "Linda is a bank teller and is active in the feminist movement." The majority of respondents ranked the second statement as more probable than the first. Doing so, they seemed to violate a basic law of probability: the probability that two statements are jointly true – "Linda is a bank teller" and "Linda is active in the feminist movement" – cannot be larger than the probability of one of them being true. Whenever Linda is a bank teller and active in the feminist movement, she is a bank teller. But she could also be a bank teller and not a feminist. The probability that Linda is a bank teller has therefore to be larger than the probability that she is both a bank teller and active in the feminist movement.

Tversky and Kahneman named this violation of the rules of probability the "conjunction fallacy" and explained it with the representativeness heuristics. The error that participants seemed to make was that the description looked more similar to what a bank teller and a feminist look like than just an

---

[16] Not that one of the most iconic biases attributed to the representativeness heuristic has not passed the test of time. The "hot hand" is the idea that basketball players can get hot (in the zone), which raises their success rate. In a very influential article, Gilovich et al. (1985) argued that this perception is a cognitive illusion. The success rate does not vary in sequences of shots, but people are not very good at understanding random sequences. As a result, they see (naturally occurring) streaks as indicative of a change in players' performance level. Recent work has shown, however, that the hot hand actually exists (Green and Zwiebel 2018; Miller and Sanjurjo 2014, 2018). People did not simply imagine it. Instead, it was the psychologists' statistical models that had a (subtle) bias masking the existence of the hot hand.

average bank teller. Participants could have relied on this heuristic to make their probability judgement, leading them to make mistakes.

However, this interpretation relies, here again, on the assumption out that the participants interpret the question in the way the experimenters assume they do. Hertwig and Gigerenzer (1999) pointed out that the term "probability" has several meanings in English. It can, for instance, mean "plausibility". Participants may not necessarily take the mathematical interpretation of the term as assumed by the experimenters. They may understand the question by forming views about the reason why this specific description of Linda is given to them by the experimenters. They may assume that it must be relevant to understand who she plausibly is. Hertwig and Gigerenzer showed that when participants were asked about frequencies instead of "probability", the conjunction fallacy pretty much disappears. The notion of frequency is less ambiguous and participants may stick to a quantitative reasoning closer to what experimenters have in mind.[17]

The second heuristic was the *availability heuristic*. It is commonly described as a poor way of making judgments that leads to distortions in the perception of probabilities. In a recent study, psychologists (Lieder et al. 2018) formally demonstrated that the availability heuristic can be seen as a good solution when having to choose between different options with risky outcomes. To decide which option to choose, the decision maker may mentally simulate possible outcomes from each alternative. In that case, sampling more of the outcomes with extreme consequences reduces the variance of the estimated difference in expected utility between the two options. In other words, if one option has a small risk of a disaster, it makes more sense to think of this disaster to evaluate this choice, even if it is improbable. Such a logic means that it can be optimal for people to remember more events that are extreme in consequences and are more "available" in their memory. Here the heuristic is actually a good solution once the decision-maker problem is understood as a minimisation of the cost of possible mistakes.

Finally, there was the *anchoring heuristic*, the fact that people are overly influenced in their estimations of a quantity by their starting point (anchor). In the experimental situations studied in the laboratory, I do not see an advantage for participants to be influenced by anchoring. However, changing the range

---

[17] The same argument was used by Gigerenzer and Hoffrage (1995) against the evidence used to support the existence of base rate neglect. In an adversarial collaboration, Mellers et al. (2001) found that it is not clear whether the conjunction fallacy fully disappears when frequency is used. The results were mixed, however, and the researchers drew different conclusions from the results.

of your perception as a function of the value you observed can make sense for a perceptual system. It is indeed one of the key ideas developed in the next chapter. If it is the case, anchoring effects may be similar to visual illusions: they are mistakes that can be observed in very specific and unusual situations. These mistakes derive from the inner workings of our perceptual systems, which are designed to work well in most of the situations we encounter.

In summary, the biases associated with these three heuristics may fall in three categories: one may be a spurious experimental effect (representativeness), one may actually be an efficient decision rule (availability heuristic), and the last one (anchoring) may be an optimal error observed only in unusual circumstances.

The Positive Role of Gut Feelings

Heuristics can be conceived as part of all the subconscious cognitive processes helping us make decisions. These cognitive processes generate the intuitions and gut feelings that influence our decisions (Gigerenzer 2007). Why would evolution make some of our decision process subconscious?

One credible explanation is that through the long process of evolution, adequate solutions to common problems can already be encoded in our DNA. Some problems are frequent and essential to solve for our survival. There has therefore been an evolutionary pressure on our ability to solve them quickly right away. Let's think about the simple act of walking. For young humans, safely fostered by their parents, it is a tedious learning process. But for most mammals in the wild, where walking is a survival requirement, babies are born with the ability to walk. After a few uneasy steps, a baby zebra or elephant will be able to follow its parents. This possibility for some behaviour to be hardwired is not limited to skills like walking. It includes the way we make decisions in the common situations we encounter in our daily life. In such situations, we may be better off equipped with automatic cognitive processes that do not need to reach our full consciousness.

To understand how automatic cognitive processes can contribute to the optimal design of a decision maker, imagine the situation where you'd have to design one yourself. Let's consider the following scenario: you are tasked by NASA to design a robot that will be sent to a planet on another solar system. Part of the challenge is that there are things you know about this planet from available observations: there is water, there is some firm ground, and so on. But there are plenty of things you do not know, such as whether there is a form of life on it and whether it could be a threat to your robot. As you design it, the way to make it optimally operational is to pre-solve the problems that you know your robot will face, using the knowledge you already have. You can encode all the rules of physics you know are going to apply on that planet in order to react quickly to a dangerous situation. For example, you can encode the rule: "if a rock is falling towards you, move quickly out of the way". You can also program your robot to recognise known objects and substances. For example, you can program it to know how an area filled with water looks like. If your robot is not amphibious, you can then add the behavioural rule: "never get into water".

But in some situations, your robot will be faced with new problems that you did not plan or foresee. In such situations, you will need your robot to carefully consider the data available to make an assessment *on its own* about the likely challenge ahead and how to solve it. For novel challenges, your robot won't be able to use pre-coded solutions; it will have to come up with its own solutions on the spot.

What you are building for your robot would be very similar to the dual system of decision-making described by Kahneman. System 1 encodes fast rules to react to situations quickly and without much deliberation. System 2 solves problems slowly by processing the available information consciously. Psychologists have frequently presented this dual system as a reflection of our human biases when making decisions. Instead, it is credible to think that this dual system can be the natural result of an optimisation process. When situations are frequent and important, there would have been evolutionary pressure to encode the right reaction in our genes. When a snake appears right in front of you, the right thing to do is not to ponder about what type of animal it is or what its intentions are. It is to avoid it, quickly. Hence our natural phobia for deadly animals like snakes and spiders. But when we are faced with a genuinely new problem, we need to look at it carefully to understand the risks and opportunities we face, and assess the different possible courses of action. In such novel situations, we are on our own. Nature would not have had a chance to encode the right answer in our genes.

Going back to the robot scenario, a further improvement would be to allow it to learn from its new experience and progressively build automatic responses that could be added to those you pre-programmed it with. For example, if your robot gets into contact with an unknown viscous substance several times and observes that it rusts its joints, it could incorporate the rule "if you see the viscous substance, avoid it".

The same process seems to characterise our learning process. In novel situations, our intuitions may not be very helpful, and we may need to slowly look at the different aspects of the situation to make a decision (System 2). But the more we face a specific type of situation, the more we learn to fine-tune our behaviour by trial and error about what works and what does not. It makes behaviour faster and more automatic (System 1). Consider our ability to become skilful at new tasks. We were not designed to drive a car, stand on a surfboard, or execute multiple somersaults on a gym mat. It is with tedious practice that humans can master such feats. Progressively, we learn (and encode in our neural connections) new automatic rules that allow us to solve very complex tasks automatically, without having to "think" about what we are doing when we are doing it.[18]

---

[18] A great example of this is the difference between how mentally straining it is to learn to drive and how automatic it becomes later on. It can become so automatic that people driving on a

This feedback and error approach has limitations. Some games are just too complex to play, like chess, for us to be able to approximate the optimal solution. But often, it will lead us to be able to automatically do the right thing in spite of the complexity of the problem.

The distinction between System 1 (automatic) and System 2 (reasoning) is simplistic, however. It can lead us to believe that our decision processes are at any moment in time governed by one or the other. When we reason with our inner voice to make decisions, we may assume that System 2 is the only one in charge. We tend to identify with this inner voice and to think that it is how we make decisions.[19] Instead of this picture where either System 1 or System 2 is active, it makes more sense to think of teamwork where our slow reasoning will be as limited as possible to the aspects that are novel in the situations we face. In any new situation, some aspects may be novel while others are familiar. Our pre-packaged information-processing systems may help give us quick feedback on the familiar aspects in the situation to help inform our reasoned decision.

In that perspective, the very influential research in neuroscience by Antonio Damasio has contributed to change our view on how we make decisions. He has shown that emotions and intuitions are key to good decision-making (Damasio 2006). A huge amount of information about the surrounding world is processed automatically by brain processes producing positive/negative values as a way to help us to make decisions. These emotions/intuitions are positive/negative feelings that are not brought to the fore of our consciousness. They are essential, however, to allow us to make even the simplest decisions. Some patients with damage to the ventromedial prefrontal cortex can lose the coupling of bodily arousal with decisions (Bechara et al. 1994). They can maintain normal intellect and are able to make rational judgements, but they may be unable to make mundane choices, such as shopping in a supermarket. Think about the simple act of choosing which type of potatoes to buy, among the many varieties available in the vegetable section. Humans with a fully functioning brain would quickly get a feeling for the best option and pick it, generally without really thinking about it. But people with such brain damage will not *feel* anything, and while being able to describe all the characteristics of the options (e.g., shape, price) and the intended use (e.g., soup), they will feel blank about which option is best. Without emotions, they are stuck in the allegorical positions of Buridan's donkey who dies of hunger and thirst, while being placed at equal distance of food and water.

---

usual route (e.g., commuting) suddenly realise that they have arrived at their destination and they don't have a recollection of their journey.

[19] In the words of Kahneman (2011), "System 2 believes that it is i n charge and that it knows the reasons for its choices." In opposition to this possibility, Jonathan Haidt (2006) famously used the metaphor of an elephant and its rider: "Like a rider on the back of an elephant, the conscious, reasoning part of the mind has only limited control of what the elephant does."

The intuitive view that the little voice in our head is in charge of the rational decisions is misleading. To give a better idea of how our brain works, Eagleman (2011) uses the metaphor of a CEO. It is true that CEOs make important decisions for their companies. But most of the decisions are de facto taken outside their control. Many decisions are taken in lower decision centres because they are of low importance. Even big decisions are not really actually made by CEOs. A big decision will require experts in the firm to produce opinions and recommendations. Most of the times, when the recommendations are just overly positive or negative, a CEO does not have really to make a decision; the decision was already generated by the results of the advisors' analyses. Only when a situation presents a complex set of positive and negative aspects will the CEO really be the key decision maker by integrating the different pieces of advice and making a choice.

Engelman points out that our decision-making process is very similar. We believe that we (the little voice in our head) make all the decisions in our life. But automatic brain processes treating the information in the background are providing us continuously with values about the different options in the form of feelings and emotions. When our feelings about an option are overly positive or negative, there is hardly the need for conscious deliberation. Only when there is a conflict between the different signals we get do we need to stop, take a pause and carefully ponder about what to do.

This process happens all the time, for minor as well as for major life decisions. Suppose you are visiting a flat to possibly live there. As you enter the flat, you are filled with impressions that are reflecting how your brain is associating the available information with a likely positive or negative outcome. Is this door creaking? Was the neighbourhood looking safe? Is the paint looking good? Is it far from my work? It is said that people can make a decision about a house/flat quickly after entering it. It is because, generally, this flow of feelings delivers a clear verdict – yes or no – and you do not need to ponder consciously about it further. The study of our gut feelings and their role in our decision-making suggests that they do not guide our actions in an irrational way. Instead, they exist to help us make good decisions.[20]

Since Damasio's contribution, the progress in neuroscience has pointed to the large amount of computations made by the brain beyond consciousness (Montague 2006). The key role of a brain is to make decisions, as only decisions have in the end an impact on the individual's fitness. Decisions require an assessment of the different options available and their value. Behind most simple choices, the human brain is processing a large amount of new information to quickly assess the best option to pick. While social psychologists

---

[20] The array of emotions we experience is rich and goes well beyond fleeting feelings. We also experience a range of social emotions such as gratitude, pride, anger, guilt, sadness, and shame that help us assess the social cost and benefits of our actions (Sznycer and Lukaszewski 2019). Some of these social emotions also help us strategically in our interaction with others. I discuss this aspect in Chapter 11.

were trying to find the many ways in which people do not optimise, research in neuroscience was finding evidence that the brain does computations in many ways very similar to those assumed by the standard economic models.

∴

By focusing on the mistakes they generate, the study of heuristics may have given the impression that humans make mindless mistakes from following imperfect rules of thumb. This view is too pessimistic. It underestimates the incredible feats achieved by the human brain in its ability to analyse very complex data to make quick decisions.

6

Reference Points and Aversion to Losses

We suffer more ... when we fall from a better to a worse situation, than we ever enjoy when we rise from a worse to a better.

—Smith (1759/2010, 311, ii)

One can even see reference-dependence as a biological solution to an environmental challenge, a kind of optimization under constraint.

—Glimcher (2011, p. 417)

Reference-dependence is not simply an arbitrary fact, but may be necessary, or at least an efficient solution, given constraints on what it is possible for brains to do, given fundamental limitations that result from their being finite systems.

—Woodford (2012a)

Summary: The homo economicus model assumes that people's utility increases with the level of their income and wealth. However, evidence from psychology suggests that (1) people care more about the deviations (gains and losses) of their income and wealth relative to a "reference point", and (2) losses have a larger impact on subjective well-being than gains (loss aversion). Such reference-dependent preferences are not strange deviations from rationality. Instead, reference-dependence is most likely evolution's solution to the problem of designing an optimal reward system.

To make decisions, people first need to be able to ascribe values to the different options they face. It seems reasonable to think that whatever the things people desire, they should value a given option for how much this option provides them with the things they like. For instance, in situations where people care only about money, they should value only an option for the total amount of money it would lead them to have.

The study of human decision-making progressively showed, however, that this is not exactly what people do. Instead of considering the *absolute amount* of what they get, people tend to value this amount *relative to a reference level*. In the case of money, people may not care so much about the level of their wealth per se. Rather, they may care about how this level compares to what they think they should have.

The existence of such reference levels seems bound to distort people's decisions in undesirable ways. Why should people care more about some specific levels in a way that could influence their decisions? The notion that our preferences over things are reference-dependent is often seen as one of the key deviations from rationality unearthed by behavioural economics.

6.1 REFERENCE-DEPENDENT PREFERENCES AND LOSS AVERSION

Bernoulli's Error: We Think in Terms of Gains and Losses

The story of our understanding of how people value they options they face starts with the study of how people should make decisions in situations where outcomes are uncertain. Uncertainty is a key component of most decisions taken in the real world. Should you take this route or another one? Accept this job offer or keep your current position? Go into this business venture or not?

Probability theory emerged in part as a way to put a value on uncertain prospects. Estimating the value of uncertain prospects is essential to determine the fair price for an insurance policy or a game of chance like a lottery. Between the end of the seventeenth century and the beginning of the eighteenth century, mathematicians like Pascal, Huygens and de Moivre were converging towards the idea that the fair price of a gamble is its *expected value*. Imagine a lottery giving you one chance in a 100 to win $100. Its fair price, if defined as its expected value, would be $100 × 1/100 = $1.

This proposition has some appeal. Suppose that you were to play this gamble a large number of times. Your average gains (total gains divided by the number of times you played) would tend to be close to $1.[1] In that sense, the expected value can be understood as the price for which, "on average", you would neither win nor lose money if you were to play this game repeatedly.

In spite of its appeal, this proposed solution to the question of a gamble's fair price quickly faced some difficulties. In a 1713 letter to the French mathe-

---

[1] This is a consequence of the "law of large numbers": the average of a large number of random draws taken from a given distribution tends to get close to its expected value.

matician de Montmort, Nicolas Bernoulli proposed a thought experiment that presented a serious challenge to the use of the expected value. Suppose you are faced with the following game of chance.

You start with a stake of $2. You toss a coin, and as long as it lands on head, your stake is doubled after each throw: 2, 4, 8 ... As soon as it lands on tail, the game ends, and you keep the amount of money you got.

Imagine that a casino was selling tickets to play this game. Consider it for an instant: How much would you be willing to pay to enter the game?

When asked this question, most people answer a number below $20, often just a few dollars. This price range may seem reasonable given that there is a high probability for this game to stop very quickly, after only a few coin throws. It is therefore very likely that the payoff you get will be small. However, what is this game's fair price if we define it as its expected value?

To answer this question, we have to think of every possible outcome and its probability. To start, there is 1/2 chance that the game stops on the first toss (tail), leaving you with the stake of $2. If, instead, you get heads on the first throw, there is then half a chance that you get tails on the second toss, leaving you $4 with a probability of $1/2 \times 1/2 = 1/4$. Continuing that way, you have 1/8 chance of getting $8, 1/16 chance of getting $16, and so on. We can formally write the expected value EV as:

$$EV = 2 \times \frac{1}{2} + 4 \times \frac{1}{4} + 8 \times \frac{1}{8} + 16 \times \frac{1}{16} + \cdots.$$

Simplifying gives:

$$EV = 1 + 1 + 1 + 1 + \cdots = \infty.$$

So the expected value is infinite! If you were using the expected value as the fair price of this game, you should be willing to give away all your wealth to participate! The gap between the limited price people are typically willing to pay for this gamble and its infinite expected value led to this problem being called the "St Petersburg Paradox".

This name came from the publication by Nicolas' brother, Daniel Bernoulli, of an article in the *Commentaries of the Imperial Academy of Science of Saint Petersburg* (1738).[2] In this article, D. Bernoulli proposes a solution, using the notion of "utility": "The determination of the value of an item must not be based on the price, but rather on the utility it yields." In other words, Bernoulli suggests that the utility of additional monetary gains progressively decreases

---

[2] Noticeably, this paradox is not related to the city of St Petersburg, besides the journal where it was published.

as one gets richer. To represent this idea, he proposed to model people's utility as the logarithm of their wealth w.[3] Using this assumption, the value of the gamble can be re-assessed using its *expected utility*, EU:

$$EU = \ln(w + 2) \times \frac{1}{2} + \ln(w + 4) \times \frac{1}{4}$$
$$+ \ln(w + 8) \times \frac{1}{8} + \ln(w + 16) \times \frac{1}{16} + \cdots.$$

In that case, this expected utility is not infinite. It has a finite value. Indeed, for reasonable values of wealth the willingness to pay for this game is quite small. Even a millionaire would pay only around $20 to play this game.

This resolution of the paradox is now considered as the earliest suggestion that people value gambles with their expected utility, instead of their expected monetary value. To practically solve the paradox, D. Bernoulli had to decide what influences utility. While it was not necessary for the resolution of the puzzle, he opted for the utility to be a function of the individual's *total wealth*. He then motivated the notion of decreasing marginal utility with the impact of wealth on the marginal utility of income: "There is no doubt that a gain of one thousand ducats is more significant to the pauper than to a rich man though both gain the same amount."

Somewhat following the steps of Bernoulli, economists have routinely assumed that the carrier of utility is the absolute level of wealth (or sometimes income). But, for Daniel Kahneman, defining the carrier of utility as the absolute level of wealth was a fundamental mistake. He dubbed it "Bernoulli's error". Before we venture into Kahneman's criticism, we should acknowledge that this choice was a natural one to make for Bernoulli. When considering utility as a measure of subjective satisfaction, it is reasonable to assume that people enjoy having a higher level of wealth. As a reflection of this, people would frequently say things like "if only I were rich", which suggests that their level of satisfaction would increase with their level of wealth. And while the saying "money won't bring you happiness" is often heard, people generally appear to behave as if they believe it will.

The evidence suggests, however, that people's subjective satisfaction is not primarily derived from absolute levels of wealth or income. Imagine the following situation (Kahneman 2003):

---

[3] The first solution to this problem appears to have been found by Gabriel Cramér, a mathematician from Geneva, in a letter to Nicolas in 1728. In this letter, Cramér proposed to use the square root of the monetary amount to represent the decreasing value of monetary gains. D. Bernoulli seems to have learned about this solution after having found his own solution.

Choice 1
Two persons get their monthly report from a broker:

A is told that her wealth went from 4 million to 3 million.
B is told that her wealth went from 1 million to 1.1 million.

(i) Who of the two individuals has more reason to be satisfied with their financial situation?
(ii) Who is happier today?

If A's and B's absolute levels of wealth determine their satisfaction, A should be happier and more satisfied today. However, our intuition tells us that it is actually B who is likely more satisfied on the day, even though A is substantially richer.

This example shows us that something is amiss when we assume that people's satisfaction is driven by their *level* of wealth. Instead, people appear to be sensitive to *changes* in wealth. People enjoy getting richer and dislike getting poorer. But rich people do not generally wake up every day thinking about how happy they are to be rich. They go on with their day, often trying to get richer (and getting frustrated if they can't).

Another telltale sign that people care not just about levels of wealth is the fact that they react asymmetrically to possibilities of gains and losses. Losses seem to be perceived as particularly unappealing, and people tend to be overly keen to avoid them. Take the following hypothetical choice also presented by Kahneman:

Choice 2
Would you accept this gamble?

50% chance to win $150
50% chance to lose $100

This gamble offers a positive expected value, but most people typically prefer not to accept it. The risk of loss trumps the possibility of gain. Suppose now that you are instead offered the following choice:

Choice 3
Which would you choose?
Lose $100 with certainty

or

50% chance to win $50
50% chance to lose $200

In this case, most people tend to opt for the gamble. The sure outcome gives a guaranteed loss. In comparison, the gamble offers a chance of avoiding a loss. Taking the gamble seems now understandable. But notice that the second

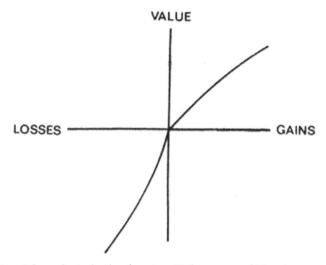

FIGURE 6.1. A hypothetical value function (Kahneman and Tversky, 1979).

choice is the same as in the Choice 2. Only one thing changed: $100 has been withdrawn from each alternative. It is hard to explain how people's risk attitudes would so dramatically change (preferring the sure outcome $0 in the first choice and the gamble in the second choice) if what they care about is their overall level of wealth or income (which is going to be very similar in both situations).[4]

To explain this pattern of preferences, Kahneman and Tversky proposed a new theory, called prospect theory, in their famous 1979 paper. Contrary to Bernoulli's assumption, Kahneman and Tversky suggested that people value outcomes as gains or losses relative to a *reference point*. Specifically, they proposed the utility function depicted in Figure 6.1 to represent how people enjoy gains (positive subjective value) and dislike losses (negative subjective value).

This utility function has several significant features. First, it presents both a decreasing marginal sensitivity to gains *and* losses. The idea of decreasing marginal utility was central to the resolution of the St Petersburg paradox by D. Bernoulli. Kahneman and Tversky propose to extend it to the area of losses

---

[4] Formally, if people use expected utility to make risky choices, their attitude towards risk (risk aversion vs risk love) is determined by the curvature of the utility function. The different answers for Gambles 2 and 3 would suggest that this curvature was dramatically different between the respondents' possible levels of wealth in the two gambles even though these levels differ by only $100.

too: in the same way that our satisfaction increases more when our gains move from $0 to $10 than from $1,000 to $1,010, our satisfaction decreases more when our losses move from $0 to $10 than from $1,000 to $1,010.

Another feature of this utility function is the substantially steeper slope in the domain of losses. The loss of $100 leads to a larger change in utility (downward) than the change in utility (upward) from a gain of $100. People are said to be *loss averse*: they feel losses more strongly than gains of the same magnitude. This loss aversion explains the choice not to take the gamble that presented some losses in the Choice 2 situation and the choice to take the gamble in Choice 3, when the only alternative was a sure loss instead.

Noticeably, it was not the first time that such an S-shaped function was proposed in economics. In 1952, Markowitz proposed a similar function with a reference point placed at the "customary level of wealth". But until Kahneman and Tversky's prospect theory, the suggestion that utility could be relative to a reference point had not attracted much interest in economics. The idea that preferences are *reference-dependent* – our utility depends on a reference point – became one of the most influential contributions of prospect theory to economics. It has since been used in a wide range of applications explaining real-world behaviour (O'Donoghue and Sprenger 2018).

Reference-dependence and loss aversion are, for instance, used to explain a phenomenon called the *endowment effect*: people value things *more* when they have them in their possession. Imagine, for example, that a big event you would love to attend is going to take place in your city. This event may be something like the concert of the most famous pop singer in the world or the final of the football World Cup. Think, for a few seconds, about the following question: What is the highest price you would be willing to pay for a ticket? Imagine now a different situation where you already have a ticket. If somebody enquires whether they could buy it from you, what is now the lowest price you would accept to give your ticket away? If you were a homo economicus, this price should be the same as the highest price you would be willing to pay: it is the price for which you are just *indifferent* between the money amount and the ticket. If the money amount is larger, you prefer to keep the money (you do not buy, or you sell if you have the ticket). If the money amount is lower, you prefer the ticket (you buy, or you do not sell). But, in practice, for most people, the price they would ask to sell the ticket is higher than the price they would be willing to pay to buy it.

Psychologists Ziv Carmon and Dan Ariely conducted exactly this experiment at Duke University (2000). They contacted students who had registered to try to get a ticket to see the highly prized basketball team of the university playing in the NCAA Final Four tournament. They asked them the highest price they would be willing to pay to buy the ticket and the lowest price they would be willing to accept to depart from it if they had one. The difference was startling: the students indicated they would be willing to pay on average $166 to buy a ticket, but to give it away, they would require to be paid at least $2,411!

The asymmetric pattern between buying and selling prices can be explained with reference-dependence. If people's belongings quickly become part of their reference point, any change in belongings will involve the feeling of losing something (e.g., the basketball match ticket) and the gain of something else (e.g., the money). If people are loss averse, the negative utility generated by the loss will trump the positive utility generated by the gain.

How Is the Reference Point Determined?

The idea of reference-dependence opens, however, a new question: How are reference points set? A natural candidate, used by Kahneman and Tversky themselves, is the status quo relative to which gains and losses are determined. In that sense, the reference point is most often considered to be *what people already have*. Intuitively, getting more or less than that level can be felt as a gain or a loss.

However, at the end of their 1979 paper, Kahneman and Tversky pointed out that reference points do not always have to be the status quo. They could be your expectations or aspiration levels:

So far in this paper, ... the reference point was taken to be the status quo or one's current assets. Although this is probably true for most choice problems, there are situations in which gains and losses are coded relative to an expectation or aspiration level that differs from the status quo.

A 1999 study of cab drivers' behaviour in New York seems to illustrate that perfectly. Camerer et al. (1997) showed that the drivers tend to drive *longer hours* on the days when there are fewer customers around and *shorter hours* on the days when there are more customers around. It may not sound particularly peculiar to you if you are not an economist, but, to an economist, it seems very wrong. To see why, we have to consider the following question: What is the best way for taxi drivers to allocate their time across different days? The answer is quite simple: taxi drivers should work *more* on busy days as they will get more customers per hours worked. On quiet days, they should work *less* and stop earlier to enjoy some leisure (instead of working for a relatively low hourly income). Over the course of the year, this behaviour would lead to the best mix of income and leisure.[5]

Taxi drivers are doing exactly the contrary: they work longer hours when the hourly income is low (quiet days) and shorter hours when the hourly income is high (busy days). This puzzling behaviour makes sense if one considers that taxi drivers set for themselves daily income targets to reach. If they do so, they reach their target earlier on busy days and later on quiet days. Once they reach

---

[5] It does not depend on whether a driver likes "leisure" (by which economists mean doing anything else besides working) a lot or not. Even if a driver prefers to work most of the time, they should not stop earlier when the number of customers per hours is higher.

their target, they may be more prone to stop if these daily income targets work as reference points: falling below the desired target will motivate them to work harder due to loss aversion. And this additional motivation can compensate for the fact that the lower hourly hour rate is in itself less motivating (as predicted by standard theory). The desire to avoid making less than their daily target will motivate them to put in the extra hours required.

Reference-dependence can be seen as a violation of rationality. One reason for this view is that people are prone to the *failure of asset integration* when considering only financial gains and losses. In short, they are missing the big picture in their financial decisions. In the case of taxi drivers, they look not at their total monthly or yearly income, but only at their daily income. This behaviour seems wrong, in the sense that it will generate decisions that lead to lower levels of overall wealth (as in the case of taxi drivers). While asset integration is not one of the foundational axioms in decision theory, it is a reasonable enough principle to consider "irrational" the failure to respect it.[6]

Examples like the endowment effect or the target-chasing taxi drivers have, among many others, convinced economists of the relevance of making utility relative to a reference point. But reference-dependence raises issues that are not answered by these empirical studies. First, why would people behave that way? Second, how are reference points set? While Kahneman and Tversky stressed that reference points could differ from the status quo, they did not provide a method to precisely determine what a person's reference point would be, in a given situation. Should it be the status quo or a target ahead? If it is a target ahead, how would it be determined?

In a very influential article, Köszegi and Rabin (2006) proposed to assume that the reference point is the level of expectation a person would rationally have in a given situation. This assumption conveniently provides a possible explanation for reference points that can be the status quo (when you expect that your wealth will stay the same) or for targets in terms of positive income (when you expect your wealth to increase). In the case of taxi drivers, the daily income target may be their rational expectation of what they should make on an average day in the year. Köszegi and Rabin's model provides a possible answer to the question of how reference points are determined.

Some questions still remain. First, *why* should we have reference points at the level of our expectations, rather than at other possible levels?[7] Second, can reference points always be explained as our expectations? There is a literature that suggests that *goals* can act as reference points (Heath et al. 1999). People sometimes set ambitious and difficult goals for themselves. Research has found

---

[6] Redelmeier and Tversky (1992) describe the principle of asset integration as "normatively unassailable even though it is not descriptively valid".

[7] Kőoszegi and Rabin's motivation to assume that reference points are set at the level of expectations was largely pragmatic: "Our primary motivation for this assumption is that it helps unify and reconcile existing interpretations and corresponds to readily accessible intuition in many examples."

that runners in marathons behave as if symbolic thresholds (e.g., finishing in under three hours) act as reference points (Allen et al. 2017). Similarly, chess players seem to exert extra effort to improve their best rating, acting as if their personal best is a reference point (Anderson and Green 2018). It is not clear that such goals are necessarily equal to their expectations a priori. In some cases, these goals may be quite hard to achieve.

Peer Comparison

One important factor seems to be at play in how we set our reference point: how people around us are doing. Imagine the following situation. John is a middle-class employee. He is fairly satisfied with his life. He and his partner have enough to repay their house's mortgage and save for the education of their two children. On a Saturday afternoon, John takes his phone and half-automatically looks at his Facebook account. A post liked by one of his friends attracts his attention. A certain Jake Smith, just gave a TV interview as a major manager of a leading company in the country. The Facebook post shows him posing on a large yacht with his family during his holidays in some tropical islands. John recognises Jake. Over twenty years ago they were in the same high school! There was nothing very distinctive about him. He was neither brilliant nor very popular. John is surprised by Jake's outstanding success. How did he become so successful? At school, John had significantly better grades and was more popular than Jake.

Put yourself in John's shoes. How do you think he is likely to feel? Happy for the success of Jake? Indifferent about somebody he has not seen for so long? Or possibly envious/bitter about how Jake's success compares to his? The psychological evidence suggests that, in many cases, John is likely to feel a bit down after learning about Jake's success.

Facebook and other social media give people access to personal information from a wide network of people. This information is self-curated and, most often, positive. People post their beautiful (and carefully chosen) holiday pictures, and announce their positive news (promotion, engagement, awards). When exposed to such news and photos, people have regularly been found to experience negative feelings (Krasnova et al. 2013), and young women, in particular, can experience a lower mood and a greater dissatisfaction with their facial appearance (Fardouly et al. 2015). It seems that a frequent reaction to others' achievements is not to feel happy for them, but to *suffer in comparison*. It may seem petty and unkind. Should we not revel in the happiness of others?

This effect makes sense if our peers contribute to shaping our reference point. When we wonder whether we should be happy or not with our current level of achievement, the achievements of others give us a natural point of comparison. Is having a university degree from a good university a success? If all my friends from my old socially disadvantaged suburb have barely made it out of high school, it may feel like a great achievement. But if I come from a selective social background and a large number of my friends have graduated from more prestigious universities, a degree from a good university may look like an underachievement in comparison.

In his book *The Social Leap*, Bill Von Hippel (2018) describes the following hypothetical situation to illustrate our concern about our success relative to our peers:

> Imagine I invented a pill that increased your intelligence by 50 percent, and I offered you one. Immediately after taking the pill, you'd feel so much smarter – all sorts of problems that had seemed complex before would now be child's play. Particle physics and calculus problems would be amusing ways to entertain yourself while waiting for a haircut. But now imagine that I offered everyone else two pills. You'd be sitting there waiting for your haircut, and everyone around you would be discussing ideas that were way beyond your capacity. In a matter of moments, you'd go from feeling like a genius to feeling like a fool.

The economists Solnick and Hemenway (1998) tested this idea in an experiment. They asked faculty, students and staff at Harvard which one of the following two situations they would prefer:

A: Your current yearly income is $50,000; others earn $25,000.
B: Your current yearly income is $100,000; others earn $200,000.

Faced with such a question, and with similar other examples, around 50% of respondents answered they would prefer solution A, the one where they have less in *absolute terms* but more in *relative terms*.

Another experiment by Zizzo and Oswald (2001) found that people were willing to pay to reduce the amount of money received by other people. The participants, mostly university students, had to play in a game with real monetary payoffs. In a first phase, payoff differences were generated between participants, and in a second phase, participants could "burn" others' money by spending some of their own money. Overall, two-thirds of participants were willing to spend money in order to decrease the amount of others, in particular, when others had more.

Beyond experiments, evidence on happiness and life satisfaction suggests that comparison to peers drives, to a large extent, whether we are happy or not. People's satisfaction with their income tends to depend on whether it is higher or lower than what other people with similar characteristics are making (Clark and Oswald 1996). Social comparisons are also observed in other domains: for a given weight, people tend to feel more overweight when other people around them have a lower average weight (Blanchflower et al. 2009); for a given height, they tend to have lower feeling of well-being when the average height is higher around them (Clark 2016).

This concern for relative comparisons also seems to explain the so-called *Easterlin paradox*: Following Easterlin (1974), economists have found that people in richer countries do not tend to be happier than people in poorer countries. However, it is not the case that income does not matter. In a given country, richer people tend to be happier than others. These facts are compatible with the idea that people care about their relative income but that this comparison mainly operates within their countries; when incomes rise overall in a country, it does not impact people's feeling about their relative position (Clark et al. 2008).

Here again, the evidence on reference-dependent preferences raises a question: What should be the level of our reference points? In the context of peer comparison, this question becomes: How are reference groups determined, and why do we care about comparing ourselves to some people and not to others? Not every comparison matters. It is usually understood that we compare ourselves to a *reference group*. It can be composed of our peers (e.g., schoolmates) but not necessarily (e.g., people having a similar profession in an industry). If John had seen on Facebook a post about Bill Gates earning another few billion dollars, he likely would not have cared. Bill Gates is not somebody John finds relevant to compare himself to.

The evidence about reference-dependence is overwhelming. But why should we have reference points in the first place, and what should their levels be if we agree they exist? These two questions have received answers from new theories in economics and neuroscience.

6.2 EVOLUTIONARY FOUNDATIONS OF REFERENCE-DEPENDENT PREFERENCES AND LOSS AVERSION

Let's go back to a fundamental problem: how an organism perceives the value of different choices. Ascribing values to different possible choices is a necessity as soon as the organism tries to make the best choices possible. An important insight is that choices are intimately associated with movement. The neuroscientist Read Montague (2006, p. 119) makes this point neatly: "Once life started to move, valuation mechanisms were an inevitable consequence. A creature that moves left one moment forgoes what it might have obtained had it moved right. This is an economic decision and it selects creatures that make more informed choices."

Efficiency of Perception

Let's think about the task of an organism having to make decisions between different alternatives (e.g., eating different pieces of food). The organism has to perceive the value of each alternative. What would be the optimal perceptual mechanism the organism should be endowed with?

Robson (2001) showed that under very reasonable assumptions about the limitations of perception, the optimal way to perceive value is to have an S-shaped function, very similar to the one from prospect theory. The key assumption from Robson is that the precision of a perceptual system cannot be infinitely precise.

Here is a highly simplified description of the type of limitations a biological perceptual system could face. Suppose that the organism's perceptual system used to assess the values of options is composed of only ten neurons. Each neuron can give only a binary signal: it can fire (on) or be at rest (off). Each neuron fires if the value from the option is above a given threshold set for this neuron. The organism's perception of value is then determined by the number of neurons firing: only a discrete number of neurons can fire at once. In that case, the organism can perceive only a limited number of different ranges of value.

Let's consider the simple situation where an organism regularly has to choose between only two options with different values. For the sake of simplicity, let's further assume that the best option possible can give a value of 100 (maximum fitness) and the worst option possible a value 0 (worse fitness possible). Any pair of options faced by the organism will be drawn from values between 0 and 100. The organism's ability to discriminate between the values of these two options will depend on the location of the neurons' thresholds between 0 and 100. If the organism has only ten neurons, it has ten thresholds of perception to discriminate the values of the options it faces.

The simplest solution would be to place these thresholds uniformly: the first neurons fire if the value is above 5, the second neuron also fires if the value is above 15, the third neuron also fires if the value is above 25, ... and the tenth neuron above 95. If the organism faces two alternatives that have very different values, it will have no problem discriminating between them. For example, think about the situation where it faces two alternatives with values 14 and 23. The first alternative will trigger only the first neuron, while the second will trigger the first and the second neurons. The organism will, therefore, be able to identify that the second alternative has a higher value, and it will be able to make the right decision and choose it. These thresholds can be conceived as creating a valuation function helping the organism to perceive the value of the options it faces. This function is a step function where the value of an option perceived (1) is equal between two thresholds and (2) jumps across two thresholds. The top left panel of Figure 6.2 shows this valuation function with a uniform distribution of thresholds.

This valuation function is useful to discriminate values, but what happens when two alternatives have similar values? Consider, for example, the situation

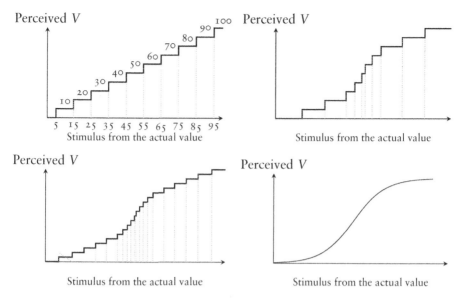

FIGURE 6.2. Why an S-shape can be an optimal solution to the problem of perception, when the organism has limited ability to discriminate between values of a stimulus. Top left panel: situation where an organism can discriminate between only ten levels of a stimulus and the thresholds to discriminate between these different levels are evenly spaced. Top right panel: if the stimulus is more likely to be observed for middle values and less likely to be observed for extreme values, it is more efficient for the threshold to be packed more densely in the middle. Bottom left panel: if the number of thresholds increases, the same logic applies. Bottom right panel: in the limit, as the number of thresholds gets larger, the perception function follows an S shape.

where the two alternatives have values 38 and 43. In that case, both alternatives trigger the firing of the same number of neurons: four. The organism is not able to discriminate between the values of these two alternatives. It is a situation similar to when you hold two pens and wonder which one is the heaviest. Each pen has a specific weight, and a highly precise balance could tell you which one is heavier. But for your perception of weight, they may seem identical. You are in that case unable to discriminate between the two and to tell which one is indeed the heaviest. In such a situation, the organism will be able only to choose randomly between the two alternatives. Half the time, it will make the wrong choice.

The problem for the organism is to allocate its ten discrete levels of perception in order to be able to discriminate between two alternatives in the best way possible. Suppose that the perceptual system is not bound to place thresholds uniformly but can place them in any way possible. What is the distribution of thresholds of perception that would minimise the number of errors? Intuitively, to make fewer errors, there should be more thresholds in the range of values that are frequently observed.

If the two alternatives in our example tend to have their values always located between 46 and 54, a uniform allocation of the thresholds is inefficient. First, most of the neurons are going to be either always on (thresholds below 46) or always off (threshold above 54). As a consequence, they will rarely be used to make decisions between options. And second, there will be lots of cases where both alternatives have close values and where the perceptual system will not be able to discriminate between them (both options will trigger the same number of neurons).

The optimal solution to minimise the number of errors is to allocate more thresholds in the range of values that the organism is most likely to observe. This solution is represented in the top right panel of Figure 6.2. Imagine now that the organism would progressively evolve a better nervous system with more neurons to be able to discriminate between a larger number of thresholds. The value function should progressively follow the distribution of the values of the options in the organism's environment (formally it should follow its *cumulative distribution function*). The lower panels of Figure 6.2 represent this progressive evolution of the value function to an S-shaped function when the likelihood to observe values is higher in an intermediate range, and lower for higher or lower values. In that case, the solution has the distinctive shape of a prospect theory utility function.[8]

Robson's theory provides a simple explanation for the S-shape of the utility function. And, with it, also comes a simple answer to the question of the location of the reference point. The location of the inflexion point of this utility function is where values are most likely to be observed. This inflection point is the reference point in the prospect theory utility function. Among the most common distributions are bell curves (symmetric and single-peaked). For such distributions, the inflection of the optimal value function will be at the expected value of the distribution. So this framework also provides a natural explanation for why people's reference points would be set at the level of their *expectations*.

This framework can also be extended to explain how we *adapt* our utility function to changing circumstances. If you move from a bright room to a

---

[8] A similar point was already made by Laughlin (1981) about the patterns of firing of a single neuron. Using a different type of perceptual constraints motivated by information theory, Woodford (2012a; 2012b) shows that a perceptual system trying to optimise its ability to discriminate would also lead to an S-shaped function. A paper by Netzer (2009) extended Robson's approach further. While Robson assumed that an organism would aim to minimise the proportion of errors, Netzer looks at what happens if an organism minimises the *cost* of errors in terms of fitness instead. He shows that it also results in an S-shaped utility function that is flatter than the cumulative distribution function to be able to discriminate extreme values more (the errors can be more costly when choosing between alternatives with extreme values).

dark room, you will initially be unable to discern anything as your eyes will only perceive everything as "too dark". It is what you would expect from a perceptual system where perception thresholds were optimally calibrated and concentrated at a high level of luminosity. When you moved to a dark room, the different shades of darkness triggered the same thresholds of perception (which are sparsely located for such low levels of luminosity). You are therefore not able to discriminate between these different shades of darkness.

As organisms come across different environments with different distributions of stimuli (e.g., dark rooms and bright rooms), it would be optimal for an organism to be able to adapt the location of these thresholds when the perceived distribution of stimuli changes. Robson et al. (2017) showed that simple and mechanical adjustments of the thresholds can lead to moving their distribution to a new empirical distribution of values faced by an organism.[9] Such an adaptation can allow an organism to fine-tune its perceptual ability to the specific context it faces. In the example of a dark room, as your eyes progressively habituate to the low level of luminosity, you may eventually start being able to distinguish shapes from the different shades of grey in the room.

This adaptation can help explain how our utility function and its reference point adapt over time. Suppose you buy a lottery ticket and win a jackpot of $10 million. On the day you win, the magnitude of this prize will likely trigger the maximum valuation estimate from your subjective reward system, given the usual range of income you enjoy. In short, you will be ecstatic. But as you progressively settle into your new life, you will get used to a different range of valuations. Soon enough the lobster and caviar dinner, which looked like the epitome of bliss to you before, now seems just fine, if not bland.[10]

These theoretical explanations are compelling. They provide a simple foundation to reference-dependent preferences and an explanation of the level of reference points and their evolution across time. Research in neuroscience has provided further support for these models. Neuroscientist Wolfram Schultz and his co-authors found that specific neurons indeed seem to estimate subjective values, by firing and releasing dopamine, the molecule coding reward in the brain (2007). These neurons fire proportionally to the magnitude of an enjoyable stimulus (e.g., size of a glass of orange juice). More importantly, neurons encode not absolute value but value *relative to expectations*. In an

[9] Woodford's (2012a) framework using information theory to model perceptual systems also has the ability to explain such adaptations.

[10] Even though Kahneman and Tversky did not delve into the evolutionary foundation of prospect theory, they made the connection with our perceptual system in their 1979 article: "Our perceptual apparatus is attuned to the evaluation of changes or differences rather than to the evaluation of absolute magnitudes. When we respond to attributes such as brightness, loudness, or temperature, the past and present context of experience defines an adaptation level, or reference point, and stimuli are perceived in relation to this reference point.... Thus, an object at a given temperature may be experienced as hot or cold to the touch depending on the temperature to which one has adapted. The same principle applies to non-sensory attributes such as health, prestige, and wealth."

experiment, if a monkey is shown a light and then given a bit of orange juice, the neurons are going to fire (reward) when the juice is received. But if this situation is repeated, the neurons will start to fire when the light gets bright, which is the surprising stimulus indicating that the juice is coming. When the (now expected) juice comes, the neurons do not fire anymore. Expected outcomes do not bring rewards. But if a light is shown and no juice is given, neurons fire on the light signal but their firing activity decreases when the juice doesn't eventuate (negative reward) as the expected positive outcome is not experienced.

In his discussion of how the brain encodes information, Glimcher (2011) points out that reference-dependence is actually directly built in to our perceptual system. Our eyes, for instance, record only differences in intensity, not absolute values: "the hardware requirements for a reference point-free model cannot, in principle, be met ... All sensory encoding that we know of is reference-dependent. Nowhere in the nervous system are the objective values of consumable rewards encoded.... Information about the objective intensity of incident light is *irretrievably* lost at the transducer" (pp. 274–275). The reference-dependence in that view emerges in our perceptual system (from the perception of basic stimuli to the perception of subjective value) as a solution to the biological constraints we face.[11]

Optimal Motivation

Rayo and Becker (2007) have proposed another reason why our utility function should have an S-shape, which complements Robson's theory. While Robson started from the idea that organisms face alternatives drawn randomly from a probability distribution, Rayo and Becker start from the idea that the outcomes faced by an organism typically result from its decisions. Organisms have to work to find food, they have to try hard not to be eaten, they have to compete to find a mate, and, finally, they often have to invest time and resources to protect their offspring.

Chilling out is not an option, or rather, those organisms whose genes gave them a taste for chilling out were less likely to pass these genes along to the next generation. Evolution will tend to foster the selection of organisms that work as hard as possible to maximise their fitness. And the way to do so is to endow these organisms with a reward system that gives them greater rewards for actions leading to higher fitness.[12]

Similarly to Robson, Rayo and Becker examine a reward function designed to discriminate between the values of different options. Rayo and Becker consider two realistic constraints when thinking about how this reward function

---

[11] "This encoding of employing a 'baseline' reflects an underlying process of optimization" (Glimcher 2011, p. 276).

[12] A reward is simply a directional signal giving feedback to the organism about what is or was good to do (positive reward) and what was not a good thing to do (negative reward).

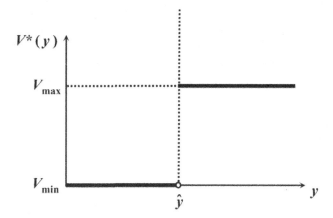

FIGURE 6.3. Optimal value function from Rayo and Becker (2007). On the horizontal axis, y is the level of fitness associated with the decision of the organism; $\hat{y}$ is just below the maximum of fitness the organism can reach.

would look. First, there is a minimum and a maximum level that this function can take. For example, if this reward function is constrained by a number of neurons firing in the brain, this number has to be finite. As a result, it is impossible to be *infinitely* happy. Second, they assume that organisms struggle to assess small differences in rewards, in the same way as we would struggle to assess the differences in weight between two similarly heavy objects.[13]

Under these restrictions, Rayo and Becker show that the optimal reward function is a step function, with a step just below the level of the organism potential in terms of fitness (the highest level of fitness the organism can reach). This function is depicted in Figure 6.3. It does not not give any rewards for choices leading to fitness values markedly below the organism's potential, and it gives maximum reward to the organism for reaching a level close to its potential. This function is the one that gives the best motivation to the organism to maximise its fitness.

Rayo and Becker then extend their model to situations where the organism's reward system cannot perfectly map all the characteristics of the state of the world into a potential level of fitness. An organism can face a wide range of situations and not all of these situations' characteristics can be encoded in the value function whose principles are hard-wired in the organism. In other words, evolution is not efficient enough to map every type of situation an organism may face in its life to a precise fitness value.

---

[13] In Robson's approach, the first assumption was implied via the assumption of a limited number of possible levels of valuation. The second assumption of imprecision of perception was then a result of this limited number of levels that can be perceived.

Consider an organism facing rainy days and dry days. Evolution may be able to encode in the organism's reward system the maximum possible fitness for an average rainy day or an average dry day. But days differ in many dimensions: temperature, wind, intensity of the rain or sunlight. There are too many possible situations for an organism to have a hard-wired reward system that identifies precisely the organism's maximum possible fitness in any situation (e.g., fairly dry, very hot and somewhat windy). This problem is compounded by the fact that the environment can change: the climate varies over time, populations migrate to new environments. While evolution may progressively tune our reward function to track more precisely our fitness potential given our specific circumstances, it may not be able to perfectly discriminate between all the situations we face.

Nonetheless, an organism may acquire additional information about its environment and its potential that evolution has not had time to encode its reward function. In that case, Rayo and Becker show that an optimal value function will be S-shaped. Instead of locating all the rewards in one location with a step function, it spreads them across a range of possible outcomes to cater to all the possible situations the organism may be facing.

One way to conceive this spread of the utility function is to see it as the ignorance of the reward system about what the organism is able to achieve. To make this problem intuitive, here is a simple comparison. Imagine a situation where Jane (a manager) wants to hire John (an employee) to sell a product. John's work consists in calling potential customers and trying to convince them to buy as many items of the product as possible.

Jane tries to find the best way to reward John for him to be motivated to make the highest sales as possible. To motivate John, Jane has a budget of $1,000. Her problem is simple: How to best allocate this budget in possible rewards as a function of John's performance? Jane knows John's CV. She has, therefore, quite a bit of information about his skills. But she is not sure about John's ability in the context of this specific market. So she does not know for sure what level of sales John can achieve. If she knew that John can sell at most 100 items if he tries his best, then she would set a $1,000 bonus for the sale of 100 items to ensure that John reaches this target. This is the solution when Jane has full information about John's potential. However, given that Jane does not know for sure John's capacity, she should divide the $1,000 bonus in several smaller bonuses spread over the sale numbers that she expects John is likely to be able to reach. For instance, suppose Jane thinks John's best possible performance in terms of sales, is somewhere around 100 items, perhaps somewhat below or somewhat above that number. She may opt to give John a bonus of $100 if he sells 80 items, an additional bonus of $150 if he sells 90, a additional bonus of $250 if he sells 100, a additional bonus of $150 if he sells 110 items and a additional bonus of $100 if he sells 120 items. By doing so, Jane has spread her budget of $1,000 over a wider range of possible outcomes. This reward system ensures that whatever John's ability is, he will always be in a situation where he can gain a bit more from trying his best. If John can only reach 80, he gets some reward ($100) for reaching his potential, and if John can reach 120, he still gets some additional reward ($100) for reaching this higher potential, instead of simply selling 110 items. Note that, the total reward received by John as a function of his performance (adding the different bonuses) is S-Shaped: it grows slower below and above 100, and faster at 100. This S-shaped function reflects Jane's uncertainty about the ability of John. And the inflection point should be located where Jane believes John's highest achievement is most likely located.

In this example, Jane faces the same problem as "evolution" faces (in some sense) when designing an optimal reward function for an organism. As evolution progressively tunes our reward system for us to maximise our fitness, it cannot encode in an organism a recognition of what its potential will be in every possible situation. As a consequence, it makes sense to design organisms with smoothed S-shaped reward functions that follow the distribution of the organism's potential.[14] A consequence of this S-shaped reward function spreading rewards is that, for each situation faced by the organism, it will have an incentive to do well due to the fact that doing better is rewarded more than doing worse. This incentive will be lower than if all the rewards were located at the right place. But given that evolution is unable to encode a precise "right place", spreading out rewards is the best it can do.

This model, therefore, gives another explanation about why our utility functions should follow an S-shaped pattern as suggested by prospect theory. Rayo and Becker's model also answers the question about where the reference point should be on this utility function: it should be around the level of achievement that the organism is able to reach. Because the organism *can* reach this level and because the value function will incentivise it to reach this level, it is also the expected level of outcome the organism *will* reach.

This model can explain adaptations and variations of the reference point: as the opportunities of an organism change, its reference point changes as well. The first pay you received on your first job may have seemed like a bonanza at the time. Soon enough, though, you stopped contemplating how much money you were making and looked forward to a promotion. As you kept experiencing receiving this income regularly, your reference point had to move upward to keep motivating you. Remember that chilling out is not an option and evolution did not design our subjective reward system to make us happy. The pursuit of

[14] We can compare "evolution", an impersonal process, to a designer who has to decide, like Jane, what is the best reward function. This metaphor was proposed by Dennett (1987) and Binmore (1994b) and used by Rayo and Becker as a way to model this problem. To be fully precise, I should point out that there is a key difference between the problem evolution has to solve and the one Jane has to solve. For Jane, the problem is that John may lack motivation because he dislikes work. Evolution does not face this problem since it designs all the aspects of an organism's reward function. It would not make sense to endow the organism with a tendency to try to dislike doing well. But an organism may face perception limitations, like the one described in the previous section. The goal of the reward function is to prevent the organism from making mistakes between choices with different fitness levels. To extend the example of Jane and John, the problem could be that John is happy to do a good job but he reacts only to the monetary rewards; if these rewards are too close, he may fail to notice the difference and opt for a low level of effort rather than a high level of effort.

a state that will deliver "long-lasting happiness" is a goose-chase. Evolution has designed us to consistently move the goal post forward once we get more successful.

Noticeably, people often fail to anticipate such adaptations. In a famous study, Schkade and Kahneman (1998) found that while people tend to believe that living in sunny California would make them happier, people living in California are not happier. Schkade and Kahneman called this the "focusing illusion", the idea that we will be very happy with the next move to a better location, a better job, a better-looking car and so on. But in the end, "Nothing ... will make as much difference as you think" (Schkade and Kahneman 1998, p. 345).

In Rayo and Becker's framework, it is natural for people to habituate to the circumstances they face. But why would people not anticipate this future habituation? Robson and Samuelson (2011) showed that it could be optimal for evolution to embed the illusion that our choice today will make us happier tomorrow in our utility functions. These utility functions should be suited to the range of outcomes relevant in each period: if you are choosing between living in California and the (cold) US Midwest, you should feel positive subjective satisfaction from choosing California. But once you moved to California and you make decisions there, just being in California is not a relevant feature to take into account to discriminate between decisions. Your subjective satisfaction for the different options you consider should not be impacted by the fact of living in California.

The tennis player Andre Agassi illustrated this myopia about how one will react to future outcomes with this great quote: "Now that I've won a slam, I know something very few people on earth are permitted to know. A win doesn't feel as good as a loss feels bad, and the good feeling doesn't last long as the bad. Not even close (2010)."

Peer Comparison

Rayo and Becker's model also explains the social nature of our reference point: our tendency to use our peers' successes to evaluate ours.[15] In their framework, this tendency and its effect on our subjective well-being comes naturally. Our peers are similar to us in many ways, and their success provides us with information about our own possibilities.[16]

In that view, we should care about others' outcomes because they tell us something about what we can do ourselves. When John sees on Facebook that his old classmate Jake became hugely successful in life, he learns that such

---

[15] A popular phrase reflecting this is the impetus to "keep up with the Joneses".

[16] An interesting paper by Samuelson (2004) can be seen as formalising a very similar intuition in the case of consumption. Evolution could lead to relative consumption effects because the consumption levels of others is informative on whether the environment is bountiful or not. If the environment is bountiful, one should try to reach a high level of consumption.

a success was likely within the realm of his own possibilities. This becomes even more clear when he remembers comparing favourably to Jake in terms of academic and social skills. "If Jake managed to be successful, why did I not? I could have done that," John may think realistically.

This information we get from peers gives a simple explanation about how we select our reference group: we choose to compare to those who are similar enough to us to inform us about what we can do. If Jake had been an outstanding genius known for winning the International Mathematics Olympiad, John would care less because Jake's later success would not be that informative about what John himself could have done.

Evolution should tune our utility function to depend on our peers' outcome to the extent that they look like us. Specifically, it should reward us for doing better than our peers as it likely reflects that we are doing things right, while it should penalise us for doing worse than our peers as it likely indicates that we are doing something wrong. In Rayo and Becker's framework, this effect takes the form of peers' outcomes contributing to shaping our reference point.

An important aspect of this explanation of peer comparison is that it is purely about *information*. We enjoy doing better than others not because we are envious or spiteful, but because doing better than others – who are similar to us – is a signal that we likely achieve close to our potential.

This explanation is very appealing, but it may miss some aspects of peer comparison. We have seen that people are willing to choose worse outcomes in absolute terms in order to be better than others in relative terms in experiments. It is hard to explain such behaviour with Rayo and Becker's framework. Evolutionary theory suggests another possible reason for peer comparison. We may care about our position relative to our peers, because natural selection selects not just for absolute success but for relative success. There is often a competitive aspect to natural selection: organisms compete to secure resources, territories and mates. This competitive aspect means that it is not enough for an organism to be well adapted to its environment; it needs to be better adapted than others of its own species. As pointed out by Darwin himself, this competitive aspect is particularly present in the quest for the best mate of the opposite sex. Success at attracting a partner depends on the ability to look like a good option *relative* to the other options available.[17]

As a consequence, it is normal for our subjective reward system to be receptive to our standing relative to others (Frank 1985). In that perspective, it is not surprising that humans care about how they look relative to others, how

---

[17] This competition leads to what Darwin called sexual selection, which "depends on the advantage which certain individuals have over other individuals of the same sex and species, in exclusive relation to reproduction" (Darwin 1871/1981). Sexual selection with its competitive aspect introduces many important strategic considerations; see Jones and Ratterman (2009) for a very clear presentation.

rich they are relative to others, what's their reputation relative others, and so on. The competitive aspect in evolution also explains why people may sometimes prefer situations where they have a worse outcome in absolute terms but a better outcome in relative terms.

These considerations suggest another way we would choose our reference group: we should be more sensitive to groups in which we are socially involved and where our social standing matters. In the case of John, he may care less about Jake's story if he learns that Jake has left to live in a country far away. Jake's success may suggest that John could have done better, but at least Jake won't be present at the next high school reunion to outshine him in front of his friends.

To sum up, there are very good reasons why we care about our relative success: information and the benefits of relative standings. These reasons help us understand which group of people we are likely to choose as a comparison point to judge our achievements as successes or failures.

Loss Aversion

One piece of the prospect theory utility function is still left to explain: the aversion to losses reflected in the utility function being steeper below the reference point than above. In the previous explanations given to reference-dependence, the utility functions are S-shaped and symmetric on each side of the reference point (the inflection point of the S). The aversion to losses has been observed not only in humans but also in great apes (Brosnan et al. 2007; Drayton et al. 2013), monkeys (Lakshminaryanan et al. 2008) and rats (Constantinople et al. 2019). These findings suggest it relies on cognitive processes that are quite ancient on an evolutionary time scale.

What could drive such a loss aversion? An optimal reward function needs to take into account the range of potential levels of fitness that the organism will be able to reach. As discussed above, the organism may be faced with a wide range of situations: some situations where it can reach a high level (favourable situations); some situations where it can't (unfavourable situations). Since all these different situations are likely too complex to be encoded in the reward function, the optimal reward function will be S-shaped: spreading the increase in satisfaction in order for the organisms to be rewarded for trying to do well over a wide range of possible outcomes.

But is smoothing the only solution? The answer is no. With my colleague Greg Kubitz, we have found that evolution can do better than just smooth the reward function. It can (1) get the organism to set itself a goal, reflecting the organism's information about its potential and (2) endow the organism with a reward function asymmetric around the goal, which acts like a reference point.

To see how it can work, let's come back to the earlier example of Jane (a manager) trying to motivate John (an employee). If Jane does not know John's potential, I described how she could spread the rewards for John with a series of bonuses if John reaches different thresholds of sales: $100 for 80 items sold, $150 for 90 items, $250 for 100 items, $150 for 110 items, and $100 for 120 items. Suppose that John faces this reward system and that, as he starts working, he realises that the sales are quite easy. He quickly understands he will have no problem selling 120 items. This level of performance is a bit outside the average prediction made by Jane, and the bonus Jane has allocated to sell 120-item items is relatively small, only $100. As a consequence, John may actually not have the best motivation to reach the 120-item target. Instead, he may opt to stop at 110 items sold, which does not require much effort and still already guarantees a reward, in total.

Here Jane is disadvantaged by her lack of information about John's potential. Whenever John's potential is higher or lower than what Jane expected, she will not have allocated large rewards for John to try his best. To prevent this to happen Jane can do better than simply spreading the rewards: she can design a reward system where John *reveals his knowledge about his ability* in the specific situation he faces. To do so, Jane can ask John to set himself a goal in terms of sales and reward him for setting a high goal. If John knows he can do well, he will choose a high goal and be rewarded accordingly. If he thinks the task is hard, he can opt for a low goal.

This incentivisation via goal setting has an important implication: the reward structure should be *asymmetric* relative to the goal that John sets to himself. In order to prevent John from picking a high target he would not be able to achieve, Jane should ensure that a failure to reach the target will lead to a penalty, a *loss* relative to the reward associated with the target. To prevent John from picking a low target he would be able to beat easily, Jane should ensure that, while there are some *gains* from going above the target, these gains will be relatively modest.

With this reward structure, if John can achieve a high target, he will get more by setting this target and meeting it than by setting a low target and reaching the level of sales of the high target. This reward structure incentivises John to set for himself the best goal he can achieve to get the most rewards.

The same logic can be built in the design of utility functions. An organism, having some information about its specific ability and challenges in each situation, should have the possibility of setting goals for which it receives subjective rewards (the higher the goal, the higher the reward). But once a goal is set, it will need to be reached. Failing to reach a goal leads to a decrease in subjective satisfaction. Going above the goal leads to an increase in subjective satisfaction, but this increase is not as large as the negative drop from failing to reach the goal.

This explanation recovers all the key ingredients of the prospect theory utility function: (1) the utility function is S-shaped; (2) it has a reference point that is set at the level the individual is expected to be able to reach; and (3) falling short of the reference point is relatively more penalised than going over it is rewarded (loss aversion). In addition, this explanation has an additional feature that is quite intuitive: there are some subjective rewards to aiming for high goals. But the cost of opting for goals too high is to set oneself up for failure and to pay the cost later on in disappointment and frustration.

Goals either can be to keep what you have (status quo) because you know you can keep it or they can be aspiration levels that reflect your understanding about your potential in a given situation. With such a design of a reward system, our utility function shifts in different contexts and keeps us incentivised to do our best in each situation. In that framework, loss aversion is not a bias; it is a part of a reward system designed to get the organism to always reach its full potential. In other words, the organism is designed to follow the maxim "if you can, you must".

∴

When the idea of reference-dependence was introduced, economists initially considered it as a mark of irrationality. Certainly, many economists still share this view. It is even more the case for loss aversion, considered as one of the main findings of prospect theory. At face value, it may seem hard to explain such an asymmetry in concerns for gains and losses.

Insights from economic theory and the empirical evidence from neuroscience cast a new light on these patterns of preferences. When trying to make decisions, organisms need to assess the values of the different options they face. Reference-dependence and loss aversion are credibly good solutions to this problem of value perception, given the constraints faced by evolution.

7

Sensitivity to Probability

I suggest, therefore, that when he contemplates this inner range of outcomes each of which carries no potential surprise, the entrepreneur does in fact concentrate his attention exclusively on the best and the worst hypotheses in this range.

—Shackle (1941, p. 251)

My psychology makes me prefer safety more strongly in the neighbourhood of certainty than I do in the neighbourhood of high risk. I am absolutely convinced there is nothing about this view that could justify it as being regarded in any way as irrational.

—Allais (1953, p. 539)[1]

Shouldn't risk attitude have something to do with feelings about probabilities?

—Wakker (2010, p. 147)

Summary: The homo economicus model assumes that people maximise their expected utility when choosing between different risky prospects. A person maximising expected utility takes into account the probabilities of the different payoffs associated with each prospect. However, empirical evidence suggests that people behave as if they distort probabilities. Specifically, people tend to give relatively greater weight in their mind to the probabilities of the extreme payoffs (close to the best and worse possible payoffs).

In the previous chapter, we saw how Bernoulli solved the paradox of St Petersburg with the assumption that people take into consideration the utility of monetary gains, not the monetary gains themselves. To solve the paradox,

---

[1] Translated in English in Allais and Hagen (1979).

Bernoulli made a key conceptual innovation: he assumed that people maximise the *expected utility* of the monetary gains. The idea that people should use the expected utility is not trivial. As we will see, there are other ways people could form preferences over risky prospects.

7.1 EXPECTED UTILITY AND ITS CRITICISM

The idea that people chose the risky prospects with the highest expected utility solution has some appeal: it is a very small deviation from the expected value solution. In that sense, it seems a very reasonable way to choose between prospects where the utility becomes a measure of *subjective* value that replaces money as a measure of *objective* value.

Until the 1950s, Bernoulli's solution did not get much traction in economics. The "utility" proposed by Bernoulli was conceived as a measure of internal satisfaction. As such, it was at odds with the fact that economics was moving away from psychology. At the start of the twentieth century, under Pareto's and Samuelson's influence, economists largely abandoned the idea of using utility as a measure of subjective satisfaction. Instead, they wanted to use this notion only as representing how people rank all the possible options they face, given their preferences. So when economists associated different options with utility values, these values had no psychological meaning. They just reflected an order of preferences: options with greater values are chosen over options with lower values.

In 1947, von Neumann and Morgenstern made a radical contribution to economics by giving a theoretical foundation to the use of expected utility. In the second edition of their book *Theory of Games and Economic Behavior*, they showed that people will behave as if they choose the gambles that maximise their expected utility, if they follow a few reasonable principles when making choices between gambles. These principles, or *"axioms"*, are the following.

First, people have *complete preferences*: they are assumed to know what they prefer. Faced with two different gambles, somebody is always able to indicate which one is preferred (or whether they would be equally happy with both). Second, their preferences are *transitive*. They are consistent in the sense that if they prefer a gamble A to a gamble B and a gamble B to a gamble C, then they also prefer A to C.[2] Third, their preferences are *continuous*: if somebody prefers A to B and B to C, the preference for B is "between" the preference for A and C in the sense that there must exist a gamble giving some probability of playing A and some probability of playing C for which the person is indifferent to B.

---

[2] These first two axioms are those used by economists to describe rational preferences when agents make decisions between goods (see Chapter 1).

If people respect these three principles, they will choose among gambles as if they give a utility V to each gamble and choose the one with the highest utility. A final principle ensures that the overall utility of V each gamble is the expected utility of its possible outcomes. It is the *independence axiom*. This principle states that the preference between two gambles should not be influenced by possible outcomes they have in common. When adding this assumption to the principles of completeness, transitivity and continuity, people will choose between the different gambles *as if* they choose the gamble with the highest expected utility. Formally, suppose a gamble composed of the possible monetary outcomes $(x_1, \ldots, x_n)$ where the probabilities of each outcome are, respectively, $(p_1, \ldots, p_n)$. When considering whether or not to choose this gamble, a decision maker following the principles above will behave if the value of the gamble is the expected utility:[3]

$$V(gamble) = \sum_{k=1}^{n} p_k u(x_k),$$

where u is a utility over possible outcomes, similar to the one defined by Bernoulli. Similarly to the expected value, the expected utility can be thought as the average level of utility a decision maker would get from playing this gamble repeatedly over time.

The intuition behind the axiom of independence is that the utility for gambles works very much like a measure of weight for physical objects: when you assess the weight of several objects taken together, when you assess the weight of several objects taken together, there is no *interaction* between the weight of the different objects. The is no *interaction* between the weight of the different objects: the weight of an object does not depend on the weight of the other objects it is measured with. For instance, the weight of an apple in a basket does not depend on whether the basket also contains another apple or an orange instead. As a consequence, the weight of bunch of objects taken together is simply the sum of the weights of these objects taken individually. With the axiom of independence, the utility of a gamble is the sum of the utilities of the different elements in the gamble.[4]

One observation that reflects this idea is that if you weigh two different baskets of goods, the difference in weight cannot be influenced by objects that are present at the same time in both baskets. The objects that are present in both baskets contribute only their own weight and do not influence the weight of the other objects. So if you remove the same objects on both sides it will not

---

[3] If you are not familiar with mathematical notations, it means that the value of the gamble is the sum of each outcome multiplied by their probability: $p_1 u(x_1 + p_2 u(x_2) + \ldots$.

[4] The probabilities act here as fractions. The weight of half an apple and half an orange is the sum of half the weight of an apple and half the weight of an orange. Similarly, the utility of a gamble giving 50% chance of getting \$200 and 50% chance of getting \$100 is half the utility of \$200 plus half the utility of \$100: $0.5u(200) + 0.5u(100)$.

change the difference in weight between the two baskets. Imagine the following example: basket *A* has three bananas and one apple, basket *B* has four carrots and one apple (identical to the one in basket *B*). You put these two baskets on balance scales and observe that basket *A* is heavier. If you remove from both baskets the apple they contain, *B* cannot become heavier than *A* as a result. Similarly, basket *A* will stay the heaviest one if you replace the apples in *A* and *B* with (identical) oranges.

The independence axiom extends this intuition to preferences over gambles: the preference between two gambles should not change when some outcomes identical in both gambles are changed for something else. Consider two gambles *A* and *B* that both contain 10% chance of getting $100. If you prefer gamble *A* (given the other possible outcomes it offers), then you should still prefer gamble *A* if this $100 outcome is replaced by $200 in both gambles.

Noticeably, the crucial independence axiom was not explicitly stated in von Neumann and Morgenstern's formal demonstration. Instead, it was an implicit assumption. The requirement for this principle was progressively understood by economists in the year following the book's publication, in particular, Marschak (1950), Nash (1950), and Samuelson (1952).[5]

Shortly after von Neumann and Morgenstern's contribution, Savage extended, in *The Foundations of Statistics*, the notion of expected utility to situations where the probabilities of outcomes are not observable. Savage showed that, if people follow a few reasonable principles of choice, including the independence axiom,[6] then they will act as if they choose the gambles with the highest expected utility relative to a subjective measure of probability. In other words, they will choose as if they have consistent beliefs about the probabilities of the different outcomes of each gamble (and try to maximise their expected utility).

These theoretical contributions from von Neumann, Morgenstern and Savage became the foundations of the economic theory of decision under uncertainty. They showed that decision makers following a few principles would pick among gambles using the simple rule of expected utility. It is an elegant and convenient result in its simplicity.

The reasonable nature of these axioms makes these theories compelling from a normative point of view: decision makers using expected utility to make choices are de facto respecting some good principles of consistency in choices. The agreement over whether these principles are descriptive of behaviour was less clear. The axiom of independence, in particular, quickly faced criticisms. While it is intuitive that the weight of a physical object does not interact with the weight of other objects on a scale, is it really the case that the utility of gambles do not interact when several gambles are mixed together?

The French economist Maurice Allais was soon going to point to serious evidence against the axiom of independence. At the International Colloquium

---

[5] See Fishburn and Wakker (1995) for a discussion of the progressive discovery of this required principle.

[6] For simplicity, I refer to the "independence axiom"; however, there were different formal versions of it that capture a similar idea (Fishburn and Wakker 1995).

TABLE 7.1. *Allais' gambles decomposed to reveal the substitution of a common element (in bold)*

	89%	1%	10%
Gamble A	**$1 million**	$1 million	$1 million
Gamble B	**$1 million**	$0	$5 million
Gamble A'	**$0**	$1 million	$1 million
Gamble B'	**$0**	$0	$5 million

on the Foundations and Applications of the Theory of Risk, which took place in Paris in 1952, he presented to fellow participants, which included Samuelson and Savage, several hypothetical choices under risk. In the most famous one, people were asked to choose between the two gambles:[7]

Gamble A: 100% chance to win $1 million
Gamble B: 89% chance to win $1 million; 10% chance to win $5 million; 1% chance to win nothing.

Like Allais' colleagues, take a few instants to consider these two options and think about which one you would prefer. Allais then offered a second choice. Once again, try to think about which option you prefer:

Gamble A': 11% chance to win $1 million; 89% chance to win nothing
Gamble B': 10% chance to win $5 million; 90% chance to win nothing.

When presented with this pair of choices, most people tend to choose *A* over *B* (possibly to avoid the risk of getting nothing) and *B'* over *A'* (possibly because the prize is much larger in *B'* and both lotteries have similar risks of getting nothing). Indeed, not only do most people tend to make this choice; *Savage himself* chose *A* and *B'* (Savage 1972, p. 103).

But this simple pair of choices has an important implication. Choosing *A* and *B' violates the axiom of independence*! To understand why, let's decompose the Allais gambles as in Table 7.1. This decomposition shows that gambles *A* and *B* are actually closely related to *A'* and *B'*. In the first pair of gambles, both *A* and *B* give 89% chance of getting $1 million. In the second pair of gambles, this possible outcome is replaced in both *A'* and *B'* by 89% chance of getting nothing.

According to the axiom of independence, a choice between two gambles cannot be influenced by the presence of 89% chance of getting something identical in both gambles. As a consequence, when 89% chance of getting $1 million is replaced by 89% chance of getting $0, the preference between the two gambles must stay the same. In other words, if you preferred *A* in the first pair, you must prefer *A'* in the second pair to respect the axiom of independence. Similarly, if you preferred *B*, then you must prefer *B'*.

---

[7] The original amounts where in millions of French francs.

The fact that most people, including economists, violate the axiom of independence in such a simple choice situation (and other similar ones) raised a big question about the validity of this principle as an assumption about how people make decisions between risky options.

These violations, which became known as the "Allais paradox", generated a search for explanations. If people do not respect the axiom of independence, and if, as a result, they do not behave as if they are maximising their expected utility, how do they behave? Is it possible to make sense of people's behaviour in situations of risk?

The solution, which later received the most attention and empirical support, was proposed by Kahneman and Tversky in their 1979 *Econometrica* article. They proposed that people do not behave as if they are using the exact probabilities in their decisions (like expected utility maximisers). Instead, they behave as if they use distorted probabilities that can be either above the real probabilities (we say that probabilities are *overweighted*) or below (we say that probabilities are *underweighted*). Looking at situations where there are only two possible outcomes, Kahneman and Tversky proposed that people choose the option maximising this weighted expected utility:

$$V(gamble) = \sum_{k=1}^{2} \pi(p_k)u(x_k), \qquad (7.1)$$

where $\pi(p_k)$ is the subjective weight given to the probability p_k of the outcome x_k.

In practice, following Kahneman and Tversky, behavioural economists assumed that people behave as if they tend to overweight small probabilities and underweight probabilities close to 100%. This assumption is backed by empirical evidence[8] Figure 7.1 represents a typical weighting function. A simple way to describe the behaviour characterised by such a function is that people are *oversensitive to small deviations from certainty*. Consider the situation where John faces a prospect of gaining $100 with a probability p. If Figure 7.1 describes how he weights probabilities, he will overweight small deviations from certainty of failure and small deviations from certainty of success. When faced with a probability of success of 10%, he may behave as if this probability was 20%. Similarly, when faced with a probability of 10% of not getting the $100 (i.e., 90% chance of success) he may behave as if this probability was 20% (i.e., 80% chance of success). John will therefore behave as if he overweights small probabilities (e.g., 10%) and underweights large probabilities (e.g., 90%).

This overweighting of small probabilities helps explain the Allais paradox. When faced with A and B, the small probability of 1% to get nothing in the lottery B may seem particularly worrying. It may loom large in the mind of the

---

[8] While this pattern is found on average, some people are also found to deviate from it (Conte et al. 2011)

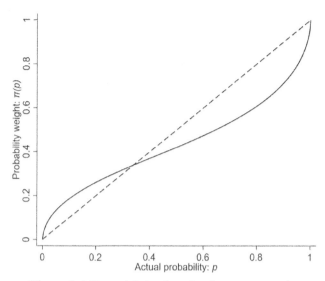

FIGURE 7.1. The probability weighting function from prospect theory.

decision maker. But in the choice A' vs B', this 1% is now added to 89% to form a 90% chance of getting nothing. As part of this 90%, the additional 1% may feel quite small. For that reason, B' is not unappealing relative to B.

Besides explaining the Allais paradox, one of the advantages of the subjective weighting of probabilities is that it can explain one of the outstanding mysteries economists were facing when using expected utility: why people both gamble and insure themselves at the same time.

According to expected utility, the attitude towards risk is purely driven by the shape of the curve of the utility function u over the monetary outcomes. Assuming that risk preferences are somewhat stable across contexts, people should be risk-averse if they have a concave utility function (like a logarithmic function). A concave utility function corresponds to decreasing marginal utility: additional amounts of money have a progressively lower and lower positive effect on utility. In that case, gambles tend to be unappealing because people care less about the chance of getting a high outcome than about the risk of getting a low outcome. People therefore tend to prefer sure outcomes to gambles. Conversely, people are risk-seeking if they have a convex utility function (like an exponential function). A convex utility function corresponds to increasing marginal utility: the utility of additional amounts of money gets higher and higher. In that case, the thrill of getting additional gains motivates the decision maker to take risky gambles.

Risk-averse people should always prefer a sure outcome to a risky outcome with the same expected value. Symmetrically, a risk-seeking individual should always prefer a risky lottery to a sure payoff equal to the lottery's expected value. However, it is commonly observed that people do gamble, which suggests risk-seeking preferences and that they also generally insure themselves (preferring to pay a sure fixed amount to avoid facing the risk of an adverse event), which suggests risk aversion.

Economists had grappled with this problem for some time. Friedman and Savage (1948) and Markowitz (1952) had even proposed utility functions with exotic shapes (concave in some places, convex in some others) to try to explain the concomitance of these two types of behaviour. Prospect theory provides a simple unifying explanation: people overweight small probabilities both when they consider gains and when they consider losses. When considering small probabilities of large gains, they overweight these probabilities, which makes gambling attractive. Similarly, when considering the small chances of large losses (e.g., house burning), they overweight the probabilities of such bad outcomes, which makes insurance attractive.

The idea that people's perception of probabilities may be distorted had been proposed before Kahneman and Tversky. In a 1948 article, Preston and Baratta described an experiment where lotteries with a probability of gain were auctioned to be sold to participants. The price could be used to infer how the lotteries' probabilities were used by the participants to value the lotteries. In their experiment, Preston and Barrata found that probabilities of less than 0.25 were subject to systematic overestimation. So participants behaved as if they used subjective probabilities, which differ from objective probabilities.

One of the key insights of Allais was that differences between "psychological probabilities" and actual probabilities is one of the drivers of the decisions to take risk. This insight motivated the creation of his examples of choices between lotteries to disprove the theory of expected utility (Allais 1953, p. 508).

Kahneman and Tversky proposed a way to model how subjective weights distort probabilities. The relative simplicity of their proposition and its articulation with the other principles of prospect theory made it quite popular. In spite of its appeal, the way proposed by Kahneman and Tversky to weight probabilities faces some problems, however, when we try to extend it beyond the simple two-outcome case they proposed. Imagine a series of gambles with three possible outcomes, as represented in Table 7.2.

TABLE 7.2. *A series of gambles to investigate prospect theory's predictions. Only the value of the amount in the second column, in bold, varies across the gambles*

	50%	25%	25%
Gamble A	$0	**$5**	$10
Gamble B	$0	**$6**	$10
Gamble C	$0	**$7**	$10
Gamble D	$0	**$8**	$10
Gamble E	$0	**$9**	$10
Gamble F	$0	**$10**	$10

Gamble *A* gives 50% chance of getting $0, 25% chance of getting $5 and 25% chance of getting $10. Kahneman and Tversky's prospect theory would predict that the probabilities of getting $5 and $10 would be overweighted because they are small (25%). The next gamble, *B*, is almost identical to *A* except that the payoff of the $5 outcome is increased to $6. This new gamble is clearly Formally, the gamble B is said to *stochastically dominate* A. We would expect a reasonable decision maker to prefer *B* to *A*. Since changing the payoffs in that way would not have any effect on the probability weighting, a decision maker following prospect theory would indeed prefer this new gamble. Consider now the gambles *C*, *D* and *E*. In these gambles, the value of the intermediary outcomes is increased progressively to $7, $8 and $9. Each time the intermediary payoff increases, the new gamble is better than the previous one. So we would expect a reasonable decision maker to prefer *E* to *D*, *D* to *C*, and so on.

But look at the last gamble, *F*, in the table. In this gamble, the intermediate payoff increases further, to $10. This last increase changes the nature of the gamble. It is now a 50–50 chance gamble between $0 and $10. Something very strange happens as a result: there are no more small probabilities, and the probability of $10 is not overweighted any more. In gamble *E*, both the 25% probability of getting $9 and the 25% probability of getting $10 were overweighted. The decrease in probability overweighting of the positive outcomes in *F* may make this gamble less appealing than *E* even though the intermediary payoff is higher by $1! When faced with gambles *E* and *F*, a decision maker following prospect theory may choose *E*, which is obviously worse.[9]

The idea that people weight probabilities potentially leads to the prediction that they could make decisions that seem obviously wrong. When presented with decisions that visibly violate stochastic dominance, people generally prefer not to do so. It suggests they themselves think it is a bad idea to make such choices. So the assumption of probability weighting seems characterised by a fundamental flaw.

Following a 1977 article by Handa on probability weighting in the *Journal of Political Economy*, an Australian graduate student, John Quiggin, sent a note to the journal with a solution to this problem. The note was eventually published in the *Journal of Economic Behavior and Organization* in 1982. In it, Quiggin proposes that people do not weight the probability of an outcome per se, but

---

[9] In this example, it is possible that *F* would still be preferred because the increase in monetary amount ($1) could more than compensate for the disappearance of the probability weighting (two 25% probabilities becoming a 50% probability). But a violation of stochastic dominance would have to happen at the limit: a gamble with 25% chance of getting $9.99 and 25% chance of getting $10 would still lead to probability weighting, while a gamble with 50% of getting $10 would not. Here the increase in monetary amount ($0.01) would be much less likely to compensate for the drop in overweighting of probabilities. And the same argument could be made comparing gambles even closer (e.g., where the middle payoff is $9.9999).

the probability of getting at least this outcome.[10] This proposition resolves the problem with the initial probability weighting: people with such preferences never choose gambles that are clearly worse (stochastically dominated).

Quiggin's solution was later adopted by Tversky and Kahneman (1992) in a revised version of prospect theory. In this new version, people overweight not small probabilities as such, but probabilities of outcomes close to the extreme outcomes. In other words, when facing gambles, people tend to overweight the chances of getting outcomes close to the worse possible outcome, as well as the chances of getting outcomes close to the best possible outcome. In practice, prospect theory is still commonly described as predicting that people "overweight small probabilities". This presentation is a bit misleading though. As long as we talk of the (typically small probabilities) of extreme outcomes it is fine, but small probabilities of intermediary outcomes are not overweighted.[11] In the case of gambles with only two possible outcomes, the initial version of probability weighting and Quiggin's solution are equivalent. It is nonetheless important to remember that when there are more than two outcomes, the overweighting characterises only the probabilities of the outcomes near the minimum and maximum of the distribution.

Empirical studies have found that models assuming people weight probabilities provide a better description of observed behaviour than the expected utility model (e.g., Conte et al., 2011). So what does this weighting (or distortion) of probabilities mean from a psychological point of view?

There are two different ways to interpret it. First, it is usually presented as a *misperception*. The weighting of probabilities is then seen as a distortion of the actual probabilities: small probabilities appear larger than they are in the mind of the decision maker. In that view, probability weighting is part of the cognitive biases that mar human decision making. It is another aspect of our imperfect ability to make good decisions. This view has typically been the one adopted by behavioural economists.

There is also a second interpretation, often preferred by decision theorists: this weighting can be seen as *part of the decision maker's preferences* over risky outcomes. Under the axioms of expected utility, and in particular the axiom of independence, risk attitudes are purely explained by the utility function. One can think of prospect theory as representing the preferences over risky prospects. These preferences emerge from both a sensitivity to outcomes (curvature of the utility function) and a sensitivity to probabilities (curvature

---

[10] Formally, people weight not probabilities but the cumulative distribution of probabilities.

[11] Instead, they are usually underweighted since people are not very sensitive to variations of probability in intermediary range (e.g., a 1% probability to get an intermediary outcome will lead only to an additional 1% of getting at least this intermediary outcome). See Wakker (2010) for an extended discussion.

of the probability weighting function).[12] This view is a bit more agnostic about whether probability weighting is a default or not in terms of decision-making.

7.2 EVOLUTIONARY FOUNDATIONS OF SENSITIVITY TO PROBABILITIES?

What could explain this weighting/distortion of probabilities? Could they be solutions to the problems we face in the real world?

In his book *Prospect Theory* (2010), Peter Wakker proposes a tongue-in-cheek evolutionary explanation. Suppose an organism has a "probability measuring module" to assess the probability of events. A very rough module would just discriminate between coarse variations, for example, certainly not, possible, certainly yes. It would lead to overweight small probabilities as very small probabilities would be considered similar to larger probabilities. Wakker surmises that as evolution progresses, this deviation would progressively disappear as organisms would become better and better at perceiving probabilities accurately.[13]

Even though Wakker proposes this explanation half-seriously, it is indeed a possible solution. The distortion of probabilities could be due to our difficulty to discern small probabilities close to 0 and 1. In that case, the distortion would simply be a bias due to the fact that the evolutionary process has not led to a perfect calibration of our perception of probabilities.

Several researchers have proposed another type of explanation: the distortion of probabilities may be a "second best" solution correcting the existence of other biases in decision making. It is, for instance, the argument made by Herold and Netzer (2010). They suggest that, given a utility function that is S-shaped, like the one proposed by prospect theory, the curvature of the probability weighting can help the decision maker to select options with higher expected values. As evolution selects decision makers to maximise their expected fitness, the existence of an S-shaped utility function may lead to the selection of probability distortions as a compensation. Herold and Netzer's argument is interesting, but it has one weakness: it relies on taking the curvature of the

---

[12] Formally, decision theorists have shown that probability weighting can be rationalised if one assumes that the decision maker follows not the axiom of independence, but a weakened version of it: the axiom of *comonotonic independence*, which restricts the principle of independence to pairs of lotteries where changing a common element does not change the order of the outcomes in either lottery (Schmeidler 1989).

[13] It is not unreasonable to think that such shortcomings could exist even though probabilities are presented to participants in experiment. As Glimcher (2011, p. 388) puts it: "It seems plausible that the symbolic communication of probabilistic events, a very recent evolutionary event in the history of our species, reflects true failures of our neural apparatus for maximization."

utility function for granted and looking at how a probability weighting function should adapt to it. Ideally, as acknowledged by the authors themselves, one would want to investigate how an evolutionary process affects the shape of the utility and probability weighting functions simultaneously. It is not necessarily the case that a distorted probability weighting would appear (and with the same features) if utility and probability weighting are optimised jointly, instead of sequentially (utility first and then probability weighting).

Another second-best explanation has been proposed by Steiner and Stewart (2016). They studied the situations when decision makers have to choose between the "status quo" (what decision makers already have) and a risky option with two possible payoffs: one above and one below the status quo. If there is noise in the estimation of the chance of getting the best outcome in the risky option, the decision makers may be victims of the *winner's curse*. That is, when the risky option looks appealing, it is often due to mistakes that the decision makers made when evaluating their chances of success. These errors can make the risky option look more appealing than it actually is.[14] In order to hedge against this winner's curse, it is optimal to slightly underweight high probabilities, and to overweight small probabilities.

Steiner and Steward's explanation is also interesting. However, it applies to a specific case of choice between a good status quo versus a risky alternative. It is not clear whether this explanation is able to account for the existence of overweighting in all the situations where it is observed (e.g., in situations where the decision makers choose between two risky options that do not include the status quo).

A third second-best explanation has recently been proposed by Price and Jones (2020). In their case, they point to a well-known fact in evolutionary biology: when organisms' choice affects their rate of population growth, their best strategy is to maximise the geometric mean of growth, which differs from the simple (arithmetic) mean of growth. Organisms that would maximise only their (arithmetic) mean growth (by simply maximising their average fertility) would, in the long run, experience a lower population growth rate. When the rate of growth is at stake, organisms should be a bit more conservative (Cooper 1989). The reason is simple: if fertility is zero in one generation, the arithmetic mean fertility may still be large, but the geometric mean is zero. Organisms should be careful of trading prospects of high fertility against the risk of very low or zero fertility. It is therefore optimal to be conservative and display some risk aversion in the choices affecting fertility. This risk aversion can take the form of a concave utility function. But it can also take the form of a pessimistic weighting of probabilities. Price and Jones point to the fact that if organisms have linear utility functions on fertility, they should have weighting functions

---

[14] As pointed out to me by Peter Wakker, this case can be seen as a specific example of the general point made by Van den Steen (2004) that when people choose an option, it is likely that they overestimated the chances of success of this option.

thats are pessimistic and overweight the worst possible outcomes.[15] As in the other two explanation, one may ask why this solution would be the one selected by evolution: why instead not have utility function curvature generating the required risk aversion?

Overall, second-best explanations are interesting, but they are partial: they start from a given a behavioural pattern and show that conditional on this bias, probability weighting may be a solution. It is not always clear why this pattern would not have been corrected in the first place, or controlled by other means.

A new explanation presents another possible alternative. Enke and Graeber (2019) suggest that the existence of probability weighting may be an emerging phenomenon due to the fact that adequately estimating the expected value of gambles is difficult. Consider Jane trying to assess the value of the gamble: 10% chance of getting $3,000. It looks like a good gamble. But how much does Jane value it? Specifically, how much would she be willing to pay to play this gamble: $100, $200, $300? This is not an easy question. To answer it, Jane may enter in some introspection to figure out how much she would like this gamble. But even after taking some time thinking about it, she may still be uncertain. She may, for instance, not be sure whether she values this gamble at $200 or less. If she is offered a ticket to play this gamble for a price of $200, she may be unsure whether she wants to buy this ticket or not.[16] If Jane faces such uncertainty, the best solution for her is to take into account the feeling she got from introspection (this feeling acts as an informative signal), but she should also give some weight to prior beliefs she may have. In the case of a binary decision, she may use an ignorant prior belief of 50–50. And so she would end up choosing as if she used probabilities shifted towards 50–50, which generates the S-shape characteristic of prospect theory.

This explanation critically depends on the type of prior belief assumed (here it is assumed that Jane's uncertainty is about the probability and that she uses an ignorant prior belief), but it suggests something credible: probability weighting could be an optimal response to the difficulty of assessing the subjective value of risky options. This idea echoes the explanation suggested by Wakker that we may not be able to process/perceive probabilities well enough.[17]

∴

---

[15] The idea that risk attitudes can be generated by probability weighting when utility is linear is not new. It is known since Yaari's work (1987) that the same risk attitudes can be obtained with concave utility and expected utility or with linear utility and probability weighting.

[16] The next chapter develops this point about the possible uncertainty of preferences.

[17] It also echoes the idea that people may be uncertain when assessing probabilities and that this uncertainty may tend to distort probabilities asymmetrically around the extremes 0 and 1 (Erev et al. 1994). Intuitively, if there is some noise in your estimation of probabilities, and if the true probability you are trying to estimate is very close from 0, your error may move your perception more upward than downward, leading to an upward bias (your perception of small probabilities would be higher than the actual probability). Symmetrically, your perception of large probabilities, close to 1, would likely be underestimated for the same reason.

When making choices between risky prospects, people behave as if they give different weights to the probabilities of different outcomes. Observed choices seem to suggest that people give more weight to the worst case and best case outcomes. This greater importance given to extreme outcomes leads people to violate the principles of expected utility. Several theories have been proposed to explain probability weighting. The ideas presented here show that there are several ways to think about the possible reasons underlying the emergence of such a pattern that don't simply present it as an irrational bias. The quest to fully understand its roots is still going on.

8

The Randomness of Choices

A man, being just as hungry as thirsty, and placed in between food and drink, must necessarily remain where he is and starve to death.
—Aristotle (350 BCE, 295b)

A mere introspection is enough to prove our hesitation if faced with a problem of choice.
—Georgescu-Roegen (1936, p. 568)

One of the most elementary findings in the area of psychophysics—the study by experimental psychologists of the relation between subjective perceptions and the objective physical characteristics of sensory stimuli—is that subjects respond randomly when asked to distinguish between two relatively similar stimuli.
—Woodford (2012a)

Summary: The homo economicus model assumes that people know what they want. They should, therefore, consistently make the same decisions when presented with the same choices. Empirical evidence suggests, however, that people do not have strictly fixed preferences between the different options they face. Some psychologists have even proposed that people do not have preferences as such. Instead, I will argue here that it is possible to explain the apparent variations in choices as reflecting that people know what they want (e.g., satisfaction), but they don't always know the best way to get it.

In one of the episodes of the *Big Bang Theory*, "Indecision Amalgamation", Sheldon agonises over a decision between two different video game consoles: a PS4 and an Xbox One. Lamenting to his girlfriend he states: "I don't feel like you're taking this dilemma seriously…. I've done all my research, I conducted an informal poll, and I've arrived at the rock-solid certainty. I've made the right choice. Although ..." More decision agony follows from then on.

To common mortals, this scene is likely to be similar to many situations frequently experienced. Faced with an important decision between two options, we worry we are not making the right choice. These worries can lead to protracted hesitation and sometimes to the postponement of the decision altogether. Surprisingly, such situations fell outside the realm of the old economic model of human behaviour. Indeed, they present a puzzle for an economist using the homo economicus model. They imply violation of one of the pillars of the theory of consumer choice: the principle of completeness of preferences (see Chapter 1). In the classic Mas-Colell et al. (1995) microeconomics textbook, the assumption of complete preference is summarised as the idea "that the individual has a well-defined preference between any two possible alternatives". Said like this, it may seem innocuous, and indeed it has been used as a mostly unquestioned assumption by economists looking at decision-making. But it means that economics does not have anything to say about situations where people find it difficult to make a choice.

8.1 DO PEOPLE KNOW WHAT THEY WANT?

The early empirical tests of economic theory of decision brought a surprising result: it was unclear whether people really had set preferences in the first place! In a classical study, Mosteller and Nogee (1951) asked participants in an experiment to accept or reject binary gambles. The authors observed that the participants did not systematically choose the gamble with the highest expected utility (as estimated from the participants' choices). Instead, their probability of choosing the gamble with the highest expected utility seemed to progressively increase from 0 to 1, following an S-shaped pattern. In later studies, researchers found that even when the same choice was offered repeatedly to participants, they often ended up making different decisions over time. Reviewing these results, Rieskamp et al. (2006) estimate that participants tend to change their mind on a given binary choice 25% of the time, when this choice is presented to them twice.

Faced with this evidence, economists abandoned the claim that preferences should translate into deterministic choices. They instead developed probabilistic theories of preferences, whereby a preference for an option A versus an option B leads to a *greater probability* to choose A.

Many of such models have been proposed.[1] The most popular one is the *random utility model*. In this model, the decision maker makes some errors when assessing the utility of the options considered. Suppose that John considers two options A and B. His preference over these two options is represented by utilities, $U(A)$ and $U(B)$. But John's perception of these utilities is affected by some noise from cognitive errors. These errors take the form of

---

[1] See Wilcox (2008) for an excellent review.

small random deviations in his perception of the options' values, respectively, ε_A and ε_B. As a consequence, he perceives the utility of the two options as $U(A) + \varepsilon_A$ and $U(B) + \varepsilon_B$. And when choosing between these options, John will pick the one with the largest *perceived utility*.

The random utility model is straightforward to use to model choices that are not deterministic. It has been widely adopted in economics to model discrete choices, following the pioneering work in this domain by McFadden, who later received the Nobel Prize in Economics (McFadden 2001).[2]

Nonetheless, this addition of errors in utility could be criticised as a way to protect the theory and make it harder to refute it with data. One could ask what these "preferences" are if people can't even make the same choice twice over a short time period. Psychologists did not miss on pointing out these issues. Building on a range of empirical studies, a number of psychologists suggested that the inconsistencies in people's choices come from the fact that preferences do not pre-exist as assumed by economists. Instead, they are "constructed on the spot" (Lichtenstein and Slovic 2006). To create these preferences, people use imperfect heuristics, which, as a consequence, leads to inconsistencies.

The point made by psychologists is well taken, and, on reflection, one may wonder how economists can have considered that the completeness of preferences was a credible assumption. Imagine a familiar situation: Jane a customer, goes to a supermarket to do her shopping. To respect completeness, she should be able to state her preference when faced with any pair of shopping lists that respect her budget constraints. These shopping lists could contain any combination of the goods in the supermarket as long as the total cost of the shopping list is below or equal to her budget. These shopping lists may contain similar products like butter and margarine or unrelated products like butter and a hairbrush. The assumption of completeness of preferences implies that she would effortlessly be able to indicate which shopping list she prefers. If you think it is a demanding task cognitively, you are right. In their criticism of the completeness axiom, Bossaerts and Murawski (2017) use this situation to illustrate the complexity of Jane's task. If there are 1,000 goods stored in the

---

[2] If the εs are distributed normally, the choices of the decision maker can be analysed with a *probit model*. And if the εs are distributed according to a Gumbell law, the choices of the decision maker can be analysed with a *logit model*. The εs are interpreted as noise/error induced by cognitive processes in behavioural/experimental economics. Note, however, that these error terms are often interpreted differently in applied microeconomics: as an unobserved part of John's utility (Train 2009). In this perspective, John's choices are not really random. They only look random to us observers because we do not know all the factors John is taking into account to choose between the two options. This explanation can look adequate in situations where John is choosing between real goods for which it is nearly impossible to characterise precisely all the features that could matter for the decision maker. However, random choices are typically observed in experiments where the options are presented with a limited number of clearly observable differences. In that setting, the "unobserved utility" interpretation of ε seems less credible than just assuming that there is indeed something random in people's choices.

supermarket, the number of possible shopping lists that Jane should be able to consider is 10^{310}, which is 10^{220} times more than the number of atoms in the observable universe! Let's appreciate these numbers, in light of the fact that an average US supermarket stores around 40,000 different products.

You may retort that, in the case of supermarkets, people have enough experience of the typical goods they buy to have close to complete preferences. Let's look then at the situations where the products are unfamiliar or unique. Imagine John looking for a new car. Every year there are around 250 models listed on the US market. With such numbers, the axiom of complete preferences would imply that John would be able to effortlessly choose between any of the 62,000 possible pairs of cars that could be presented to him. Saying that it is unlikely is an understatement.

But before we condemn economists for having so quickly adopted an unrealistic assumption, it is worth reading how Mas-Colell et al.'s (1995) textbook discussed the completeness assumption. Just after presenting it, it states:

The strength of the completeness assumption should not be underestimated. Introspection quickly reveals how hard it is to evaluate alternatives that are far from the realm of common experience. It takes work and serious reflection to find out one's own preferences. The completeness axiom says that this task has taken place: our decision makers make only meditated choices.

The problem is not that economists never considered the strength of this assumption, but that they often overlooked it in their research and teaching.

Does abandoning the assumption that preferences over existing options are complete imply that they are inconsistently constructed on the spot? I don't believe so. Like Sheldon looking for the best console, or like a customer looking for a new car, the person looking for the best option will "work" and engage in "serious reflection". This work generally consists in looking for additional information about how the features of the products will likely be associated with future satisfaction. Some of this search will involve looking for external information, and some can also involve some introspection (e.g., using memory and reasoning to improve one's expectations about the project).

This perspective gives us another way to look at Sheldon's problem. His anxiety does not come from the fact that he ignores what he wants. Indeed, he knows what he wants: having fun playing. What he does not know is which product is the best to have the most fun. He faces two options with unknown values (amount of fun experienced in the future). In short, he does not have *perfect information* about the different options he is considering. As a consequence, he is uncertain about which product is the best. With some search of information, such as looking for consumer reviews and asking friends, he may be able to reduce this uncertainty and reach an informed decision likely to deliver the best choice for him.

8.2 OPTIMALLY FORMING PREFERENCES

Optimal Sampling of Information

Given that Sheldon does not have perfect information on the two types of consoles, he has the choice, at any moment in time, to buy one of them or to wait a bit more and collect more information. When should Sheldon stop? This problem is very general: What is the optimal amount of information to acquire before making a decision?

The famous mathematician Abraham Wald (1945) gave a formal solution to this problem. Whenever Sheldon gathers more information about the two products, he updates his beliefs about which option is the best. If gathering information is costly in time, effort and money, Sheldon should stop when he has reasonable confidence about what the best product is. But how should he define "reasonable"? Wald showed that there is a straightforward solution to this problem if Sheldon wants to have some probability of making the right decision. Suppose that for each product, Sheldon wants only 5% chance of making the wrong choice (e.g., buying the PS4, while the Xbox would actually give him more satisfaction). Then the solution to his problem is to stop searching for information once his confidence in the best product crosses a specific threshold in terms of probability (e.g., Sheldon buys a console only when he is 95% confident that the Xbox is the best product).[3] This optimal stopping solution will minimise Sheldon's search duration, given his preference for a small chance of error (Wald and Wolfowitz 1948).

Amazingly, this same principle was also used by Alan Turing during World War II, in his quest to crack the Enigma, the German coding machine (Gold and Shadlen 2002). Enigma was an incredibly complex machine with an enormous amount of possible settings. Turing and his cryptographer colleagues had to find the machine's settings, which were renewed each day. To do so, the team worked on cracking the code using different documents, and it had to decide how long to try on a given document before moving to another one. Using an optimal stopping approach similar to the one described above allowed them to optimally allocate their time (a very scarce resource in that context) to crack the codes used by the German army to communicate.

The fact that Abraham Wald and Alan Turing, two of the most famous mathematicians of the twentieth century, found the solution to this problem is one thing. But the complexity of this problem could suggest that this solution is out of reach for most people. However, remember the argument I presented in

---

[3] The example given here is a special case of the general problem solved by Wald. It implies a symmetry when aiming for making errors only 5% of the time either way. Wald's solution also gives the desired threshold when there is no symmetry (e.g., when some types of errors are more costly than others).

Chapter 4: if a problem has been met frequently in our ancestral past, evolution will have had time to shape our decision-making processes to approximate the optimal solution. Now think about it: there is hardly a more generic problem than the one consisting of considering different options and deciding which one is best or opting to think a bit more about it. This problem has been met not only by our primate ancestors, but even well before that by life forms that have much more limited cognition than we have. So evolution has potentially had plenty of time to design and fine-tune decision-making processes that approximate the optimal solution.

Is it the case? The evidence suggests it is reasonable to assume it is indeed the case! Neuroscience studies have found that the brain seems to make decisions approximating the decision rule described by Wald (Gold and Shadlen 2002; Bogacz et al. 2006). When asked to choose between two simple options, neurons behave as if they progressively accumulate the weight of evidence in favour of each option. The decisions are well explained by models assuming that the final choice is triggered when the accumulated weight of evidence crosses a threshold (in favour of the option chosen). Many neuroscientists now model brain processes as using Wald's optimal stopping solution and related models to determine how long to look for information and using this information to form beliefs in a Bayesian way (Knill and Pouget 2004). It is hard to be further away from the idea of inconsistent choices simply made up on the fly.

A consequence of these models is that choices should be in part random. Indeed, Webb (2018) showed that if our brain follows the optimal stopping rule described above to accumulate evidence and make choices, our choices will look like they are generated by a random utility model. At first sight you may find this suggestion strange. Suppose Jane is choosing between a large or a regular size coffee at her preferred café on a given morning. In a split second, she opts for the regular size. How could Jane's brain have accumulated information during the short duration of her decision process? She did not read any article on coffee choice or not did she ask a friend for advice. However, during that split second, several cognitive processes likely worked together to assess the value of the two choices of coffee. Some processes recovered an estimation of her need for coffee: feeling of tiredness. Some recovered information from her memory: whether a large coffee was too much last time Jane had one, whether Jane has a long meeting today where she needs to stay sharp. Some cognitive processes may have generated some simulations about what is likely to happen next: how she is likely to feel after a regular versus a large coffee. The result of these processes quickly provided some signals in favour or against each coffee option. The accumulation of these informative signals was progressive over the short time Jane spent thinking about it. When the accumulated signals became clear enough in favour of the regular option, she stopped and indicated her choice. In such a process, the arrival of informative signals is in part random. Even if Jane would really prefers a large coffee, she may on a given day get a few more signals (memory, simulations) that happen to be a bit more in favour of the large coffee. Because of this randomness of informative signals, Jane's decision will also be in part random: her decisions will be determined by the signals that Jane's brain happened to accumulate before reaching the required level of confidence. Webb shows that the Wald model can generate decisions that look almost exactly like those from random utility models.

These models of optimal accumulation of information have an important feature: they predict that we make mistakes. Indeed, they imply that *we should make mistakes*. Aiming for zero mistakes is too costly; one may want to be sure to choose the best product between two video game consoles, but one may also not want to spend tens of hours thinking about it. At some point it is rational to put the issue at rest, make a decision and accept that, while it may have been the best decision given the available information at the time, it may not end up being the right one eventually. So the first insight we have from these models is that it is optimal to make mistakes. Therefore, making mistakes as such should not be an argument used to prove that a decision maker is making poor decisions. The decision maker will appear to be making random mistakes, but those mistakes are part of an optimal decision-making process. The optimal proportion of mistakes should depend on the cost and benefits present in each situation. A decision maker should make fewer mistakes when the stakes are high, and they should make more mistakes when the costs to collect information is high.

These models can also explain a puzzling fact: we tend to make *more* mistakes when we take more time to think about a decision. This surprising pattern, observed by psychologists (Luce et al. 1986), has sometimes been considered to justify the idea that humans' decision-making processes are flawed. Indeed, it may seem that impulsive and intuitive decisions are better than carefully considered decisions. But Fudenberg et al. (2017) showed that it has a simple and intuitive explanation, once we appreciate the fact that people progressively assess the value of different options before making a decision. When the values of the options are very different, making a choice between them is easy and it does not require too much time to process. Suppose you win a prize that gives you the opportunity to choose between two cars: a Ferrari and a Fiat. Given the difference in value between the two cars, you are likely to make up your mind very quickly. But choices between options that are more similar in value will require more time to find out which one is the best. If the two cars you face are, instead, a Volkswagen and a Fiat, it is less obvious which one is best and you may need time to think about your choice.

When the two values are very close, the decision maker is also more likely to make mistakes. The greater number of mistakes for decisions that take more time is therefore the result of a *selection effect*.[4] Quick decisions take less

---

[4] The optimal solution is indeed to make more mistakes when the values are close because the reduction of the cost of mistakes is small and does not compensate as much as the cost of collecting information.

time because they are easier to make, and because they are easier, they are also more likely to be correct. On the contrary, decisions that are harder take more time and are characterised by more mistakes. We should not interpret this as indicating that people's hunches are better than people's careful thinking. Instead, we should appreciate that people take more time to choose when the choice is more difficult. The increase in error rate with the decision time is what should be expected from an optimal decision-making process.

Does it all mean that the brain always makes optimal decisions like a Bayesian computer? No. Researchers have mostly looked at very simple situations of choices between perceptual stimuli. Such situations have been ubiquitous in the life of our ancestors. For more complex tasks such as choosing between two products in a supermarket, it may be harder for our brain to approximate the optimal solution. However, our own research has found evidence that when faced with complex choices repeatedly, decision makers tend progressively to get closer to the optimal solution (Descamps et al. 2019).

The Need for Exploration

In the situation we just considered, the sampling of information can be made prior to making a decision between the options. In the case of Sheldon, he can acquire information about the two types of consoles from user reviews, technical guides and friends' recommendations. In some cases, the best way to acquire information is to sample the options themselves. The problem then becomes twofold: how to choose what to sample, and how long to sample.

Consider John, who moves from London to Bangkok. He is not fully familiar with Thai food and now faces a new problem: how to choose a meal in a local restaurant. Let's assume that John goes to the same restaurant every day and that the restaurant has a long menu of different options. On the first day, John can pick an option and see whether he likes it. Then on the second day, he faces a simple problem: Should he take the same option or try another one? Suppose that he really liked the dish he tried on his first day. What should he do on the next day? It is not a simple problem. On one hand, it would seem that John's experience would justify choosing the same dish again. But if John really enjoyed his first meal, it may suggest that he could enjoy the food in this restaurant in general. It may make sense to try out a few other options instead of stopping on the first one he tried.

John is faced with a classical *exploration-exploitation* trade-off. He needs to decide how much time he should spend sampling the different options in the menu (exploration) to make his mind about his preferences and then opt for his preferred options on a regular basis (exploitation). It is reasonable for John to invest some time exploring the different options, perhaps sampling each of them several times to form a clear opinion about how much he likes each of them. This exploration of the different options may induce randomness in John's choices (Cohen et al. 2007). The day-to-day variations in John's decisions are not in that case due to an error; they stem from the fact that he is acquiring information about his preferences between the different options.

This acquisition of information via the sampling of options should persist as long as sampling may bring more benefits from discovering the value of better options relative to those already known. If the options that John faces are always the same and if John's tastes or needs are always constant, he should eventually acquire enough observations about most of them and stop his exploration. With a good (even if not perfect) knowledge about his preferences between the different options he faces, he would make his decisions accordingly, every day.

However, it is reasonable to think that engaging in some exploration may always be optimal because the options we face are unlikely to always stay the same. In John's case, the quality of the restaurant may change over time, or his own tastes may vary with age. Some residual exploration may then still make sense to provide from time to time additional information on the options that are not chosen. This exploring behaviour would lead to what seems like random choices for external observer. For the decision maker, like John, it would reflect a trade-off: sometimes choosing different options to keep learning about the value of the different options available.

Using Contextual Information

We have seen that the apparent randomness of choices can be the result of good decisions, if decision makers have imperfect information about the value of the options they face. The challenge from the psychological literature, however, goes beyond the fact that our choices are partly random. The empirical evidence unearthed by psychologists also suggests that our preferences are influenced by irrelevant elements of the context. These contextual effects are perhaps why there is some randomness in choices: a given choice between two options is never made twice in exactly identical circumstances. Even if the choice is the same, slightly different circumstances could mean different contextual effects that influence the choice made.

A clear example of this fact is that our choice between two options is often influenced by the presence of other options *that we do not intend to choose*. It seems irrational: these options should be irrelevant. Economists widely accept that a rational decision maker should make choices that respect the principle of *independence of irrelevant alternatives*. Contrary to this view, the evidence suggests that this principle is frequently violated by our choices.

Compromise Effect
Consider again the situation where Jane enters a café. This time we will assume that she is hesitating between three possible sizes for her coffee: regular, large and extra-large. Research has shown that the simple presence of an expensive extra-large coffee may increase Jane's propensity to take the large option,

even though she may never consider taking the extra-large one. This has been called the "compromise effect" by psychologists (Tversky and Simonson 1993). The presence of the extra-large option places the large option as the middle one, which can seem a very reasonable choice. As a way to investigate this compromise effect, Soman (2015) created an experiment in a coffee shop in Hong Kong. He proposed coffees sized 8, 10 and 12 ounces. The most popular size was the middle one, and when asked about their choices, the customers indicated that 8 was too small and 12 too large. But when Soman increased the size of all coffees by two ounces (to 10, 12 and 14), the most popular choice became the 12 ounce coffee. And customers having picked this option motivated their choice by saying that 10 is too small and 14 is too large.

For sure, such behaviour seems irrational. Here again, some psychologists have heralded this effect as evidence that preferences do not exist and that they are made on the fly and can be influenced by irrelevant features of the decision situation (such as the other unchosen options in the menu).

But let's take the perspective we have described above. We do not have inbuilt preferences for coffee cups. But, as I have discussed in Chapter 6, we have a subjective reward system that has been designed for us to maximise our fitness (or at least that was designed for our ancestors to maximise their fitness).[5] In any decision situation, our brain tries to determine the choices that are associated with the greatest expected subjective satisfaction. In that process, our brain should use all the possibly relevant information to make the best decision possible. When choosing a coffee, this information may not just be the cups of coffee considered but also the context. Is it a reputed café? Or a café that looks like it could be reputed? What are other customers having?

In the process of using the available information, the list of other items on the menu can also be noteworthy (Luce and Raiffa 1957, p. 288). In a market situation, there is a good reason why a menu of options can be informative: it can reflect what people usually tend to choose. If you know how your tastes compare to others in general, the menu available may provide you with valuable information to make your choice (Wernerfelt 1995; Kamenica 2008). The use of such information can explain the compromise effect. If you know that you have middle-ground tastes relative to other people you know, it may make sense to choose one option in the middle of the menu of choices. As Kamenica (2008) states, in the case of buying a computer:

Goldilocks may not know how many dollars she is willing to pay for an additional megahertz, but, as long as she knows she is in the middle of the distribution of taste for speed, she will do well purchasing the computer that is neither too slow nor too fast.

---

[5] Formally, we can say that our reward system endows us with preferences over the outcomes from the experience of consumption.

Decoy Effect

Another example of how the context of a choice can influence a decision is the "decoy effect" (Huber et al. 1982). The presence of an option that is clearly not attractive (decoy) may increase your chance to choose an option that looks better, in comparison. A good illustration of decoy effect is the way different sizes of a product are usually priced. Suppose you go to the cinema and see that you can buy a large box of popcorn for $6. The evidence suggests that the cinema can increase your propensity to buy this box of popcorn simply by adding an option that is clearly worse. For instance, it can add a "small" box that is only half the size of the large one and costs $5.50. If you are willing to pay $5.50 for a small box, you are most often willing to pay $0.50 more to have double the size. So you likely won't choose the small box, but its presence can increase your propensity to buy the large one. In comparison to the small box, the large box looks like a good option. The small box acts as a decoy and changes your preferences even if you never considered choosing it.

Li and Yu (2018) proposed an intuitive way in which context can influence our choices and generate a decoy effect. When an organism has to make choices over several periods, the type of choices available at one period may reveal something about the type of choices likely to be available in the future. If a bad option is present in a choice set at a given period, it may suggest that the options that will be available in the future are less likely to be appealing. As a consequence, upon seeing a clearly less desirable option, a rational decision maker may view the better option to be a good opportunity that may not be available in the future.

To appreciate the logic of this argument, imagine that Jane is moving to a new town and she is looking for a new flat. On the first day, she sees a flat A which is just okay. She may choose to wait for a better option to see over the next days. But if she has seen a much worse option, flat B, before seeing flat A, she may have different beliefs about the range of possible options available in the town. Being more pessimistic after seeing flat B, she may rationally choose A. Doing so, Jane may seem to violate the independence of irrelevant alternative, since her choice changes with the addition of an option, flat B, which she does not want to choose.[6] This logic may have tuned us to be tricked in seeing opportunities when a poor-looking decoy is paced in the options we face.

Learning about the Person Proposing the Choices

In a social context, when somebody offers some choice to us, it can also signal something about this person. Is she trustworthy? Reputable?

---

[6] Note that this model does not explain all the possible decoy effects. In particular, when a decision maker chooses between several options, a new option can act as a decoy even though it is a relatively good option in the choice set. To act as a decoy an option only has to be just a bit worse on visible dimensions compared to one specific choice.

Sen (1993) gives the example of a situation where somebody invites you to have a drink at their place. You have two choices: accept a drink or decline the invitation. Suppose that you are inclined to accept. Your choice may change if the person inviting you says there is also the option of taking drugs. The addition of this third option may change your view of the value of the other two options considered.

The same logic applies to companies selling products to customers. When you are in a restaurant, your belief about the likely quality of the food may depend on the list of dishes on the menu. The presence of a dish that, in your view, is associated with poor taste may make you wary about the rest of the menu: you may become more conservative in your choices.[7]

In such situations, our choices may seem to violate the independence of irrelevant alternatives, when taken independently. But these choices may be perfectly reasonable if we have incomplete information about the person/organisation proposing the options we have to choose from. In that case, we can learn about the proposer from the menu of options offered.

General Contextual Effects

The previous arguments share a similar idea: context should matter because it brings information to the individual. Samuelson and Swinkels (2006) proposed a general argument along the same logic: context should generally matter because evolution would have designed our decision-making processes to tap into the information present in different contexts. The reason is that evolution is unlikely to be able to encode in our utility function all the information available in each specific situation.[8] As a consequence, our tility functions should take into account contextual information that can help make better decisions.[9] For that reason, the framing of a decision situation with a menu of options may influence our decision.

The trick here is that it is optimal in general for us to be influenced by the context to make good decisions. But when businesses, like coffee shops, discover how we adapt our decisions to the menu of options we face, they may design their menus in order to influence us to make the best decisions *from their point of view* (i.e., to buy the larger, more expensive option). It is a very specific case of evolutionary mismatch: when our decision processes designed to work well most of the time have some weak spots used by others to their benefits. As we

---

[7] Such a mechanism was recently modelled by Bhui and Xiang (2021).

[8] For example, our ancestors would not have seen enough red-berries-under-an-oak-tree-when-it-rains situations for evolution to have led humans to have utility functions pinpointing the value of red berries in this specific context.

[9] In Wernerfelt's and Kamenica's approaches, the context does not change the decision makers' utility as such but their information about which option is most likely to be their preferred one.

have not yet been selected to make good decisions in a café, coffee sellers can use attention to framing to distort our choices.

$$\therefore$$

The fact that people's decisions between different options vary over time can naturally seem a clear indication that they do not know what they really want. In particular, it has been found that elements of context influence decisions. This observation has been interpreted as suggesting that "preferences" are not something that characterise people, but that, instead, they are made on the fly, often under the influence of arbitrary aspects of the environment. Such behaviour can easily be interpreted as being irrational, something people would not want to do. But this interpretation relies on a very specific assumption about situations when people choose between different options: they have *perfect information* about the satisfaction each of them will deliver. It is obvious that, if you have perfect information about the options in that sense, your choices should not change over time. If you know that hot chocolate gives you more satisfaction than coffee, you should always choose hot chocolate, and your choice should not be influenced by irrelevant things such as other less preferred options being present or not on the table.

But once the hypothesis of perfect information is clearly stated, it is evident that it is not realistic. People cannot know perfectly the satisfaction they will derive from each option. For a start, this satisfaction will generally depend on future evolutions in the environment, which are uncertain. For instance, I may prefer hot chocolate in general, but there is a chance for me to be called in a meeting at work where I will need to stay sharp and coffee will be the best option in that case. Or, when choosing between different video game consoles, it may depend on the quality of games released in the future and on the consoles my friends will choose. Even when the future is fairly certain, there may still be residual uncertainty about which option is best for me. This uncertainty is likely greater for choices that are faced infrequently.

Once we model choices as made under imperfect information, it is possible to explain why and how there should be some randomness in decisions. Even if a decision maker were to be faced with the same choice situation several times, the information available or collected to make a decision may differ each time (even if it is just the recollection of past experiences from memory). Decisions can therefore be expected to vary somewhat from situation to situation, particularly when the likely satisfaction derived from the possible choices is relatively close.

9

Impatience

> If anyone objects that there is a great difference between present pleasure and pleasure or pain in the future, I shall reply that the difference cannot be one of anything else but pleasure and pain.
>
> —Plato (490–420 BCE)

> All men certainly seek their advantage, but seldom as sound reason dictates; in most cases appetite is their only guide, and in their desires and judgments of what is beneficial they are carried away by their passions, which takes no account of the future or of anything else.
>
> —Spinoza (1670/1958, chapter V)

> It is one of the most pregnant facts of experience that we attach a less importance to future pleasures and pains simply because they are future, and in the measure that they are future.
>
> —von Böhm-Bawerk (1891)

Summary: *The homo economicus model assumes that when people make a plan for the future (e.g., consumption, savings, work), they stick to it. The empirical evidence suggests, on the contrary, that the inability to stick to one's plans is a major feature of human psychology. This inability reflects a greater preference for getting rewards now and postponing unpleasant things to later. Such a pattern of behaviour can be explained by the fact that present and future opportunities come with different degrees of risk.*

In many situations, we face options involving some costs and benefits over time. For example, we go through years of education only to get rewards when we leave the education system with a diploma. These years of education involve costs to start with: subjective costs (e.g., work, forgone leisure) and material costs (e.g., tuition fees, forgone wages). They provide benefits only later on by offering better opportunities on the job market. Similarly, we go through diets to improve our fitness. A diet will typically involve some costs now (e.g., forgone opportunity to eat tasty meals) with the perspective of getting benefits later on (being fit and having a slim figure).

How do we compare these costs and benefits, which happen in different periods, when choosing a course of action? An intuitive and well-established fact is that people tend to be *impatient*.

9.1 IMPATIENCE

One of the most iconic studies on impatience is the "marshmallow experiment". Looking to understand how children manage to delay gratification, Mischel and Ebbesen (1970) placed children from a Stanford nursery, aged three to four, in a room with the prospect of getting a treat of their choice if they could wait while the experimenter left for some time.[1] If they did not want to wait, they could have their second preferred option at any time. Less than a third of the children waited up to the maximum of fifteen minutes to get their preferred treat, and most children preferred to have their less preferred treat right away. With their choice not to wait, these children illustrate the impatience that is commonly observed in human preferences. We generally prefer to get rewards (e.g., treats) now and to face costs (e.g., work) later.

The ability to delay gratification is essential to make decisions that will pay at a later date (e.g., getting a good university degree, saving to buy a house). The fame of the marshmallow experiment largely came from the follow-up studies that seemed to make this point in a striking manner. The benign decision to wait for this treat at ages three to four was able to predict success at a much later age! Researchers found that the choice to wait is correlated with school test scores at age fifteen (Shoda et al. 1990). This choice seems also associated with a more active prefrontal cortex when having to inhibit an impulsive action (Casey et al. 2011). These results are striking, and they raised a lot of interest in how such a simple test at an early age could say so much about our chances of success.[2]

---

[1] The name of the treat is actually absent from the paper, which became known as the marshmallow experiment. Marshmallows are mentioned only in a follow-up paper (Mischel et al. 1972) and the following studies.

[2] A recent replication of the marshmallow experiment found these effects at fifteen to be smaller than initially found (Watts et al. 2018). It also found that these effects are largely explained by things like family background. Nonetheless, these new results are compatible with the existence of early differences in impatience, correlated, to some extent, with success later in life.

To think about how people allocate rewards and costs across time, economists had for a long time a simple and very convenient model: people (1) discount the utility of future rewards and (2) use the sum of these discounted utilities to assess the overall utility of a stream of future rewards. Let X be a stream of future rewards, a decision maker getting X will receive x_0 now, x_1 in one period, x_2 in 2 periods, ... The overall utility of this stream of rewards for a decision maker would be:

$$U(X) = u(x_0) + \delta u(x_1) + \delta^2 u(x_2) + \delta^3 u(x_3) + \cdots .$$

The utilities u are the utility for rewards in each period, and the "discounting" factor δ represents the degree of impatience of the decision maker between two consecutive periods. It is usually assumed that $\delta < 1$, which reflects the idea that people give less value to future rewards than present rewards. Consider the case where $\delta = 0.9$. The discounted utility formula above says that, compared to the present, the utility of a given amount is perceived as only 90% as good if it is received the next period, 81% if it is received in two periods, 73% in three periods, and so on. The lower δ is, the more impatient the decision maker is.

This model was initially proposed by Ramsey (1928) in a theory of saving and later adopted by Samuelson (1937) in a general note on decisions over time. Samuelson did not claim that this discounting model was empirically true (he recognises its "arbitrariness"), nor did he claim that it has a normative value.[3] But this "exponential discounting" model has appealing features, which led it to become the main model used by economists to study decisions over time.

First, it has the great advantage of being very simple and easy to use when trying to study decisions over time. All the impatience is fully encapsulated in a single parameter, δ. Simple experiments can then be used to measure time preferences by asking people the amount of rewards x_t and x_{t+1} between two periods t and $t+1$ for which they are indifferent: $u(x_t) = \delta u(x_{t+1})$. The discounting factor is then simply $\delta = u(x_t)/u(x_{t+1})$.

Second, this model has a very desirable property for economists looking for a model of rational decisions. A decision maker with exponential discounting is *dynamically consistent*.[4] Imagine the following situation: Jane learns that a friend is bringing her a box of chocolates on Monday morning. Looking forward to this treat, she decides not to eat them too quickly. On Sunday night, she sets her mind on spreading her consumption over the week by eating

---

3 "Any connection between utility as discussed here and any welfare concept is disavowed" (Samuelson 1937).

4 In addition, Koopmans (1960) showed that this model can be justified as what would result if people were following a few (specific but) reasonable principles. It helped cement further the appeal of this model (see Frederick et al. 2002 for a discussion).

the same number of chocolates every day. When Monday comes, if Jane has exponential time preferences, she will follow the plan she initially set out and stick with this schedule of consumption.[5] In other words, Jane will have no desire to change her mind as time passes. If ever Jane were to decide to change her mind and to eat, let's say, a few more chocolates early in the week than she initially scheduled, she would not have exponential time preferences.

Dynamic consistency is undoubtedly a desirable property. Violating it would mean that a decision maker sets out a plan at some point but does not respect it later on (see Ericson and Laibson, 2018). However, simple introspection, as well as ample empirical evidence, points to the fact that dynamic consistency is routinely violated. It was recognised in economics by Strotz (1955), well before the advent of behavioural economics.[6] A few intuitive examples are enough to make this clear: people set their mind on going on a diet (eat less each day) to improve their fitness (at a later date), but they keep pushing back on starting it or fail to maintain it; people set their mind on stopping habits (like smoking each day) that are bad for their health (at a later date), but they keep falling back into it; people set plans to work regularly (e.g., each week) to progress on a long-term project (which will pay at a later date), but they end up pushing back work and falling behind schedule; people plan to save regularly (e.g., each month) to be able to buy a house or car (at a later date), but they struggle to keep up with their saving plans.

A common feature to all these situations is that plans for long-term rewards requiring regular efforts/sacrifice in the present are made initially but not respected later on, when opportunities for short-term rewards (e.g., a small treat now) are preferred, instead of the required effort (e.g., diet). This pattern suggests that people are not just equally impatient between consecutive periods; they are also particularly impatient when considering a specific period: the present. Whenever they make choices for the future, they are happy to make efforts later: "I'll start a diet tomorrow." But when tomorrow becomes today, the possibility to opt for immediate gratification now often leads to *preference reversals* (change in plans): "I'll just get a treat today ... I'll start the diet tomorrow."

These *present-biased preferences* are one of the main causes of poor choices in a modern world where lots of the decisions we make involve long-term horizons: investing in education, repaying a mortgage, saving for retirement, staying healthy over a long lifetime. It has been one of the major areas of

---

[5] We assume here that preference, do not change over time; they are *time invariant* (Halevy 2015). It is a natural ceteris paribus condition mostly assumed implicitly in economics.

[6] Strotz showed that any deviations from exponential discounting would lead to some inconsistency of preferences over time. In other words, only an exact exponential discounting guarantees a perfect consistency.

research in behavioural economics. And behavioural economists have played an influential role in designing policies to help people reduce their inconsistent choices: procrastinating less, saving more, adopting a more healthy lifestyle.

One interesting aspect of these preferences is that human behaviour suggests a certain naivete about the inconsistency in time preferences. Evidence suggests that people set working plans ahead while underestimating how much they will procrastinate in the future (Ariely and Wertenbroch 2002). People set up plans to go to the gym regularly and opt, accordingly, to pay a yearly gym fee. But they end up not going enough, to the point where they would pay less for temporary access (DellaVigna and Malmendier 2006). When DVD rentals were still popular, people rented high-brow movies and documentaries along with commercial movies, but the high-brow DVDs were more likely to gather dust unwatched than the low-brow movies (Milkman et al. 2009).[7]

To explain these patterns, economists developed new models. The most commonly used is the "quasi-hyperbolic discounting" model (Laibson 1997), which adds a parameter, β, in the standard model to explain the specific preference for the present:

$$U(X) = u(x_0) + \beta \left(\delta u(x_1) + \delta^2 u(x_2) + \delta^3 u(x_3) + \cdots \right).$$

The parameter $\beta < 1$ represents a greater discounting of all future rewards relative to present rewards. The discounting rate between period 0 (now) and period 1 is $\beta\delta$, while it it only δ between period 1 and period 2. So whenever people consider today (period 0) whether to go on a diet tomorrow (period 1), which will bring benefits later (period 2), they may be willing to start in period 1 as the expected rewards in period 2 are discounted only by δ. But when period 1 becomes today, the future rewards from the diet are now discounted by $\beta\delta$ and opting for a treat now looks relatively more attractive than when the diet was initially planned.

The name "quasi-hyperbolic" comes from the fact that it is a simple way to approximate *hyperbolic discounting*, which produces the type of preference reversals described above. The "quasi-hyperbolic" function presents the same pattern of discounting while being very similar to the exponential discounting function and therefore easy to work with. Figure 9.1 shows a comparison of how these three different types of function discount the value of future rewards.

---

[7] Beyond movies, it may explain many other patterns like the tendency to buy more books than one reads. The Japanese word "tsundoku", originated in the nineteenth century, describes this tendency to acquire reading material and let it pile up without reading it.

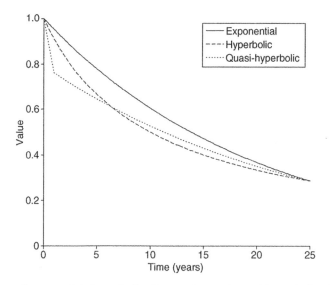

FIGURE 9.1. Exponential, hyperbolic discounting and quasi-hyperbolic discounting functions. The hyperbolic and quasi-hyperbolic discounting model show a greater discounting of future rewards relative to the present, compared to exponential discounting.

9.2 WHY DO WE HAVE IMPATIENT PREFERENCES?

Humans do not seem to be the only ones to be affected by such preference for immediate rewards. In influential studies in the 1970s, Ainslie showed that the same behaviour (and possibly preferences-reversal) is present in pigeons (Ainslie 1975). And later, present-biased preferences have been observed in a wide range of animal species: monkeys and apes, lemurs, rats, jays, chickens and bumblebees (Hayden 2016). There is a possibility that the behaviour observed in humans is widespread in the animal world.[8]

Resources Are More Useful Now

Why should we, and other organisms, discount the future? Several reasons have been proposed. The first one is that getting something now is often more valuable than getting something tomorrow. Suppose you get $1,000 today. You would be able to put it in the bank and get interest on this amount, say, 5%. If you get $1,000 in one year from now, you will have then just that amount. But if you get it today, you will have $1,050 then, which is $50 more. The same logic

---

[8] See, however, Hayden (2016) for a counterpoint, criticising the ability of animal studies to measure time preferences similar to those observed in humans.

can take place without banks: eating more today can give you more strength to work more today and collect more food, which will be available tomorrow. More generally, any time you are engaged in a process where positive outcomes build up from past positive outcomes, it makes sense to want positive outcomes earlier as they will "fructify". There is an *opportunity cost* of delaying rewards. This cost is the gains that you would have made in the future if you had been able to get such rewards today.

Note, however, that this explanation does not usually imply the type of preference reversal I described earlier. If the return rate on what you have now is constant in time (e.g., 5%), then your discounting of future amounts should be exponential. As a consequence, your preferences should be dynamically consistent.

The Future Is Uncertain

There is another reason why it makes sense to discount future payoffs: the future is typically somewhat uncertain. In some cases, future rewards never eventuate. Following this idea, Robson and Samuelson (2007) start from the most basic uncertainty: our time of death. Consider the most important decision an organism has to make: to have offspring now or later. There can be a trade-off between having a few offspring now or potentially more offspring later.[9] The risk of waiting longer is that the organism may die before getting the opportunity to produce these offspring in the future. Looking into this trade-off, Robson and Samuelson show that under reasonable assumptions, evolution would select between reproduction strategies as if offspring were discounted exponentially over time. If the number of offspring is a positive function of the level of consumption reached (e.g., of food), the organism could also discount consumption exponentially.[10]

In a follow-up paper, Robson and Samuelson (2009) showed that if the risk of death is not simply at the individual level but at the population level (e.g., because of natural catastrophes), then under some conditions, it may become optimal for organisms to have a greater preference for the present than in the model with exponential discounting.[11]

Even without going into such fundamental considerations about reproduction, uncertainty can play a role because a specific opportunity considered in the present may disappear in the future. This possibility is well described by the proverb: "a bird in the hand is worth two in the bush". This maxim is at

---

[9] A simple example of this trade-off is the time spent raising offspring. An organism can have offspring and leave them from birth to survive by themselves, or it can stay with them and protect them until their probability of survival has increased. The second approach takes more time to produce surviving offspring.

[10] Though the discounting pattern may be more subtle as the quantity of offspring may depend on how consumption is spread over different periods.

[11] This present bias does not lead to preference reversals, however, unlike when discounting is hyperbolic.

least as old as ancient Greece (Ammer 2013). The role of uncertainty has long been proposed in biology to explain discounting: when foraging, animals may prefer smaller rewards sooner, as larger rewards later may never eventuate due to interruptions, such as the arrival of a predator (Kagel et al. 1986; McNamara and Houston 1987).

This insight is also valid for human behaviour. Imagine that John promises a payment of \$100 to Jane. Consider the situation where each month there is a risk of 1% chance that this payment opportunity disappears. This 1% is a *hazard rate*. It reflects all the events that, each month, could lead Jane to see her payment prospect vanish: John could forget and move beyond reach, he could have an accident and be unable to pay, he could go bankrupt. With such a 1% hazard rate, the probability that Jane would eventually get the \$100 if John makes a promise to pay in one month is 0.99 (there is 99% chance that Jane will get it). If the promise is in two months, the probability is $0.99 \times 0.99 = 0.98$ (there is 99% chance that the \$100 do not disappear in the first month, and 99% chance that they do not disappear in the second month). In 12 months, it is $0.99^{12} = 0.89$. In 24 months, it is $0.99^{24} = 0.79$. If Jane follows the principles of expected utility, she would de facto follow the exponential discounting utility model with a discount factor $\delta = 0.99$ per month: \$1 in one month would only be worth as much as \$0.99 today, because of the hazard rate of 1%.[12]

The fact that future is uncertain can explain why people would discount future payoffs. But note that, if the hazard rate is constant over time, this explanation leads to exponential discounting. It still does not justify the existence of preference reversals.

We Overreact to Uncertainty

Given that the future is uncertain, a possible reason for hyperbolic-like discounting may come from *the way people react to this uncertainty*. Halevy (2008) and Epper and Fehr-Duda (2012) show that the weighting of probability assumed by prospect theory (see Chapter 7) can generate behaviour similar to what would happen if people perceived a decreasing hazard rate.

To see why, consider the above example where Jane receives John's promise of a payment in the future, with a hazard rate of 1% chance that the payment opportunity disappears every month. If Jane overweights extreme probabilities, she may be overly sensitive to a 1% chance of losing a future reward in the first month. This 1% would reduce her probability from getting a reward from 100% to 99%. In comparison, she may be less sensitive to the additional risk from waiting one more month after month 24. With a hazard rate of 1% Jane's probability to get her reward goes from 78% to 77% between month 24 and 25. This additional 1% in chance of losing her payment may not feel as important as the 1% change from 100% to 99% in the first month. For that reason,

---

[12] She would value the prospect of a payment at month t as the product of its probability $p_t = 0.99^t$ and utility $u(100)$.

if Jane overweights the probabilities of extreme outcomes, she may be more sensitive to delaying a payment one period after the present than to delaying it one period later in the future. As a consequence, she may behave in a way that looks like hyperbolic discounting: her discounting factor would be highest in the first period in the future and decrease afterwards.

In support of this explanation, Keren and Roelofsma (1995) have found that people are much less impatient when the reward considered at different points in time is a lottery with uncertain rewards. For uncertain enough rewards, no dynamic inconsistency was observed. Such a phenomenon would naturally arise if the overweighting of a small subjective risk initially drives the preference for short-term rewards. People may be overly sensitive to a small chance of future rewards not happening. But the additional uncertainty from waiting has a smaller psychological effect when they are considering, for example, a lottery with 30% chance of not receiving anything and only 70% chance of getting a payment. In that case, the additional uncertainty from waiting does not induce a departure from certainty, just a small increase in uncertainty. People may then find it easier to wait for larger rewards later, as they are only slightly less likely than the smaller reward now.

Epper and Fehr-Duda (2012) show that such an explanation can account for many of the patterns observed in decisions under risk and over time. It is an appealing explanation. It reduces the cause of inconsistencies in time preferences to how we subjectively handle risk and distort probabilities, as discussed in Chapter 7. In that view, the bias for present rewards could potentially be simply the consequence of the fact that we overreact to the uncertain nature of future rewards: "something may go wrong".

We Perceive the Future with Uncertainty

Another possibility recently, proposed by Gabaix and Laibson (2017), is that hyperbolic discounting may be driven not by the uncertainty of the future as such, but by the uncertainty in our *perception* of the things that will happen in the future.

Consider Jane, who lives in London and is facing a choice between a holiday in Kent, in the south of the United Kingdom, now or in a seaside town in Italy in four months. Suppose that Jane would prefer the Italy holiday if the choices were at the same date and that she does not have time preferences as such. She may still face a problem when comparing the two options. The holiday in Kent is very easy to picture as she faces this option now. In comparison, the Italy option may seem fuzzier in her mind. To imagine how much she would enjoy it, she may need to spend some time thinking about her state of mind in four months, and perhaps about the state of the world then (e.g., will the weather be still as good as it is now?). Jane's ability to predict how she will feel about a trip in Italy in four months is unlikely to be perfect. As a consequence, Jane's perception of how much she would enjoy a holiday in Italy in four months may be less precise than her perception of how much she would enjoy a holiday in Kent now.[13]

If Jane forms her beliefs in a Bayesian way, she will discount somewhat her impression about how much she would enjoy a holiday in Italy. The reason is that her impression is an *imprecise signal* of how much she would enjoy the holiday. Noticeably, this discounting of her subjective estimation can create hyperbolic discounting. Consider a simple situation where Jane has initially no idea about whether she would enjoy Kent or Italy. Suppose then that, when starting to think about it, both destinations appear appealing to her. As a consequence her newly formed subjective impression is positive for both destinations. But while her subjective impression about the Kent holiday (now) is quite clear, her subjective impression about the Italy holiday (later) is imprecise and therefore discounted. Gabaix and Laibson (2017) show that it can lead Jane to discount her positive feelings about the Italian holiday as if she had hyperbolic time preferences.

Importantly, this may lead to preferences reversals. If Jane had to choose between Kent in one month and Italy in five months, she may choose Italy: when both Kent and Italy are perceived with imprecision, Italy may seem relatively better. But when offered to choose between Kent now and Italy in four months, she may opt for Kent. In that new situation, the uncertainty affects only her perception of the Italian holiday.

The mechanism leading to time discounting here is just the Bayesian updating of beliefs, associated with a growing imprecision of the perception of the value of experiences that are considered further in the future. There are two ways to interpret this growing imprecision of perception. First, it may be the result of cognitive limitations: it is harder to think about the future when it is further away in time. A second interpretation is that the context, which will define the utility of each experience, is indeed more and more uncertain as we anticipate it to be further and further in the future. In that view, discounting is not generated by a cognitive error or an overreaction to the uncertainty associated with the future. It is generated by an appropriate reaction to how uncertain we are about how much we will experience future goods and rewards.

This model makes interesting predictions. In particular, people more experienced about the types of choices made or people who invest more effort thinking about the problem should display less hyperbolic-like discounting. This type of effect seems to have been observed in an experiment (Gershman and Bhui 2020).

---

[13] Formally, this impression is a signal that is more noisy when the option assessed happens further in the future.

The Highest Risk Is Foregoing a Present Opportunity
Finally, a possible explanation for preferences reversal is that the hazard rate, the risk that the reward will disappear, is not constant, but decreases over time (Kagel et al. 1986; Green and Myerson 1996). In other words, if you consider waiting for the opportunity of a larger reward later on, the risk of losing the opportunity would be greater in the first moments when you start waiting and then be lower as more time passes.

Several models have been proposed to explain why the hazard rate could credibly decrease over time. One possibility is that it is the *perception* of the hazard rate that is decreasing. Sozou (1998) proposes a model where the hazard rate is not perfectly known initially. As time passes without the opportunity of future rewards disappearing, the decision maker's belief about the level of this risk can progressively be revised downward. It leads to a decrease of the perceived hazard rate.[14] Note, however, that this decreasing hazard rate cannot generate preference reversals between two different rewards facing the same hazard rate: an initial choice to wait for a larger reward later will be proven right as time passes (the belief about the risk of losing this opportunity decreases over time).

An alternative explanation is that the hazard rate really decreases over time, possibly because there may be specific risks associated with letting a present opportunity go. Imagine that John promises to pay Jane $110 dollars in one month instead of $100 now. If Jane accepts, as time passes, there are risks that John may forget or simply get out of touch for some reason ($\delta < 1$). But there may also be a risk ($\beta < 1$) that John is lying, and the opportunity is lost as soon as Jane accepts.[15] Any time there are such risks specific to letting a present reward go, there is a specific difference between the present period and all future periods. When such an asymmetry between the present and the future exists, we can expect a decision maker to have a stronger preference for seizing the rewards that are available now. The image of one bird *in the hand* expresses well this intuition that there is a specific risk that occurs in the first instant after choosing to forgo the present reward.[16]

[14] And it generates precisely hyperbolic discounting if the prior belief of the decision maker about the hazard rate followed an exponential distribution.
[15] This example taps into the importance of social trust for many of our decisions between present and future rewards. In modern times, we often have near certainty about what is going to happen in the future. When you put your money in the bank, you can safely assume that you will be able to access it tomorrow or, for that matter, five years from now. Similarly, when John promises to Jane to repay $110 in one month, this promise may be set in a contract that is enforceable by law and by the law enforcement institutions (police, justice). In comparison, most of the history of humankind has taken place in times when uncertainty about the future was likely much greater and impossible to eliminate. The institutions enforcing agreements over time were generally much weaker and less reliable.
[16] Benson and Stephens (1996) provide a possible framework to understand such a risk pattern. They use a Markov process to model the transitions experienced by animals when searching for prey, attending to prey that has been found and catching and consuming it. This model creates a

In such cases, it makes perfect sense not only to discount future opportunities, but also to make a psychological distinction between the opportunities available now and the opportunities that may eventuate only at a later date. This psychological distinction could be what drives a bias towards present rewards in our choices.

∴

Impatient and present-biased preferences have been one of the main areas of research of behavioural economics. It is also an area where behavioural economists have been most influential in helping design policies and institutions to help people make better decisions for themselves, for example, in dieting or saving.

Such preferences make sense when we appreciate that the prospect of future outcomes is always associated with some uncertainty. The greater the uncertainty about future rewards, the more we should prefer to have rewards earlier rather than later. An evolutionary perspective suggests that, in modern times, people's preference for present rewards is likely too pronounced, as a result of a *mismatch*. In ancestral times, life was shorter, riskier, and there was typically no institution able to guarantee future streams of rewards without uncertainty. Nowadays, banks, pension funds and governments offer such guarantees. People's lifespans are much longer than in the past. As a result, we have to make financial choices that will impact us in a time horizon that was uncommon for our ancestors to consider (e.g., 40 years). We can expect people to have too high preferences for present rewards in ways that are not best suited for modern societies. It is because our preferences have likely been tuned in an environment that, on an evolutionary scale, was still present only a moment ago. Understanding exactly why we behave the way we do can help us design better models of behaviour and better solutions to improve our decisions in today's world.

preference reversal, possibly simply because choosing not to consume prey now involves going to search situations, which can involve waiting some time before another opportunity arises. This idea echoes a model by Dasgupta and Maskin (2005), who explain hyperbolic discounting with a model where the timing of the future reward is uncertain.

PART III

SOCIAL INTERACTIONS

10

Kindness and Reciprocity

There are evidently some principles in [man's] nature, which interest him in the fortune of others, and render their happiness necessary to him, though he derives nothing from it, except the pleasure of seeing it.

—Smith (1759/2010)

Under certain conditions natural selection favors ... altruistic behaviors because in the long run they benefit the organism performing them.

—Trivers (1971)

Noble human tendencies ... not only have survived the ruthless pressures of the material world, but actually have been nurtured by them.

—Frank (1988, p. ix)

Summary: Economists for a long time relied on the assumption that people are primarily driven by self-interest. One of the main aspects of the behavioural revolution has been to accumulate a tremendous amount of evidence showing that people care not just about themselves but also about others. Initially, economists often deemed such behaviour irrational. But it is easy to show that behaviours like kindness and reciprocity seem puzzling only when social interactions are modelled in an overly simplistic manner. Once we appreciate the rich complexity of social interactions, these prosocial attitudes can be explained as good and sensible ways of navigating them.

In a cross-cultural study looking at pro-social behaviour, Henrich et al. (2005) criticised "the canonical model of self-interest" that relies on "the selfishness axiom – the assumption that individuals seek to maximize their own material gains ... and expect others to do the same". The impressive data collected in small pre-industrial societies around the world shows that prosociality (the fact of caring about others' interests) seems to be widespread across cultures. This study was adding to a large body of evidence from experiments run in Western universities with students showing that people often do not choose the actions that are in their own material interest without regard for the consequences to other people.

To many, this rejection of the "selfishness axiom" is proof that the economic model of human behaviour is wrong. The self-centred rationality assumed by the homo economicus model is misguided. In an answer to this study, the game theorist Ken Binmore begged to disagree: "It is not true that 'textbook predictions' based on homo economicus incorporate a 'selfishness axiom'. Orthodox economic theory only requires that people behave consistently" (Binmore 2005a). It must be said that Binmore's statement is entirely right. As discussed in Chapter 1, the core hypotheses of the economic model of rationality do not make any prediction on the content of preferences, just on their coherence. Many economic theorists have no qualms assuming that people care not only about their own material well-being but also about the distribution of resources in society. Formally, Binmore is accurate with this comment.

But in practice, critics of the homo economicus are entitled to raise concerns about the importance of selfishness in the economic approach. If it is not part of the core of economic theory, it has clearly been part of the set of auxiliary assumptions overwhelmingly adopted by economists when modelling human behaviour. Predating the modern economic approach, classical economists stressed that an ordered society could simply emerge as the result of actions of self-driven individuals. One of Adam Smith's most famous quotes is about the motives that drive economic agents to cooperate with each other:

It is not from the benevolence of the butcher, the brewer, or the baker that we expect our dinner, but from their regard to their own self-interest. We address ourselves not to their humanity but to their self-love, and never talk to them of our own necessities, but of their advantages. (Smith 1776/2019)

Smith used his well-known expression, the "invisible hand", to express his marvel at the fact that a society constituted of self-interested individuals can work in the interest of all:

Every individual ... neither intends to promote the public interest, nor knows how much he is promoting it ... he intends only his own security; and by directing that industry in such a manner as its produce may be of the greatest value, he intends only his own gain, and he is in this, as in many other cases, led by an invisible hand to promote an end which was no part of his intention. (Smith 1776/2019)

The importance of the assumption of self-interest in economics was clearly stated, a century later, by Edgeworth (1881): "The first principle of Economics is that every agent is actuated only by self-interest."

At the start of the twentieth century, Pareto, Hicks and then Samuelson vowed to remove any assumption on the content of preferences from economic theory.[1] Economists opted not to make any assumption about *what* people prefer but to assume only that people's preferences are *coherent*.

In spite of this theoretical revolution, the assumption that decision makers are selfish remained widely used by economists as a default assumption when modelling human decisions in applied work. As I discussed in Chapter 1, such a restrictive definition of preferences could even be conceived as a sound scientific approach. By restricting themselves to strictly material motives, economists avoided the possible risk of explaining any type of behaviour with suitably tailored exotic preferences. This methodological approach was explicitly stated by Stigler and Becker in their classic paper "De gustibus non est disputendum" (1977). In a later text, Stigler addressed explicitly the question about the possibility for people to have "ethical values". He stated that he believes altruism exists and that it is "strong within the family and towards close friends and diminishes with the social distance of the person" (Stigler 1981). Nonetheless, whether people act according to "effective ethical values" is for Stigler an "empirical question". And his prediction is that, when testing behaviour in situations where self-interest and (alleged) ethical values are in conflict, "Much of the time, most of the time in fact, the self-interest theory ... will win." Even if "in a set of cases that is not negligible ... the self-interest hypothesis will fail".

This position, at the heart of the approach of the Chicago school of economics, has undeniably been extremely influential in economics. It has been instrumental in the proposition of novel and provocative explanations for behaviours thought to be outside the realm of economic decisions: marriage, crime, political actions. The "economic imperialism" has mostly consisted in the extension of this approach to other neighbouring disciplines such as sociology (rational action theory) and political science (rational choice theory).

Nonetheless, the idea that people can be motivated with moral principles and that they can care about others has also been present in economics since the start of the discipline. Adam Smith was a moral philosopher, and besides his work on economics, where he focused on the role of self-interest, he also wrote *The Theory of Moral Sentiment*, a book where he argued that people are motivated to behave morally by a feeling of sympathy for the fortune of others (Smith 1759/2010).[2] More recently, Gary Becker himself

---

[1] This movement is described as the "ordinalist revolution". This term refers to economists adopting an ordinal instead of a cardinal view of utility. The idea that utility reflects a measure of subjective satisfaction is referred to as *cardinal utility*. In comparison, the notion of *ordinal utility* represents the idea that utility does not measure anything as such. It just reflects the order of preferences of the decision maker. See Moscati (2018) for the history of this revolution. I discuss this debate further in the Epilogue.

[2] The passage quoted as an epigraph at the start of this chapter comes from this book. It shows that Adam Smith's thought about human motives is much more subtle than the "butcher" quote, so frequently mentioned, could suggest.

defended that evolution would select altruism as a possible strategy in human interactions (Becker 1976).

Over time, substantial empirical evidence has been accumulated showing that the self-interest theory is not a good model of human behaviour. I'll present here three important ways in which our behaviour deviates from this model: we care about others' *outcomes*; we care about others' *intentions*; and we act as if caring about these others and their intentions is required by *rules of morality* that are objective (i.e., universally true, not relative to people or situations).

While such behaviours have often been considered as "irrational" by economists, research has now provided critical insights into how non–strictly selfish behaviours are adaptive in social environments (therefore, they would have likely been selected by evolution).

10.1 FROM HOMO ECONOMICUS TO HOMO MORALIS

We Care about Others' Fate

The selfishness "assumption" has been a target of criticism for a long time in economics. Non-economists typically find it evident that people are not purely selfish. Don't we observe charitable behaviour in the real world, or people helping others out of good will? How could economists be so wrong about something so obvious?

But the selfish assumption is, in fact, more resilient to criticism than it could seem at first sight. Whether genuine altruism exists is a difficult question to settle. Let's consider John giving a coin to a homeless person in the street. It seems, at face value, an altruistic action. But we cannot exclude that acting that way in public may be associated with some benefits for John, like looking good in front of other people. If such benefits exist, they can motivate John to look altruistic in public in order to build a reputation as a good person. Even if the action is not done in public, carrying out the action creates an event that John may be able to mention truthfully later in some social situations. This action may thus still bring benefits from the positive image associated with this action.[3]

The fact that such motives exist is not contentious. Nowadays, many charitable organisations provide the opportunity for contributors to mention

---

[3] If nobody observed the situation where the action took place, one may wonder why John would not simply lie about it. One possible reason is that the probability that nobody will ever find out what really happened is rarely precisely zero. To realise this fact, you have to picture what would be an altruistic action where John could credibly lie and know that nobody would ever be able to find out. Since an altruistic action would imply interacting with others in some way, it would be hard for him to come up with a credible story that would not run the risk of being contradicted by others at some point in the future. Lying may create a risk of being found out. Carrying the action itself is perhaps more costly for John, but it is a riskless way for him to build a mentionable record of good deeds.

their gifts on their social media accounts as a way to give extra motivation to give, besides pure altruism. In a field experiment on giving behaviour, economists found that Yale alumni were more likely to give to an alumni association if a promise of public recognition for the gift was mentioned (Karlan and McConnell 2014). Such self-image concerns are not lost to observers. When people's charitable behaviour appears possibly a bit too conspicuous, they can be criticised for "virtue signalling" (the attempt at looking good by publicly adopting a virtuous behaviour).

The altruistic nature of an action is usually open to question as it is hard to exclude the possibility of non-altruistic motives. The selfishness assumption is much harder to disprove than just quoting a few examples of seemingly altruistic behaviour. The difficulty of dispelling the selfishness assumption was faced by the psychologists and behavioural economists who contested the homo economicus model. Their initial evidence of altruistic behaviour was often rejected as not sufficient to exclude selfish explanations. The continual push-backs from these economists led psychologists and behavioural economists to improve the design of their experiments to address the criticisms. In the process, they progressively accumulated overwhelming evidence that, in its raw form, the selfishness assumption is unlikely to be a credible description of people's behaviour.

To study behaviour in social interactions, economists use the tool of *game theory*. It consists in studying well-defined situations where people's choices of action lead to rewards as a function of the actions of others. These well-defined situations are called *games* and the people engaged in them *players*.[4] One of the most famous games, where a deviation from systematic selfishness has been observed, is the "ultimatum game" (Güth et al. 1982). In this game, a "proposer" offers to a "receiver" a way to split a sum of money, for instance, $10. If the receiver accepts, each player receives the corresponding amount. If the receiver refuses, both players get nothing.

The prediction from the selfishness assumption is pretty striking: The senders will keep the largest amount for themselves (e.g., $9.99) and send the lowest amount possible (e.g., $0.01) to the receivers. Faced with this offer, the receivers will always accept it. Remarkably, these choices stem automatically from the assumption that people want only the largest amount of money possible. With this motive in mind, the receivers should accept any positive amount of money, even the smallest possible amount. Being aware of the responders' willingness to accept anything, selfish proposers should then propose the lowest possible amount to them.

Perhaps unsurprisingly, when economists asked real people to play this game, the observed behaviour did not look at all like these predictions. First, the offer most frequently made by the proposers was a 50–50 split. Second, when the

---

[4] See Binmore (2007) for an introduction to game theory.

proposers ventured into offering an unequal split in their favour, the receivers often outright rejected it. Studies have found that people tend to reject offers below 30% of the total amount, even when this amount is substantial (Camerer 2011). This result, in particular, the second one, shocked economists. Receivers preferred not to receive any money rather than to receive an unequal share of the sum to be divided. This clearly suggested that the receivers were not just driven by a concern for money and that monetary incentives could be trumped by what looks to be a concern for *fairness*.

What about the proposers? Perhaps they are not so much altruistic as simply responding to the threat of rejection they face if they make a low offer to the receiver. The proposers making offers close to 50% could simply be selfish: They could aim to maximise their expected gains from the game by limiting the risks of rejection. To investigate the proposers' motives, an alternate version of this game transformed the proposer in a "dictator" who decides for both players, without the receiver having any say in the split. In this version, a selfish proposer would simply take all the money. The first recorded dictator experiment was run by Kahneman et al. (1986). Their experiment, as well as many others afterward, revealed that proposers tend to offer a smaller but still significant proportion of the total amount (Camerer 2011).

One may still be worried that the game imperfectly neutralises the possible image concerns for the proposer. Indeed, there is always at least one observer in the experiment: the experimenter. It is therefore possible that a desire not to look selfish drives the participants' decisions to give some money to the receiver. To eliminate this possible motive, economists ran this experiment as a "double-blind" one, where neither the receiver nor the experimenter know the actions of the proposer. In such situations, proposers tend to offer less money. However, a significant proportion of proposers still offer a positive amount to the receiver (Hoffman et al. 1996).

The importance of these experiments is that they can be seen as representative of strategic interactions present in many social situations, such as when people have to decide how to allocate resources between themselves and other people. Such situations are commonplace. A good example is when we have to share a single cake.

Alongside the ultimatum and dictator games, economists developed many other experiments where people have to allocate resources. In these experiments, participants generally tend to distribute resources equally. These results eventually convinced economists that most people act as if they have "social preferences": they care not only about their own interests but also about others' interests. As a consequence, many economic models of social preferences have emerged. Most of them assume that people do not like inequality per se (Charness and Rabin 2002): they have preferences for distributions of outcomes that are more equal. People are said to be *inequality averse*.

We Care about Others' Intentions

This departure from the selfishness assumption was only the start. Very soon, the empirical evidence made it apparent that people care not only about the distribution of outcomes but also about how this distribution is reached.

Let's look at the following "mini-ultimatum" game: you are the receiver, and a proposer can choose between two offers: 5–5 or 2–8 (in favour of the proposer). Suppose the proposer opts for 2–8. Try to imagine how much you may be tempted to reject the $2 offer, and opt for a 0–0 outcome instead. Now consider a slight variant: you are told that the proposer's choice was instead between 0–10 and 2–8 in favour of the proposer. Suppose again that you get the 2–8 offer. Do you think that you would be as tempted to reject the offer now? If you are like most people, you are likely to feel less aggrieved in the second situation. In a lab experiment studying these two situations, the rate of rejection by the receiver was around 45% in the former case versus only 10% in the latter case (Falk et al. 2003).

This reaction suggests that people do not just care about what they and other people get. They also care about whether others try to be *kind or unkind* with their choices. If an offer of $2 was the smallest the proposer could offer, it is perceived as unkind, and the receiver is more likely to reject it. If, instead, the same offer was actually the largest the proposer could make, the proposer looks kind. Even though the outcome may seem disappointing, the receiver is less likely to reject it.

In other words, people don't only care about others' outcomes; they also care about their intentions. Evidence of reciprocal behaviour shows that people tend to be kind with people who are kind to them and unkind with people who are unkind to them. Such preferences over intentions present a tougher challenge for economic theory than preferences over distributions of outcomes. Conceptually, extending the notion of individual preferences from preferences over the individual's own outcomes to preferences over everybody's outcomes is straightforward.[5] But intentions are not "things" that can be allocated and measured like material outcomes. It is not even clear what they are and how to define them. To model such preferences, economists have proposed new models departing further from the standard homo economicus assumptions (Rabin 1993; Levine 1998; Dufwenberg and Kirchsteiger 2004; Cox et al. 2008). These models characterise intentions in different ways, but each of them

---

[5] Indeed, they are formally similar. Think about a consumer choosing how to allocate a budget I (for income) between N goods. Suppose every good has the unit price. Then the consumer has to rank by order of preference vectors $(x_1, x_2, \ldots, x_N)$ where $\sum_i^N x_i = I$. This problem has the same formal structure as somebody having to distribute an amount of money I among N different people.

assumes that people want to be kind with people they perceive as being kind and unkind with people they perceive as being unkind.

We See Moral Imperatives as Rules

Beyond others' outcomes and intentions, there is also evidence that people may have preferences to follow some rules dictating what is right or wrong to do in given situations. In a review of the experimental evidence on cooperative behaviour, Dawes and Thaler (1988) pointed out that many of the experiment participants who deviated from the prediction of the self-interest theory justified their action by saying they wanted to "do the right thing".

In some cases, people seem motivated to do the right thing even if, most likely, nobody is affected by their decision. One of the most evident examples of such situations is the seemingly trivial action of voting. In general, more than 50% of eligible citizens vote in the elections in modern democracies (e.g., local, parliamentary, presidential). This simple action is, however, one of the most puzzling facts for the homo economicus model.

Consider Jane, who is wondering whether and for whom to vote at an election. She cares only about the consequences of her vote. Jane's incentive is the expected impact of her vote on the types of policies that will be implemented after the election. If she cares only about her own material payoffs, she may prefer the candidate who proposes the mix of tax and benefits most beneficial to her. If Jane has social preferences, she may prefer the candidate with the best policy for her vision of a fair society. Note, however, that, whatever Jane's preferences over the different candidates, voting makes sense for her only if she has a chance of influencing the outcome. But voting is not free. To vote, Jane would need to spend time travelling to the polling station; sometimes she may have to queue. She could easily spend one or two hours in the process. Instead of voting, she could have spent this time working or having leisure. So to justify Jane's decision of voting, even considering the possibility of social preferences, we need to look at the chance that she will influence the outcome of an election.

In most elections, this chance is small if not negligible. Think about the situation where Jane lives in a large country with several million eligible voters having to choose between two candidates. In almost all likelihood, her vote will have *no effect* on the final outcome: whether she goes to vote or stays at home, the result will be the same. For her vote to be decisive, the country's vote would need to be perfectly split between the two candidates, with Jane casting a decisive vote between the two. The Nobel Prize–winning economist Roger Myerson has proposed a formula to estimate the chance of being pivotal. For a country with 5 million voters with two candidates closely tied in the polls, 50.1% versus 49.9%, it would be 0.000000008%. So if voting costs even just $0.01, the expected benefit of electing one's favoured candidate would have to be greater than $80 million dollars (or its equivalent in subjective value) to justify going to the polling booth (Feddersen 2004).

Given the probability calculations above, it seems hard to reconcile the choice of voting with any type of consequentialist behaviour (i.e., motivated by the consequences of one's actions). The widely observed fact that people regularly vote in modern democracies has therefore been called the *paradox of voting*. A possible solution is to think that people vote because they care about *principles*. They may believe that people living in a democracy should vote. As they are living in a democracy, they are simply doing the right thing.

Such behaviour has been considered by the Nobel Prize–winning economist John Harsanyi under the name of "rule utilitarianism" (Harsanyi 1982) and it has later been used to model voting behaviour (Coate and Conlin 2004; Feddersen and Sandroni 2006). Rule utilitarianism further deviates from the usual assumptions about the homo economicus. And it opens new questions: How to define the set of possible rules over which an agent has a preference, and why agents do have preferences over rules in the first place?

10.2 THE EVOLUTIONARY FOUNDATION OF MORAL BEHAVIOUR

Even though the homo economicus' assumptions look naive in retrospect, they had the merit to be easy to explain: people make choices that are good for them. In comparison, the existence of preferences over others' outcomes, others' intentions and even over the rules one should follow is less straightforward. Why such preferences and not others?

Why We (Should) Care about Others' Fate

If these preferences have puzzled a large proportion of economists, it is because they have overly focused on behaviour in stand-alone situations or "one-shot games". In these situations two people meet and engage in a specific interaction only once. These situations are easier to study formally than repeated interactions, but they are likely a poor guide to understand human behaviour. Social interactions take usually place over time, in repeated settings. Whether in the family, at school or at work, people tend to interact with the same group of people over and over again. It was even more the case for our ancestors who lived in small groups of typically less than 150 people.[6] Economists do not ignore these facts. Unfortunately for them, repeated interactions do not lend themselves to an easy formal investigation.

---

[6] Note that I leave aside here all the considerations relative to altruism towards kins (e.g., children, siblings). These considerations are important to explain human behaviour, but altruism towards kin would not generally be considered as irrational, even by the old economics standard. Gary Becker is famous for having used the hypothesis of parental altruism, in spite of his attachement to limiting preferences to material incentives (Becker 1981). Altruism towards kins is easily explained by evolutionary theory due to the genetic proximity between kin (Stewart-Williams 2018, chap. 5).

One-Shot Games and the Dilemma of Cooperation

To investigate what happens in games, economists use the notion of *Nash equilibrium*: a situation where nobody has interest to unilaterally change one's actions given the actions of others. An example of Nash equilibrium is the choice to drive on a given side of the road in a "driving game" where several players share a road between two locations and want to reach their destination without an accident. If all the players drive on the left on the road, nobody has an interest to switch side unilaterally. The same is true if all players drive on the right. When players are in an equilibrium, their actions are a *best response* to others' actions. In the case of the driving game, if I know that all other drivers intend to drive on the left of the road, driving myself on the left road is the best decision I can make (even if I come from another country where everybody drives on the right).

Actions outside an equilibrium are not a best response to others' actions. As a consequence, one expects that when players' actions are not reflecting an equilibrium of a game, players will adjust their actions to try to best respond to each other. If the game has an equilibrium, it is often reasonable to expect that players will end up will end up playing the strategies corresponding to this equilibrium because it is stable: once reached, nobody has an interest to change the way they behave.[7]

For this reason, economists look for a game's equilibria when trying to identify the likely actions players will adopt. In one-shot games, there are often one or a few equilibria. The fewer equilibria, the better for the economist: the predictions become sharper about what type of behaviour should be expected. But when a one-shot game is repeated indefinitely, things become very different. Instead of having one equilibrium or a few equilibria, there will possibly be an infinite number of equilibria.

Let's look at one of the most studied games: the prisoner's dilemma. While the canonical form of this game involves two prisoners, I'll discuss an alternative presentation involving two criminals engaged in a transaction.[8] One of the criminals has diamonds and he would prefer to sell them for money,

---

[7] The sharp reader will have noticed an apparent contradiction in my explanation of how players are likely to reach the equilibrium by trial and error over repeated situations of the game and the statement that we are going to use the notion of equilibrium for stand-alone games. We are entering here some non-trivial interpretation about why we should expect players to play the equilibrium strategies. If the players play the game only once, how could they have expectations about the likely actions of others? One possible argument is to assume a large population of players who meet only once to play the game and never interact afterwards again. Hence the game itself is common, but the players have no shared history between themselves. For them the game is a one-shot interaction. Another interpretation is that only strategies part of a Nash equilibrium are rational in the sense that nobody could recommend to select actions outside a Nash equilibrium (Binmore 2007, pp. 13–14). For further discussion on this point, see Binmore (1987), Binmore (1988) and Osborne and Rubinstein (1994), sections 1.5 and 3.2.

[8] This presentation is adapted from Hofstadter (1983). The framing of the prisoner's dilemma as a briefcase exchange was also adopted in the classic book on the topic by Poundstone (1993).

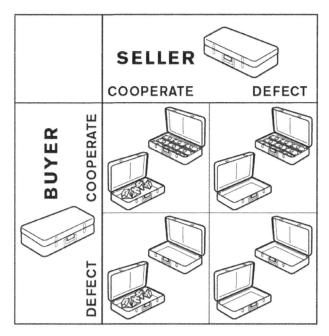

FIGURE 10.1. Prisoner's dilemma game as a briefcase exchange. Image(s) by Chris Jensen and Greg Riestenberg.

and the other criminal has money and would prefer to get diamonds instead. Unfortunately, these criminals have no way to organise a safe transaction enforced by the rule of law in their country. Let's assume that, as a consequence, they have to quickly exchange briefcases in a public place without having the opportunity to check the content of the cases at the time of the transaction.

The structure of this interaction creates a dilemma. Each criminal could opt to either cooperate (bring a briefcase with the intended content) or defect (hand out an empty briefcase) and give away nothing while possibly receiving a briefcase with valuable content. This game is presented in Figure 10.1. It is obvious in this game that *whatever* the other player does, a player is better off giving out an empty briefcase. Take the point of view of the buyer. If the seller is bringing a briefcase full of diamonds, the buyer is better off not paying anything for them. And if the seller brings an empty briefcase, the buyer is better off giving away an empty briefcase too. In each possible situation, the buyer is better off not bringing the money. Take now the point of view of the seller. It is easy to see that he faces the same problem. Like the buyer, the seller is better off bringing out an empty briefcase, whatever the choice of the buyer.

The dilemma is that these choices lead to a situation where no real transaction takes place. The equilibrium is the situation where only empty briefcases are exchanged: both players defect! It is unfortunate, given that both criminals would prefer the full exchange to take place, rather than no exchange at all.

This frustrating outcome is, however, *unavoidable*. Faced with this problem, many have tried to argue that cooperating may be in some way the right strategy. But as Binmore stresses: "cooperation cannot result from rational play in the one-shot Prisoner's Dilemma" (1994b).

Repeated Games and Cooperation

If we change this one-shot interaction for a repeated one, things can change radically. Suppose that instead of a single transaction, the seller has now regular access to new diamonds, and that the buyer and the seller have agreed to meet once a week, from now on, for an exchange of briefcases.[9] What is now the best strategy they each should adopt?

It does not take long to realise that giving away an empty briefcase one week may result in the other player refusing to engage in any future transaction in later weeks. If each successful transaction is valuable for the player, the threat of an end to such transactions may be enough to motivate the player to cooperate in each period.

This logic was perfectly demonstrated by the first-ever instance of a prisoner's dilemma experiment, which was organised, in January 1950, by Merril Flood and Melvin Dresher, two scientists at the RAND corporation (Flood 1958). They invited two friends, the economist Armen Alchian from UCLA and the mathematician John Williams from RAND, to play a game very much similar to our briefcase exchange, 100 times in a row. The way the game developed is illuminating. First of all, the outcome when both players defect appeared only 14% of the time. In comparison, the outcome when both players cooperate appeared 60% of the time!

Most interestingly, Flood and Dresher recorded comments from Alchian and Williams all throughout the game. These comments help understand the logic behind the choices of each player. The economist Alchian initially expected both players to defect and hence defected himself. Instead, Williams hoped for Alchian to cooperate. On his first move, as he chooses to cooperate, Williams writes: "Hope he's bright." As Alchian does not cooperate initially, Williams sets on the goal to educate him ("he'll wise up") by alternatively punishing him through defection and then, later on, giving him another chance by cooperating again ("I'll have to give him another chance"). Even though Williams was sometimes frustrated in his endeavour ("This is like toilet training a child, you have to be very patient"), he was eventually mostly successful. On the other side, Alchian was initially dumbfounded by Williams' choice to cooperate ("What is he doing?!!"). But after a few periods, he progressively understood that there

---

9 Formally, they play an *indefinitely repeated game*: the briefcase exchange is repeated ("every week") and there is no end foreseen to these interactions ("from now on").

was a logic behind Williams' moves ("Is he trying to convey information to me?") and eventually ended up cooperating most of the time.[10]

So, unlike the predictions of the one-shot game, these two very smart players ended up cooperating most of the time. I suspect that, for most readers of this book, it would not seem odd or surprising. Indeed, the logic of cooperation in repeated interactions is very intuitive. In 1739, David Hume provided in his *Treatise of Human Nature* an insightful description of how cooperation can emerge from the expectation of future interactions: "I learn to do service to another, without bearing him any real kindness; because I foresee, that he will return my service, in expectation of another of the same kind." A layman version of David Hume's insight is the maxim: "You scratch my back, I scratch yours." This maxim does not sound to our intuitions irrational, and it should not.[11]

When John Nash was asked by Flood and Dresher to comment on the result of their experiment, he pointed out that repeated games have more equilibria than simply the one consisting in playing each time the equilibrium of the single game (Binmore 2012). In the repeated prisoner's dilemma, it means that there are more equilibria than just defecting all the time. Indeed, it can be rational to cooperate, even though it is not the case in the one-shot game. This insight was formalised as the *folk theorem*, which states that in an infinitely repeated game, players can approach the payoffs from repeated cooperation.[12] It is possible because the threat of a future withdrawal from cooperation acts as a deterrence to defection in the present. This deterrence is mutual. Payoffs approaching the average full cooperative payoffs can be sustained with an equilibrium where no player has an incentive to deviate.

The intuition behind this result is straightforward and an example makes it easy to understand. Consider the "grim strategy"; it is simple and it can lead to full cooperation. It consists in starting with cooperation and continuing to cooperate as long as the other player does the same. However, if ever the other player defects, then the player playing "grim" switches to an uncooperative attitude for all the future interactions. In the setting of our briefcase game, a player following this strategy would bring a full briefcase to the exchange, as long as the other did the same. But he would stop, forever, as soon as the other player brings an empty briefcase. This strategy is akin to the one

---

[10] The transcript of this game can be found in Poundstone (1993), pp. 108–116. It has to be noted that the payoffs were slightly asymmetric in favour of Williams, which may partly explain the resistance of Alchian to cooperating. This little game interested Albert Tucker, a Princeton mathematician. He decided to frame it as a game between two prisoners in classes on game theory. From there, the game became known as the Prisoner's Dilemma. Interestingly, it was first created as an experiment, and played repeatedly.

[11] The more formal expression "quid pro quo" refers to the same process of exchange of favours.

[12] Or more formally, payoffs approximating those of repeated cooperation can be sustained by strategies forming an equilibrium of the repeated game. If the discounting of future interactions (because of the risk that interactions will stop or because players are impatient) is small enough, the possible payoffs can be as close as possible from the average payoffs from full cooperation.

I described above: if you betray the other player once, this one will refuse to cooperate forever afterwards. The grim strategy is harsh: it punishes heavily any deviation from cooperation. But interestingly, if both players follow this harsh strategy, suddenly neither of them has interest to defect. Both are locked into an equilibrium where they *always cooperate*.[13]

The implications of the folk theorem are profound. It means that even purely self-interested players would rationally engage in sustained cooperation over time. The only requirement for this to happen is that the probability of future interactions is high enough. So the traditional economic approach does not predict that human interactions should be dominated by systematic uncooperative behaviour because players are selfish.

The folk theorem's name comes from the fact that, in the 1950s, game theorists became aware of the idea of the theorem without knowing exactly who precisely had come up with the idea in the first place. Earlier statements of the possibility to cooperate in repeated interactions were made by Luce and Raiffa (1957), Shubik (1959), and Aumann et al. (1960) is considered to have published the first formal statement of the theorem (Friedman 2000). In their early discussion of this question, Luce and Raiffa (1957) expressed that it did not seem "reasonable" to single out the joint defection as the "solution" of the prisoner's dilemma when it is repeated. Instead, the choice to cooperate appeared to be a "quasi equilibrium" that "is extremely unstable; any loss of 'faith' in one's opponent sets up a chain which leads to loss for both players" (chapter 5.5).

Aware of these discussions in economics (and of Luce and Raiffa's reflections, in particular) the biologist Robert Trivers published in 1971 one of the most influential articles in the history of biology, "The Evolution of Reciprocal Altruism." In it, Trivers builds on the insight that cooperation can emerge when interactions are repeated to propose an explanation of altruism between strangers. Trivers' article presents a rich set of ideas about how individuals would regulate cooperation through the reward of cooperative behaviour and the detection and punishment of uncooperative behaviour.[14]

In economics and in biology, the idea that cooperation can emerge as a rational behaviour between self-centred players progressively became accepted. The folk theorem, however, was raising a problem for economists. It doesn't just say that cooperation is perfectly sustainable but also that there are *an infinite number of ways of sustaining cooperation* and that different ways may allow players to get closer to or further from reaching average payoffs from full cooperation.

---

[13] Note that a somewhat puzzling aspect of a Nash equilibrium is that it can involve strategies that specify actions that are never observed. In the case of an equilibrium with grim strategies, since nobody ever defects in equilibrium, the retaliation is never observed.

[14] I recommend to any behavioural scientist to read this paper, which is unfortunately not well known in social sciences.

It may sound nice to say that there are an infinite possible number of ways to cooperate, but for economists it just looked like a failure of their formal approach. Having an infinity of equilibria means that game theory did not lead to a model with clear predictions about behaviour. Remember our discussions about scientific methodology (Chapter 1): having a model that can predict anything makes it relatively weak and unable to make predictions that can be tested empirically. So, as a consequence, economists typically preferred to look at one-shot interactions where there is typically a limited number of equilibria. But by focusing on one-shot games, economists may have not given enough attention to the question of how, in practice, people play in repeated games.

The way to play these games may be to select one equilibrium (among all those possible). If social interactions are characterised by many equilibria, the problem people face could be to find which one to choose. Some equilibria seem better than others. For a start, some equilibria make it possible for people to cooperate repeatedly. All the cooperation-sustaining equilibria, however, are not equivalent; some bring higher payoffs than others. Let's consider the equilibrium with grim strategies. If players never make mistakes, it works well: both players cooperate all the time and receive the payoffs from full cooperation. But suppose that players sometimes make mistakes. For instance, one of the criminals may have taken the wrong briefcase among all those he possess. Or he may have erroneously switched their briefcase with another person on their way to the exchange (e.g., in the train). After such mistakes, the grim strategy implies that no cooperation will ever take place again. In other words, there are no second chances. This solution to enforce cooperation may lead to missed opportunities for cooperation to resume after a mishap in one given interaction. Like Williams in Flood and Dresher's experiment, one may want to be somewhat forgiving and willing to give a second chance in order for cooperation to restart after some time.

So what should be the best strategies to sustain high cooperation (and therefore high payoffs) for both players? It is not an easy question. In a hugely influential study, the political scientist Robert Axelrod organised a tournament to try to answer it through the test of a wide range of strategies (Axelrod 1980a, 1980b). He invited experts in game theory to submit strategies for the repeated prisoner's dilemma game. Each strategy played against every other strategy once, over 200 moves.

Economists, sociologists, psychologists, mathematicians and political scientists submitted strategies to the tournament. Some strategies were quite complex, trying to model the strategy of the other player from past action to infer the best action to play.[15] The result from this study was astonishing. The most successful strategy ended up being one that even a three-year-old toddler

[15] The authors give this example of an "intricate" strategy: "one which on each move models the behavior of the other player as a Markov process, and then uses Bayesian inference to select what seems the best choice for the long run".

can understand: *tit-for-tat*. This strategy starts by playing nice (cooperating) in the first period. After that, it follows a simple rule: it is nice to players who have been nice in the previous period and it is not nice (defect) to players who have not been nice in the previous period.[16] When people cooperate in the first period and then follow the tit-for-tat strategy, they are clearly in an equilibrium: none of them has interest to change. As long as the other cooperates, they cooperate.

This result is fascinating for two reasons. First, it is a surprisingly simple strategy among all the possible strategies one could think of. Second, it is surprisingly *intuitive*. Tit-for-tat is a simple rule or reciprocity that can easily guide us in our daily social interactions. It has a few simple properties. It is nice: it starts cooperating and continues to cooperate with cooperators. It is not a pushover: it retaliates against defectors. It is forgiving: it retaliates only once after a defection then cooperates again.

Expressions reflecting a tit-for-tat logic for social interactions are found all throughout history. The *Law of Talion*, one of the oldest recorded laws, which can be traced back to Babylonian times, famously states that retaliation should be in proportion of the offence: "an eye for an eye" (Frymer-Kensky 1980).

In following studies, Axelrod and others found strategies that do better than tit-for-tat. An interesting feature of these winning strategies is that they are also intuitive. For example, Nowak and Sigmund (1993) proposed a strategy that is similar to tit-for-tat with some small adjustments. It switches back to cooperation if *both* players defected in the last period. This new strategy makes it possible to avoid being locked up in a tit-for-tat feud. The *gradual* strategy by Beaufils et al. (1997) seems to be the most successful so far. It consists in behaving like tit-for-tat, but it has a perfect memory of the other player's past defections. It punishes any new defection by defecting a number of times equal to the number of past defection from the other player. After the first defection, the gradual strategy answers by defecting once; after a second defection, gradual defects twice, and so on. Then it cooperates twice in a row to reinitiate cooperation. This strategy can be seen as ramping up punishment towards players who do not change their behaviour after being sanctioned for their uncooperative behaviour.

The fact that these automatic rules can be easily understood using moral concepts such as *reciprocity* and *forgiveness* raises the prospect of a fascinating change of perspective. If we have the moral intuitions we do, it may be because they are solutions to the problem of cooperation in repeated interactions. It would then make sense that we find the strategies successful at this game "intuitive"; these rules may actually form the foundations of our moral intuitions. Armed with such intuitions, we may be able to successfully cooperate with others in games with repeated interactions. These intuitions may make us better players by helping us navigate the complex decisions of whether to cooperate or not and with whom to do so.

---

[16] This strategy was originally proposed by the psychologist Anatol Rappoport.

A person who never cooperates would certainly be a very poor player in social interactions, missing out on the opportunity of gains from cooperation and unable to get consistent benefits from uncooperative behaviour (because other people are not pushovers). The best way to play in repeated interactions is to care about others and about what they get.

Why We (Should) Care about Others' Intentions

The previous explanation of why people should care about others' outcomes has used the case of repeated interactions between two people. In such situations, it is the perspective of future interactions that creates the possibility to sustain cooperation in present situations. For that reason, strategies where people care about others' outcomes can emerge. We can understand an even wider range of social behaviour by extending this simple setting to situations where interactions can take place with different people.

A simple extension of the repeated prisoner's dilemma game between two players is to think that there is a multitude of players who are randomly matched and play the game. In such situations, cooperation can also emerge as an equilibrium of the game (Nowak and Sigmund 2005). A solution is for people to decide to cooperate with people who have a record of having previously cooperated with others. This cooperation towards people who cooperated with others was proposed by Alexander (1987), who called it *indirect reciprocity*, in comparison to the direct reciprocity from the tit-for-tat strategy.

Such a strategy requires keeping track of the past cooperation of others. The past record of a player acts as a *reputation*, which will determine whether people decide to cooperate with the player or not. A reputation can increase from past cooperation, and decrease from past defections. But it is also possible to have equilibria where reputation changes in more subtle ways as a function of past actions. For instance, players who do not cooperate with players who have a low reputation may not lose their own reputation (they may even gain some reputation in that case). Determining the reputation of somebody can therefore require understanding their *motives* in past interactions.

Suppose we observe Jane not helping John in a situation where he is in trouble. To determine whether and how this should impact her reputation as a cooperator, we need to understand the motives that drove this behaviour. Did she mean to be unkind or did she mean to punish John because he had himself been unkind in the past? If John has the reputation of being unkind, not helping him could have been justified as a punishment. In that case, it should not hurt Jane's reputation.

In real social settings, we are not matched randomly with the people we interact with. An important decision we have to make is to *choose with whom to interact*. The choice of suitable partners – lovers, friends, colleagues, commercial partners – is an important one. For this reason, we are cautious about choosing our acquaintances. When doing so, we have to form a view on their likelihood to cooperate in the future (Baumard et al. 2013). Here again we can use other people's reputation, based on their past actions, to guide such decisions.

A key aspect of social interactions is that there are many of them and that circumstances change frequently, meaning that while interactions are repeated, the specific payoffs and risks are going to vary over time. The future circumstances in which we will be in a situation where our fate depends on the actions of our partners are hard to foresee. It creates an incentive to look carefully for partners who are inclined to cooperate and on whom we may be able to rely on, whatever happens. In lay terms, we will look for people who show *good character* in their past actions.

For this reason, when we choose social partners, it is not just what they do that matters, but the intentions that led to their actions. We can infer intentions by comparing what people did in the past with all the other things they could have done instead. Observing that somebody's action led to a positive outcome for you does not tell you much about this person's kindness if you do not know the other actions this person could have taken. In the mini-ultimatum game, if you receive an offer 2–8 (you get $2 and the other person gets to keep $8), it does matter whether the other choice possible was 5–5 or 0–10 in favour of the proposer. In the first case, the player making the offer chose the worst option for you, even though a symmetric split was possible. In the second case, the player chose the best option for you, even though you are not getting much. If you had to choose with whom to cooperate, you should certainly prefer players who made this choice when the alternative was 0–10. Their choice signals intentions that are more likely to be caring about you than if the alternative was 5–5. Understanding the options that others had when making choices helps us ascertain their intentions (Falk et al. 2003; Engler et al. 2018). And it helps us predict their behaviour in the future.

The fact that people care about others' intentions explains a lot about the intricate patterns of social interactions. For example, it creates incentives to exchange information about others' actions and motives to find out what they are really up to. Such information is useful to ascertain whether somebody can be trusted as a cooperating partner. A typical form of such information exchange is *gossip*, which pervades social interactions across human societies and is even observed among primates (Dunbar 2004).

The importance of partner choice also explains some seemingly quirky human behaviours as signalling strategies. Think about somebody who wants to be seen as a good partner, likely to cooperate in the future. What is the best way to do so? Stating "I am a good partner" is unlikely to work. Anybody, including potentially uncooperative partners could make this statement. It is *cheap talk*. As I will develop in Chapter 13, signals convey information when they are costly. One option is, for example, to show that you are a good cooperator by making kind gestures conspicuously (e.g., charitable giving).

But a kind gesture that is made as a public signal of kindness is somehow problematic. People want to find real cooperators who act kindly because they are intrinsically motivated to do so. If someone acts kindly to look kind, it may actually be the action of somebody who is just trying to look like a good cooperator without necessarily being one (Iredale and van Vugt 2012). This problem explains the suspicion and even scorn that can be raised by overly public acts of good deeds. A perfect example of such concerns is how the term *virtue signalling* has now been imported from the evolutionary textbooks to be used to criticise others' moral positions as grandstanding to get public approval.

These considerations imply that observing a good deed that was intended not to be observed is much more valuable than observing a good deed that was intended to be made in public. A classic example of such a situation takes place in Jane Austen's *Pride and Prejudice*. Elizabeth's affection for Mr Darcy grows markedly when she unexpectedly learns that he acted to rescue the reputation of her family[17] *while asking for his role not to be acknowledged.* The observation of a person secretly acting altruistically is a common trope in novels and movies, allowing the "real" character of a good person to be revealed.[18] Anonymous benefactors are seen as the epitome of kindness. Their only motivation is in their actions and not in people observing their good deeds. The value given to these unobserved acts of kindness can explain another subtle aspect of social behaviour: it creates incentives to engage in acts of kindness that are *not too conspicuous.*[19]

Another implication of this search for intrinsic motivation is the preference for people who engage in kind behaviour without calculations. This fact is observed in a wide range of situations. A person who does not take time to think before deciding to help is seen as nicer than somebody who takes a long time to make the same decision to help. In social interactions, splitting something equally without clearly looking at everyone's cost and benefits is often preferred to the feeling of awkwardness associated with engaging in the required accounting. A good example is when people split the bill in restaurants without looking at it to determine the precise amounts corresponding to each person's meal. Another one is when researchers opt for signing their papers in the alphabetical order of co-authors instead of allocating the order based on each author's contribution.

People may prefer to avoid calculating precise costs and benefits with close social partners because it may signal a concern for the short-term benefits of the present interaction rather than the long-term benefits from future interactions. People with short-term motives may be kind today, but they may be unreliable

[17] After one of Elizabeth's sisters eloped with a soldier, Mr Darcy paid him to convince him to marry her.
[18] The reverse situation is also very common: a hypocritical character is unmasked for acting badly in a situation the person thought was not public.
[19] See the notion of buried signals in Chapter 13.

when short-term benefits to defection appear in the future. Hoffman et al. (2015) looked at this question with a small model of repeated interactions where one player can take a chance to look at the cost of cooperation before cooperating. If the cost is too high, this person has an interest not to cooperate. A player has therefore an interest to look at the cost to decide whether to cooperate or not in the present interaction. But the player may gain from not looking in the present period. Players who do not look signal to the other players that they will cooperate *unconditionally* in each interaction. This signal can increase the confidence of the other player, who may be more likely to cooperate in the next interaction. For that reason, not looking at the cost in the first period can be an equilibrium strategy in this game. In the case of a restaurant dinner, splitting a bill may reflect a preference for being kind and willing to incur some costs for others. It indirectly signals that one's kindness in the future can be safely expected; it is not conditional on the costs and benefits present in each specific interaction.

Finally, the screening of intentions also helps explain the extensive presence of gift exchanges in human interactions, from small gifts such as paying for your colleague's coffee or inviting your friend for dinner to large ones like when someone gives an expensive ring to their partner. Why so much gift-giving? Possibly because it may be a good strategy to build relationships when people can change partners fairly easily. In such situations, people who tend to trust others right away could be vulnerable to con artists who make a living from "fooling everybody once" in early interactions and then move to other partners afterwards. One way of screening out these possible untrustworthy partners may be to build trust slowly. But Carmichael and MacLeod (1997) show that another solution is to engage in gift exchange to start a cooperating partnership. The gift exchange is costly, and it screens out untrustworthy partners interested in a quick benefit from a betrayal of trust. The mutual gift-giving creates bonds of trust that sustain long-term cooperation.

Gift exchanges have somewhat peculiar characteristics: "gifts" are not entirely free, they somewhat create a duty of reciprocity. This reciprocity, however, is expected not right away, but at a later date. These characteristics are easy to explain when one understands the signalling games behind gift exchanges. Mutual gifts allow potential partners to signal to each other an intent to engage in long-term cooperation, in opposition to a care for short-term costs and benefits. For gifts to build trust of each partner in the other, there must be some symmetry. If a gift exchange was asymmetric, with one partner making smaller gifts than those received, the signalling value of the exchange would be under threat. The smaller contributor could engage in the gift exchange for the benefits it provides, therefore removing the signalling value of participation in the gift exchange. In addition, for a gift to work as a signal, the temporality of the exchange matters. A gift acts as a signal because the giver indicates that they can incur short-term costs for the sake of the relationship. Reciprocating a gift too quickly erodes the signalling value of the initial gift by not allowing the giver to display their willingness to wait before receiving a reciprocal gift. Reciprocating right away, or even refusing the gift, can be perceived as an unfriendly gesture, indicating an unwillingness to engage in a process creating bonds of mutual trust to sustain friendly interactions.[20]

This role of gift-giving in the creation of social bonds was famously discussed by the sociologist Marcel Mauss in his essay "The Gift" (1990), studying ritualised systems of gift exchanges such as the *potlatch* among Native American populations in the Northwest Coast of North America and the *Kula ring* in the Trobriand Islands on the East Coast of New Guinea. Mauss argued that behind the apparent generosity of the gift-giving practices, there were strict rules of obligations: the timing and the level of the reciprocation mattered greatly, and refusing to reciprocate was akin to declaring war.[21] In the absence of an overarching state regulating and adjudicating conflicts between individuals and between groups, these systems of gift exchange helped sustain mutual trust and limit conflicts.[22]

Why We Care about Following Rules

The last feature of moral behaviour I identified earlier is the fact that people often see morality through the angle of "rules" that need to be followed. Trivers describes very clearly one advantage of moral rules:

Multiparty altruistic systems increase by several-fold the cognitive difficulties in detecting imbalances and deciding whether they are due to cheating or to random factors. One simplifying possibility that language facilitates is the formulation of rules of conduct, cheating being detected as an infraction of such a rule. In short, selection may favour the elaboration of norms of reciprocal conduct. (Trivers 1971)

Fairness Norms as Ways to Coordinate on Cooperative Solutions
The existence of many equilibria in repeated games where cooperation is possible implies that, a priori, many types of repeated interactions can be sustained over time. For example, people can be stuck in a feud where they are unkind and keep retaliating against each other. They could instead sustain cooperation

---

[20] It is certainly why the idea of offering to pay friends for their gifts (e.g., invitation for dinner) seems either incongruous or ill-mannered.

[21] "To refuse to give, or to fail to invite, is – like refusing to accept – the equivalent of a declaration of war; it is a refusal of friendship and intercourse ... The obligation of worthy return is imperative. Face is lost forever if it is not made or if equivalent value is not destroyed ... Time has to pass before a counter-prestation can be made" (Mauss 1990).

[22] Interestingly, Mauss saw his analysis of gifts as contradicting the homo economicus model already discussed at the time: "this economy of gift-exchange fails to conform to the principles of so-called natural economy or utilitarianism ... Homo economicus is not behind us ... we are still far from frigid utilitarian calculation". As I have argued in this section, gift-exchange contradicts the narrow homo economicus assumptions but it does not contradict economic principles per se, when applied in repeated interactions.

by being kind and reciprocating. The existence of many cooperation-sustaining equilibria in repeated games should not be seen as the death knell of economic analysis. On the contrary, it should invite economists to investigate how we end up coordinating on specific equilibria, rather than others, to split the benefits of cooperation.

In a fascinating investigation of this question, Ken Binmore (2005b) notes that one rule is widely shared across human societies to help people cooperate and limit conflicts, the *Golden Rule*: "treat others the way you would like them to treat you". This rule is present in Confucianism, Hinduism, Ancient Greece, Christianity and Islam:

Never impose on others what you would not choose for yourself.
Confucius

Treat others as you treat yourself.
Mahābhārata

Avoid doing what you would blame others for doing.
Thales

Do to others what you would want them to do to you.
Bible

The most righteous person is the one who consents for other people what he consents for himself, and who dislikes for them what he dislikes for himself.
Hadith

The presence of this same rule across such different times and places suggests that it reflects some fundamental aspects of human morality. A possible reason is that it may help people coordinate on one of the cooperation-sustaining equilibria. Taking the other's point of view, and anticipating that the other person will do the same, may allow people to reach a joint understanding about how to interact with each other in repeated interactions.

It is important to note that the Golden Rule does not specify precisely *how people should treat each other*; instead, it states that they should treat others the way they would like to be treated. The "right" way to share the gains from cooperation is neither trivial nor unique. In particular, it is not always a rule of strict equality. Imagine a situation where Jane and John face every day the same situation: they have to decide whether they want to work together on that day and, if so, how they want to split the product of their work. One possibility is for them to work together every day and to split the gains from their work evenly, 50–50. It is indeed what is typically observed in sustained cooperation, and we intuitively feel that it is *fair*. However, suppose that Jane and John are different. Jane is much more efficient at the task than John, and she is the main reason their joint work creates large gains every day. Should they still split the gains from their cooperation evenly? Suppose, alternatively, that they are both equally skilled, but John works ten hours every day, while Jane works only one hour. Should they still spit the gains evenly?

Here our moral intuitions are less clear, indeed, we are likely to feel that an even sharing of the gains from the project may be *unfair*. Aristotle famously pointed out that it is not necessarily equality that is required, but ensuring that shares are determined according to each person's merit: "this is the origin of quarrels and complaints – when either equals have and are awarded unequal shares, or unequals equal shares" (Aristotle 340 BCE). It then begs the question of how to determine who merits more. Should the strong get more, or the weak? Should the old get more, or the young? Should the skilled get more, or the unskilled?

We have to answer these questions all the time. When we allocate public recognition for collective work (e.g., "I would like to thank …"). When we decide who can be the first to take something from a dish on the table and who can get the last bit remaining at the end. When we have to decide who gives way in a narrow corridor or a small elevator. When we decide who should speak first in a conversation and when others can interject to make a point (and for how long). In all these situations, we have to decide how to split gains and costs among different people.

Potentially, such situations could lead to endless negotiations to determine who should get what. Having to renegotiate each time would be inefficient and tiresome. Indeed, we do not engage in such negotiations in daily situations. Instead, we seamlessly solve them by having a shared understanding of how such a situation should be resolved. For instance, in a small corridor, the priority is likely to be automatically given to an older person or to a slower person (e.g., a person with impaired mobility). It can also be given to a person of higher status (e.g., your manager if you work in a company).

How do we manage to coordinate in such situations, without conflict or negotiation? Binmore puts forward a compelling explanation: *fairness norms* guide us into coordinating on a specific equilibrium of the game. As fairness norms are shared and mutually understood, they are not required to be stated or discussed. They are generally used without being mentioned, often without even being consciously considered by the people involved. In the same way as you do not think, "I am driving on the right," when you drive in a country where it is the norm, you do not need to think, "I am letting my manager speak uninterrupted," when you are in a work meeting.

Fairness norms are, in that view, a grammar to help us navigate and solve ubiquitous social interactions where gains and costs have to be shared. When we say, "It is fair," it is a recognition that the way gains and costs were shared in a situation complies with the mutually accepted norm. In many cases, *fair* will mean equal, but in others it won't. The fact that fairness norms are collectively shared ensures that we agree on how unequal things should be when people don't have necessarily the same status or contribution.

While fairness norms solve our daily interactions without needing to be mentioned or considered, they are nonetheless always here in the background, structuring our actions. Their presence and importance is often revealed when they are violated in situations where people fail to respect them. A person who jumps a queue may be at the receiving end of a reminder of the prevailing social norm: "Sorry, but I was here first." Fairness norms also become visible when people disagree on their application or about their respective claims. Somebody wanting to jump queue may have to argue about the right to do so: "I am sorry, but I am late for my appointment and it is important." Different claims will lead to possibly different responses as they mobilise different assessments of what is fair, given the prevailing norms. A man asking to jump the line to go to the hospital to see his wife giving birth is more likely to be successful than another one saying he is simply late for work.

In that view, failing to comply with a norm of fairness is a violation of the cooperative equilibrium, which typically leads to punishment. In social interactions, punishments of norm violators often start with mockery, signalling to the culprits that they deviated from the norm. If John never pays for his friends' drinks in a pub while they frequently pay for his, he risks ending up being at the receiving end of jokes about his stinginess. If mockery does not work, stauncher punishments are bound to take place, like the simple withdrawal from future cooperation. In the case of John "forgetting" to take his turn paying for drinks, others may end up not inviting him to their social drinks any more.

Because fairness norms are equilibria of repeated games, they are *self-enforcing*. Not following the norms leads to social sanctions. This is an important point. The fact that people engage in reciprocal altruism and respect fairness norms in social settings is not a puzzle. People have an interest to follow the norms and not to deviate.

So if the solution to the problem of selecting a cooperation-sustaining equilibrium is to follow fairness norms, how are these norms determined? Why do they point to a given equilibrium rather than others? To answer this question, Binmore suggests that the specific tuning of fairness norms is likely to be determined by the historical and cultural realities of a given society. Different societies have different norms, which reflect different equilibria. The relative bargaining powers of the different society members may, in practice, determine that equilibrium can be sustained in the long run. Fairness norms about how to share things would then tend to reflect the equilibrium that can be sustained given the bargaining power of the different group members. It would explain why, as societies have become more democratic with a more equal distribution of political and economic power, fairness norms have become more egalitarian.

The Objectivity of Fairness Norms

Fairness norms are part of the social norms that indicate to people how to behave in society. But not all social norms are the same. Some norms are clearly conventional: we understand that they exist only because we agree on them. We are aware that we could have agreed on different norms instead. A good example would be norms of fashion.[23]

Fairness norms tend to feel different from conventional norms. They are associated with an impression of objectivity: moral preferences are often experienced as *truth* rather than preferences. An action that violates a fairness rule will be perceived as unambiguoulsy bad not because we have some preference over it but because *it is* bad. This feeling of objectivity is easy to understand in ethical philosophies supported by religious beliefs where a deity can give an objective nature to a moral rule. But even secular ethical philosophies have relied on the notion of objectivity, such as the idea that individuals have *natural* rights.[24]

This aspect of moral behaviour may seem peculiar, but the feeling of objectivity creates constraints on moral behaviour, and, as pointed out by Schelling (1960/1980), the restriction of possible actions may give an advantage in social interactions by allowing one to commit to some course of action. For example, you may trust people more in business transactions if you know that they believe that unfair deals are forbidden by some objective rule (therefore removing for this person the option to engage in unfair behaviour).[25]

Stanford (2018) has recently theorised further how this feeling of objectivity can provide an advantage by making cooperation unconditional. As I have discussed previously in this chapter, we interact with social partners in new and different situations over time. It would be difficult to predict our partners' behaviour if their choice to cooperate was driven by a cost-benefit comparison between selfish and prosocial preferences. Observing someone having behaved kindly in some past situation would not necessarily mean that they would do the same in other contexts, where the relative strength of their preferences may lead to different choices. If, instead, people understand moral behaviour as the unconditional respect of rules, observing whether somebody follows moral rules in one context is a good predictor of what this person will do in another context.

Furthermore, the objectivity of the rule helps people to coordinate their expectations. Supporting morality based on subjective preferences could make it hard for somebody to request others to act morally as they may claim

---

[23] For an extended discussion of the different type of social norms, see Bicchieri (2005).

[24] The idea that there are natural laws of justice that ascribe natural rights to people was developed by Hugo Grotius (1625). He argued that these laws can be found using human reason. Famously, Grotius stated that the existence of such laws would still stand even if there were to be no God. The notion of natural rights played an important role in the French Revolution and the Declaration of the Rights of the Men and of the Citizen of 1793. It was famously criticised by Bentham: "Natural rights is simple nonsense: natural and imprescriptible rights, rhetorical nonsense, – nonsense upon stilts" (Bentham 1832/1998).

[25] I develop this idea in Chapter 11 with Frank's (1988) argument that our moral emotions exist at least in part to bind us to moral behaviour, making us more trustworthy partners.

other tastes or motivation. The belief in the objectivity of the fairness norm means that each person expects others to be similarly motivated and that these expectations are common knowledge.

Using an evolutionary game-theoretic model, Alger and Weibull (2013) found that evolution could select agents who are torn between acting in their self-interest and acting morally by following rules (*homo moralis*). A greater probability for such a homo moralis to interact with others would likely lead them to give more weight to the importance of following rules rather than their self-interest.

Following rules may be, in practice, what people do when they behave morally. As we have seen, there are very good reasons why people would follow commonly understood and shared rules. And acting as if these rules are objective may also help facilitate cooperation. Such behaviour departs significantly from the standard assumptions of economic models, and more work is certainly needed to study the role of unconditional rules of morality in human cooperation.

Explaining Observed Moral Behaviour

Explaining Cooperation in Behavioural Experiments

The elements presented in this chapter allow us to make sense of the prosocial behaviour observed in carefully controlled lab experiments. People are equipped with social norms that do not leave them when they enter an economic laboratory. Even though the situations people face are often novel, sometimes a bit puzzling, people will try to solve them using their understanding of what is right. The widespread concern for fair distribution of outcomes in the lab is therefore not surprising. Games usually played in the lab have an embedded element of symmetry: participants are randomly allocated to different roles. If Jane is allocated the role of proposer in an ultimatum game or in a dictator game, she understands that this role was not given to her due to her merit in some way, but to the luck of the draw. This symmetry between the players can foster the feeling that an equal distribution of outcomes is the fair allocation of the monetary amount. The role of social norms in the process is further evidenced by the fact that proposers are much more likely to offer nothing when the allocation of the roles, or the money to be split, has been earned from the performance in an earlier task (Hoffman et al. 1994; Barber and English 2019). When the advantage of a player can be interpreted as being derived from some merit, norms of fairness dictate that the fair outcome may deviate from equality to reflect the different merits of the two players.

The fact that concerns for fairness are shaped by norms helps explain one of the features of the reactions to unfair treatment. People react to unfair allocations perhaps not so much because of the amounts in the allocation per se, but because it is a violation of the *respect* they deserve given the prevailing fairness norm. In his *Theory of Moral Sentiments*, Adam Smith

(1759/2010) submitted that "What chiefly enrages us against the man who injures or insults us, is the little account which he seems to make of us, the unreasonable preference which he gives to himself above us." In line with this explanation, Yamagishi et al. (2012) found that the propensity to reject unfair offers in the ultimatum game did not correlate with the propensity to adopt prosocial behaviours in other games. They conclude that the rejection of unfair offers is not driven by a propensity to have prosocial feelings in general. Instead, it is better explained by the hypothesis that players receiving unfair offers respond with a "wounded pride" to the lack of respect shown by the offer (Straub and Murnighan 1995). In a recent review of literature on fairness concerns in children, Engelmann and Tomasello (2019) also pointed out that their response to unequal distributions was based not on material interest but rather on a desire to receive equal respect. In this perspective, players rejecting an unfair offer are refusing to accept an action that violates the respect they are due.

One may retort that the behaviour observed in the lab cannot be explained by a model where people are inherently self-centred. Interactions in the laboratory are generally one-shot and anonymous. Therefore, it does not cost anything to play selfishly. There is no loss of future cooperation opportunities with others. So, shouldn't people simply play ruthlessly in one-shot games?

The key to answer this question is to point out how unusual laboratory experiments are. They are carefully designed to create one-shot anonymous interactions. Such interactions mean that you will *never* know with whom you played; other players will *never* know what you did; and your actions will *never* influence how other people decide to engage with you in future interactions. There are several reasons why social norms, as described above, are likely to still have some bite in these laboratory experiments.

First, while the experiment is designed with the aim of creating anonymity, there is no guarantee that the players fully believe it. Believing in the full anonymity between players requires confidence in the trustworthiness of the experimenter. And even if the experimenter is trusted to have designed the experiment to be anonymous, the participants still need to trust that there won't be any data leaks that could reveal later their actions in the experiment. These are not trivial issues. Some academic disciplines routinely deceive lab participants. The participants' beliefs in the trustworthiness of the experimenter is therefore not guaranteed. And leaks of numerically recorded "private" data have now made it apparent that a zero risk may not exist. Having said that, these risk perceptions may be relatively minor, in particular, in economic experiments where researchers strive to build a reputation for trustworthiness.

Second, the players' actions are de facto not entirely anonymous in any situations where the experimenter can match the behaviour of players and their identity. Even though chances of future interactions with the experimenter may be small, they may not be absent, in particular, when the experimenter is a professor in the department and the participants are students. As I previously mentioned, the altruistic behaviour displayed in dictator games tends to be less pronounced when the experiment is run as a double-blind one (Hoffman et al. 1996). When participants are told that the experimenter will not be able to know what they did, they tend to behave more selfishly.

Finally, it is most likely that participants simply import in the laboratory their moral feelings, which are tailored to solve games of repeated interactions. People may not be able to turn off these feelings when participating in an experiment. The one-shot anonymous interactions significantly depart from our typical social experiences. How often do we engage in interactions that can be genuinely one-shot and anonymous? Most interactions take place with family members, friends and colleagues, and such interactions last over years and decades. Only a limited number of interactions can take place with perfect strangers in modern large cities. But even interactions with strangers are not clearly one-shot as we may meet them again, and how we interact with strangers can be witnessed by others. Indeed, the widespread use of hand-held cameras has led to many people being "shamed" after their unkind behaviour towards a stranger was recorded and posted on social media.

Most importantly, even though large cities now offer some interactions with strangers that are likely to be one-shot, it is a very novel and unusual type of interaction on the time scale of human history. Most of our ancestors have lived in small groups of up to 150 people for tens of thousands of years. The big anonymous cities appeared in the last 200 years, which is a blip in human history.[26] It is not unreasonable to assume that evolution may not have had time to design us to discriminate between purely one-shot interactions with a stranger and interactions that are likely to be repeated (or that are likely to be witnessed by, or communicated to, other people with whom you may interact later). Evolution may have endowed us with a moral compass and a way to care about social norms that does not turn itself off in the one-shot interactions designed in experimental labs.

It is particularly likely to be the case when laboratory games are played only once and participants do not have the opportunity to learn, therefore relying more on their moral intuitions. In support of this view, we observe that participants tend to increasingly display a more selfish behaviour when they play these (one-shot) games several times with different players each time. Playing these games more than once gives participants the opportunity to learn how to play (Fischbacher and Gachter 2010). Such a pattern is easily explained by the perspective I propose here: as participants repeat the same game over time, they have the opportunity to learn that they can get away with less kind behaviour than would be prescribed in usual social interactions.

---

[26] While cities are obviously older than that, it was most likely harder to be anonymous in the social fabric of old cities.

Human Moral Behaviour and Evolutionary Explanation

There is often an implicit (and sometimes explicit) belief that an evolutionary explanation would lead to the prediction of a narrowly selfish homo economicus. This is a misconception. There is no contradiction between our moral attitudes and an evolutionary explanation. Evolution should not necessarily select for selfish preferences. Instead, it is more likely that evolution led us to have moral preferences to help us navigate successfully the opportunities of repeated cooperation with others. Reading these lines, some readers may feel unsatisfied by this explanation of moral attitudes as having an instrumental value to be successful in social situations. Giving an evolutionary explanation (which relies on a selfish agent) to moral behaviour may feel misguided, if not disturbingly wrong. Aren't people simply intrinsically altruistic? Isn't it that, by definition, altruism cannot have an instrumental value?

This criticism is understandable but not warranted. It is indeed possible to say that people can have genuine moral feelings while also giving an evolutionary explanation to these moral feelings. The way to do so is to distinguish the two ways to explain behaviour in biology. First, there are the *proximal causes* of a behaviour. To find these causes, we look at an organism's behaviour today and try to understand the mechanisms (e.g., psychological and physiological) that cause it. For instance, to explain why a bird sings, we may describe how it enjoys singing.

The second type of causes are *ultimate causes*. To find them, we ask a more fundamental question: Why are proximal causes here in the first place? How did they come to be? The question here is: Why does the bird like to sing? The answer to ultimate causes has to be found in the evolutionary process that shaped organisms to be the way they are. If birds like to sing, it is because singing is, among other things, a way to get in touch with possible mates (and to compete with other rivals in displaying one's skills).

The two explanations are not in contradiction with each other. A bird most likely genuinely enjoys singing, but if it enjoys it, it is because there is an evolutionary reason behind this behaviour. The satisfaction of singing is an evolved reward for doing something that is good for the fitness of the individual.

In the same way, there is no contradiction between saying that humans have genuine moral feelings and that these feelings have been shaped to guide them when playing games of social interactions. Paradoxically, because we have these moral feelings that are genuine (proximal cause), the idea of explaining them as instrumental (ultimate cause) can feel distasteful. My preferred answer to this is to compare our moral feelings to other tastes that we also genuinely feel. Take the taste for chocolate. Most people enjoy chocolate. The subjective feeling associated with the taste of chocolate is the proximal cause of the behaviour "choose to eat chocolate". The ultimate cause though has nothing to do with chocolate per se. We like sugar-rich food because sugar is high-energy, and, for our ancestors, such high-energy food was scarce and highly valuable. Developing a taste for sugar was evolutionarily adaptive. Saying this does not imply that our taste for chocolate today is disingenuous. Similarly, explaining our moral feelings as evolution's solution to make us good at social interactions is not saying that our moral feelings are fake. On the contrary, the evidence supports that they are very real.[27]

∴

In conclusion, there are excellent reasons to think that humans should not be selfish in the way often described by the homo economicus model. Indeed, in retrospect, the assumption of selfishness seems a bit naive. It would characterise more a kind of sociopath than somebody likely to navigate successfully their way through society. Social interactions require collaboration and cooperation with others, negotiation of who should do what and who should get what. Within a household, a family has to decide who does the chores and how leisure time is spent. At work, colleagues have to decide who does a given job and how to allocate the benefits of collective work. When moving around other people, you have to decide when to give way, to whom and how much. When living in a house, you may have to decide how much to prune your tree overhanging the neighbour's fence. When living in a flat, you have to decide when to stop a noisy party on Saturday night. The list goes on and on. The type of selfish attitude described by the homo economicus model would characterise an individual particularly inept at finding the right behaviour in such situations. On the contrary, typical humans usually navigate these fairly complex social situations seamlessly. They sense when it is okay to do something, and when it is not; when some actions will be widely accepted by others, and when some others will be frowned upon.

Humans are social animals; they are pretty helpless alone and face large potential benefits from cooperation. It is therefore reasonable to expect that they will have evolved preferences helping them interact with others in ways that can be mutually beneficial. These considerations explain why people care about others' fate, why they care about others' intentions, and why they care about following fairness norms that, in a given social context, point to commonly accepted ways to share the benefits and costs from cooperation.

---

[27] Beyond the evidence from economic experiments, research in neuroscience has shown that the brain regions activated when observing another person's emotion, such as pain, overlap with those activated when experiencing these emotions themselves (Singer et al. 2004; De Vignemont and Singer 2006).

11

Emotions and Commitment

It may be perfectly rational to wish ... for the power to suspend certain rational capabilities in particular situations.

—Schelling (1960/1980, p. 18)

Being known to experience certain emotions enables us to make commitments that would otherwise not be credible.

—Frank (1988, p. 5)

Using rational emotions and commitment as tactics is especially common in bargaining and negotiating. Emotions such as anger and insult, but also empathy, can all be identified in common negotiation situations. They influence the relative bargaining power of the negotiators.

—Winter (2014, chap 1)

Summary: Peoples' propensity to fall prey to social emotions such as anger or love often leads them astray from reasonable and sensible decisions. It is frequently described as blatant evidence that people are irrational. In this chapter, I show that these emotions can help us in social situations by tying our hands and limiting the type of actions we can take. The paradox of commitment shows that, sometimes, it is penalising to have the option to make the most reasonable choice. Being committed to some course of action, hereby limiting our options, can be beneficial. For this reason, these emotions do not make us weaker; they make us better at negotiating our way in social interactions.

Thinkers and philosophers have often described emotions as conflicting with reason. While reason allows us to make good decisions, emotions are feelings that may drive us to make very costly choices. People get into physical fights and engage in acrimonious exchanges on social media because of anger. They refuse business opportunities because they feel they are not getting their fair share. They are willing to sacrifice a substantial amount of their time and resources for somebody else when they are in love.

These facts are far from benign. In their book on lethal violence in America, Zimring and Hawkins explain that most of gun deaths do not occur from criminal activity such as robberies but from "arguments and other social encounters between acquaintances" (1999, p. 16). The availability of guns in these situations leads to homicides as a result of outbursts of anger. These arguments are frequently triggered by jealousy in love affairs or hurt pride in regard to someone's status.

Emotions can drive behaviour in a way that seems out of control. Indeed, the etymological root of the word *emotion* comes from the Latin word for moving. An emotion is something that makes you feel as if you are being moved by an external force. It is understandable why thinkers may have disparaged emotions as being in conflict with reason and as something one needs to overcome to make wise decisions.

11.1 THE PARADOX OF COMMITMENT

If emotions are impairing our decisions, why have they been selected by evolution? And why are they so entrenched in our psychology? One reason we have already discussed in Chapter 5 is that emotions such as fear or elation can contain information that is valuable in our decision processes. Here I will present another reason why emotions can be helpful: they can provide a credible commitment to specific courses of actions in social interactions.

The importance of commitment was stressed by Thomas Schelling in his book *The Strategy of Conflict* 1960/1980. The critical insight from Schelling is that in many strategic situations, it can hurt you to have too many choices at your disposition. Think again about the briefcase exchange situation described in Chapter 10. Each criminal has an interest to bring an empty briefcase to the exchange location. As a consequence, no exchange will take place. Anticipating this, the criminals may even decide not to go to the exchange meeting in the first place, since it would be a waste of time to show up. This outcome is unfortunate, given that both of them would prefer for a real exchange to take place. Here, the criminals are penalised by the fact that they have the option to defect. The existence of this possibility makes the exchange impossible.

Suppose now that the two criminals could credibly commit beforehand to eliminate the option to defect. Then they would be able to proceed with the exchange, in their best interest. It is the *paradox of commitment*. In many strategic situations, agents can gain an advantage by tying their hands and reducing the options they have at their disposition, such as the option to defect later on.

The issue of possible defection underlies most of our economic interactions. Businesses could fail to deliver the goods we paid for or lie about the quality of what they are selling. Such actions would be equivalent to the choice of defecting in our diamonds versus bank notes game. In most of the economic situations we encounter, the constraint not to defect is provided naturally by the institutions enforcing the rule of law (police, justice). These institutions make defecting costly in a way that eliminates defection from the set of profitable options. A business not delivering the goods it sells would soon find itself facing very costly court trials.[1] In societies where the rule of law is less firmly established, people are wary about the risks of defection, and they only carefully grant their trust to potential partners in business exchanges. Such situations greatly reduce the opportunity for mutually beneficial cooperation. For that reason, possibilities for players to commit to cooperation can play an important role in allowing cooperation to take place.

One possibility is for people to reduce their material incentive to defect by increasing the cost of defection. In his book *Codes of the Underworld*, Diego Gambetta (2011) illustrates this fact with the strategies used in communities of criminals where, by definition, legal constraints cannot be used to prevent defection. In a situation like the briefcase exchange, one option could be for criminals to reveal their whereabouts, or the whereabouts of somebody from their family, to create the possibility of retaliation in case of defection.[2] Doing so would make defection an unappealing option. It would make it possible for the criminals to trust each other and to engage in a mutually beneficial exchange.

Another possibility to reduce the material incentive to defect is to increase the *subjective* cost of doing so. One type of institution that helps doing so is religion. It is particularly the case for religions with *moralising gods*, divine beings who wish for humans to follow moral rules and who punish deviations. In his classical study of the effect of religion on the economy, Max Weber pointed

---

[1] Beyond the rule of law, the prospects of future interactions limit defection (e.g., the desire of businesses to retain the trust of their consumer base). Note that, even in societies with good rule of law, many transactions feature an asymmetry of information, which prevents the customers from knowing for sure whether the goods/services they paid for are really delivered. Is a car mechanic really charging for the right pieces to be changed in the engine or is this tradesperson proposing unnecessary changes? Is a restaurant really respecting the health and safety regulations in its kitchen? The greatest risks for customers are in transactions where there is a large asymmetry of information and limited prospects of repeated business in the future. Examples include hiring a builder for a house, hiring a surgeon for cosmetic surgery or buying a second-hand car from another person. In such interactions the issue of trust can become very obvious in the transaction.

[2] The use of family members as collateral to ensure trust in bargaining situations has been observed throughout history in a wide range of situations, from economic interactions between individuals (e.g., to secure a loan) to international relations between states (e.g., to secure a treaty).

to this fact as one of the effects of Protestantism in the United States. It created a common understanding that, in the Protestant community, people believed in an all-powerful and omniscient God who was able to observe all the actions and intentions of everyone. The Puritan Protestant was characterised by "trust, especially his economic trust in the absolutely unshakable and religiously determined righteousness of his brother in faith" (1915/1953).[3]

Religion may increase the credibility of people's commitment to cooperation by creating subjective costs to defection. If it is the case, could other types of subjective costs also have the same effect? In his influential book *Passions within Reason*, Frank (1988) proposed that emotions can play this role and credibly constrain some of the choice people have. The types of emotions that can play this role are *social emotions*, those emotions that arise specifically in the context of our social interactions. I'll explain this point using three of these emotions: anger, guilt and love.

11.2 ANGER

Anger can be a very destructive emotion. It can lead people to engage in verbal abuse or even physical violence. An old French idiom states that "anger is a bad advisor". Indeed, at first sight, there is not much positive in people experiencing anger.

It is widely acknowledged that anger somewhat reduces a person's ability to make reasoned decisions. This recognition underlies, for example, the difference between voluntary manslaughter and murder. The former is often committed "in the heat of passion" (Dressler 1982). This fact is interpreted in courts of law as a mitigating factor when deciding on a conviction. On the contrary, murder is defined as premeditated – and therefore reasoned – killing.

Because of anger, people can engage in very costly behaviours. They tell others things that may hurt their long-term relations. They may engage in public arguments that have a costly impact on their reputation. In many instances, people have lost their job following ill-tempered public outbursts.

Isn't this type of behaviour the epitome of irrationality? How could something so negative have been selected by evolution (or not been eliminated by it)? Schelling's point on the importance of commitment helps provide insights on the role of anger in our social interactions. Let's look at how this insight can explain apparently irrational behaviour in many situations.

The Paradox of Commitment in Conflicts
Many social situations are conflicts where only one party can win at best, and everybody can lose if the conflict lasts too long. Such situations can be represented with the "game of chicken". The most famous depiction of this

---

[3] The effect of religion that has moralising gods may explain their success and evolution (Johnson and Bering 2006; Norenzayan and Shariff 2008).

TABLE 11.1. *The game of chicken in Rebel without a Cause*

	Jimmie jumps first	Jimmie jumps second
Buzz jumps first	Draw	Jimmie wins
Buzz jumps second	Buzz wins	Jimmie and Buzz die

game in popular culture is the drive to the cliffs in the movie *Rebel without a Cause* (1955): Jimmie (James Dean) and Buzz challenge each other to drive stolen cars at high speed towards a cliff. The one who chickens out first, by jumping out of the car, loses the challenge. In the movie, Jimmie jumps just before the cliff, while Buzz gets stuck in the car and falls to his death.

Let's use this movie scene to discuss the strategic structure of a game of chicken. I will use a simplified version of this game and suppose that the players have only two possible strategies: "jump first" or "jump second". With the strategy "jump first", the player does not wait for the other player's decision and jumps right away. It is the "chicken" strategy. With the strategy "jump second", the player first waits for the other player to jump before doing so. Table 11.1 presents the payoffs for the players as a function of their joint choices. Each player should jump second if the other jumps first. But if both wait for the other to jump first, they are driving to their mutual death.

The structure of this game reflects the nature of many conflicts in the real world. Consider a strike where workers are fighting for a raise in their wages. If the workers back down, the employer wins, and if the employer backs down, the workers win. But if nobody backs down, the firms' economic activity suffers. In the worst-case scenario, the firm goes bankrupt.

Games of chicken are also very in common international relations where costly economic or military conflicts are the possible end points of confrontations. The most iconic example is the episode of the Cuban missiles crisis. In 1962, the United States found out that Russia planned to install nuclear missiles on Cuba, within firing range of the US mainland. The American President United States John F. Kennedy ordered a naval blockade of the island to prevent Russian ships from reaching Cuba. The confrontation lasted thirteen days during which the stalemate could either end in the United States or Russia backing down or in a nuclear warfare between the two countries. Eventually, Russia agreed not to place missiles on Cuba against a US pledge not to invade the island.

These situations all have in common that a player wins by getting the other one to back down. One way to convince the other player to do so would be to convince this one that you are never going to back down first. If indeed you are never going to chicken out, there is no benefit for the other player to push the conflict to the end; it is more reasonable to stop first. The plight of rational players is that they cannot credibly convey the belief that they will never back down. They may claim that they won't back down, but it is evident why they could have an interest in making this claim, even when they would be willing to back down.

But suppose that evolution would have endowed some players with emotions that makes them angry when they play this game, to the point where, in spite of the risks involved, they would be willing to stick obstinately to never backing down. Then the emotion of anger would serve as a commitment device to eliminate the backing-down strategy from the set of possible moves. These players would fare better against cool and rational players who would back down if they expect the other player to be madly obstinate.

This commitment effect seems to provide a good idea of how anger can help. However, it is not enough. To work out as a strategy, a commitment needs both to exist and to be explicitly revealed to the opponent. This point was made comically in Stanley Kubrick's movie *Dr Strangelove*. The Russians, understanding the importance of commitment, had built a "doomsday machine" that would launch an immediate and unstoppable nuclear counter-strike to answer any nuclear attack. This commitment device should serve to deter the Americans from ever considering striking first. Unfortunately, they set up the machine without informing their American opponent, and before they did, a rogue US general decided to launch an attack himself.

To deter opponents, anger needs to convey the visible signs of its existence. And indeed, anger is not a quiet emotion. It comes with visible signs such as redness in the face, clenched fists, loud outbursts. These signs can help inform the other player that backing down is indeed not an option for you.

To the extent that such signs can be imitated, there is an incentive for players who are not actually committed to a course of action to mimic these signs of anger and give the impression that they are committed. If they can convince their opponent, they can win even though they were not really angry. These considerations explain why real-world games of chicken are typically characterised by a competitive display of anger where both players may seem irrational. At the same time, both players monitor the signs displayed by the other to assess how much they are really committed versus how much it may simply be grandstanding without real resolve.[4] The ability to play these games masterfully is rightfully called *brinkmanship*: the ability to drive close enough to the brink of the cliffs to convince the other player to jump first.

Making Credible Threats in Negotiations

Anger can be helpful in a wide range of situations where it creates a credible threat that deters other people from taking advantage of you. One type of such

---

[4] This scrutiny for tell-tale signs of real intent behind the grandstanding is reflected in the expression "he blinked first", which is commonly used in such situations to describe a player giving signs of anxiety, which betrays a lack of commitment to the most radical course of action.

situation are negotiations, where players disagree on how to divide costs and benefits.

Think about a very specific type of negotiation: a customer trying to get compensation for a service or product perceived to be unsatisfying. Often, the customer may engage in such a negotiation with subtle (or not subtle) signs of anger.[5] Companies ignore these signs at their peril. The story of Dave Carroll and his guitar, which became viral in 2009, gives a good illustration of that fact. That year, Dave travelled by plane within the United States, using United Airlines. He is a Canadian musician, and he was carrying a $3,500 guitar in his luggage. During a stopover in Chicago, he heard passengers saying that ground staff in charge of the passengers' luggage were throwing guitars without much care. Upon arrival to his destination in Omaha, Nebraska, he found that his guitar was broken. When raising the issue with the airline staff, he felt that they showed "complete indifference" towards him. He then filed a claim with United Airlines, who answered that he was not eligible for compensation because he had not made a claim within twenty-four hours.

If Dave Caroll had been a homo economicus, there is nothing more he would have done about it. Sure, he would likely be unhappy with the loss of his guitar and disappointed in the company's handling of the situation. But complaining further would serve no purpose. It would likely be a waste time and effort for little expected gains. As a homo economicus he would not even stop using the company in the future as he would still choose future plane trips based on the best offers for any given trip.[6]

But Dave Carroll is not a homo economicus, he is a *Homo sapiens*. He persisted over several months, trying to get compensation for his lost instrument. Eventually, angered by the lack of consideration shown by United Airlines' employees, he wrote a song, "United Breaks Guitars", where he describes his misfortune and warns potential passengers of the risk they face using the company. The song's refrain contains the line "I should have flown with someone else, or gone by car, 'cause United breaks guitars." His video, posted on YouTube on July 6, 2009, received 150,000 views in its first day. At the end of 2021, it had reached over 21 million views. The success of the video is undoubtedly a terrible public embarrassment for the company. The public relations damage was worth much more than the $3,500 Dave was looking compensation for. The company ignored Dave's grievance, and paid a dear price for it.

Dave Caroll went to a considerable length of effort to write and record a song to complain without much prospect of it being ever successful. In 2009, it was

---

[5] Or with signs of displeasure, which can indicate that they would get angry if no satisfying solution is found.

[6] He would possibly slightly modify his future behaviour, given his updated beliefs on the risk of getting his luggage damaged. However, his future choices would not be influenced by a grudge against the company as such. Instead, he may opt to invest in a reinforced suitcase for his musical instrument.

estimated that 50% of YouTube videos were getting fewer than 500 views.[7] In other words, most videos posted online are barely ever noticed. But Dave most likely was not driven by economic rationality in his endeavour; rather, he was angry at the company, and it's what motivated him to produce this video.

It is what anger makes people do. People are willing to engage in costly behaviour to retaliate when they feel they have been wronged. While this could be seen as irrational at first sight, it provides a benefit: it makes your threat of retaliation *credible*, because people know you are likely to carry on a threat if you have angry feelings. This credibility increases people's bargaining power relative to a homo economicus. Companies could safely ignore a "rational" consumer's complaint, knowing that the consumer would not engage in costly retaliatory behaviour. But most companies know they face humans with emotions and try to handle unsatisfied customers with care (in particular, when they have a valuable brand reputation to protect).

Here as well, anger has to be communicated visibly to be effective as a credible threat. The outburst and rage from angry customers are the signs that give credence to the future (or even imminent) retaliatory behaviour if their grievance is ignored. While an onlooking observer may think that an angry customer has "lost it" or is "out of their mind", it is precisely what is effective at making a threat credible and therefore at influencing the company to take the grievance in consideration.

Building a Reputation as a Way to Deter Others
An even better solution than showing signs of anger when one is wronged is to build a reputation for anger and retaliatory behaviour in order to deter others from even trying to wrong you. Building such a reputation makes sense in situations where the rule of law is fragile and where opportunities of wrongdoing against you are frequent.[8]

In their book *Culture of Honor*, Nisbett and Cohen (1996) investigate the roots of the greater level of violence in the US South. They see its origin in the lower level of property rights protection in the early times of settlement. The South was settled by herdsmen whose main property was their cattle. Relative to crops, animals are much easier to steal. At the time, the government had less power to enforce compliance with the law. Citizens had to create "their own system of order". One effective strategy to adopt was to build a reputation

---

[7] Estimated by TubeMogul, an advertising software platform.

[8] Today, unlike our ancestors, we rarely solve our disputes through violence and even less often through murder. The fact that such a way of resolving disputes was part of our ancestral past is reflected in the relatively high number of people who engage at some point in an "aggressive fantasy" where they imagine hurting or harming somebody else. In a survey in the United States, psychologists found that two thirds of respondents had experienced such fantasies (Poon and Wong 2018). Nowadays, the rule of law limits the availability of weapons and/or associate, large penalties with the use of violence.

for toughness and a propensity to retaliate: "To maintain credible power of deterrence, the individual must project a stance of willingness to commit mayhem and to risk wounds or death for himself" (p. xv). To deter crime, this reputation has to be built ahead of time before any major wrongdoing is committed. The culture of honour that developed in the South leads to people reacting violently to small slights. Indeed, there is much more at stake than it would seem in small interactions. Your *reputation* is on the line. "When someone allows himself to be insulted, he risks giving the impression that he lacks the strength to protect what is his" (p. xv).

In his book on the strategies used in the underworld, Gambetta (2011) also stresses the importance of building a reputation for toughness, to the point of being seen as ready to do anything. It is notoriously the case of Mafia bosses who will use graphical crime scenes when getting rid of a traitor as a signal for others who could be tempted to betray them. The strategic portrayal of irrationality in the underworld is also well illustrated by a scene from *The Godfather*. Don Corleone issues an implicit threat to other families when stating that he wants his son to come back safely from Sicily: "I'm a superstitious man, and if some unlucky accident should befall him – if he should get shot in the head by a police officer, or if he should hang himself in his jail cell, or if he's struck by a bolt of lightning – then I'm going to blame some of the people in this room. And that, I do not forgive." Doing so, Don Corleone wants to deter any attempt at killing his son, which could be masqueraded as due to external causes. He states a tendency to blame others irrationally as a pre-emptive threat.[9]

Another example presented by Gambetta, possibly more extreme and less well known, is the use of self-harm in prisons. The carceral environment is often structured by an unforgiving social hierarchy. Prisoners who are not part of a group risk ending up at the bottom of this hierarchy. Low positions in the prison's social order may lead to being the target of systematic violence. In such an environment, some criminals engage in acts of self-harm, such as lacerating their arm with a knife, to build a reputation of irrationality and unpredictability. These acts show both an ability to resist pain and a readiness to go to mad extremes if needed.

Building a Reputation in International Conflicts

International relations is one of the areas where there is no overarching rule of law to limit the misdemeanour of other players. While diplomacy is generally polite and subtle, there are situations of tension in international relations where it can be important to make credible threats: the indication that your country would retaliate in case another country does something bad. But countries face a credibility challenge when trying to make a threat. Any retaliation for

---

[9] For a general discussion on how blame can be used strategically to deter pre-emptively, see Gurdal et al. (2013). The example of Don Corleone was pointed out to me by Joshua Miller.

a small unfriendly act may be overly costly and not be in the interest of the country. This problem was discussed in length in Schelling's book, written in the middle of the Cold War, and it is perfectly illustrated by a scene in the classic British political series *Yes Minister*. Discussing with an army expert at the start of the 1980s, the British prime minister is considering spending a lot of money on British nuclear armament as a way to deter the risk of aggression from the Soviet Union. The slightly frightening expert starts, with a comical German accent, quizzing the PM about the utility of the nuclear weapons to deter the USSR to attack. The surprised PM answers that nuclear weapons simply deter the Russians from attacking, a seemingly obvious answer. But the expert does not let it go, and he starts unpacking the PM's logic. Why does it deter the Russians? he asks. The PM, still puzzled, answers: "Because they know that if they were to launch an attack I would press the button." To which the expert retorts, "You would?" Pressed to go into the detail of when and how he would use nuclear weapons, the PM, now slightly uneasy, says that he would do it "as a matter of last resort". But what is a situation of last resort? asks the expert, unrelenting. "If the Russians were to invade Western Europe", the PM retorts. This answer seems straightforward enough. But the expert continues challenging the PM about his willingness to "press the button". He starts describing some scenarios of aggression. In reality, he says, Russia would not launch a full-scale invasion of Europe. It would proceed slice by slice, using a "salami tactic". For instance, the PM should consider a scenario where riots erupt in West Berlin, buildings are in flames and an East German fire brigade crosses the border to help. Would the PM "press the button"? The PM declines. Suppose now the East German police come to "help"; would the PM press the button? No again. The expert continues: "Then some troops, more troops, just for riot control, they say, and then the East German troops are replaced by Russian troops. But the Russian troops don't go. They are invited to stay to support civilian administration. The civilian administration closes roads and Tempelhof Airport. Now you press the button?" The PM, now quite uncomfortable, shakes his head to indicate he would not. The expert continues to describe scenarios where Russia progressively takes over Western Europe slice by slice. Each time the PM balks at the idea of using the button at any specific step forward taken by the Soviet Union. The expert's point is that the costs involved in using nuclear weapons limit their ability to deter aggression.

Here again, the weakness of the British prime minister comes from his rationality and his understanding of the deadly consequences of initiating nuclear warfare. An effective strategy to make a threat of retaliation credible is to convince your opposition that you are not rational and could very possibly retaliate disproportionately in case of limited aggression. An important condition for it to work is for you to be able to send credible signals of anger to inform the other player that you would very likely act upon your threats. Displaying a tendency to be erratic, unpredictably angry and unreasonable may be a good way to keep an opponent wary about not trying to do anything that could trigger a disproportionate reaction on your part. Such a strategy was somewhat theorised by the US President Richard Nixon during the Cold War:

I call it the Madman Theory, Bob. I want the North Vietnamese to believe I've reached the point where I might do anything to stop the war. We'll just slip the word to them that, "for God's sake, you know Nixon is obsessed about communism. We can't restrain him when he's angry—and he has his hand on the nuclear button" and Ho Chi Minh himself will be in Paris in two days begging for peace. (Haldeman and DiMona 1978)[10]

11.3 GUILT

We have seen in Chapter 10 the potential gains from cooperation when you interact with other people over an indefinite amount of time. But it is also clear that *pretending to cooperate* rather than really cooperating can bring rewards as long as it is not found out. If John shirks instead of pulling his weight in a group task, he may benefit from the collective work without having to contribute to it. Similarly, if Jane is in a situation where people expect everybody to be truthful, she can gain an advantage by providing others with alternative representations of reality that conveniently fit her interest.

The possible gains from defection mean that there is always a latent conflict in incentives, even between cooperators. This conflict creates a motive for deception as someone could only pretend to be cooperating while actually defecting. Such behaviour presents some risk if found out by others. When people are found to have lied to others and betrayed their trust, it damages their reputation, and it lowers the trust they receive from others. It typically leads to less opportunity to benefit from cooperation with others in the future.

Guilt as an emotion certainly exists partly to keep us aware of these possible negative future consequences associated with a defection in the present. This point was made by Trivers: "It is possible that the common psychological assumption that one feels guilt even when one behaves badly in private is based on the fact that many transgressions are *likely* to become public knowledge" (Trivers 1971, p. 50). In doing so, guilt acts as a *shadow cost* of defection. It conveys useful information to the agent, in the same way as other emotions, as discussed in Chapter 5.

But guilt also has another effect: it can limit ex ante a person's willingness to engage in some wrongdoing: "Consider, for example, a person capable of strong feelings of guilt. This person will not cheat even when it is in her material

---

[10] In his Discourses on Livy, Machiavelli suggested another type of situation where it may be "wise to feign folly": when they could have incentives to connive against their ruler. To avoid the ruler's pre-emptive strike, they may feign folly so that it appears that conniving is not part of their options.

interest to do so. The reason is not that she fears getting caught but that she simply does not *want* to cheat" (Frank 1988, p. 53).

By eliminating some possible moves, guilt can provide an advantage by making a person more trustworthy. The key, as for anger, is for others to be well aware that the person is prone to guilt. Indeed, as described by Darwin himself, there are visible signs of guilt, at least in children: "In one instance the expression was unmistakenly clear ... an unnatural brightness in the eyes, and ... an odd, affected manner, impossible to describe" (Darwin 1897, p. 262). Another possible giveaway is the act of blushing.[11] As a consequence, the tendency to blush can act as a signal of trustworthiness. Illustrating this point, Darwin reports the statement of a Spaniard quoted by Humboldt: "How can those be trusted, who know not how to blush?" (Darwin 1897, p. 318).

The emotion of guilt, with the visible cues it generates, credibly signals to others that one is trustworthy. It is why guilt can be felt and expressed in relatively minor violations in social interactions. We have seen that anger may emerge after small wrongdoings of others to indicate that future and possibly larger wrongdoings should not be attempted. Similarly, guilt may emerge after small wrongdoings on our part to indicate that we can be trusted not to be willing to engage in possibly larger wrongdoings in the future.

11.4 LOVE

Love is undoubtedly one of the strongest emotions felt by human beings. Love can generate both tremendous fulfilling happiness as well as the darkest sorrow. It can drive a person to make the greatest sacrifices motivated by a feeling of abnegation in favour of a loved one.

Love seems to be opposed to rationality, and many would not expect love to appear in a discussion on the optimal strategies behind our behaviour. However, like anger and guilt, the strength of the feeling of love can bind an individual's behaviour in a way that eliminates some moves. Love can act as a commitment device.

This argument was developed extensively by Robert Frank (1988).[12] He noted that a monogamous partnership requires a very demanding investment from both partners. Let's consider John and Jane forming a typical monogamous partnership. They have to abandon other possible partnering options, present and future. And they have to invest resources in their being a couple. In the case of Jane, it includes a substantial physiological investment if the couple makes children. If John and Jane were homo economicus, they would re-assess at every moment in time whether their investment is best placed in

---

[11] Blushing is also associated with shame, which differs from guilt: shame arises when someone becomes aware that others know about a wrongdoing. Guilt is a feeling that is perceived even when a wrongdoing has not been found out by anybody else.

[12] It was also raised at the same time by Buss (1988).

this specific partnership. And they would be open to, if not looking for, other possible partners becoming available. The challenge for them is that the possible defection at any moment of the other partner would make it very risky to invest much in this specific relationship. The lack of trust between John and Jane would lead to a low level of joint investment in the partnership.

Love provides a possible solution to this difficulty by binding partners with feelings that eliminate defection, or at least makes it very unlikely. When in love, people feel and act as if their partner is the only person they value in the world. They not only neglect other possible partners; they often purposely stay away from them.

As for other emotions, love can work as a commitment device if it gives visible and credible signs of its existence. Indeed, somebody infatuated with another person can show visually discernible signs of these feelings (even sometimes involuntarily). Love also leads a person to behave in costly ways that act as credible signals of love.

Nonetheless, as showing a feeling of love can enhance the others' trust, there can be an incentive for people to mimic the signals of love to benefit from the partners' trust to one's advantage. This is particularly true in the case of men, who have a relatively lower cost of defection.[13] In a discussion of the evolutionary roots of love, David Buss quotes the Roman poet Ovid, saying that "duplicity is used in order that a man might win his way into a woman's heart and subsequently into her boudoir" (Buss 2006, p. 72)

As a consequence, the process of selecting a potential partner and deciding to form a partnership is more intricate than it would be without this risk of deception. Women tend to require more time to screen potential partners and make a decision before forming a partnership than men (Buss 2019). This time of screening has, in the past, taken the form of *courtship*.[14]

The strong feeling of love, guaranteeing the commitment to a long-term partnership, is paralleled by the less intense feeling of benevolence, which can enhance trust in everyday partnerships like friendship. The fact that benevolence can act as a guarantor of a later kind behaviour was initially pointed out by Hirshleifer (1987). The shared emotion of benevolence between members of a partnership can help sustain their trust in their mutual intentions. To do so, benevolence has to be associated with credible signals that cannot be easily generated without benevolence. As pointed out by Ho (2021), genuine signs of benevolence like smiles and laughter are hard to fake. Our difficulty in generating such signs at will while they come so naturally when we enjoy our

---

[13] The biological definition of sex comes from the size of the gamete. Males are the ones with the smallest gametes and the lowest investment in the process of producing offspring. It is less costly for them to leave a partner after having offspring than it is for females. In the human species, women carry the offspring in their body over several months at great physiological cost (Trivers 1972).

[14] I discuss courtship in more detail in Chapter 13.

interactions with others could be seen as a puzzling limitation. But it is because these signs are hard to fake that they are credible, and therefore that they have value to convince others of our benevolent intentions.[15]

11.5 EMOTIONS AS STRATEGIC MOVES

We have seen how the complex and often seemingly irrational behaviours generated by the emotions of anger, guilt and love can actually be explained as good answers to the actual strategic challenges faced by humans interacting with each other.

But this explanation seems to miss something. How can emotions be something that comes from the individual, but over which the individual has no or limited control? I have described emotions as constraining the individual's actions, but how can such self-constraints exist without the individual being able to override them?

One way to answer this question is to use a *principal-agent metaphor* (Binmore 1994a).[16] Instead of designing a simple decision maker, evolution could lead to decision processes that work as if a person's brain host two players: an agent who makes a decision in the instant and a principal who has the goal to make the agent better off, in the long run.[17] In the interest of the agent, the principal may reduce the agent's possibilities as a way to commit this one to a specific course of action.

This metaphor is not just an image; the autonomic nervous system indeed does just that. It helps regulate body processes such as blood pressure, heart rate, breathing, digestion as well as emotional arousal. The physiological processes regulated by the autonomic system are vital for survival, and they are basically kept away from the control of your conscious decisions. You do not control your heartbeat: you can't decide to stop it or accelerate it. likewise, if you try to stop breathing, a gasping reflex will soon give you the uncontrollable urge to do so. It makes perfect sense. In the same way as you do not give children the freedom to play with knives, your autonomic nervous system does not give you the ability to experiment with your life by altering your breathing or heart rate. Similarly, emotional arousal is triggered by clues in a way that you do not

---

[15] We'll see in Chapter 12 how emotions generated by a shared identity can also help sustain trust and cooperation in a group.

[16] A principal-agent relationship describes a situation with two players, where one of them (the principal) wants the other (the agent) to do something (e.g., an employer wants an employee to work well).

[17] The metaphorical description of evolution as a designer trying to make the agent as efficient as possible dates back to Darwin himself: "Natural selection is daily and hourly scrutinising, throughout the world, every variation, even the slightest; rejecting that which is bad, preserving and adding up all that is good; silently and insensibly working ... at the improvement of each organic being" (Darwin 1859, p. 133). This metaphor was also promoted by Dennett (1987). For a discussion of the validity and limitation of such a metaphor, see Okasha (2018, chapter 2).

control consciously. It is precisely this lack of control that makes it beneficial by credibly committing you to not engage in some course of action (e.g., backing down, defecting).

This lack of conscious control is not a bug; it is a feature. And the principal-agent metaphor gives us more insight into how emotions work: while the triggering of emotions is beyond conscious control (the agent), it does not mean that it is totally non-strategic. On the contrary, the cognitive processes in charge of triggering them (the principal) would gain from using this possibility as a function of the costs and benefits in each situation.

Indeed, the emotion of anger is not just triggered by the characteristics of an offence. It is responsive to the expected costs and benefits that would ensue. Evidence supports this prediction. For instance, men's tendency to display anger depends on their chance to come up on top, if a physical conflict was to ensue. They tend to be more prone to anger against others if they are more formidable than them (Sell et al. 2009). One can expect that the expression of other emotions is also sensitive to the context faced. Even though emotions are beyond our conscious control, they may still be triggered in a somewhat strategic manner, reflecting the opportunities and risks associated with binding the behaviour of your conscious self in a specific situation.

Schelling defined a *strategic move* as a move, prior to a game, that gives an advantage, by committing to a course of action. Emotions can be seen as your principal's strategic moves in social games. And it makes sense for such strategic moves to be made (at least in part) strategically. In the words of Frank (1987), if our emotions make us irrational, they may make us *shrewdly irrational*.

∴

Emotions such as anger and love are undoubtedly the source of much turmoil in the world. They are passions that often blur the mind of decision makers. They can drive some people to hurt themselves or to hurt others in irremediable ways. They seem to be the best examples of how irrational human beings are. Nonetheless, they can be conceived as adequate answers to the nature of some of the strategic interactions with which we are engaged. Emotions offer a way to solve the paradox of commitment, the fact that renouncing the freedom to engage in some actions can actually provide an advantage to the agent.

12

Social Identity

In order that primeval men ... should become social ... [t]hey would have felt uneasy when separated from their comrades, for whom they would have felt some degree of love; they would have warned each other of danger, and have given mutual aid in attack and defence. All this implies some degree of sympathy, fidelity and courage.... A tribe rich in the above qualities would spread and be victorious over other tribes.

—Darwin (1871/1981)

In the social jungle of human existence, there is no feeling of being alive without a sense of identity.

—Erikson (1968, p. 38)

The real conflicts of group interests not only create antagonistic intergroup relations but also heighten identification with, and positive attachment to, the in-group.

—Tajfel et al. (2004, p. 33)

*Summary: The traditional homo economicus model depicts agents as individual atoms driven by their self-perspective. In opposition to this vision, people seem driven by their membership in groups, in many social situations. The feeling of belonging to a group is typically associated with warm feelings towards other in-group members and sometimes with negative feelings towards the out-groups' members. These feelings are far from being inconsequential. For the sake of their groups, people can decide to make substantial sacrifices.**

* This chapter, written in 2021, is one of the most important chapters to understand social interactions, as it looks at some of the bleakest aspects of human sociality. The mass war crimes committed during the Russian invasion of Ukraine in February 2022 painfully remind us of the importance of understanding the mechanisms leading individuals to participate into intergroup conflicts and commit violence against outgroup members.

On 11 September 2001, several terrorists crashed two planes into the World Trade Center in New York. This moment shocked the world, and most of those who remember it can still picture where they were when they learned this shocking news. By hijacking two planes and piloting them towards the Twin Towers, the terrorists were devising the deaths of thousands of people. But in the process, they were also actively planning their own deaths. Such a plan seems in blatant contradiction with the idea of rationality. It was, however, not the result of an impulsive decision. The hijacking had been planed for months and several terrorists had taken weeks-long piloting lessons.[1]

Suicide attacks have, unfortunately, been quite recurrent in the twenty-first century. But looking back, we can see that voluntary participation in a suicide action to fight for a cause is not specific to our times. At the end of World War II, when Japan had all but lost the war. The Japanese Army sent, as a last resort, suicide attacks on the US Navy. Locked in a plane charged with explosives and without parachute or landing gear, Kamikaze soldiers aimed to crash their planes on US ships. In total, it is estimated that around 3,800 pilots died in these attacks. While the process of recruitment is not always clear, it seems that a proportion of these pilots were volunteers, willing to sacrifice their lives.

Modern terrorists and Kamikaze suicide attacks seem to conflict with our intuitions about reasonable behaviour. But our intuitions may be tainted by the fact that, for most of us, modern terrorist groups and the Axis powers in World War II are the wrong side. Think, instead, about the fictitious story from the movie *Saving Private Ryan* where Captain Miller and his seven soldiers go to rescue a single soldier, Private Ryan. In the end, Ryan is saved but after taking great personal risks: most of the men who came to his rescue die in the operation. Instead of feeling like a senseless sacrifice, many viewers may instead have perceived it as heroic. The movie received five Academy Awards.

Heroic sacrifices in battles have taken place all over history. One of the most famous examples is the Battles of the Thermopylae, which happened 2,500 years ago in Greece, between a small army led by the Spartan King Leonidas (7,000 men) and the massive Persian army led by King Xerxes (100,000–150,000 men). The small Greek Army blocked the Persians on a narrow coastal pass in 480 BCE. In the end, the Persians found a detour to reach behind the Greek lines. When the Greeks became aware of it, they had to choose whether to flee or not. According to the Greek historian Herodotus, the Oracle of Delphi had told Leonidas that only the death of a Spartan king would save the city of

---

[1] As an attestation that he was aware of the final goal of this training, one of the terrorists famously stated to his instructors that he did not need to learn how to land.

Sparta from destruction by the Persians. Leonidas decided to stay, with 2,000 soldiers, to fight in what was a certain-death rearguard battle to protect the retreat of the rest of the army. Leonidas and most of his soldiers died in a battle, which has become famous in history as a symbol of heroism.[2]

The real battlefield of the Thermopylae and the fictional battlefield of *Saving Private Ryan* share something in common: they feature people willing to die for a cause and, I would argue, a cause carried by a group of which they are a member. I would even be more specific: the people ready to sacrifice themselves in these situations were willing to do so for a group to which they belong and that they represent.

Being willing to die for the cause of a group can seem extreme. I started this chapter with such examples to show how far group loyalty can push people away from their narrow self-interest. These sacrifices are just extreme examples of a much larger type of situation where individuals are willing to pursue costly behaviour for the sake of a group. Members of ethnic and cultural groups can go to great cost to mark their identity to a group. They frequently continue to follow norms from their groups, even when they live in foreign countries. They may show great care for key symbols of their group like a flag or anthem. Sports fans invest their time and money to support their team (club/country). They invest in jerseys, hats and scarves wearing the colours of their club and travel long distances to support their team. Members of political groups can spend a lot of their time as activists to distribute leaflets, make phone calls and post on social media to support their organisation and its cause.

In these different examples, individuals' support for these groups sometimes goes beyond marking ones' membership and leads to engaging in violent confrontations with members of other groups. Physical violence between members of different ethnic or cultural groups is still common all over the world. Violent conflicts even occur between supporters of different sporting clubs. In Europe, fights between staunch supporters has been the cause of numerous injuries and deaths. While many of these fights take place in the hot emotional moments of a football match, in some countries like Poland, Holland or Russia, groups of supporters *pre-organise* mass brawls between themselves. It may strike an external observer as confounding given that sport "is all just a game". In the arena of politics, violence is also not that rare. Over the last few years, several deaths have occurred in countries like the United States and the United Kingdom due to political conflicts.[3]

---

[2] The awe inspired by this story of heroism is amplified in a fictionalised retelling of this story where the size of Leonidas' force is heavily underestimated as in the movie *300*, where Leonidas' army is composed of only 300 Spartan soldiers.

[3] Without attempting to be exhaustive, here are a few famous cases. In June 2016, British MP Jo Cox was murdered by a far-right activist. In August 2017, a far-right activist drove a car into a left-wing demonstration in Charlottesville, killing one person. In 2020, two Trump supporters were shot dead by far-left activists (one Portland and one in Denver).

Some of these behaviours may be explained as part of the prosocial behaviour we discussed in Chapter 10, like the attachment to a moral cause. It is in particular the case for religious and political groups. However, such defences of a cause are generally articulated through group membership. And this group membership motivates members to act for the group and its cause. The feeling of being part of a group, of belonging to a group, can raise strong emotions that do not seem to be simply about moral or religious values. On the positive side, there are feelings of elation when sharing positive moments as part of a crowd: singing in a church, cheering after one's team victory. There are also feelings of pride when one's group is successful (or when some members of one's group are). On the negative side, there are feelings of anger against others who seem to hurt or disrespect one's group.

12.1 SOCIAL IDENTITY THEORY

The social psychologist Henri Tajfel has been one of the most influential researchers looking at how belonging to a group influences individual behaviour. Born in Poland in a Jewish family in 1919, Tajfel later studied at the Sorbonne in Paris, and, during World War II, he joined the French Army. Captured, he spent several years in a prisoner-of-war camp. While his family died in the Holocaust, Tajfel survived by hiding his identity as a Jew from Poland and presenting himself as French. He later stated that he was aware that no matter what his personal characteristics were, once his true social category membership would have been revealed, his fate would have been sealed (Turner 1996). This personal history certainly explains his interest and insights in the mechanisms underlying prejudice between groups.

In a 1970 paper, Tajfel describes his personal experience hearing a "Slovene friend", coming from the richest constituent country of the (then) Republic of Yugoslavia, describe the stereotype of the poor Bosnian immigrants there. When, shortly later, Tajfel described this stereotype, without context, to a group of students at the University of Oxford, they almost unanimously thought it was a description of the immigrants from the West Indies, India and Pakistan in the United Kingdom (Tajfel 1970). This anecdote seemed to suggest to Tajfel that attitudes between groups were perhaps not about the actual characteristics of each specific group but about general psychological attitudes towards in-group and out-group members. If so, these attitudes may present regularities across a wide range of group interactions.

A key intuition from Tajfel is that an important part of an individual's identity is the fact of belonging to social groups. He used the term *social identity* to characterise "the part of an individual's self concept which derives from his knowledge of his membership of a social group (or groups) together with the emotional significance attached to that membership" (Tajfel 1974). Tajfel initiated a research program on social identity that has led to the identification of several effects of group membership on individuals' behaviour.

In-Group Favouritism/Out-Group Discrimination

According to social identity theory, group membership can potentially affect an individual's behaviour towards others in the group (*intragroup behaviour*) and towards others from other groups (*intergroup behaviour*). To study the intragroup and intergroup behaviour in general, Tajfel designed experiments using what became known as the "minimal group" setting. The idea is to divide participants in new arbitrary groups and to study whether these artificial groups change their behaviour. One of the famous approaches followed by Tajfel was to ask participants their taste between paintings from two modern art painters, Klee and Kandinsky. Participants were then told that they would be divided in two groups as a function of their preferred painter (the allocation was actually random). After the formation of groups, Tajfel asked the participants to make a few decisions about how to allocate amounts of money between two other participants. In some cases these two other participants were both *in-group members* (from the same group as the participant making the decision), in other cases they were both *out-group members* (from the other group) and finally in some cases the pair was composed of one in-group and one out-group member. Even though the groups were artificial, Tajfel found that these groupings changed participants' behaviour. In particular, participants were more likely to deviate from norms of fairness and to allocate more money to in-group members and less money to out-group members.

Research on intragroup/intergroup behaviour has consistently found evidence of *in-group favouritism* across a wide range of situations. The origin of this favouritism is not entirely clear. Social identity theory, and the minimal group setting, suggests that the simple fact of being a member of a group leads people to be biased in favour of other in-group members. But research has found that intragroup favouritism depends on what people know about others in the group. People are more likely to display in-group altruism when their membership in a group is known, and when they can expect other group members to possibly reciprocate (Balliet et al. 2014; Yamagishi and Mifune 2016).

Research has also found evidence of *out-group discrimination*, where people engage in unkind behaviour towards out-group members. Such behaviour, however, is less systematic than in-group favouritism. Individuals do not seem to go out of their way often to harm the interest of members of other groups. Such behaviour is mainly seen in situations where there is a conflict with the other group. In absence of conflict, individuals favour the members of their own group but act in a neutral way towards members of other groups where there is no advantage to be gained for in-group members (Balliet et al. 2014; Yamagishi and Mifune 2016; Abbink and Harris 2019).

I will return to these characteristics of intragroup and intergroup behaviour when I discuss intergroup tensions below.

Outgroup Stereotyping

Further research on social identity showed that group membership does not just influence behaviour; it also influences *perception*. Once part of a given group, it seems that people overestimate how much people from other groups are alike (Goethals and Darley 1977; Mullen and Hu 1989).

Imagine the following situation. John, who is English, is on holiday in Spain. While there, he sees somebody litter by throwing a can of soda in the street. Let's imagine two scenarios. In the first scenario, John hears the person speaking in Spanish as a native speaker. In the second scenario, John hears the person speaking English with an accent from England. Would John draw the same type of conclusion from the two scenarios?

Research in psychology suggests that John would most likely draw *different* conclusions. In the case where the person sounded English, John may conclude that *this person* is uncivil. In the case where the person sounded Spanish, John may conclude that *Spanish people* are uncivil. Note the difference. If the littering act is done by somebody from another group, John may tend to draw conclusions about the traits about other members of this group. If the same action is done by somebody from John's in-group, he may draw conclusions about this specific individual, not about the group itself.

This way to form views about one's in-group and out-groups leads people to overestimate the variance of traits in their own group relative to the variance of traits in other groups. Said otherwise: people look like different individuals in your own group, but they tend to seem alike in other groups.

The reduction of the perceived differences between people from other groups is associated with *stereotypes*: "beliefs about the attributes, typically personality traits, that define a group" (Yzerbyt 2016). The psychologist Susan Fiske (2015) has proposed that stereotypes are generally about two types of things: how warm and how competent members of another group are. The traits reflecting warmth include seeming trustworthy, friendly, sociable and well intentioned. Competence includes seeming capable and skilled. Beyond warmth and competence, stereotypes can broadly be any type of generalisation that seems to characterise the members of an out-group. They can sometimes be wildly inaccurate about average group characteristics, but not always (Jussim et al. 2009). Their main characteristic is likely to be associated with a perception of homogeneity when considering the members of an out-group (underestimation of individual differences within the out-group).

Group Culture

Social groups are often characterised by a distinct culture. A great deal of what people do is shaped by traditions, practices and norms that are shared by members of their community and transferred from generation to generation.

The adoption of a group's cultural symbols and practices contributes to representing one's membership of this group. Adopting cultural symbols and following specific cultural practices can act as visible signs of membership to in-group as well as to out-group individuals.[4] Belonging to a group often requires behaving in a certain way, not in others. The disrespect of such symbols and practices by members of the group can raise suspicion about their allegiance to the group. Some practices may seem inconsequential at first sight, like what to eat or what to wear. But imbued with a group membership meaning, these practices can become a litmus test of group loyalty. Hence, even those group members who do not care so much about the practices themselves may carefully respect them, in order not to raise doubts about their attitude towards the group.

Cultural practices can also be a way to enforce boundaries within a group. When the membership of a social group is exclusionary, out-group members can be prevented from wearing signs of membership in the group. An explicit example are *sumptuary laws*, which have been historically used to prevent commoners from imitating the appearance of members of higher social classes (Gambetta 2011).

When disrespect for the group's cultural symbols comes from out-group members, it can cause strong emotional responses. Many intergroup conflicts are triggered by symbolic actions such as disrespecting a flag or the image of a revered figure in the group. Nowadays, mockery of the symbols of one group in one corner of the social media often leads to outrage in the group, even if people involved are not socially connected and even if, sometimes, they don't even live in the same country.

It is easy to take such events as evidence of senseless irrationalities whereby "tribal" mentality makes people angry for actions that are unimportant ("who cares one person burned your flag in another country?"). But we saw in Chapter 11 that individuals may have developed a propensity for anger in order to have a reputation of not being pushovers. The same logic may have fostered angered reaction at the group level: reacting strongly to early hints of a challenge may help prevent further antagonistic steps from other groups.[5]

Choice of Identity

All the elements above point to the important role played by social identity in the way people perceive others and behave towards them. But how do people end up having a given identity rather than another one? And do people have only one identity?

---

[4] It is one of the main themes of the work on social identity by Akerlof and Kranton (2010).

[5] The reader trained in biology may be concerned that I am here smuggling in some kind of group selection argument. I am indeed but it is a cultural group selection one, which is not the old, and discredited, group selection. I develop this point later in this chapter.

Consider Jasmin, a doctor living in New York. Her parents were born in Tunisia; she was herself born and raised in Paris and is a French citizen. Her family is Muslim, but she is not religious herself. What is Jasmin's identity? At a broad level, she may feel French as she was raised in France and is a French citizen, though she may also be connected to the culture and identity of her parents. At a more local level, she may identify as a Parisian, though she may also now identify as a New Yorker. Finally, professionally, she may identify as a doctor.

We can think of Jasmin as facing a menu of possible identities. To understand how she could form her personal identity, we have to answer two questions. First, where does this menu of possible social identities come from? Second, given a menu of possible identities, how much freedom does Jasmin have to shape her own identity?

Let's think about the first question. In a given society, there are typically some fairly well-defined groups with which an individual can identify. There are two extreme views about the origin of such identity grouping: essentialism and constructivism (Sayer 1997). On the one hand, essentialism is the view that identity stems from underlying pre-existing characteristics that are fixed in a population, such as culture and language. According to that view, Jasmin's identity will be determined by her origin in ways that cannot be changed. For instance, she may never be fully French because her family's origin is from another country with different ethnic and cultural roots. On the other hand, constructivism is the view that identity is purely constructed. The social categories people identify with are simply socially constructed by old traditions and modern practices and discourses. In that view, Jasmin can identify with any social group, independently of her origins. To sum up and simplify, essentialism posits that people are tied to an identity that reflect who they (and their ancestors) are, while constructivism posits that it is more the social context that determines the type of identity an individual is likely to have.

The second question is about the freedom that Jasmin has to choose her identity. One possibility is that people do not choose their identity because they are tied to innate characteristics or to the social context they live in. Another possibility is that people can at least in part choose their identity. The answers to the two questions are connected. Somebody who believes in strict essentialism would think that Jasmin does not have a choice. But note that it can also be the case for someone who believes in constructivism, if identity is seen as entirely shaped by the social context in which Jasmin was raised.

The evidence from studies on social identity gives us some idea about how to answer these two questions. Social identity seems not strictly determined by innate characteristics. The minimal group experiments show that simply creating artificial groups can lead to in-group/out-group behaviour. Other research has shown that feelings of group identity can be triggered or fostered by making an existing group membership salient (Charness and Chen 2020).

In the case of Jasmin, her feelings about her possible identities may depend on the contexts she faces. Different group identities may become salient in different contexts. When she watches the French team in the final of the football World Cup, she may feel French. When she returns back to Paris, and remember her childhood memories, she may feel Parisian. When she reads a book about the experience of Tunisian migrants in France, she may feel Tunisian. If she visits a mosque during a trip in Tunisia, she may feel that Islam as a religion is part of her heritage, even though she is not religious herself. Then, back in New York, she may feel like a doctor when attending a professional conference for medical professionals. People can credibly have different possible identities, without being tied to a specific one.

The existence of multiple identities does not, however, provide an answer to the second question about how people choose their identity. In the examples above, Jasmin does not choose her identity; she is simply influenced by the context. But there are good reasons to think that she may have some choices between the different identities. Suppose that Jasmin is in a situation where she has two identities and one is likely to make her feel better than the other one. In that case, she may *opt* for the identity that makes her feel better. For instance, if Jasmin observes the French football team losing repeatedly, her feelings about how much she cares about the team may change. She may progressively feel that she does not care that much about it. If the Tunisian team happens to do pretty well at the same time, she may switch to follow it. Having made this choice, she may feel a stronger attachment to her Tunisian identity as a result.

Moses Shayo (2009) proposed an interesting model of how such choices of identity can take form. When having to choose between identities, a person takes into account the status associated with each identity. Shayo proposes that when choosing an identity, an individual will trade off the benefits of adopting a group identity given the relative status of the group and the costs of adopting this identity, which is harder if the individual's characteristics are far away from the average characteristics of the target group. The idea that people can choose their identity as a function of their best interest runs counter to the typical view, according to which the notion of social identity is incompatible with the model of an economically rational decision maker. But as we discussed in Chapter 1, it's maybe a case where assuming that people make choices with agency helps us understand better what they do than assuming that their actions are the mere consequences of external influences.

Let's use these insights to see how Jasmin could navigate her different possible identities. Jasmin's tendency to feel more or less attached to her French identity may be influenced by external circumstances making this identity more or less attractive. Her choice may also depend on the nature of the links that associate her with specific groups and the type of status it would give her in each of them. If Jasmin learns that her Tunisian grandfather was a member of the royal family, it may make her Tunisian identity appealing. She would have a somewhat flattering status from her prestigious ancestry within the Tunisian community and possibly outside. If, instead, she learns that her grandfather was a common criminal, she may prefer to move on to identities associated with her current social circles.

Jasmin's choices will also be constrained by her personal characteristics. She can easily feel French because of her objective ties to that country. She would find harder to identify with a country with which she has little in common. Suppose that Brazil wins the World Cup. It would be a good time to identify as a Brazilian. However, Jasmin is unlikely to do so. In spite of her diverse life experiences, she does not have much in common with the average Brazilian: she has never been there, she does not speak Portuguese, she does not know much about the Brazilian culture. She may find it hard to convince herself that she has a special bond to this country. Making such a special bond real would actually require some costly investment to learn Brazilian culture. She would likely face even greater costs convincing others that she is indeed Brazilian and that she feels a genuine loyalty to this group. So saying that people can choose their identity does not mean that anything goes. These choices are constrained by the individuals' resources and life histories that make it easier or harder to identify with a specific group.

It is hard to observe people's identity in the real world and therefore how they can change based on their choices, but it is possible to find evidence backing Shayo's model. Let's consider religion, one of the aspects of identity that seems the least likely to be affected by choices driven by personal interest. In a fascinating study, Saleh (2018) looked into a puzzling fact: in Egypt, the Christians (Copts) form a minority of around 10% of the population, which tends to be much better off economically than the Muslim majority. One may wonder why it is the case. Could it be because the Christian religion and culture help people to be more successful in life? The historical evidence suggests a very different explanation. Before the Arab conquest in 641, Egypt was mainly Christian. Since in- and out-migrations have been limited, modern Christians and Muslims in Egypt are mostly descendants from the pre-641 population. For that reason, the change in the proportion of Muslims and Christians has to reflect the *conversion* of Coptic Christians to Islam in the past. Saleh shows that this conversion was likely very much influenced by economic incentives. From the Arab conquest to 1856, an annual poll tax was imposed on every adult Coptic male. Converting to Islam therefore afforded a way to avoid paying this tax. The evidence suggests that poorer Copts opted to convert so they would not have to pay this tax, leaving only the richer Copts as part of a well-off minority of Christians in Egypt. Religious identities were here shaped by economic incentives.

Another aspect of identity that seems unlikely to be affected by choice is ethnicity. But ethnic groups have often blurry boundaries. If somebody has parents from ethnic group A and from ethnic group B, this person may preferentially identify with one group, both or neither. Former US President

Barak Obama, born from a black father and a white mother, identified himself as black. Asked about it, he answered:

I always felt as if being black was cool. That it was not something to run away from, but something to embrace. Why that is, I think, is complicated. Part of it is, I think, that my mother thought black folks were cool, and if your mother loves you and is praising you – and says you look good, are smart – as you are, then you don't kind of think in terms of How can I avoid this? You feel pretty good about it. By the time I was cognizant of race, American culture had gone through enough changes that as a child, I wasn't just receiving constant negative messages about being black. (Coates 2016)

The choice of identification with an ethnicity is influenced not just by one's good feelings but also by economic interests. In a recent paper, Green (2021) looked at the influence of political outcomes on ethnicity identification in Africa. African presidents tend to favour their own ethnic group economically in countries with multiple ethnicities. Green found that an ethnic presidential change leads to an "upward shift in the percentage of respondents identifying with the new ruling ethnic group" in countries that are autocratic.

The notion that people can choose their social identity is also relevant for Western countries where it likely helps explain the rise in nationalism in Europe and the United States over the recent years. Moses Shayo (2020) used his model to propose a possible explanation of this phenomenon. Poorer categories of native workers in Europe and the United States have seen their economic situation deteriorate relatively, with income inequality widening. Immigration from poorer countries has also made the poorer social categories more ethnically and culturally diverse. These two phenomena have made the identification of poorer categories of native workers to a working class both less appealing (lower status) and less straightforward (greater heterogeneity). At the same time, the identification with a national identity that has a higher average status and a greater ethnic homogeneity may have seen its relative appeal grow. This explanation is in line with the observation that the growth of nationalist parties has largely benefitted from the migration of voters originally supporting left-wing parties with redistributive policies (Oesch 2008).

12.2 APPLICATIONS: INTERGROUP TENSIONS AND LEADERSHIP

Equipped with this understanding of the rich and subtle nature of social identity, we can understand better some key aspects of human behaviour in society: the nature of intergroup tensions and of group leadership.

Intergroup Tensions within Society

Violence
As indicated above, group tensions surface from time to time in developed countries, such as in political demonstrations, sporting events or riots between

different ethnic groups. A cursive glance at history quickly makes it evident that such tensions are not unusual within societies.

Conflicts between groups identified along their socioeconomic status have been observed throughout societies around the world. It was already the case in the Roman Republic. The opposition between the plebians (poorest citizens) and the patricians (members of the minority of richest citizens) structured many of the political fights. In a famous move, the *secession of the plebs*, plebeian citizens, unsatisfied with their smaller political rights, would occasionally withdraw from the city, refusing to defend Rome as soldiers from potential external attacks.

Tensions between different ethnic or religious groups have also been a recurrent feature of history. Indeed, modern tensions and the occasional violence that comes with it are nowadays very limited compared to the type of conflicts observed in the past. When considered through the lenses of modern moral norms, the past violence of group conflicts can be striking. History is littered with mass killings of members of one group by members of another, following wars, unrest or religious conflicts.

In the extreme, there are the organised mass killings of one group by another. The term *genocide*, introduced in 1944, is defined by the UN as actions aiming to "destroy, in whole or part, a national, ethnical, racial or religious group". The Holocaust, the mass killing of Jewish people by Nazi Germany, is the largest genocide in history by its magnitude. It is estimated that six million Jews died between 1941 and 1945. This genocide is, by no means, unique in history. The list of past events that can be described as genocides is, disturbingly, substantial. The historian Norman Naimark (2017) starts his book on the topic with the following statement:

Genocide has been a part of human history from its very beginnings. There is little reason to think that our prehistoric forebears were either more or less civilized than ourselves when confronting and eliminating other peoples and suspected enemies. Extended families, clans, and tribes routinely engaged in genocidal actions against their rivals, just as ancient empires and modern nationstates enacted their murderous hatred for imagined or real enemies in mass killing.

Beyond the extreme case of genocides, the mass killings of some members of one group by another as part of warfare has also been frequent in the past. It has been the case of innumerous armies defeated, and civilian populations in conquered cities. In a review of the evolution of violence throughout history, Steven Pinker (2011a) points out how past violence is documented in the Bible, the most printed book in history: "The Bible depicts a world that, seen through modern eyes, is staggering in its savagery.... Warlords slaughter civilians indiscriminately, including the children."

The well-documented history of ancient Rome also provides numerous descriptions of massacres. The Latin expression *vae victis*, woe to the vanquished, reflects how a group defeated in battle was at the mercy of their conquerors. In 55 BCE, Julius Caesar, the most well-known Roman figure, claimed to have killed 430,000 members of two German tribes, the Usipetes and Tencteri, by attacking their camp by surprise (Gilliver 2004). The victims included men, women and children. Modern historians estimate that the death toll must have been much lower (Roymans 2017). It is telling, though, that Caesar chose to inflate this number.

The historian Matthew White collected in his *Great Big Book of Horrible Things* (2011) a long list of mass violent events in history. Among these, the Mongol conquest, in the thirteenth century, stands in a category of its own. It was accompanied by the systematic killing of civilians in many conquered cities. In Baghdad alone, between 200,000 and 800,000 residents were killed when the city was captured in 1258. In total, the Mongol expansion is associated with an estimated 40 million deaths, a number comparable to the estimated 55 million deaths from World War II.

Besides these deaths, emerging from military conflicts, there are violent events that are even more striking to our modern eyes: mass killings that were carried out by *civilians* from one group against another group. In situations of conflict, suspicion and feelings of threats and conspiracies, mob violence has, from time to time, erupted and turned into massacres. One of the most famous examples in Western history is the *St Bartholomew's Day massacre* of Protestants in France in 1572. At a time where tensions were high between Christians and Protestants (around 10% of the French population at the time), the Queen Catherine de Medici and her son the King Charles IX seem to have decided to kill the prominent Protestant nobles to eliminate them as a political threat. The killing started in the night of 23–24 August. While it seems to have targeted initially only a few dozen of nobles and their entourages, the crowds of Christians in Paris spontaneously joined in gathering and killed Protestants of all ages and genders. It is estimated that between 5,000 and 30,000 Protestants were killed over the next few weeks in France.

It can be hard for us to understand how large numbers of civilians could voluntarily join such actions. Closer to our times, the discovery of the death camps at the end of World War II begged the question: How could such a thing as the Holocaust have taken place without the participation/collaboration of a large number of people? In her book *Eichmann in Jerusalem: A Report on the Banality of Evil*, Hannah Arendt (1963/2006) famously suggested that the answer was perhaps not to be found in the abnormal psychological traits of the perpetrators. Instead, evil-doing may very well be within the possibility of very banal personalities. She describes in her book the trial of Eichmann, one of the key administrators who organised, until the last minute of the war, the logistics of trains conveying Jewish people to extermination camps. Strikingly, Eichmann did not fit the description of an evil mastermind. He "was not Iago and not Macbeth", Arendt concluded, referring to two famous evil Shakespearean characters. Rather, he seemed like a methodic and lacklustre bureaucrat doing his best in his daily job to be efficient and to be promoted.

Arendt's observation is supported by the historical accounts of the social life in the death camp of Auschwitz. Over 1.1 million people, including children, lost their lives there. Sixty years after the war, a former SS guard and clerk at the camp, Oskar Groening, remembered a positive social atmosphere, illustrated by the (in)famous photos taken in 1944 by Karl Höcker of SS camp guards laughing and enjoying themselves (Kühne 2011).[6]

The fact that mass violence towards an outgroup can involve a large number of in-group members raises an uncomfortable prospect: these behaviours may not just be the results of a small minority of sociopaths. Rather, normal people may end up involved in such actions in situations where the logic of intergroup conflict takes a turn for the worse. A look at humanity's history suggests that it is not our past that is strange, but our modern times, which, in comparison, stand out with their limited tolerance for violence and homicide (Pinker 2011a).

Discrimination

In modern societies intergroup conflicts rarely lead to such mass violence, but tensions can arise and wane between different social categories, different ethnic groups and different religions. A key issue that has become prominent in liberal democracies has been the protection of ethnic and religious minorities from discrimination.

Public discussions about *discrimination* often interpret differential treatments of in-group and out-group members as mostly or entirely driven by antagonistic feelings. The evidence, however, is more subtle, and to understand it, I'll unpack the notion of discrimination.

In a famous book, Gary Becker (1957) incorporated the possibility of negative feelings towards people from an out-group by assuming that discrimination based on taste can influence the choice of consumers or employers. One of the insights from Becker's model is that if such *taste-based discrimination* exists, it may be limited by market competition. For instance, if firms discriminate when they hire employees, they will be disadvantaged compared to companies who hire only the best employees. As a consequence, the presence of people willing to discriminate against members of a group may actually have a limited effect on the outcomes of the members of this group when a market is fairly competitive.

This idea that competition tends to eliminate discrimination was criticised by the economist Kenneth Arrow, who stated: "Becker's model predicts the absence of the phenomenon it was designed to explain" (Arrow 1972). In response to Becker, Arrow (1972) and Phelps (1972) developed a model of discrimination that does not disappear with competition. In their view, discrimination can arise because of the incomplete information decision makers have. This idea is called *statistical discrimination*.

---

[6] Describing his feeling when he left the camp, Groening stated, "I'd left a circle of friends whom I'd got familiar with, I'd got fond of" (Kühne 2011, p. 237).

Let's think about the following scenario. Jane is looking to buy a second-hand mobile phone. She visits a website to buy second-hand items where people place ads. One mobile phone description and price sound right for what she is looking for. Jane is interested and she clicks on the ad to have more details and see a photo of the item. Once she has done so, a picture of the phone appears, held by what must be the hand of the seller. The phone looks in perfect condition. It is exactly what she is looking for. Something attracts Jane's attention, however. It is the hand of the seller. Or rather, it is the fact that this hand, seemingly from a man, reveals a large tattoo on the wrist. Jane does not care about tattoos as such, but she wonders about what it may say about the seller. From her understanding, tattoos are relatively more frequent among "tough guys" who are not always entirely reputable.[7] Jane is slightly concerned. To secure the deal, she would have to send the money first to receive the phone afterwards. It would be possible for the seller not to deliver the phone, or for the phone, not to be as good as the one displayed. Jane could potentially lose her money and not have a phone, if the transaction does not proceed well. To be on the safe side, Jane decides to opt for another ad where no tattooed hand is visible. She pays a bit more, but she thinks it is better to be safe than to take some risks.

Note that in this story, Jane's decision was not driven by a dislike of tattoos. It is because Jane lacks information about the seller that she uses the tattoo as information about the possible trustworthiness of the seller (which she cannot observe). As a consequence of Jane's decision, the seller with a tattoo has been discriminated against. He lost an opportunity to sell his mobile phone.

Now think about what would happen if, instead of seeing a tattoo, Jane was seeing a hand that reveals that the seller is a person of colour. As for the tattoo, Jane may have nothing against the members of this group. But suppose that in Jane's city, members of this group are economically disadvantaged and tend to live in poorer neighbourhoods. Suppose also that poorer neighbourhoods tend to have higher crime rates than other neighbourhoods, simply because socioeconomic disadvantages tend to be associated with higher crime rate (Tanner et al. 2013).

Even though Jane has nothing against members of this group as such, she may use the information in the same way as she would for a tattoo. She may, as a consequence, be less likely to proceed with the sale and look for another advertisement.

In a fascinating research paper, the economists Jennifer Doleac and Luke Stein (2013) implemented an experiment exactly along the lines of the scenarios above. Advertisements for electronic items (iPods) were posted on US websites with a hand holding the items. The researchers looked at three treatments: the hand had either white skin, Black skin or white skin with a tattoo. They

---

[7] There would potentially be some ground to her belief. Tattoos are indeed frequently used as a signal of membership in a criminal gang (Gambetta 2011).

found that both Black and tattooed sellers were discriminated against. They received, respectively, 18% and 16% fewer offers. Looking at how prospective buyers interacted with the sellers suggested that a lack of trust was driving this behaviour: buyers were less likely to give their details and to be willing to pay online before receiving the item.

It is easy to see how such behaviour can lead to systematic discrimination of some categories of population.[8] When hiring people for a position, employers may use visible traits, including membership in a social or ethnic group, as an indication of the likely success of the applicant on the job. As a consequence, members of disadvantaged groups may be discriminated against, even in cases where employers have no negative feelings towards this group as such.[9]

The notions of taste-based discrimination and statistical discrimination provide two radically different motives for discrimination. On the one hand, taste-based discrimination seems closer to the notion of discrimination commonly discussed in public debates. It implies an unkind intention towards the person discriminated against. On the other hand, the notion of statistical discriminations explains discrimination as a rational behaviour devoid of unkindness as such.[10]

---

[8] This exact argument is made by Nobel Prize winners Abhijit Banerjee and Esther Duflo in their 2019 book "Good economics for hard times" about discrimination in the US and India (Chap 4). "what looks like naked racism does not have to be that; it can be the result of targeting some characteristic (drug dealing, criminality) that happens to be correlated with race or religion. So statistical discrimination, rather than old-fashioned prejudice—what economists call taste-based discrimination—may be the cause. The end result is the same if you are black or Muslim, though.

[9] With the rise of artificial intelligence algorithms, this type of discrimination has attracted new concerns. A lot of decisions affecting us are now taken by algorithms trained on big data. Even if they have no intent as such, they can carry out statistical discrimination by design. Consider an algorithm used by a bank to score customers' applications to get loans. It may be designed to use all the information it has about the customers to estimate their likelihood of repayment and make the best decision accordingly. But this information may include the customers' postcode, their ethnicity, their gender. On average, people from different postcodes, different ethnicities or different genders may have different probabilities of repayment. The decisions by the algorithm may be influenced by the social categories you belong to and you may be discriminated based on your geographical location, ethnicity or gender.

[10] Statistical discrimination arises when your membership in some group is used by others to form views about your traits. Interestingly, Cornell and Welch (1996) have shown that when, on the contrary, your membership in some group makes it harder for others to form views about your traits, another type of discrimination can take place: *screening discrimination*. When screening applicants for a job, employers may be less likely to select applicants from another social group, simply because they are less able to assess their ability and credentials compared to somebody from their in-group. It can happen even when employers have neither ill-feeling towards out-group members nor beliefs about the existence of average differences in ability between in-group and out-group members.

The opposition between the taste-based discrimination and the statistical discrimination explanations has led to a lot of research in economics to assess which model explains discrimination best. An important aspect of this debate is that the two models reflect different types of *intent*. Taste-based discrimination implies that some people can be blamed for their intentions, while statistical discrimination implies that there are no unkind intentions to blame. For the reasons described in Chapter 10, we are very attentive to identifing and punishing others' negative intent towards us. As a result, taste-based discrimination seems to be the default interpretation when patterns of discrimination are discussed in public debates. Economists, by contrast, have certainly felt some appeal for the statistical discrimination model, which is more compatible with the homo economicus model where people simply follow their material best interest.

It is hard to fully disentangle taste-based and statistical discrimination. A major difficulty is that we do not observe all the possible beliefs that may be driving some statistical discrimination. There is a risk that using a statistical discrimination explanation as a default may seem to absolve the people engaging in discrimination from their responsibility. Behind a technical discussion, there is, in short, a question of whether or not blame can be attributed for the existence of discrimination. The sensitivity of the issue and the political implications of the conclusion often influence the debate on this question.

Complementing these explanations of discrimination, behavioural economists have recently suggested a new possible way it can arise: *inaccurate statistical discrimination*. The notion of statistical discrimination relies on people being really good at inferring likely unobserved traits (such as skills or trustworthiness) from observed traits (such as group membership). But behavioural economists have shown that people can form inaccurate judgements. What if such judgements could be inaccurate when judging group characteristics? In a recent study, Bohren et al. (2019) showed that discrimination can arise from stereotypes about groups that are inaccurate. In an experiment, they found that people were more likely to expect that Indian participants would be better at maths than American participants. As a result, when hiring participants to perform a maths tasks, people were more likely to favour Indian participants. As a matter of fact, Indian and American respondents performed equally well at the task. The discrimination in favour of Indian participants was therefore seemingly driven by inaccurate beliefs.

It is easy to see how such inaccurate beliefs could lead to negative discrimination against certain groups. Suppose that there is an economically disadvantaged group. Low socioeconomic status has been found to be one of the major risk factors associated with criminal activities (Tanner-Smith et al. 2013). And criminal activities tend also to be selected for news stories by the media. It is thus possible to have a situation where the news features a disproportionate number of negative stories about people from this group. Even though group membership may have in itself nothing to do with the propensity to be involved in crimes, people from another group may form distorted beliefs due to the way news stories are selected and due to the group stereotyping bias I described above.

The evidence suggests that taste-based discrimination, statistical discrimination and inaccurate statistical discrimination all exist. However, it is likely that the mechanisms behind discrimination are more complex than the existence of these three distinct explanations. It is indeed reasonable to expect that taste-based, statistical and inaccurate statistical discriminations are linked. In situations where members of a group A have negative feelings towards members of a group B, group A members may be inclined to form negative beliefs about group B members. Forming beliefs that members of another group have negative traits can help justify a negative feeling towards members of this group.[11] And similarly, negative beliefs about members of another group can foster antagonistic feelings. Beliefs and tastes are therefore most likely intertwined.

Multiple Equilibria

The entwinement of beliefs and tastes leads us to an interesting implication: between two given groups, different types of relations may emerge and persist over time.

A key insight comes from the study on social preferences. People care about others' intentions. More specifically, people usually want to be kind with other people they perceive as kind and unkind with people they perceive as unkind. These types of mutual concerns can lead to the existence of multiple equilibria (Rabin 1993): the same people can end up in very different types of relations. Consider John and Jake, who work as colleagues. If John believes that Jake is unkind to him and Jake believes John is unkind to him as well, both may want to be unkind towards the other as a consequence. Their intention confirms each other's beliefs. We can call this situation an *unkindness equilibrium*. But think about a different situation: What if John believes that Jake wants to be kind to him and Jake believes that John wants to be kind to him too? Then, because of their beliefs, they will want to be kind to each other, which also confirms their beliefs. We can call this a *kindness equilibrium*.

These two opposite situations are equilibria because, once John and Jake are in such a situation, it is hard to move away from it. When two people are bitter from their perception of the other's intentions, they may engage in antagonistic behaviour, which feeds the bitterness of the other person. When two people are kind to each other, they may engage in kind behaviour, which fosters the mutual kindness in the pair. A key insight is that *the same two people* can end up in either a kind or an unkind equilibrium. It is not due to who they are. It was not *written in advance*. Sometimes, unexpected events can push a relationship either

---

[11] Many negative comments about people from another group often take the form: "I have nothing against people from this group, but it is true that ..." Such statements justify attitudes towards members of another group on objective facts rather than subjective tastes. I discuss in Chapter 14 how people's beliefs may be biased in the direction of their motivations.

in the direction of confident cooperation or in the direction of bitter resentment and lack of mutual trust.

The possibility of multiple equilibria between two people can be (intuitively) extended between two groups when relationships between groups are largely determined by beliefs and preferences. If members of a group think that the members of another group are kind towards them, they are likely to want to be kind too. But if members of a group perceive unkindness, they may react negatively in a way that is perceived as unkind by the other group, leading to an equilibrium where relations are antagonistic. Such an equilibrium is described by Adida et al. (2014) in a study of the relations between Muslims in France and the rooted French. The authors described a situation where many rooted French exhibit taste-based discrimination against Muslims, and where this discrimination contributes to make Muslims reluctant to assimilate, which, in turn, contributes to foster the taste-based discrimination from the rooted French.

Given the interrelation between tastes and beliefs, it may be very hard to move away from such an equilibrium, once groups are locked in it. This possibility has important implications for societies composed of members from different cultures, ethnicities or religions. Intergroup tensions can likely appear faster than they can disappear. Consider the case of political discourses pitting some groups against others. Fostering an antagonism between different groups may push society into a conflictual equilibrium. It may be hard and take time for social tensions to eventually recede and for society to move back to a non-conflictual equilibrium.

Leadership

One of the most interesting new insights from the research on social identity is, in my view, a renewed understanding of what makes leaders successful.

The Elements of Successful Leadership

In a fascinating book, Haslam et al. (2010) propose a new psychology of leadership where social identity plays a key role. The authors reject the "old psychology of leadership". By this term they describe the most commonly held view that what makes a good leader are key individual traits such as charisma, or the ability to shine when talking to other people. In that view, great leadership is achieved by "great men" and the key to understanding their leadership success is to understand their personality.

The authors reject this view to propose that successful leadership is articulated around the group's self-perception. A leader is somebody who is accepted as such by a group. It is somebody the members of the group are willing to follow and to trust to represent them.

For this to happen, Haslam et al. propose several principles. First, leaders must be perceived as "one of us" by members of the group. It means that, independently of personal skills, individuals are more likely to be successful leaders if they have the characteristics of a *prototypical* member of the group they aim to lead. This simple principle is fundamental, as distances from prototypicality will make it harder to naturally generate support and trust from members of the group. Prospective leaders therefore tend to put forward their prototypicality and to downplay what could be perceived as differences.

A great example is Barack Obama's speech at the US Democratic National Convention in 2004. This speech is widely seen as having propelled him to the top of the list of future possible nominees for the Democratic Party presidential primaries. As a mixed-race American, Obama did not a priori fit the prototypical image of a person from a primarily white country. He built his speech around his family story, described as a typical American story where the prototypicality is about the experience of migrants building success from scratch:

I stand here knowing that my story is part of the larger American story, that I owe a debt to all of those who came before me, and that, in no other country on earth, is my story even possible. Tonight, we gather to affirm the greatness of our nation, not because of the height of our skyscrapers, or the power of our military, or the size of our economy. Our pride is based on a very simple premise, summed up in a declaration made over two hundred years ago, "We hold these truths to be self-evident, that all men are created equal."

A second principle of leadership is that leaders need to be seen to "do it for us". The role of a leader is to be a champion for the group. Many personal defects can be overlooked as long as a leader is seen as defending the interests of the group. On the contrary, being seen as having divided loyalties with another group is a big concern. This principle is often reflected in greater eligibility restrictions for being a leader than for being a simple group member. In many modern democracies, politicians face constraints on their citizenship and origin to be elected. In the United States, not every citizen can be president of the country. You have to be born in the United States and to have been resident for at least fourteen years to be eligible.[12] In Australia, citizens can have as many citizenships as they want, but Members of Parliament cannot have any other national citizenship. In 2017–2018 a "parliamentary crisis" erupted in Australia when it was found that several MPs had other nationalities, from Canada, New Zealand or the United Kingdom. These citizenships had been acquired either by birth or by descent. They were sometimes apparently

[12] It led to a famous attack on Barack Obama's suitability for the office when unsubstantiated claims that he was born in Kenya were leveraged against him.

unbeknownst to the MPs themselves. Even though Australia has good relations with these other countries, the MPs had to resign as a result of their dual citizenship.[13]

Besides being "one of us" and "doing it for us", leaders need to be *entrepreneurs of identity*: they need to "craft a sense of us". Masterful leaders are not just inheriting a group; they are contributing to building the group's narrative. Sometimes they can contribute to building as they carve out a group from a complex social reality, with an appealing new narrative. Haslam et al. give several examples of such entrepreneurship. One of the most iconic ones is Mandela's strategy of recasting the national rugby team as a new symbol of a syncretic identity.[14]

During apartheid, the all-white Springboks and their fans had belted out racist fight songs, and blacks would come to Springbok matches to cheer for whatever team was playing against them. Yet Mandela believed that the Springboks could embody – and engage – the new South Africa. And the Springboks themselves embraced the scheme. Soon South African TV would carry images of the team singing "Nkosi Sikelele Afrika", the longtime anthem of black resistance to apartheid.... South Africans of every color and political stripe found themselves falling for the team. When the Springboks took to the field for the championship match against New Zealand's heavily favored squad, Mandela sat in his presidential box wearing a Springbok jersey while sixty-two-thousand fans, mostly white, chanted "Nelson! Nelson!" (Carlin 2008, p. i)

Another great example is the case of Muhammed Ali Jinnah, who played a key role in the creation of the new nation of Pakistan:

He brought together the disparate peoples who made up Pakistan into a single entity through his dress. This was seen when, on August 4, 1947, Jinnah stepped out from his plane and onto the soil of an independent Pakistan for the very first time. On his head he wore the karakuli, a black sheepskin cap as worn by the Muslims of North India. On his back he wore the sherwani (a knee-length black coat as worn by the Muslims of Aligarh). On his legs he wore the shalwar (baggy trousers worn by Muslims in the west of the country). Altogether his attire thus constituted the national dress and helped constitute the nation itself – not just the meaning of Pakistan, but the very reality of a Pakistani entity. (Haslam et al. 2010, p. 153)

Behavioural Political Economy of Identity
This new understanding of leadership also shows that group identities are much more than simply fixed in a social setting. Group identities can be shaped by

---

[13] History provides a long list of events where (perceived) divided loyalties from a leader weakened their authority. In Ancient Rome, Mark Anthony's relationship with the Queen of Egypt Cleopatra was used by Anthony's rival, Octavian (future Augustus), as a way to undermine his loyalty to Rome. In eighteenth-century Russia, Peter III, a German-born Emperor, lasted only six months on the throne as his intention to adopt a pro-Prussian policy undermined the trust in his leadership. A few years later in France, the foreign origin of Queen Marie-Antoinette, who was born in Austria, a rival country, played an important role in her downfall.

[14] This approach was depicted in the 2009 movie *Invictus*.

leaders, and leaders have an incentive to shape groups and their identities. Aspiring leaders have an interest to carve out a group of which they are prototypical and to present themselves as the defender and promoter of its identity.

In situations where people's traits differ in many aspects, there are many ways different groups can be defined. Either through the extension or restriction of group boundaries or by splitting or merging groups, aspiring leaders can articulate narratives about a group and its identity, for which they can be the best champion. The strategy of aspiring leaders will depend both on their personal characteristics, which make them more or less prototypical of some potential groups, and on the size of these potential groups, which makes these groups more or less appealing to an aspiring leader.

Recent US history is illustrative in that regard. In 2008, Barack Obama was elected US President, not as a champion of Black Americans but as a representative of all Americans, with a narrative about the American identity that transcends racial differences. In 2016, Donald Trump was elected, presenting himself, de facto, as a defender of the white American working class. The white American working class is therefore faced with two competing narratives: one where they are encompassed in a broader identity as Americans, and another one where they form a smaller, more exclusive group. The competition between group identity narratives is an important feature of political conflicts. It emerges as a result of the competition of aspiring leaders trying to delineate the best group where their personal characteristics can be suited for them to be supported as a leader.

Competition for identity narratives and group definitions is everywhere when you start looking. One frequent competition is between a local and an overarching national identity as in the competition to appeal to Scottish versus British identity in the debate on Scotland independence from the United Kingdom. Another frequent competition is the appeal to a working-class identity versus a national identity by politicians aiming to receive support from low-income workers in Europe. Finally, another one is the appeal to a religious identity versus the appeal to an identity based on a shared national history like what can be seen in recent times in Lebanon where the embattled political system is based on a division of citizens in different religious groups.

Social identities are not fixed; they are fluid and are at the centre of a competition from entrepreneurs who have incentives to shape identities in ways that suit their personal position. These insights should perhaps lead us to be prosaic about identity. Groups and identities are not primordial elements; they keep changing. In the same ways as some entrepreneurs of identity have incentives to promote exclusive identities where smaller groups have tight boundaries excluding others, it is possible to promote overarching identities where people feel that they belong to a common group.

12.3 EVOLUTIONARY FOUNDATIONS

We have seen that from sports club supporters to religious, national and ethnic groups, social identity plays a very important role in society. People are willing to give their time, money and sometimes their lives to promote their group's interests and defend them from out-groups in situations of conflict. These costly actions seem to contradict the self-interested model of the homo economicus. Self-interested agents should not be willing to incur these costs for other people. The "membership" in a group should be irrelevant as long as it does not bring benefits for the individual. So, how can we explain the prevalence and importance of social identity feelings?

Coordination

In Chapter 10, I described how opportunities for cooperation can foster the emergence of kindness and reciprocity. The large literature on cooperation has heavily used the prisoner's dilemma game. In this game individual and collective interests are in conflict when the game is played once or a few times, but playing this game repeatedly creates an opportunity for mutual gains. The tension between individual and collective benefits is what makes this game interesting as a model for many social interactions.

But other games also capture relevant aspects of social interactions. One of them is the *stag hunt game*, whose name comes from a social dilemma described by Jean-Jacques Rousseau in his *Discourse on the Origin of Inequality* 1755/1999. Discussing hypothetical primordial times where humans were unable to cooperate consistently, Rousseau gives, as an example, the situation of two men hunting a deer. For the hunt to succeed, each man "must abide faithfully by his post". But the success of a man staying by his post would critically rely on the decision of the other to do the same. If one decided to stop the deer hunt to capture smaller prey, like a hare, the other hunter would get nothing and he would have been better off choosing to hunt a hare too in the first place.

Figure 12.1 represents a stylised version of this problem as a simultaneous game between two players (the hunters). Each player can choose to cooperate on the deer hunt project or to defect on an individual hunt for a hare. This game looks at first sight similar to the prisoner's dilemma. There is, however, a key difference: both the defect-defect and the cooperate-cooperate situations are equilibria! If the other player defects, there is no incentive to go deer hunting as the lone hunter would be unsuccessful. But unlike in the prisoner's dilemma, the cooperate-cooperate situation is also an equilibrium. If both players cooperate, they do not have an incentive to switch to the hare hunt, which would give them less than splitting the spoils of a deer hunt between two hunters.

Since mutual cooperation is an equilibrium, you may wonder why it is a dilemma. Isn't it the end of the matter? Cooperation is obviously the best

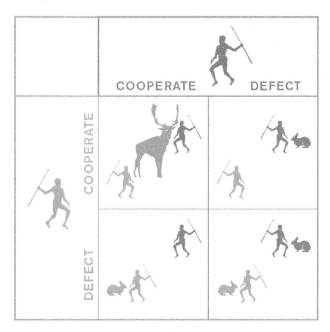

FIGURE 12.1. The stag hunt game: two hunters choose either to cooperate and hunt a deer together or to defect and hunt a hare on their own. The payoffs for each player are indicated by the animals in each cell.

outcome. Both players should realise it and choose to play accordingly. The problem is that if cooperation pays more, it is also *risky*. It requires being sure that the other player will also choose to cooperate. In comparison, defection pays less, but it is *safe*. The payoff for defecting does not depend on the choice of the other player. If you are unsure about the other player's ability to reason like you, you may be worried that, as in Rousseau's story, he could mindlessly pursue a hare instead of choosing to cooperate on the deer hunt. If you are uncertain enough about the other player's mindset, you may opt to defect, just to be safe. Cooperation requires you to be sure enough about the other player's intentions. But successful cooperation requires more than your confidence in the other player. It also requires that the other player is sure about your own intentions. So even if you trust that the other player understands the game, you need to be sure that he knows that you understand the game. Otherwise, he may defect by fear that you would. In that case, you are better off defecting even though you perfectly understand the game!

The prisoner's dilemma is different from the stag hunt game. However, Skyrms (2001) pointed out that once the prisoner's dilemma is repeated, the existence of cooperation equilibria changes the game to something that has the same logic as a stag hunt game. There are several equilibria, and the problem is how to coordinate on a good equilibrium.

The stag hunt game is not entirely trivial to solve successfully between two players. It becomes extremely hard to solve between a large number of players. In cases where success requires that nobody defects, the probability that somebody may defect (because they do not understand the game or because they fear that somebody else may not understand it) increases quickly. Hume described a multi-player version of the stag hunt game in his *Treatise* 1739/2003:

Two neighbors may agree to drain a meadow, which they possess in common; because 'tis easy for them to know each others mind, and each may perceive that the immediate consequence of failing in his part is the abandoning of the whole project. But 'tis difficult, and indeed impossible, that a thousand persons shou'd agree in any such action …

These collective coordination problems are likely to have played an important role in our ancestral past. Let's consider two of them: the organisation of large social projects with the example of irrigation and the case of intergroup conflicts.

Early civilisations from the Indus Valley, Mesopotamia, Egypt and China all had one thing in common: they arose in valleys with recurring flooding rivers where great gains could be achieved from irrigation systems, allowing the control of floods and the spreading of rich river sediment to fertilise the soil (Mann 1986). Building these systems required the contribution of the work of many individuals, beyond usual agricultural activities. The benefits were large, but only if the endeavour was successful and enough people contributed. Irrigation systems have certainly represented an important milestone in human history. Their emergence required early societies to find a solution to a large coordination and cooperation problem similar to Hume's meadow example. In present times, several thousand years later, it has been found that locations that were then propitious to irrigation are now characterised by more collectivist mindsets, placing the group above the individual (Buggle 2020).

Another major type of coordination problem are intergroup conflicts. Human groups, such as tribes, cities and states, have historically engaged in many types of warfare. The outcomes of these conflicts had very important consequences on the success of these groups. A characteristic of a collective conflict is that cohesion plays a major role in the success of a group. For instance, pitched battles' outcomes often depend on a "weakest link" strategic aspect. If a group guards a position under attack, success requires all members of the group to stand their ground. Defeat typically occurs when one part of an armed group cedes under pressure and flees the battle, with the routing then spreading to the whole group.[15] Similarly, keeping a fortified place requires

---

[15] "In ancient battles any movement backward was apt to become a rout, and the fleeing soldiers were apt to infect those behind them with their fear" (Lendon 2005).

every part of the defensive position to resist attacks. The ability of every part of an armed group to stand ground and resist as long as possible was frequently key to success.[16]

Such situations are similar to a multiplayer stag hunt game (again, like Hume's meadow example). Full cooperation can be an equilibrium. If everybody stands their ground, the chances of victory can be high, and nobody has an interest to defect. But full defection can also be an equilibrium, as nobody has an interest to fight if one expects others won't. The outcome of close battles is often the result of a shift in equilibrium whereby fighters decide to flee as they believe others are also retreating. A key challenge to be successful in such games is to ensure the coordination of beliefs on the cooperating equilibrium across a large number of group members.

The economists Michael Bacharach (1999) and Robert Sugden (2003) have proposed a solution to collective stag hunt–like problems: when having to coordinate between several equilibria with some being better than others, players may benefit from following *team reasoning*. That is, they can benefit from thinking what *we* should do, so that the outcome is best for *us*. Team reasoning provides a natural answer to the stag hunt game. If we ask what we should do and we think of the players as a team, then the best strategy is to cooperate. Similarly, in a battle, the answer is to stand our ground and not flee.

The emergence of team reasoning requires players to understand and appreciate that they belong to a group whose members are aware that they all belong to this group. In short, team reasoning requires a common trust in each other's belief that we will act as a team, with a common aim. Bacharach (2006) defended the view that group identification is the proximate behavioural mechanism that evolved to help sustain cooperative behaviour in groups. By identifying with a group, members can solve problems by thinking "what would be good for the group" and be confident that other members who share the same group identity will behave in the same way. Group identity can help solve the problem of large-scale coordination between many individuals.

Altruism towards the Group

This justification of the emergence of group identity provides a possible explanation for a wide range of behaviour where in-group cooperation can lead to better outcomes for all. But it does not give a natural explanation for

---

[16] Cohesion can also deliver success without battles. Individuals in a cohesive group would have a decisive advantage over individuals in a loose group divided in semi-autonomous subgroups. Subgroups may be unsure about what other subgroups will do. A typical example of such situations in history are the many cases when a unified army conquered very large swaths of territory by beating autonomous groups, such as tribes or cities, one after the other, while these different groups would have likely prevailed had they been united.

situations where some group members engage in actions that benefit the group but are costly to the individual. The extreme of such situations is when some specific group members accept to sacrifice themselves for the group, as in the case of kamikazes.

It is common to hear that evolution would favour groups where people are willing to selflessly sacrifice themselves for the group. Groups with more altruists would thrive more. This idea is often labelled *group selection*. It was initially put forward by biologists Wynne-Edwards and Konrad Lorenz in the early twentieth century. In the 1960s, the idea faced fierce criticism from mainstream evolutionary biologists. The reason is simple: it is individuals who are selected, not groups. If there are altruists and non-altruists in a group, the altruists who sacrifice themselves would simply disappear in favour of the non-altruists who are less noble in their actions but more likely to survive and have offspring. After facing such criticisms, the term "group selection" became a repellent phrase in scientific discussions about evolution.

The idea of group selection has later been revived in ways that are more rigorous than its initial version. A key idea of the new group selection theories is that the individual costs of altruistic behaviour within a group can be beneficial to the individual if the individual benefits indirectly from it via the benefits for the group. Intuitively, if the group's benefits are large enough, group members may benefit from being altruistic. Consider a battle situation. An individual could choose to flee, but if the benefits from cooperating and taking personal risks in a battle are likely to help secure a victory, the individual can benefit from the collective benefits as a consequence. If groups with more cooperators are more successful, they may become more prevalent, as stressed by Darwin himself in the *Descent of Man* in epigraph to this chapter.

The new theories of group selection do not ignore the individual costs of altruism (Wilson and Sober 1994; Bowles and Gintis 2013). Indeed, within a group, non-altruists may be more successful: they benefit from the altruism of others without paying the costs. But as the groups with more altruists grow, the number of altruists can grow in the overall population, even though it tends to decrease in each group. There is obviously a tension here. This theory of group selection requires hypotheses about the importance of group contests to explain a high prevalence of altruism in the population.[17]

The altruism being selected here is specifically targeted to the in-group, and it can be associated with a willingness to be antagonistic towards other groups and to incur personal costs to fight their members. This theory therefore predicts the emergence of a specific type of altruism: *parochial altruism*, which

---

[17] Whether ancestral conditions were indeed similar enough to those assumed in these models to generate such group selection is still a matter of debate. But these theories have the merit of articulating rigorous models explaining how such a group selection could have taken place.

blends altruism towards in-group members and antagonistic attitudes towards out-group members (Choi and Bowles 2007).[18]

While these theories of group selection have articulated a justification for the possible emergence of cooperative behaviour, they rely on simple models where individuals' propensity to be (parochial) altruists is fixed as if they were genetically determined to be either altruists or not. In that view, the choice to cooperate or not in the stag hunt game is determined by one's type. Somebody who is a cooperator will always cooperate and a non-cooperator will never cooperate. The question is whether the proportion of cooperators will grow enough in the population for cooperative situations to become common. I find these models interesting. However, they critically underestimate humans' cognitive ability. Even though people may have different prosocial preferences, they can *decide* to cooperate or not depending on social circumstances. For instance, in situations where everybody believes that others will cooperate, cooperating is the best choice, even for those who don't have strong feelings in favour of cooperation per se.

As discussed in Chapter 10, social norms can be seen as means to coordinate on the right equilibrium in a game like the stag hunt game. This view naturally leads to the idea that groups with better social norms will be more successful. Imagine a population with many groups; some manage to stumble on social norms that are associated with more socially effective equilibria like cooperating in the stag hunt game. When these groups compete with other groups, they will be more likely to prevail, either because they are more effective in collective fighting or because they have better resources from their sustained cooperation. Another kind of group selection operates then: *cultural group selection* (Henrich 2004; Binmore 2005b). The groups with the better social norms and institutions tend to replace others.

This view leads to blend the notion of group identity and parochial altruism with the models of reciprocity we discussed in Chapter 10 (Yamagishi and Mifune 2016). Parochial altruism can be a social norm that is an equilibrium of the game played in the group. Individuals displaying altruism with in-group members and a willingness to fight against out-group members, if needed, can

---

[18] Note that the term "altruism" is often confusing: it suggests a costly action that does not benefit the individual. Is the altruism emerging from group selection really altruism if it benefits the individual? As pointed out by Wilson and Sober (1994), the discussion about altruism is made difficult because "any trait that is selected at the group level can be made to appear genuinely altruistic by comparing relative fitness within groups, or only apparently altruistic by averaging fitness across groups". This quest for a pure altruism, however, is misguided. Nothing that does not somehow benefit the individual could be selected in the long run. But it does not mean that the ingroup altruistic feelings are not genuine. Here again it is important to distinguish between proximal causes of behaviour such as motives and feelings and ultimate causes that explain how some behaviour was selected because it benefits the individual. Individuals can have genuine altruistic feelings even though these feelings have been selected because they benefit the individual. The theory of parochial altruism suggests, however, that, similarly, individuals may have genuine feelings of hostility towards out-group members.

be rewarded with resources and status, while individuals trying to avoid such responsibilities may be penalised by punishment and loss of status. With such an explanation, cultural group selection eschews the criticism against the old notion of group selection. In each group, following altruistic social norms is the best response for group members because these norms are an equilibrium. Prosocial group members are therefore not selected against.[19]

Once groups with more cooperation-inducing social norms are selected, they may influence the selection of individual characteristics through a *culture-gene co-evolution process*. In the long run, individuals living in groups with such social norms may be more successful if they have natural proclivities that align with these norms. In other words, if people live in a society where it pays to be prosocial, people who have naturally prosocial attitudes may be more likely to thrive than others who are not intrinsically motivated, but try to play along with the prevailing social norms. Cultural institutions like social norms can therefore influence the long-term selection of genetic characteristics, leading people to have innate predispositions aligned with these norms and institutions (Henrich 2004; Binmore 2005b).

Equipped with this rich explanation of how pro-group attitudes could be selected, we can look again at situations where individuals decide to engage in costly behaviour in favour of their group. A first explanation for such behaviour is that they may actually be rational when considering the cost-benefit analysis under the prevailing social norm.

A soldier deciding to take tremendous risks on the battlefield may be taking a shot at earning glory and status in the case of success. Choosing to engage in a heroic action may be similar to choosing a lottery where the willingness to take great risks to advance the cause of the group is rewarded with great benefits in the case of a favourable outcome. Even if most would-be heroes fail, the large benefits awaiting the few successful ones may be worth the risks. Groups that reward their heroes adequately could be coordinating on a better cooperative equilibrium, by providing the right incentives to bold individuals to take personal risks that benefit the whole group.[20]

Conversely, a soldier may avoid fleeing as the cost in status, and sometimes life, associated with such a decision makes this option very costly. As an extreme example, in military history, soldiers fleeing battles have often been killed by their own group when caught. The modern word *decimation* comes from the practice in ancient Rome of killing every tenth man in an military cohort who was guilty of crimes, including cowardice and desertion.[21]

---

[19] Only those who are altruistic over and beyond what is required from the group social norms may face negative selection.

[20] The best social norms would obviously be those that provide enough incentive for heroic actions but not too much to limit reckless risk taking.

[21] The term comes from Latin word for ten, *decem*.

We can further explain the extent of the willingness to take personal risks and make sacrifices if we broaden this perspective to the idea of kin selection. In that perspective, individuals should be willing to take great risks and even possibly to sacrifice themselves for their group if the group rewards their kin as a result. In history, families of heroically fallen soldiers have frequently been substantially rewarded, while families of disgraced soldiers were penalised by loss in social status.

I believe these mechanisms help make sense of most of the sacrificial behaviour observed by individuals taking risks and often incurring great costs for the sake of their group. I suspect that such cost-benefit analysis cannot explain all the most extreme forms of sacrifices that some individuals are willing to engage in for their group. Once again it is useful to look at the distinction between proximal and ultimate causes of behaviour. The ultimate causes of individuals' pro-group behaviour may be that it benefits them and their kin in groups where social norms favour such behaviour. The proximal causes for such behaviour may actually be the emotional feelings of common identity with other group members. In specific situations such feelings may overcome personal considerations and motivate individuals to engage in costly actions in favour of their group. I conjecture that some of the most drastic acts of individual sacrifice are the consequences of such feelings, triggered in unusual extreme situations, in a way that led to choices that were not associated with overall expected benefits for the individuals and their kin. In other words, it is possible that the prosocial feelings that help motivate people to act in favour of their group in many situations could lead to overly costly behaviour in rare and extreme circumstances. It is, for instance, possible that the emotions sustaining parochial altruism may lead some individuals to commit to dying as a hero or a martyr for their groups' cause, even in cases where – after taking into account possible rewards for the individual's family – such actions have a negative impact on their inclusive fitness.[22]

Finally, an evolutionary mismatch may explain some of the costly behaviours people pursue nowadays, for the sake of their perceived group identity. Consider modern sports fans who are willing to engage in physical fights with members of other groups. They may gain status within their small group, but the overall costs and benefits in modern society may not be worth it. Alternatively, think about people harbouring feelings of racial animus against members of another ethnic group. In modern liberal societies, such feelings likely come at a cost. They lead to losses in opportunity for cooperation with members of the out-group and often to social shunning when expressed in the open.

The roots of the evolutionary mismatch lie certainly in the pacification of social relations between and within societies. In our relatively non-violent modern societies, it is easy to forget that the physical elimination of opponents

---

[22] Costly errors from proximal mechanisms may not be eliminated by natural selection if they occur in situations that are unlikely enough.

was typically one of the options as the end result of a violent conflict. The level of emotions that our feelings of group identity can generate may reflect the emotional levels needed to motivate the participation in conflicts where victory meant the possible physical elimination of the other group. In short, we may be equipped with a propensity to feel emotions of group identity that can reach magnitudes suited for the type of violent resolutions of conflict that were observed in the past. In the space of only a few centuries, the level of violence has markedly decreased in developed countries. Intergroup conflicts still exist, but they are almost never resolved by mass killings anymore. The psychological machinery of social identity we have inherited may come with the possibility to generate high emotions, ill-calibrated for the peaceful nature of modern environments.

Groups opposed to each other, like sports fans, ethnic groups or political factions, can express hatred at each other in a way that seems not to make sense in modern societies. People engaged in violent group conflicts are often perceived as senseless. But another way to look at it is that this propensity to be swept by such feelings is likely part of who we are. It is a ghost of our ancient times, where readiness to stick to one's group and violently fight other groups was key for survival.

In modern societies, physically eliminating an opponent (whether it is from another sports club, another political party or another ethnic group) is no longer an option with favourable outcomes for the perpetrator and the perpetrator's group. As a consequence, our group identity feelings may be creating too many costly conflicts and tensions from the point of view from the point of view of the groups involved themselves. Today, engaging in violence with another group will not make this group disappear. Two opposed groups will still have to co-exist in the future. It is one instance where understanding the roots of our behaviour may help us make better decisions now. Our emotional apparatus is likely designed to accompany a greater level of antagonism than would be optimal now.

∴

The study of social identity has been one of the latest additions to behavioural economics. While the homo economicus model paints the picture of a self-centred individual, research on social identity from psychology showed the importance of the feelings of belonging to a group in shaping individuals' preferences and behaviours. While considered for a long time peripheral to the main economic motives, recent events such as the rise of nationalist political movements or terrorism have pointed to the fact that people can choose to make decisions that go against their economic interest for the sake of their perceived group.

These group identity feelings make sense when we consider the cooperation and coordination problems that our ancestors faced in groups. Feelings of social ties and common shared bonds can help individuals to act as a team and be more successful as a group.

13

Impression Management

The individual who presents himself before [others] ... may wish them to think highly of him, or to think that he thinks highly of them, or to perceive how in fact he feels toward them, or to obtain no clear-cut impression ... It will be in his interest to control the conduct of the others, especially their responsive treatment of him.

—Goffman (1959, p. 3)

Naive communication – where a speaker states literally all that he thinks, and/or an audience accepts his representations at face value – is rare, and foolish, in politics.

—Loury (1994)

Most things that seem irrational don't seem so irrational once you understand signalling theory.

—Geoffrey Miller (Twitter post, 9 October 2019)

Summary: Humans are equipped with the most complex language among all animals on earth. It allows us to communicate our knowledge and ideas to others. But human communication does not take the form of a simple exchange of clear statements between people. In many cases, people use not words but actions to communicate with others. Some other times people do not say explicitly what they want to say (e.g., innuendos, euphemisms). These features of communication seem strange and irrational only if we ignore that our means of communication are primarily designed to negotiate our interactions with others. In this process, transparent communication is sometimes not enough to influence others, and it is sometimes not desirable when people may react adversely to our intentions.

A popular trope in science fiction movies is the feature of a highly rational agent confused by humans' ways of communicating with each other. Famous examples of such agents are *Star Trek*'s Mr Spock and Data. A typical scenario involves humans using irony or innuendos. These forms of communication puzzle the rational agent who takes the humans' words at face value. Such scenes usually give us to laugh at the highly rational agent. However, if we think about the fictional agent as a benchmark of rationality, should we not question the humans' behaviour instead? Why engage in interactions where things are said that are not intended (irony) or where things that are intended are not said but only implied (innuendo)? These types of interactions seem to be another sign that human behaviour is hard to explain with a rational perspective.

In this chapter, I want to show how the opposite view is most likely true. The "quirkiness" of human interactions can generally be understood as good responses to the true nature and complexity of social situations. In this perspective, the fictional robot is not a perfectly rational agent. Rather, it is an agent limited in its understanding of the different strategic layers present in social interactions. An early clue that it is the case is that the same perplexity in situations where irony and innuendos are used is often featured in scenes with an agent having autistic traits.[1]

This chapter looks at a wide range of strategic interactions where people care about the beliefs that others form about them. I chose to name this chapter "impression management" as a nod to the work of the sociologist Erving Goffman, who looked, with fascinating acuity, at the games embedded in everyday life where people aim at managing the impressions others form about them (1959), (1971).

The need to manage others' impressions arises when two conditions are met. First, others have imperfect information about us; second, the beliefs others have about us matter for our prospects.

The first condition is not only very frequently respected; I will argue that it is most often respected. People differ on a range of psychological traits: some people are more meticulous, some are more cynical, some are more caring about others.[2] These traits are not directly observable. Other people cannot know a priori how kind, trustworthy or diligent we are. They can only form a belief about our traits from our actions that they observed, or that they heard about. When trying to form an impression about whether Jane is kind or not, John

---

[1] Good examples are the sitcom characters of Sheldon in the *Big Bang Theory* or Shaun in the *Good Doctor*.

[2] Even without a grand theory for such variations, we would expect, from the simple genetic variations across individuals and genetic mutations from one generation to another, *some* differences in traits (Mitchell 2020). For instance, even in a population of reciprocal altruists as described in Chapter 10, some children could be borne with more or less proclivity towards prosocial behaviour.

will think about the situations where he saw Jane act kindly or not. He may also remember discussions where Jane's actions were described by others.[3]

This first condition should be understood to be not just about others' imperfect knowledge about our traits but also about their imperfect knowledge of our intentions and beliefs. Suppose you are a criminal looking to make transactions with another criminal. If you meet another well-known criminal in a bar, there may be limited uncertainty about your willingness to engage in criminal activities. But you both may be unsure about each other's intentions. Suppose you meet to carry a transaction like the briefcase exchange in the prisoner's dilemma in Chapter 10. It matters for you to assess your counterpart's intentions. Does he intend to proceed with the exchange as stated, or does he intend to cross you over? It also matters for you to understand what your counterpart believes about your intentions. Let's say you want to proceed with the exchange as planned. The chances of a successful exchange will depend on whether the other criminal trusts your intentions or whether he is suspicious.

This example may seem far from daily life, but the problem it describes is present in common social interactions. Suppose John and Jane are office colleagues. Jane invites John for coffee to discuss the project they are working on. John may wonder about Jane's intentions with this meeting: Does she want to take over some of John's responsibilities or to help facilitate the project by working more efficiently? John may wonder about Jane's beliefs about him: Does she trust him to do his job properly, or is she worried he may not be efficient enough? It is fair to say that the imperfection of our information in regard to others and their intentions and beliefs is pervasive in social interactions.

The second condition is that others' beliefs matter for our own prospects. It is also most often the case. The beliefs that others have about us influence their behaviour towards us. In the case of an exchange between two criminals, the beliefs of the two protagonists will determine whether the exchange takes place smoothly (e.g., when both criminals trust each others' intentions) or whether they fail to do so, possibly ending in violence. In Jane and John's coffee scenario, the belief they have about each other's intentions will influence whether they can coordinate successfully on improving their work on the project considered, or whether they fail to do so. Consider the case where Jane's only aim is to improve their work organisation. If John is worried that Jane may be trying to take over some of his responsibilities, he may thwart Jane's attempt at re-organising the project. To prevent this, Jane would need to care about John's beliefs about her intentions. In general, our success in what we undertake in life heavily relies on the decisions of other people going our way: stakeholders, bosses,

---

[3] John may also associate some characteristics of Jane to some likelihood of being kind: for example, the fact that Jane is a member of a church believing in a God rewarding people for being kind.

partners, colleagues. The decisions of these people depend on their beliefs about us. Therefore, it makes sense to care about these beliefs and to invest time and resources to influence them.

I will look at two broad types of situations: when we manage the impressions of others about our unobserved traits, and when we manage the impressions of others about our intentions and beliefs.

13.1 IMPRESSIONS ABOUT US

Let's consider here the situations where people have different traits. Economists use the word *type* to describe the set of traits of a person. Traits have many dimensions. Nonetheless, in many situations, we can often rank people according to how their traits give them a relative strength. We will then use terms as strong/weak or high/low to describe different types. Consider a situation where people engage in a competition, like a match of basketball. If one participant is a professional player, we may describe him as having a "strong type", while other players who are just amateurs may be described as "weak types".

In the context of a basketball match where people know who is and who is not a professional player, the types (strong or weak) of the players are known. But in many situations where relative strength in some dimension matters, people's types are not known. Imagine a game of poker with players you have never heard of before. You may not be able to tell at first sight whether a player is a "strong" player or not. In the case of poker, a strong player may prefer not to be known as such. Letting others being confident about their chances can be a good way to let them take too much risk.[4]

Signalling
Unlike in poker, in many situations, strong players want others to know about their strength. Imagine the following scenario. John, a black belt in a martial art, comes back late from a party on Saturday night. On his way home, he sees another man trying to rob a woman's handbag. John steps in to try to fend the attacker off. John is fairly confident that, in a fight, his skills and strength would most likely allow him to get the upper hand. Nonetheless, a fight is risky. John could take a blow. In the worst-case scenario, the attacker could pull a knife, and the situation could get more dangerous. The best thing for John would be to let the attacker know about his martial arts training. The attacker would most certainly back down without fighting. This situation would be better for both

---

4 A comical illustration of this strategy is given in the comedy *Odds and Evens* (1978). Terence Hill initially plays dumb at the start of a poker game by asking his counterparts: "Which is higher, ace or king?" Having safely built the confidence of the other players, he later beats them easily as they underestimate him.

of them. Unfortunately, John's strength is not immediately visible. So John's faces a challenge: How can he *signal* to the attacker his strength?

What about just stating it? John could say, "I have a black belt in martial arts." It is a true statement. Unfortunately, *anybody* could say that, even someone like me who does not have training in martial arts. This fact would be well understood by the attacker. Such a statement would not be a very convincing signal of strength. What John needs, to be *credible*, is to do something that sets him apart from people who are not experts in martial arts. To do so, he could make a technical move that only a person well trained in martial arts could pull off. This example illustrates a critical property that *signals* need to have to credibly reveal something about your strength: they need to be something that only a strong type would be able to generate or to afford (if it is a costly action).

The previous example seems reasonable: if you have martial arts expertise, signal it by executing a move that would be hard to do without the appropriate training. But signalling games often lead to behaviour that may seem counter-intuitive or irrational at first sight. One is the "handicap principle", initially proposed by the biologist Amotz Zahavi (1975). A straightforward way to credibly signal that you are strong is to impose a handicap on yourself to show that your strength allows you to afford this handicap. In the animal world, the peacock tail is the typical example of such a handicap. It is a large appendage without a clear survival function. It is costly to produce and maintain. It also has potentially a cost in terms of mobility, which may increase the risk of being caught by predators. A peacock tail seems a very poor investment in terms of fitness. But the handicap principle helps make sense of it. By being able to generate such a costly display, the peacock signals its quality as a potential mate. Only peacocks with good health, strength and agility can display a large and useless tail.[5] In a world with complete information, males would not grow such costly tails and females would just pick the best ones. But in the real world, females have imperfect information about their possible mates. The tail is a costly signal that emerges as a solution to the mate choice problem in that setting. The handicap principle provides the main explanation for the costly – and apparently pointless – ornaments used by animals to entice potential mating partners.

In human interactions, there is at least one well-known case where valuable resources are invested in costly and unproductive signals: luxury goods. At first sight, the consumption of luxury goods can seem strange. It is reasonable to assume that better-quality products are more expensive. But luxury goods' prices seem out of proportion with the actual functions they serve. Sure, quality clothes may be more comfortable and good looking than others, but can this fact explain how a luxury pair of trousers could be worth thousands of dollars

---

[5] The aesthetic aspect of the tail is also part of the signal quality. Peacocks that are not healthy may only be able to display scruffy feathers.

compared to a $100 pair from a reputable brand in a standard shop? Sure, a quality watch may be more precise and agreeable to wear than a standard one, but can it justify a price of several $100,000 compared to a $200 watch that may not look so different? Sure, a quality car may be faster, more beautiful and safer than a standard car, but can these features be worth several million dollars for the most expensive cars instead of paying $20,000–$100,000, the price of most cars on the road? Being surprised at the apparent nonsense of spending so much money on goods, which are unlikely to be that much better than standard goods, is missing one thing. People buying luxury goods are buying more than the goods themselves. They are also buying the signal that they can afford these expensive goods. The high price of luxury goods is one of the main reasons why these goods are consumed in the first place!

Veblen (1899/2017) famously wrote about this "conspicuous consumption" used to signal wealth. While everyone could pretend to be rich, visibly being able to spend large amounts of money on expensive goods is a sign of wealth that people who are not rich cannot fake.[6] Conspicuous consumption happens not only with the most expensive luxury goods. Signalling concerns are widespread, and they are not restricted to the very upper end of the social ladder. If people within a social group want to signal small differences in wealth through consumption, firms will have an incentive to provide goods differing in price even though the quality does not differ much. For example, a recent study by Bursztyn et al. (2018) found that between two credit cards with the same services, one with a visible "platinum" name is more likely to be chosen. It is then also more likely to be used in social situations, like in restaurants.

The qualities that people may want to signal in social settings are not limited to strength or wealth. We have seen, in Chapter 10, that people may also want to signal their quality as potential cooperators. If you want to convince potential partners to trust you and to cooperate with you, you may want to signal that you are trustworthy. Hoffman et al. (2015) point out that an important aspect of trustworthiness is the propensity to stay committed to a given partnership without defecting when profitable opportunities to do so arise, from time to time. They showed that such a concern can explain the fact that people often choose not to calculate when cooperating with other people. When a friend asks you whether you can help, you typically answer "sure" instead of asking a detailed description of what is involved before making your mind. Somebody who is visibly not looking at the costs before helping signals being more likely to help unconditionally in other situations. Somebody checking the cost of helping signals that, if this cost is too high in the future, they may opt not to help then.

One of the most significant situations where people try to find a reliable partner is the search for a life partner. In such a search, one typically wants to

---

[6] In some situations, fake versions of the luxury goods can become available. These fake goods erode the ability of the original versions of the good to signal wealth. It may lead wealthy customers to switch away from these goods to other luxury goods harder to imitate.

avoid partners who could abandon the partnership easily for other options. Robert Trivers (1972) proposed the theory of parental investment. If you consider a heterosexual couple, the asymmetry in parental investment in offspring means that women are usually more wary of the sincerity of the stated dedication of potential male partners than the reverse.[7] Men truly interested in a long-term relationship therefore have to signal dedication in a credible way (which cannot be easily imitated by those interested only in a short-term relationship). As pointed out by Dawkins, "by insisting on a long engagement period, a female weeds out casual suitors" (Dawkins 1976).[8]

Historically, periods of courtship have existed in societies where women enjoyed some agency in the choice of their partner (Monger 2004). The time spent by a man in a courtship is a credible signal of interest because it is costly. Since courtship is generally somewhat socially transparent, a man usually does not court several women at the same time.[9] Courtship therefore signals a man's willingness to forego alternative opportunities in terms of partnership. Courtship also frequently features gifts to the courted woman such as flowers, or jewellery. Sozou and Seymour (2005) modelled this interaction as a signalling game. A potential male partner signals his dedication by making costly gifts to his intended female partner. The gifts need to be costly to signal a credible intent from a long-term partnership (a man usually does not make such gifts repeatedly to other women). But Sozou and Seymour also note that these gifts will have, most often, low resale value (you cannot sell flowers, and the resale value of a piece of jewellery is relatively low). This apparently peculiar characteristic makes sense from the man's perspective: these types of gifts protect men from possibly being taken advantage of by women collecting valuable gifts without a real intention of becoming a partner.[10]

[7] The theory of parental investment explains how the degree of investment in offspring by members of each sex will influence the strategies of males and females when trying to find a partner. In species where males invest limited resources in rearing offspring, females care only about choosing the best males and males compete to show their strength or to beat possible competitors (e.g., sea lions). Humans are, however, characterised by mostly monogamous, long-term pair-bonding relationships where men also invest a substantial amount of resources in the raising of children. Both men and women, for that reason, care about the commitment of the other partner when forming a bonding relationship. Women's physiological investment is nonetheless larger than men's, and they should care relatively more about the propensity of a partner to be committed to a long-term investment in the relationship. The risk for them is to fall prey to a philanderer who will not stick around and quickly look for other partners.

[8] The existence of courtship interactions does not preclude more casual types of interactions between possible partners. Evolutionary biologists have proposed several reasons why both men and women can have short-term mating strategies (see Buss, 2019).

[9] It was pretty much impossible in ancient times given the small social circles people were navigating into. Modern urban life, with its non-overlapping social circles, made this possibility greater. But social media are making it harder again to keep different private lives in separate social circles.

[10] The duration of courtship has decreased substantially in Western countries. The logic presented here nonetheless explains the persisting gender asymmetry during the dating process. In a survey conducted in 2015 in North America, 69% of the respondents stated that the man should pay

The investment of time in relationships is not just to romantic partnerships. It also exists in a smaller degree with friends and colleagues. One aspect of it is *small talk*, the act of engaging in light discussions without any specific purpose. Such discussions can seem, at first sight, vacuous. They often do not involve the transfer of meaningful information. People engaging in small talk discuss about things such as today's weather, yesterday's TV program, or the number of coffees they already had that day. So one may wonder why small talk is so pervasive in social interactions. The answer is most certainly that language is not used just to convey information. It can also be used to coordinate our beliefs about our intentions without any transfer of information. This role is called the *phatic function* of language, a term coined by the Russian linguist Roman Jakobson. When John asks his colleague Jane in the morning "how are you doing?" he does not literally mean to know how she is doing. Indeed, Jane generally understands that the question is used as a mark of consideration, and she does not go on describing the issues she is facing at the moment. Discussions devoid of exchange of information can help shape others' beliefs about our friendly attitude because talk is actually not fully cheap (Sally 2005). Engaging in any talk takes time (and also presents some cognitive costs). Hence, through short costly acts of discussions, people can signal to each other their shared consideration.[11]

Counter-signalling

Situations where signalling games take place can explain lots of seemingly irrational behaviour used to signal strength or commitment. But the rich nature of these games does not stop here. In some cases, it can also explain why people may decide *not to send signals* of strength, as a way to signal strength (Feltovich et al. 2002).

Suppose that people can have three types in terms of income: low, medium and high. There may be some public information available – such as people's professions – which gives an idea about the likely type of each person. This public information may, however, not be enough to identify precisely each type. For example, a profession is often not enough to identify whether a person belongs to a medium type or to a high type. Somebody known to be a shopkeeper in a small retail shop is unlikely to have a very high income, but this information is not enough to know whether this person has a relatively low or medium income.

for the first date, 66% stated that he should also pay for the second date, and 87% stated that he should bring flowers to the first date (Cameron and Curry 2020). To some readers in large cities, this description of courtship/dating may seem at odds with the so-called hook-up culture, which looks nothing like the courtship process described here. As explained by Birger (2015) this culture is likely the result of an imbalance in the sex ratio among the educated population where women outnumber men significantly (because women are now graduating in larger numbers than men). Whenever the sex ratio is balanced, or in favour of women, the dating process presents the type of gender asymmetry in costly signalling described here.

[11] Note that small talk does not have to be devoid of information by design. While it is often the case, small talk can also feature exchanges of valuable pieces of information, in particular, about other possible partners in social interactions (*gossip*).

In such situations, people belonging to the medium type may benefit from engaging in costly signalling to differentiate themselves from the low types. But, as a consequence, the high types may engage in *counter-signalling*: sending a cheap low signal as a sign of confidence indicating that they do not need to differentiate themselves from the low types because they are not a medium type. Counter signalling is *proving that you have nothing to prove*, which sets you apart from those who care about proving their worth.[12]

Counter-signalling situations are everywhere when you start looking. They are the rich CEOs who wear seemingly casual clothes instead of visibly expensive ones. They are the famous university professors who wear grubby outfits, while the junior academics, who are looking to get a tenure position, are well dressed. They are the smart students who visibly engage in leisure activities to show that they do not need to cram for the next exam.

An example of signalling and counter-signalling, which will be close to the experience of academic readers, is the signal of intellectual skills through the use, or not, of complicated techniques or language. Nietzsche insightfully said, "Those who know they are deep strive for clarity. Those who would like to seem deep to the crowd strive for obscurity" (1882/2001, III). The obscurity of some writing is often just a signalling trick used by writers to look good. But while Nietzsche is critical of this behaviour, the signalling/counter-signalling model does not blame the obscure medium type and praise the clear high type. This model explains these different behaviours as the best strategy for each type, given the situations they are in. If you are a famous scholar, you can write clearly. People already recognise you for your qualities and will be amazed at your ability to explain in simple terms things that are complex (arguably, you are likely talking about complex things given the already recognised depth of your expertise). But if you are a young scholar, presenting your topic of research in a very clear manner may backfire. If you boil down a very complex problem in simple terms, the audience may not be able to appreciate the difficulty of the task you carried out. Instead, the audience may think that what you said looked fairly simple. They may wonder what was really the importance of your contribution.[13] A recent study illustrates these different strategies: looking at more than 60,000 research theses and talks, Brown et al. (2020) found that authors from less prestigious schools tend to use more technical jargon than authors from more prestigious schools.[14]

---

[12] A similar argument was made in finance to explain that firms with better prospects may be more willing to disclose bad news as a way to signal their confidence in their future prospects and distinguish themselves from their less confident competitors (Teoh and Hwang 1991).
[13] They may also make the inference that if you, a young scholar, were able to present a problem in simple terms it must be because the problem was simple.
[14] Another case of signalling/countersignalling in academia is the use of titles such as "Dr" or "PhD" to present oneself. Academics in PhD-granting institutions (typically more prestigious) are less likely to stress the use of their title than academics from non-PhD-granting institutions (Harbaugh and To 2020).

Counter-signalling can take the form of self-modesty, where people avoid boasting about their success. It is frequent to hear winners of prizes saying how limited their achievement would have been without a large number of colleagues who made their success possible. It is rarer to hear such a discourse from people *aspiring to win* such prizes, but still on the waiting list.[15] The fact that self-modesty can be instrumental is well illustrated by this quote from the former Israeli prime minister Golda Meir, who once said: "Don't be so humble, you are not that great," allegedly to General Moshe Dayan, who had played a central role in Israel's victory in the Six-Day War of 1967.[16]

Finally, a variation on the idea of counter-signalling is the notion of *buried signals*. The possibilities available in terms of signals are not limited to sending a signal or not. Sometimes it is possible to generate valuable signals but to choose not to send them. These signals may be more valuable when discovered by others. Consider a situation where somebody could impress others by revealing a valuable signal indicating some personal quality. It may be even more impressive for others to discover this signal themselves and to realise that the person had chosen not to reveal this signal in the first place. This idea was proposed by Hoffman et al. (2018). They give the example of charitable giving. Giving is costly and, thus, can act as a credible signal of kindness. But the visibility of the act of giving decreases its value.[17] When a benefactor makes a gift in a visible way, people may wonder whether this action results from the benefactor's desire of appearing kind rather than from this person being genuinely kind. Giving without making it public can therefore be even more valuable as a signal, *if there is a chance that it is revealed publicly later on*, without the benefactor having acted to disclose it in the first place. In another context, it may be better to avoid bragging about a success but still make it possible for the information to be found out later. A successful person may not need to brag about this success publicly, and get more benefit from this success being revealed later on, along with the fact that the person had chosen not to boast about it in the first place.

Signalling games are pervasive and add a rich layer of complexity to social interactions. In a world where we would have complete information about other people, we would only aim to understand how others' action impact us. In a world with imperfect information, we also try to understand what others' actions tell us about them (their beliefs, their intentions).

[15] Another example, pointed out to me by Jason Collins, is the willingness to admit your shortcomings. The physicist and Nobel Prize winner Richard Feynman was known to say that his IQ was "only" 125. And, in an answer to a junior high school student worried about her ability in mathematics, Einstein famously said in 1943: "Do not worry about your difficulties in mathematics, I can assure you that mine are still greater."

[16] The success of self-modesty as an enhancement strategy works only if the person benefits from a strong enough public signal that removes any doubt on the nature of the low signal. If a Nobel Prize winner says that, for a long time, they did not understand a simple idea, people are likely to praise this refreshing and reassuring modesty. If a graduate student utters the exact same words, people may think that it indicates that the student is likely not very bright.

[17] We already saw this in Chapter 10 when discussing the case of the anonymous benefactor.

Part of the confusing aspect of signalling games is that they are typically denied being played. People rarely state that they buy expensive goods to show how rich they are. Instead, expensive purchases are typically given other motivations. People state that they buy novel technologies at an expensive premium because they are techies who like innovations. They buy expensive sports cars because of the quality features of the car. They buy an expensive penthouse because they really like the view. Signalling strategies tend to be concealed because signals are often more convincing when they are seen as emerging naturally as a reflection of people's characteristics. When signals are perceived as purposefully produced, they may indicate that the signaller is a "try-hard", investing a disproportionate amount of effort in the signals themselves to unduly influence our impressions. It explains a paradox of signalling games: these games are everywhere but rarely played explicitly. It is a major reason why they produce behaviour that may seem puzzling: because their actual motivations are often consciously or unconsciously concealed.[18]

13.2 SECOND-ORDER BELIEFS: IMPRESSIONS ABOUT OUR BELIEFS AND INTENTIONS

In the previous section, I discussed why we care about what other people think about us. Similarly, other people care about what we think about them. Their beliefs about our thoughts will influence their attitude towards us. As a consequence, we also care about what other people believe we think about them. Our beliefs about these beliefs from other people are called *second-order beliefs* to distinguish them from beliefs about things (like traits), which are called first-order beliefs.[19]

Second-order beliefs are very important in social situations. You generally care about whether others believe you have a high or low opinion of them. This concern is particularly vivid when a colleague asks another, "What do you think of my work?" or when a wife asks her husband, "How do I look in that dress?" Faced with such a question, you may feel the need to choose your words carefully. What you say could be interpreted as signalling a positive or negative opinion about the person asking the question.

The management of others' second-order beliefs matters because their behaviour towards us typically depends on their beliefs about our disposition toward them. As I have discussed in Chapter 10, people tend to act kindly towards us if they believe that we are inclined to act kindly towards them.

Consider the briefcase exchange situation from Chapter 10. Suppose that both the buyer and the seller want to play it straight and to cooperate if the

---

[18] Signalling strategies do not need to be conscious, and, as Chapter 14 will show, being oblivious to the strategic consequences of our actions can, in many cases, make them more effective.

[19] Formally, first-order beliefs are beliefs about the state of the world, which include the types of the players you interact with. Second-order beliefs are the beliefs of the players about the beliefs of the other players.

other cooperates. However, they each ignore the intention of the other player. Suppose that some communication takes place before the exchange. Let's take the point of view of the buyer. He may try to infer whether the seller wants to cooperate from the seller's verbal and non-verbal cues. But the buyer will also need, during the communication, to be careful about the impression *he* gives to the seller about his own intentions. Indeed, if the buyer fails to convince the seller of his good intentions, the seller may not trust the buyer and therefore decide not to cooperate. The transaction would fail, even though both players would like the exchange to proceed.

A quick introspection reveals that our concerns about others' beliefs about our intentions pervade our social interactions. Erving Goffman gives an insightful example of the intricate considerations people have about each other's beliefs and intentions in a description of what happens in an elevator ride. When people arrive in an elevator, they adjust their position to give each other reasonable space given the number of people inside.

But departure leads to somewhat more complex behavior, since an individual who leaves his current niche to take up a freed one produces an open sign that he is disinclined to be as close to his neighbor as he was. (When the two are of opposite sex, there exists the added complication that failure to move away when possible can be taken as a sign of undue interest.) ... Thus, as the car empties, passengers acquire a measure of uneasiness, caught between two opposing inclinations to obtain maximum distance from others and inhibit avoidance behavior that might give offense. (Goffman 1971, p. 31)

Even in such simple settings, people would care about how others interpret their actions as suggesting something about what they think about these other people.

This concern for how others interpret our actions as signalling our intentions has another interesting consequence. The meaning of what you say is contained not just in what is said. This meaning also comes from all the surrounding context, which contributes to making sense of why you said what you said at that particular moment. A good illustration of this principle is that the way people react to what we say generally depends on who we are. Let's imagine the situation where Jane has written a report for her manager at work. Her friend Sally gets to read it and says, "It is interesting, but you need to improve the writing; at the moment it is a bit fuzzy." Jane may welcome this as useful feedback from a friend willing to help her. Suppose now that the same words were uttered by Julie, with whom Jane has a long-term conflict in the office. Now Jane may interpret the same statement as an attempt at undermining her. The start of the statement "It is interesting" may be interpreted as sneering and passive-aggressive, rather than genuine and well-meaning feedback. Finally, suppose that the feedback comes from John, a male colleague. Jane may wonder whether John's feedback does not reflect some prejudice against her because she is a woman. She may wonder why John is using the word "fuzzy". Does he mean women can't think and express themselves clearly?

Another noteworthy illustration that similar statements will be interpreted differently as a function of who makes them is the *intergroup sensitivity effect* (Hornsey and Esposo 2009). This term refers to the fact that you are more likely to find criticisms of your group reasonable if they come from within your group itself. Suppose that John is a citizen of the country of Syldavia. If Jane, another Syldavia citizen, states: "I have never seen a country with so much corruption and incompetence than in Syldavia," John may well agree that Jane has a point. But if the same argument comes from Sally, who is not a citizen from Syldavia, John is more likely to react negatively to the same feedback. This effect explains why, in multicultural societies, jokes about a given group are often perfectly fine when they come from within the group but a no-no if they come from somebody who does not belong to the group.

We are naturally aware of these considerations. When we give feedback, as in the example of Jane's report, we are typically careful of how feedback can be perceived *given who we are*. To convey the same informational content, different people express things differently. Julie may need to be much more friendly/polite when giving feedback to Jane to avoid any perception of possible animosity. And John may decide to be specifically cautious about his feedback, not leaving some possibility of being perceived as prejudiced against women. It is for this reason that you often observe that friends can be rougher with each other than strangers can be. Bantering and mocking each other is common in groups of friends where such behaviour can be safely interpreted as not signalling a negative intent. If anything, the ability to banter and mock each other can then become a signal of real closeness in friendship, and somebody who stays too polite may signal a lack of confidence in the closeness of the relationship.[20]

13.3 HIGHER-ORDER BELIEFS: THE IMPORTANCE OF MIND READING

The complexity of belief management does not stop at second-order beliefs. Beliefs about second-order beliefs (e.g., others' beliefs about your beliefs about their beliefs about you) are third-order beliefs. Beliefs about third-order beliefs are fourth-order beliefs and so on. Such higher-order beliefs also play an important role.[21] They may seem complicated, but they do matter for strategic

---

[20] A related popular trope in comedies is when somebody who is not close to another person tries to pretend to be close by bantering/mocking in a way only a real friend could. Such behaviour is then welcomed with an air of disapproval, revealing that the person clearly misjudged how close they were.

[21] Higher-order beliefs have been formalised by Mertens and Zamir (1985). In that framework, higher-order beliefs represent our knowledge of our lower-order beliefs and a measure of probability on others' lower-order beliefs. Dekel and Siniscalchi (2015) provide a clear presentation of this formal framework, which features a sequence of state spaces with measures of probability over types and lower-order beliefs.

FIGURE 13.1. Higher-order beliefs in the suitcase game. In that case, the seller always want to cooperate if the buyer wants to cooperate. The successful cooperation depends on the seller's belief about the buyer's intentions and on the chain of corresponding higher-order beliefs.

reasons, and our intuitions are well designed to help us appreciate when they are important. In situations where it matters, we can spend a lot of time trying to understand and manage them. The management of others' higher-order beliefs is certainly one aspect of human interactions that generates much complexity and apparent quirkiness of our behaviour.

Going back to the briefcase exchange situation, suppose again that both the buyer and the seller wants to cooperate. For simplicity, let's assume this time that it is well known that the seller always wants to cooperate if the buyer cooperates. The remaining uncertainty is about the desire of the buyer to also cooperate. This situation is represented by Figure 13.1. The belief of the seller about the intention of the buyer is a first-order belief, the belief of the buyer about the belief of the seller is a second-order belief and so on.

These higher-order beliefs matter for the transaction to take place successfully. Suppose that the seller believes that the buyer wants to cooperate (first-order belief). The buyer will not bring his suitcase if he believes that the seller doesn't trust him (second-order belief). But even if the buyer is confident in the seller's trust, the seller may not know that fact and be wary that perhaps the buyer may believe that the seller lacks trust in the buyer (third-order belief). In the mind of the seller, that could lead the buyer to not cooperate. The seller may be worried that the buyer expects the seller to not cooperate (due to his assumed lack of trust in the buyer). Therefore, the third-order belief of the seller also matters for the cooperation to take place successfully. In turn, the buyer should anticipate the importance of this belief from the seller and not cooperate if he believes that the seller wrongly thinks that the buyer is not confident in the seller's trust (fourth-order belief).[22]

These considerations are complicated, and navigating such situations well may require some intense thinking. People likely invest cognitive effort in carefully forming accurate higher-order beliefs in situations where relationships matter a lot to them. A great example is when someone has a romantic interest in another person, as in the movie *When Harry Met Sally* (1989). Suppose that Harry is interested in Sally and says something which could be picked up by Sally as indicating a romantic interest. Harry cares about Sally's first-order beliefs: "Did she understand I like her"? He can form a second-order belief: "I believe that she understands I like her." And he can also care (and form beliefs) about Sally's third-order beliefs: "Does she know I am aware that she understands?" In such situations, we can get suddenly much better at climbing the order of beliefs. It is cognitively demanding and it is certainly one of the reasons explaining the time and effort spent by teenagers trying to ascertain what potential partners think and think they think, and so on.

Consider the situation where you say a moderately provocative joke to your boss, and this one does not laugh. Perhaps your boss believes you intended to be disrespectful (your boss' first-order belief). You may be worried your intentions were perceived as disrespectful (your second-order belief). Should you inquire about the joke's reception and possibly apologise? It could be risky. Your boss could realise you were not even sure your joke was being perceived as disrespectful (your boss' third-order belief). Should you apologise without inquiring then? But what if your boss was not offended in the first place? That would reveal to your boss all these concerned beliefs you were forming out of thin air.

Pinker et al. (2008) show how these considerations help explain one of the most puzzling features of human communication: the use of *indirect speech*, such as ambiguous statements and innuendos. As they observe: "When people speak, they often insinuate their intent indirectly rather than stating it as a bald proposition. Examples include sexual come-ons, veiled threats, polite requests, and concealed bribes." For instance, a driver attempting to bribe a police officer may say, "Sir, it would be great if we could find a way to sort it out here." Another example would be inviting a date for a drink upstairs as an implicit overture in order that the evening end up in a non-platonic way.

---

[22] Ariel Rubinstein (1989) famously showed that two rational players could fail to cooperate in such a situation even if they have the correct first-, second-, third-... order beliefs but are unaware about the kth-order belief with k being as large as possible. This result is paradoxical since it seems we would be pretty confident in our joint understanding of the situation if our second- or third-order beliefs are compatible with cooperation. Higher-order beliefs beyond these levels (fourth and above) are hard for us to parse and to think through.

But why do people communicate that way even though it seems much less efficient than just stating what you mean in an understandable and obvious manner? A key insight from Pinker et al. is that "human communication involves a mixture of cooperation and conflict". If communication was, as we often assume, present only in situations of cooperation, there would not be any incentive in being ambiguous. Whatever information/intent you have, you would want the other person to be fully aware of it. For example, if you plan a meeting with somebody in New York, it is in both your interests to be entirely clear about where and when you want to meet. You may opt for a statement such as: "Let's meet at Grand Central Station in front of the information kiosk in the centre of the main concourse at 12 pm." You would not say something like: "It could be a good idea to meet near Grand Central Station at some point tomorrow." There is no reason to use an ambiguous statement, which would risk creating some misunderstanding.

But in many interactions, incentives are not necessarily always aligned. Think about the bribe situation. If the police officer is corrupt, then the driver's and the officer's incentives are aligned. They would both benefit from the bribe taking place. The driver would avoid a fine, and the police officer would get some financial reward. But if the police officer is honest, the driver's and the officer's incentives are not aligned as the latter has no interest in being bribed. An attempt at a bribe could lead the driver to be arrested. The use of an ambiguous statement allows the driver to convey the intended information (the bribe offer) while retaining *credible deniability* (the bribe offer is not certain enough to warrant an arrest).

A key feature of indirect speech is that it can convey information about your intent without establishing *common knowledge* about it. Common knowledge is when several people know something together and know that they all know and that all know that they know. In short, they all share the same higher-order beliefs. It greatly simplifies the coordination of actions. When you know that you have aligned incentives (e.g., two people who want to meet at Grand Central Station), you make clear statements to gain common knowledge with others about your plans. But when you are not sure that your incentives are well aligned (e.g., driver and police officer), making your intentions or beliefs common knowledge may be risky.

A great example used by Pinker et al. to illustrate this fact is a scene in in a movie I already mentioned: *When Harry met Sally*. In the movie, Harry *admits openly his romantic interest in Sally* even though he is currently dating a girlfriend of hers. As Sally reacts negatively, Harry says: "Okay, I take it back." To which Sally retorts: "You can't take it back, it's already out there." One way to understand Sally's answer is that now that Harry explicitly admitted his interest, it is common knowledge. There is no way to pretend it did not happen.

Let's consider the alternative situation where, instead of making an explicit overture, Harry had used a more ambiguous statement, *possibly suggesting* an interest. Let's assume Sally declined the overture. Figure 13.2 shows how the

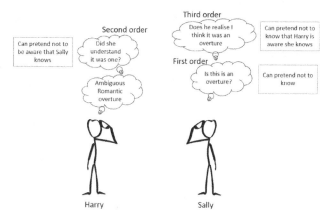

FIGURE 13.2. Harry and Sally navigating an ambiguous romantic overture.

ambiguous nature of the overture affects Sally's and Harry's beliefs about the situation. Sally cannot be sure about Harry's intent (first-order belief), and she may not be able to call him out. Once declined, Harry could understand that Sally knows it was an overture (his second-order belief), but Sally may not know that Harry has this understanding (her third-order belief). So Harry may pretend that he believes Sally is not aware she rejected an overture with her negative answer (he is faking his second-order belief to influence her third-order belief). Similarly, Sally may pretend to be naive, feigning to believe no overture was made, so none was rejected. De Freitas et al. (2019) show that when ambiguous statements are made, people's confidence in their beliefs tend to fall as we climb these higher-order beliefs from first-order beliefs to second, third and so on. So there is a stark difference between an unambiguous statement about an intent that leads it to be "out there" and an ambiguous statement that leaves much more uncertainty about the extent to which people know what other people know about the intent.

Without common knowledge, Harry and Sally could continue their previous friendship relationship, pretending nothing happened. But pretending that nothing happened is not possible when Harry's overture is made common knowledge, is out "in the open".

These concerns for conveying information about our intentions while retaining credible deniability, if ever these intents were not welcome, are widespread. They explain why people frequently convey their views and desires not explicitly through direct statements but through indirect cues. John may want to ask a raise to his boss Jane, but would be worried for it to be made explicitly as it could be perceived as pushy. Judith may want Jake to organise something for their marriage anniversary, but she may prefer for Jake to understand her wish without having to state it explicitly, not to be perceived as demanding.

One prominent domain where others' impression management is critical is politics where actors try to get the backing from others by convincing them that they will deliver policies aligned with their interests and values. In a country, voters' interests, opinions and priorities can differ widely across different dimensions. Some citizens may care about environmental policies; some may prioritise economic growth and employment; some may care more about reducing inequalities; some may want to uphold traditional values; some may be swayed by patriotism. Convincing a majority of voters to support you is difficult. The things that some voters want to hear may displease others. In the signalling game of politics, "one abandons ambiguity at one's peril" as the French Cardinal de Retz said in the seventeenth century. Euphemisms and ambiguities offer the cover of plausible deniability, while naive candour would expose politicians to situations where their exact positions are common knowledge and can therefore not be denied in case of criticism.

In an excellent discussion of such signalling games of impression management in politics, Loury (1994) explains how they can naturally lead to the emergence of *political correctness*.[23] Consider the situation where the majority of the population considers some political ideas despicable. Let's call that position X.[24] Suppose that, as a consequence of the public disapprobation, people rarely dare to express ideas associated with X in public. Because people harbouring these ideas do not express them, they will hide their true beliefs behind euphemisms or innuendos. They will also tend to explain their position on specific issues as driven by reasons other than the real one. People opposed to a given policy because of their X ideas may state their opposition to it in terms of other reasons, for example, the policy is not good enough (for reasons unrelated to X).[25]

A consequence of this hiding strategy by X supporters is that the exposition of concerns of some sorts against policies rejected by X supporters may then become suspicious in the eyes of other people. Such concerns may be perceived as possibly signalling a *hidden* support for X ideas. Think about a person who does not support X ideas but agrees with some other ideas that are also favoured by the supporters of X ideas. This person may prefer to self-censor rather than appear as possibly harbouring X ideas under the veneer of a reasonable defence of these other ideas.

The same logic goes for the use of expressions and the discussions of some issues. Suppose the expressions explicitly signalling a support for X ideas are taboo. Other expressions that become used as substitutes by X supporters can progressively also become unacceptable, as they may raise too much suspicion

---

[23] Morris (2001) later modelled Laury's intuition formally.

[24] For example, racist or sexist ideas.

[25] Another possible strategy is to use *dog whistles*: to say things that are understood by X supporters as signalling X ideas, without these ideas being expressed aloud. The expression comes from the fact that dog whistles use ultrasound, which cannot be heard by humans, for whom they are not intended.

about whether the person using them harbours X ideas. This phenomenon is not without caveats. Politicians may end up shying away from discussing some valid questions or concerns for purely signalling purposes. Paradoxically, on some important issues, it may lead the discourse to be limited to platitudes that everybody agrees on. In some cases, everybody may even realise that only platitudes are being mentioned but also understand why it is the case: these are the only kinds of things that can be safely said in public.

Loury shows how, at a smaller level, the same mechanisms operate when people who do not know each other get to talk and have to decide which topics and ideas to discuss. Imagine John and Jane sitting near each other in a plane and starting to chat. The start of the conversation will usually feature small talk unlikely to cause any friction. The weather condition is, for that reason, a prime topic to start a discussion with a stranger. On the contrary, politics is a risky topic. A candid political statement early in the conversation could create some tension and lead to a long awkward situation for the rest of the flight. Loury insightfully describes the typical dynamic of such interactions:

Each speaker, seeking recognition and reinforcement, looks for the positive feedback which encourages that candor in discussion possible only among the like-minded. The dialogue may evolve into an intense and intimate exchange, or it may lapse into vague and meaningless banter, depending on what the speakers are able to learn about one another. If real communication eventually occurs, the path to it will have been paved by overtures of calculated imprecision.

∴

To sum up, the management of others' impressions is one of the most complex, subtle and fascinating aspects of human interactions. It generates lots of behaviours that are puzzling only at face value, when one does not appreciate the actual depth of the games being played. Seemingly strange behaviour appears when people try to manage uncertainty about higher-order beliefs. People may be overly eager, or mysteriously unclear, relative to the situation faced, because people care about what other people think about their intentions.

In the movies where a rational robot interacts with humans, these intricacies of human interactions are used for comic effect with the robot offending its listeners with candid but untactful statements or with the robot not understanding humans seemingly failing to communicate what they mean in rational ways. But this movie trope gets the level of rationality wrong. It is not the robots who are the most rational. They just do not understand the real games being played by humans. The seemingly puzzling human behaviours are good answers to the actual games in which humans are engaged.

14

Selection of Delusion

The overweening conceit which the greater part of men have of their own abilities is an ancient evil remarked by the philosophers and moralists of all ages.... There is no man living who, when in tolerable health and spirits, has not some share of it. The chance of gain is by every man more or less overvalued, and the chance of loss is by most men undervalued.

—Smith (1776/2019, Book I, Chapter X, Part 1)

Most men have an irrationally high confidence in their own good fortune, and that this is doubly true when their personal prowess comes into the reckoning, when they are betting on themselves.

—Knight (1921, p. 366)

If ... deceit is fundamental to animal communication, then there must be strong selection to spot deception and this ought, in turn, to select for a degree of self-deception, rendering some facts and motives unconscious so as not to betray – by the subtle signs of self-knowledge – the deception being practiced.

—Trivers (1976)

Summary: People tend to exhibit systematically self-serving biases in their beliefs. They tend to think that they are better, smarter, nicer than they are. They attribute their success to themselves and their failure to external factors. They rationalise their errors and misdeeds but cast a critical judgement on others' missteps. Surely, it is a sign that people are just poor at forming judgements about themselves and the world. In contrast to this view, we can explain these belief distortions by the fact that evolution likely selected us to form not accurate beliefs, but beliefs that can be useful. Research has shown that overconfidence, over-pessimism and warped reasoning may be selected features of our cognition, giving us advantages in a range of situations.

Economists assumed for a long time that people collect and process information in a way that gives them an accurate perception of reality. Contrary to this view, empirical research has shown that most people often form beliefs in a systematically biased fashion. They are often overconfident; other times they are overly paranoid.

Having inaccurate beliefs has a cost. An overconfident person may take too much risk in some situations, and pay the price for it. A person overly worried may fail to grab available opportunities. It seems hard to justify such beliefs. If there is proof that humans' ability to make judgements and decisions is flawed, that must be it. Or is it really? If these tendencies to form wrong beliefs have a cost, how did they withstand natural selection? The fact that inaccurate beliefs, like overconfidence, have made their way through evolution suggests that they may not just involve costs. They may also have some benefits. Indeed, I am going to describe here how beliefs that are slightly off from reality may sometimes be useful.

14.1 BIASED BELIEFS

Paranoia

It seems that people can be overly paranoid. One of the best illustrations of this fact is the prevalence of conspiracy theories, whereby some people wrongly believe that other people (usually powerful) are leagued against their interest.

Conspiracy theories are innumerable and they are surprisingly popular. In a 2004 poll, 49% of New York City residents answered that they believed officials of the US government "knew in advance that attacks were planned on or around September 11, 2001", and in a 2006 poll, 36% of US respondents supported the claim that "federal officials either participated in the attacks on the World Trade Center or took no action to stop them" (Sunstein and Vermeule 2009). In a 2013 study on a representative sample, 37% of US respondents agreed with the statement "the Food and Drug Administration is deliberately preventing the public from getting natural cures for cancer and other diseases because of pressure from drug companies", and 12% agreed with the statement that "the global dissemination of genetically modified foods by Monsanto Inc is part of a secret program, called Agenda 21, launched by the Rockefeller and Ford foundations to shrink the world's population" (Oliver and Wood 2014).

Sunstein and Vermeule defined a conspiracy theory as "an effort to explain some event or practice by reference to the machinations of powerful people, who attempt to conceal their role". But one could extend this view to a much broader type of situations. For instance, in organisations like firms, people often form the belief that other colleagues or managers are out to get them. In a study on "organisational conspiracy theory", Douglas and Leite (2017) found that respondents frequently agreed with statements about their organisation such as "a small group of people makes all of the decisions to suit their own interests" or "a small group of people secretly manipulates events".

Obviously, in some cases, the perception of a conspiracy happens to be true, such as in the Watergate scandal. However, successfully coordinating a powerful conspiracy across many actors, without any leakage of information, is hard. The risk of defection is real in conspiracies, and it is greater with larger conspiracies. The high profiles of defections from the highly controlled secret agencies by Daniel Ellsberg (1971), Bradley Manning (2010) and Edward Snowden (2013) illustrate this fact. Maintaining successful conspiracies is difficult, and the price to pay when one is uncovered can be substantial. Examples of famous conspiracies, like the Watergate and the Volkswagen emission cheating scandal, illustrate this fact. Nixon lost his position as president of the United States following the Watergate, and, similarly, the CEO of Volkswagen had to resign when the company's cheating scheme on car emissions was found out.

It would, for these reasons, be surprising for large networks of individuals to frequently engage in hidden conspiracies, with these going unnoticed most of the time. When faced with suspicious facts that could be interpreted as emerging from a conspiracy, it is wise to adopt the ironic "Hanlon's razor": "Never attribute to malice that which is adequately explained by stupidity."

But if successful conspiracies are not likely to be so frequent, why are beliefs in conspiracies so widespread? Are people just delusional without any reason? The psychologists van Prooijen and van Vugt (2018) proposed another explanation. The eagerness to resort to conspiracy explanations may be a good defence mechanism because conspiracies are very dangerous, *if they indeed exist*. The risk of failing to notice a real conspiracy is more dangerous than the risk of being a bit overly paranoid about non-existing conspiracies.

The evolutionary psychologists Haselton and Buss (2000) and Nesse (2001) proposed that this asymmetry in costs may have been selected to lead us to overly detect dangers. Let's consider the case of house fires, as an example of very dangerous events. They come with considerable risks to our well-being and safety. Suppose you observe some signs of a possible fire (e.g., smoke). There are two types of mistakes you can make. You could decide that a fire is unlikely and ignore it. If you are right, you are not wasting your time. If you are wrong, it is a *false negative* error: there was a fire, and you missed it. The consequences could be deadly. Alternatively, you could decide to act, call the firefighters and evacuate the building. If you are right, you escaped from a fire. If you are wrong, it is a *false positive* error: you wasted time while there was actually no danger. When the risky event is dangerous, the cost of making mistakes is generally asymmetric: it is much more costly to ignore a danger than to protect oneself even though there is no danger. Table 14.1 shows the typical costs of each action either protecting from a risk or ignoring it, in each possible situation (whether the danger is real or not).

TABLE 14.1. *Costs when deciding to protect oneself or not from a danger*

	Danger is real	Danger does not exist
Take protective measures	Safe (no cost)	*False positive* (minor costs)
Ignore	*False negative* (large costs)	Safe (no cost)

When the costs are asymmetric, it makes sense to take protective measures even when the danger is less than 50% likely to happen. The higher the cost of a false negative versus the cost of a false positive, the more one should be cautious and take protective measures, even if only weak signals of risk have been observed. Nesse calls it the *smoke detector principle*: smoke detectors typically get triggered too easily. They will get triggered by the smoke from cooking, which is interpreted as a possible risk worth being signalled and acted upon. Having a smoke detector that warns you too often can be annoying. But it is safer than a smoke detector that does not warn you often enough. The 2019 fire in the Notre Dame cathedral in Paris is a striking illustration of this fact. On 15 April 2019, a fire alarm sounded at 18:20 in the cathedral. The alarm was not designed to notify the firefighters automatically; they were called only afterwards and arrived around 19:00 when the fire was already out of control. The 800-year-old building nearly collapsed in the disaster.

The smoke detector principle also explains why we may overreact to potential threats, in particular, threats that were more severe in our ancestral past (Neuberg et al. 2011). The emotion of fear helps us react to perceived threats, and it can be overly triggered in situations where threats are only possible rather than likely. It is the case with dangerous animals. Some people have panic reactions when faced with spiders or snakes. And anybody going camping may become anxious hearing animals outside even in countries where humans have no known predators.

One of the largest threats humans have always faced comes not from large animals but from microscopic germs, which can cause illness and death. While germs are not visible, objects and people carrying them have noticeable features we are designed to detect. Disgust is the emotion warning us to stay away from risks of contamination. Disgust can be overly sensitive in situations that are most likely benign in terms of risk. Consider John and Jane, who look healthy and are present at the same dinner party. The chance that John is carrying germs that could affect Jane is likely low. But when John double-dips their corn chip in the bowl of salsa, Jane may feel disgusted at the idea of dipping her corn chip in the same bowl. A further indication that our sense of disgust is designed to help us stay safely away from contamination is the fact that women's sensitivity to disgust grows in the first semester of pregnancy. At that time, infections could be more dangerous for the offspring they carry (Fessler et al. 2005).

The smoke detector principle does not only work for dangers; it can be reversed for opportunities. This point was made by Haselton and Buss (2000), who coined the term *error management theory* to describe how our tendency to make errors should answer to both the asymmetry in potential costs and the asymmetry in potential benefits of mistakes. They used this argument to explain the differential attitudes of men and women considering potential mates of the other gender. As men tend to have a greater demand for casual encounters, women tend to face more potentially interested partners than men do. As a consequence, opportunities are scarcer for a man and missing an opportunity such as failing to notice that a woman is romantically interested is costly (he may have to wait a while for another opportunity to eventuate). The cost of wrongly inferring that a woman is interested can in comparison be smaller: facing a rebuke. Error management theory suggests that this asymmetry in the cost of errors explains why men have a tendency to be overly optimistic when inferring women's romantic interest.[1]

The asymmetry in benefits was used by Johnson and Fowler (2011) as a justification for the evolution of overconfidence in competitions where the gains associated with joining the competition and winning can be greater than the risks of joining the competition and losing. In such situations, overconfidence may help nudge the individual towards the most competitive attitude.

The asymmetry in costs and benefits also explains another type of perceptual bias: the tendency to over-detect agency. The environment faced by our ancestors was a dangerous one. In many places, pre-humans were potential prey for predators. And the risk of physical violence and death at the hands of other people was substantial. The evidence on small-scale hunter-gatherer societies suggests a level of violence without comparison with our modern societies (Allen and Jones 2016; Keeley 1996). The anthropologist Napoleon Chagnon (1988) famously estimated that, in the Yanomami, a tribe he studied in the Amazonia, nearly half of the males aged twenty-five or older had committed homicide and that a third of them ended up a victim of warfare or crime.

In that context, where threats from animals and other humans were common, detecting the presence of agency in one's surroundings is critical. The information we get from events around us is usually noisy, and we need to make inferences about what this information means. Are these tree branches moving because of the wind, or because of a predator lying in the tree? Are these cracking sounds behind me some twigs naturally falling from a tree, or the indication that somebody is following me? In such situations, it would make sense for evolution to have made us overly cautious and paranoid about perceiving agency. Here too, our ancestors may have been better safe than sorry.

Similarly to our overreaction to snakes and spiders, we may today overreact to the possible presence of agency. In modern homes, people often wake up in the night worried about noises suggesting somebody could be in the house (even in countries where home intrusions are rare). Another bias, possibly associated

---

[1] Such costs have certainly substantially increased since the publication of Haselton and Buss's paper. These changes in cost would predictably lead to changes in courtship behaviour.

with our tendency to over-detect agency, is the phenomenon called *pareidolia*: our tendency to see faces in random patterns such as clouds, stones or the crinkles of our carpet.

This propensity to overly detect agency in our surrounding environment has been proposed as the main explanation for the emergence of religions around the world (Barrett 2000; Boyer 2008). When encountering patterns of mysterious events, people tend to look for explanations involving agency. The mysteries looking for an explanation can be about big questions, such as what are the sun, moon and stars seen in the sky, or more mundane events, such as why John's house burned down last night. The bias in favour of explanations relying on agency can lead to the emergence of beliefs in mischievous spirits behind small-scale unexplained events and in mighty gods behind large-scale mysterious events.

The "error management theory" and the "smoke detector principle" are compelling ideas. They can explain a large range of seemingly puzzling behaviours. Nonetheless, the acute reader may perceive an issue with this line of argument. There is no question that asymmetries in costs and benefits should lead to different tendencies to make decisions one way or the other. But one may wonder why individuals would need to have *false beliefs* to make the right decisions?

With accurate beliefs, people would make the right decisions, if they were making the right cost-benefit analysis. Making more "smoke detector" types of mistakes would then be the best thing to do. Consider Jane, who is a surgeon in a hospital. She receives a test suggesting that John, a patient, has a 10% chance of having a deadly illness. She can order a different test to confirm or disconfirm the first one. Even though the probability of John having a deadly illness is only 10%, the risks involved imply that ordering another test is the right solution, in spite of the costs that may be involved with additional tests. To make this decision, Jane does not need to believe that John is very likely to have the illness. She just has to understand that it is reasonable to order a new test, even when the risks suggested by the first test are fairly low.

The question for the smoke alarm principle and error management theory is, why would evolution's solution to this problem be to endow us with wrong beliefs? Perhaps it is the case because distorted beliefs can be easy and quick solutions leading to the right adaptive behaviour. But wrong beliefs will also have costs. So this question is something that deserves more inquiry from future research.

Overconfidence

Many of the world's greatest catastrophes, avoidable conflicts and ill-conceived enterprises have been linked to overconfidence. Overconfidence is indeed one of the most documented human biases in judgment and decision-making.

Individuals tend to overestimate their abilities and how they compare to others: most drivers believe they are more skilful than average (Svenson 1981); most students think they are smarter than the average student (Gabriel et al. 1994); and in a well-known survey, over 90% of US university professors believed themselves to be better teachers than their colleagues (Cross 1977).[2] Such prevalent misperceptions persist, even when they lead to substantial costs: overconfident traders take too much risk (Barber and Odean 2001); overconfident CEOs make poor decisions regarding investments or mergers (Malmendier and Tate 2005).[3]

Overconfidence occupies a particular place in the collection of behavioural biases. The widespread presence of inflated self-beliefs presents an instance where people are not just making random mistakes; it appears instead as a systematic tendency to venture in self-serving delusions.

The standard viewpoint in psychology and economics has been that overconfidence is a costly strategy that is maintained because of the hedonic and mental health benefits it brings to the overconfident individual, such as enhanced self-esteem, self-efficacy or happiness (Kunda 1987; Taylor and Brown 1988). In short, people simply enjoy basking in the belief that they are better than they actually are. Economists sometimes summarise this idea by saying that overconfidence has a "consumption value".

There are reasons to doubt such an explanation. If overconfidence has only a consumption value, how can it have sustained natural selection? Overconfident organisms trying to increase their subjective satisfaction based on inflated self-beliefs would make costly mistakes. Imagine that Jane has to decide whether or not to climb a mountain to get a financial prize. Climbing presents a risk, but success comes with a reward. If the climb is too challenging for her skills, she would be better off not taking the risk of attempting it. But if she is good enough for the risks to be limited, she should not miss the opportunity to grab the reward. The choice, climbing or not climbing, that will maximise Jane's expected fitness depends on her self-belief about her climbing ability. If she is overconfident, she may opt to climb the mountain when the risks of doing so are too large in comparison to the expected reward. It is easy to see how overconfidence would reduce the expected fitness of individuals in this type of decisions, for example, going hunting after animals that are too dangerous, venturing into an exploratory expedition when the chance of success is too low or trying to swim in a river that has strong currents.

There must be a cost of having systematically mistaken beliefs. It is thus reasonable to expect that natural selection should push beliefs to be accurate.

[2] Besides their abilities, people also tend to be overconfident about their health (Weinstein 1980) and their attractiveness (Epley and Whitchurch 2008).
[3] Overconfidence is also likely to contribute to the fact that most road accidents are due to risky decisions, such as speeding, drinking and using a mobile phone (World Health Organization 2018).

As pointed out by Quine (1969): "Creatures inveterately wrong in their inductions have a pathetic but praiseworthy tendency to die out before reproducing their kind." As a consequence, it is reasonable to think, like Dennett, that: "Natural selection guarantees that most of an organism's beliefs will be true" (1987).

The idea that evolution will naturally select decision-making organisms with accurate beliefs is wrong, however, when the evolutionary process involves *strategic interactions* between these organisms. Heifetz et al. (2007a, 2007b) have shown that in that case, there are always possibilities for the organisms to get higher payoffs by deviating from trying to accurately pursue payoff maximisation.[4] To understand, why let's go back to Jane's overconfidence. When Jane is facing a mountain, there is no gain from being overconfident. Jane's beliefs will arguably have no effect on making the climb easier or harder.[5]

---

[4] It is often assumed that natural selection would create a pressure to select organisms who aim to maximise their expected fitness. This is not always true. When risk of death exist, evolution would also select organisms that may opt for conservative strategies with lower average fitness but lower risk of death (Rubin and Paul 1979; Hintze et al. 2015). Nonetheless, the argument seems reasonable in many situations when risks of death are not large. The equivalent of this argument was explicitly stated by Alchian (1950) and Friedman (1953) in economics: the selection pressure on firms should lead them to maximise their profit. Friedman stated:

Let the apparent immediate determinant of business behavior be anything at all – habitual reaction, random chance, or whatnot. Whenever this determinant happens to lead to behavior consistent with rational and informed maximization of returns, the business will prosper and acquire resources with which to expand; whenever it does not, the business will tend to lose resources and can be kept in existence only by the addition of resources from outside. The process of "natural selection" thus helps to validate the [profit maximization] hypothesis.

Alchian also said that the evolutionary argument "is applicable equally to utility maximization by consumers". The results from Heifetz et al. (2007a) show that the Alchian-Friedman conjecture does not stand when there are strategic interactions between the players (firms, individuals, organisms) being selected. They show that "in almost every game and for almost every family of distortions of a player's actual payoffs, some degree of this distortion is beneficial to the player, and will not be driven out by any evolutionary process". The intuition here is that there are radical differences between a selection process where agents are confronted only with the external environment and a selection process where agents are confronted with other (strategic) agents. In the latter case, deviations from payoff maximisation can have feedback-loop effects by influencing other agents' behaviour, in a way that is beneficial to the agent deviating from payoff maximisation.

[5] One could think that confidence could help make Jane a better climber, but one would then have to explain why evolutionary pressure needed for Jane to believe that she is better than she is for her to increase her ability. A bias in beliefs would be used to compensate for a bias in performance (inability to reach full potential performance under accurate beliefs). This form of "second-best" approach has sometimes been proposed, without giving an explanation about why the performance bias would be selected in the first place. For instance, an influential paper by Bénabou and Tirole (2002) explains overconfidence as a way to enhance the individual's motivation.

But imagine a situation where Jane, walking in the street, faces a robber who wants to take her purse. The robber is stronger than she is and would certainly have the upper hand in a fight. The rational thing to do, if Jane has accurate beliefs about her strength, is to hand over her purse. But suppose that Jane is overconfident and believes she could successfully fight back. Through her stance and statement of confidence, she may be able to successfully signal her belief to the robber, who now has to decide whether or not to engage in a physical fight. He may be aware that he is stronger, but a fight could be costly; it may take too much time to get the purse and another passer-by may intervene. Jane may be able to hurt him in the process, or he may have to hurt Jane and then risk penalties above and beyond the crime of a robbery. Even though the robber knows he is stronger than Jane, Jane's overconfidence may act as a deterrent and lead the robber to back down.

Formally, whenever there are strategic interactions, the misbeliefs of agents about their traits have an indirect effect on the behaviour of other agents who optimally answer to these misbeliefs. Heifetz et al. (2007a) focused on the situations where agents can observe the beliefs of others. In such situations, there are always some misbeliefs that are beneficial to the agent, and these misbeliefs are not eliminated through evolution. When an agent competes with others, being overconfident can help deter others. When an agent works with others towards the same goal, overconfidence can help motivate others to put more effort towards the collective goal.

One way to get the intuition why overconfidence can be beneficial is to see that, when others can observe a person's overconfidence, it can serve as a commitment device (as seen in Chapter 11). By credibly committing the person to act in a way that is different from what would be the "rational" way, it can give the individual a strategic advantage. Note that it is the case even though other people may be aware that these beliefs are wrong and that the agent is just overconfident.

What if people cannot perfectly observe others' beliefs (which is usually the case)? In the extreme case where beliefs are fully unobservable, it is unclear why you would have an interest in being overconfident, since whatever you believe would not influence others. But it is credible to think that beliefs are not fully unobservable. In some cases, it seems that your beliefs can lead you to give cues in your behaviour that can be picked up by others. The fact that poker players opt to wear sunglasses is a tell-tale sign that even facial expressions may potentially leak information about our state of mind. If beliefs are, to some degree, observable, then we may expect that overconfidence can play some role in influencing others. Heifetz et al. (2007b) extended their approach to situations where beliefs are only partially observable and they found that overconfidence can indeed be beneficial in such situations. The next section looks further into the role of overconfidence when others can only imperfectly observe our beliefs.

14.2 THE FORMATION OF BIASED BELIEFS

Self-Deception

In the foreword to Dawkins's *Selfish Gene* (1976), Robert Trivers proposed, in one sentence, a reason for our inaccurate and self-serving beliefs: truly having self-serving beliefs may help to deceive others in social interactions. Trivers' argument is that deception is ubiquitous in animal communication. There is therefore an evolutionary "arms race" between the selection of the ability to deceive and the selection of the ability to detect deception. As a consequence, there must be some selection for an ability to self-deceive in order to mask the signs of deception. There is possibly no other instance where an idea mentioned in the foreword of a book has had so much intellectual influence. In a comment on Trivers' argument, the psychologist Steven Pinker simply stated, "This sentence... might have the highest ratio of profundity to words in the history of the social sciences" (2011b).

The importance Trivers gives to deception in animal communication is supported by the empirical evidence. As stated by Dawkins (1976): "It may well be that all animal communication contains an element of deception right from the start, because all animal interactions involve at least some conflict of interest." Consider one of the frequent situations of conflict in the animal world: a contest for a patch of land. If the two animals claim the land, only one can win. If none of them backs down, the end result may be a costly fight. To avoid such an outcome, which can be hazardous for both of them, they will frequently try to signal their strength to deter the opponent by showing that they would likely have the upper hand in a physical struggle. But they do not have an interest in being honest. A not-too-strong animal has an incentive to bluff, like a poker player with a weak hand, trying to lead other players to believe his hand is strong. If a weak player can convince others that he is the strongest, he can lead them to back down and win the game without a fight. Deception and bluff are common in the animal kingdom. For example, crayfish develop large claws, which suggest a formidable strength in case of a fight, but, in some cases, these claws do not have much muscle in them. They are only a fake display of strength (Angilletta et al. 2019).

The Cues People Give Away When Deceiving
Successfully deceiving others, however, is not straightforward. A key challenge is that others have ways to detect signs of deception. In the case of humans, von Hippel and Trivers (2011) list three types of cues: nervousness, signs of suppression and cognitive load. Nervousness can be associated with deception arguably because deceiving comes with the risk of potential costs if found out (e.g., retaliation). Signs of suppression can become apparent when people try

to mask signs of deception, such as signs of nervousness. Finally, a person's cognitive load may substantially increase when trying to hold a consistent fictional story together while being aware of the truth at the same time.

In an arms race between deception and detection of deception, organisms would get better at both masking these signs and unmasking them. Folk psychology often suggests that there are universal tell-tale signs of deception, such as avoiding eye contact. This idea may have motivated early research on the detection of deception, which frequently consisted in a simple set-up: some people are asked to make a true or false statement in front of a camera, and other people are asked to watch the video and try to detect whether the statement is a lie or not. In such research, the detection of deception is barely above chance: in a meta-analysis of nearly 25,000 participants, psychologists Bond and DePaulo (2006) found an average accuracy rate of 54% in detecting liars from truth-tellers when pure chance already gives a 50% chance of success. This result is not surprising. The existence of universal signs giving away deception is highly unlikely. They would be easy to find out and they would be eliminated in an arms race between skills to deceive and skills to detect deception. Instead, signs of deception are likely noisy, and unveiling deception requires effort.

Imagine that Jane is trying to figure out whether her husband John is deceiving her about his whereabouts last evening. She may be looking carefully at his face and body language while asking him where he was, but she will also typically base her judgement on the facts provided by John to her different questions: Why were you late? Why did you not let me know earlier? Why is it the first time you ever mention to me this issue that required you to stay late at work? Part of the task of finding out whether John is engaged in an act of deception is to figure out whether his factual statements and descriptions of motives and beliefs are credible, given what Jane knows about how John usually behaves. If John tends to be quite absent-minded and does not contact her much, it may be credible that he did not warn her about being stuck at the office late. On the contrary, if John is usually careful of notifying Jane of what he is doing, his lack of notification last evening will seem outside the ordinary. Jane may wonder: Would he credibly do that in normal situations? Would he credibly not expect me to want news from him? It is this assessment that will lead Jane to form a view on the credibility of John's description of where he was.

The research on lying detection using minimal settings where somebody says a lie in front of a camera without being interrogated may stack the odds in favour of the liar. In real-life situations, a liar would have to answer to inquiries (explicit and implicit) in a way that never betrays deception. Furthermore, the stakes are larger in real-life situations: in the artificial setting of an experiment where the participant was asked to lie, the participant may not care whether he is found out to be lying (and this is likely to be understood by the experimental audience). But in our example, the stakes may be high for John if he is found to be deceiving Jane about his actions and whereabouts.

So what happens when studies look at lying detection in situations where observers have the opportunity to counter-interrogate the speakers? It seems that they get much better than chance at finding out who is truthful and who is not. In an experiment, Frank et al. (1993) had participants playing a one-shot prisoners' dilemma game (see Chapter 10). They were told that the purpose of the experiment was to determine whether people can predict who will defect and who will cooperate. Participants were divided into groups of three. Each participant played once with each of the other people in the group. The experimental design ensured that the behaviour of participants was unobservable: the players' final payoff was the sum of the payoffs with the two other partners plus a random variable taking either positive or negative values. This design made it impossible for participants to deduce, from their own payoffs, the behaviour of their partners. As a consequence, it gave anonymity (and potentially more moral impunity) to players to defect in the game. The players had then thirty minutes to discuss before playing the game. During this time they could say what they wanted about their intended actions in the game and plead with others to be cooperative. Given the anonymous setting, there was no way to credibly commit to cooperate, and the verbal exchanges could be considered as cheap talk. These exchanges were not binding in any way the future decisions of participants to cooperate or not. At the end of the thirty minutes, players were taken in to different rooms where they chose their actions in the game and predicted the actions of the other players in their group.

Overall, and in spite of the anonymity, nearly 74% of players cooperated. The question, though, is how well players did at predicting defection or cooperation. And the result is clear: they were very good at predicting whether other players were going to cheat or not. Among the players who were predicted by others to cooperate, 81% did cooperate, and among those predicted to defect, 57% did. These numbers are much better than chance. They suggest that players who intended to defect were not able to perfectly mask their intention and that they gave away their intent over the duration of the discussion.

In a recent experiment, to which I contributed, we found a similar result when participants are asked to detect a deception that had taken place during a prolonged interaction within a group (von Hippel et al. 2016). Groups of friends worked together to find the solution to a problem. Unbeknownst to other group members, one of the participants was secretly asked to try to sabotage the group's effort. While the participants were oblivious to the presence of a saboteur in the group during the task, they were much more accurate than chance when they were told that there was a saboteur and asked to find this one (66% accuracy). The participants became even better when given the opportunity to cross-examine each other over several minutes to discuss their decisions and suggestions in the game (70% accuracy).

These experiments suggest that deceivers are likely to give away signs of deception when trying to convince others. It may be not so much about a twitch in their eyes or a drop of sweat on their forehead, but rather what they say and how they manage to argue and back up their cases. In a recent study on participants' promises and lies in a prisoner's dilemma game played in a game show, Turmunkh et al. (2019) found that participants who intend not to cooperate are less likely to make clear promises about cooperation (e.g., "I will cooperate"). Instead, they are more likely to use implicit promises (e.g., "It would be great to cooperate") and conditional statements (e.g., "Cooperating is best if we both do it").

Therefore, the way people communicate their intent can reveal something about whether their intent is genuine or not. Such communication may not be mere "cheap talk". Conveying a convincing deceptive signal may be more difficult than conveying a convincing truthful signal. If so, self-deception can help convince others, because deceptive signals can become easier to send if you actually believe in them yourself.

Self-Deception and Persuasion

The idea that self-deception can help persuade others has been investigated in experiments. Smith et al. (2017) incentivised participants in an experiment to write a text to convince others about the likeability of a person named Mark. Participants had first to watch videos where Mark engaged in kind behaviour in some videos or unkind behaviour in others. There were many videos, and participants had the choice when to stop watching. When participants were incentivised to persuade others that Mark was likeable, they stopped watching videos earlier when the first videos showed a kind behaviour. On the contrary, when the first videos showed unkind behaviour, the participants watched more of them. This pattern was the same (in reverse) when participants had to persuade others that Mark was not likeable. In short, participants stopped gathering information about Mark when the initial information they received was in the "right" direction (the one they were incentivised to persuade other people). When the initial information was in the "wrong" direction, participants looked for more information to potentially get another view of Mark.

Further studies extended this result to situations where people can gain from lying about themselves. Schwardmann and Van der Weele (2019) incentivised participants in an experiment to convince others about their performance at a task. They found that people tend to form overconfident beliefs. In a related study from our team of researchers, we found that participants were more likely to *select information* supportive of the fact that they had a good performance (Solda et al. 2019). In both studies, more confident participants were eventually more likely to persuade others about their achievement. The formation of overconfident beliefs provided an advantage when participants faced the challenge of trying to persuade others about their performance.

Self-Deception in Bargaining

Another type of situation where self-deception and overconfidence can potentially provide an advantage is bargaining. An important insight from Thomas Schelling is that most interactions present some aspect of cooperation and conflict. Bargaining is a perfect example. Consider a bargaining situation between Jane and John, both have a joint interest in reaching a deal (rather than having no deal). It is the element of cooperation. But there is range of deals possible. Some are more advantageous to Jane and some to John. This tension between Jane's and John's interests is the element of conflict.

Schelling (1960/1980) discussed how bargaining is partly a coordination game where the credibility of claims is critical to determine which solution people will accept to settle for. Persuasion plays a key role here, and one may think that self-deception and overconfidence could help to get better outcomes in bargaining situations.

If self-deception can help convince others, negotiators may benefit from overestimating how much they deserve in a negotiation. Such self-serving biases are indeed observed in situations where bargaining takes place (Babcock and Loewenstein 1997). It has been found, for instance, that when people work together towards a goal, the sum of participants' perceived contributions tends to be *more than* 100%. It is the case in couples, when partners are asked to assess their personal contribution to household chores (Ross and Sicoly 1979) and in groups of scientists asked to assess their personal contribution to a published article (Schroeder et al. 2016).

To investigate the effect of confidence in bargaining, our team of co-authors working on self-deception created an experiment where pairs of participants bargain to split a pot of money. This money comes from their work: in each pair, both participants answer a general knowledge quiz, and their right answers add money to the amount to be shared (Solda et al. 2020). By design, we made sure that participants cannot figure out their exact contribution to the pot of money. We then provided them with pieces of information about their performance, which, on average, were accurate, but which were sometimes erroneous: somebody who did very well would most of the time receive positive feedback but also, sometimes, receive negative feedback. This "noisy" feedback changed the confidence of the participants about their contribution to the pot of money. Those participants who got positive feedback became more confident and those who got negative feedback became less confident. We then placed the participants in a bargaining situation where they had to agree about splitting the pot of money in a markedly unequal manner: a 70%–30% split. Participants had to agree on who would get the large slice and who would get the small one. If they failed to agree, the pot of money progressively diminished, until it reached zero.

What we found was that the variations in confidence we generated with our "noisy" feedback had a significant effect on the participants' outcome in the bargaining process. The ideal scenario was for a participant to be confident following positive feedback and to be facing a less confident player who had received negative feedback. It therefore paid to be *relatively more confident* than the other player to secure a larger payoff. Unfortunately, while confidence paid at the individual level, it was costly at the level of the pair. When both players were confident after getting positive feedback, they ended up worse, as the costly bargaining process took longer.

It is here important to point out that we would expect evolution to select traits that increase *relative fitness* (having greater fitness than others) rather than absolute fitness. In the words of biologist Allen Orr (2009), "natural selection is a differential process: there are winners and losers. It is, therefore, the difference in fitness that typically matters." For that reason, even though generalised overconfidence may be bad for everybody, it may be selected by evolution if being relatively more confident brings relative benefits, as in our experiment. Generalised overconfidence may be an *inefficient evolutionary equilibrium*: being overconfident can be the best response to others being overconfident, but everybody may be worse off as a result.

Self-Deception Helps Us Understand Conflicts

The theory of self-deception as being adaptive and the existing empirical evidence suggest that self-deception may be widespread. It is an important insight to realise that we may be designed not to see the world as it is but instead to see it in a way that is possibly always a bit self-serving.

Consider the following situation: Jane is an engineer working on a personal project to develop a new type of product to solve problems of type A. She mentions this project and her ideas about it to John, who works in the same company. Later on, a meeting is organised in the company to look for ideas for a possible client interested in products solving problems of type A′ (which is related to A). Jane was due to be part of the committee, but she was ill on the day. John is present in the committee and he proposes some interesting ideas about problem A′, in part influenced by his discussion with Jane. As a consequence of his positive contribution to the discussion, he is given the leadership of the team to think of product ideas for the client. When Jane learns this, she is very unhappy with John. She told him about her ideas, and instead of mentioning her project to the committee, he mentioned related ideas and got the leadership of the team. From Jane's point of view, John is using her initial ideas without giving her credit for it. He is doing it knowingly, given the explicit discussion they had together. When Jane let John knows what she thinks, he is genuinely surprised. It's true, he remembers Jane mentioning a project to solve problem A, but these seemed very early ideas and problem A′ is different anyway. He did not think precisely about Jane's project in the meeting. Now thinking about it, he admits to himself that problems A and A′ are quite related, but they are also different, so he finds Jane's reaction disproportionate, and he tries to explain to her that he did not intend to steal her ideas to take the leadership away from her.

This situation will undoubtedly be familiar to many people who have worked in organisations where apportioning blame and merit is critical for career progression. People can spend a lot of time and energy trying to assert who was right and how to interpret what happened in such situations. Our naive psychology tends to look for black and white interpretations and suggests two types of behaviour: honesty and dishonesty. An honest person (let's say, Jane) would look at the objective evidence and make up her mind based on facts; a dishonest person (let's say, John) would hide his ulterior motives and act in a devious way while pretending that it was not the case.

The prevalence of self-deception suggests that, instead, the reality most often comes in shades of grey. On the one hand, Jane may tend to overestimate how clearly she stated her ideas to John, and how close problems A and A' are. This belief bolsters her claim that she should have been considered for the leadership of the project. On the other hand, John may overly minimise the relationship between Jane's ideas and the discussions in the meeting. He may overly emphasise the differences between problems A and A' in his mind. This view strengthens his feeling that his leadership of the team is fully earned and that Jane's reaction is out of proportion. These thought processes may not be fully disingenuous. A key insight from the prevalence of self-deception is that we may all engage in the formation of such self-serving beliefs such that we really believe the world is suitably closer to what would match our interests than it actually is. Jane may tend to believe her entitlement to being selected as team leader is larger than what her existing contribution would objectively warrant. John may tend to overly deny that it would have been natural for him to mention the extent of Jane's contribution in the area, when the leadership position was discussed.

One of the most puzzling insights of the research on self-deception is that we are likely not designed to see the world as it is. Instead, we all tend to see the world with rose-tinted glasses. This certainly explains the frequent differences in people's understanding and expectations about merits and demerits in social situations. These differences are one of the main sources of conflicts in families, in the workplace and in politics. These distortions in our perception of reality are not accidental or random; they serve our interests.

Rationalisation

After doing or experiencing something, we often wonder why we acted or felt that way. In such situations, the evidence suggests that the explanations we come up with are not necessarily the right ones. They are credible sounding *rationalisations*. Rationalisations may be part of the self-deception I just described, but some rationalisation does not seem very helpful to deceive others.

To understand how people reason about their choices, Sharot et al. (2010) designed an experiment using "subliminal choices". Participants were told that the names of two destinations, such as Thailand and Greece, would appear side by side on their computer screen for 2 milliseconds, a duration too short for participants to consciously perceive these names. After this subliminal exposure, participants were asked to choose whether their preferred destination was the one that had been presented on the left of the screen or the one that had been presented on the right of the screen. The corresponding destination was then revealed to them. At the end of a series of such choices, participants were asked to give a rating of the different destinations they had faced in the choice task. The researchers found that participants gave higher ratings to the destinations they had chosen in the subliminal choice task. It seems to make sense that the participants had higher ratings for the options they had chosen. Except there was no real choice in the subliminal task. Participants had been presented with "nonsense scribbles", and a random choice had been selected for them. The belief that they had chosen the options presented to them changed their ratings of these options afterwards. In short, people who believed they had chosen Greece thought they like it more afterwards.

These experimental results are another example of situations where people seem not to know what they like (an issue already discussed in Chapter 8). After observing, being reminded or even being wrongly told about past choices, people may try to find reasons for them and build explanations making sense. This making up of reasons after the choices does not seem rational. Intuitively, reasons should drive choices, not the reverse.

In a thought-provoking article, Cushman (2020) suggests that such rationalisation may be rational. To understand why, let's appreciate that we do not have conscious access to all the factors driving our decision making. As pointed out in Chapter 5, a lot of our decisions are influenced by valuations that are done by cognitive mechanisms beyond our consciousness. In a given situation, we get the information from these mechanisms in the form of emotions. In the example of visiting a flat to possibly rent it, you may *feel* that it is better, safer, more exciting than the others you have visited, without having a clear conscious access to all the factors that have driven these feelings.

This incomplete information about the reasons that drive your choices means that you can recover information from your choices themselves. For instance, consider the situation where you have just chosen a flat to rent, after visiting a few other ones. I may ask you "Why did you choose this one?" And your answer could be: "I don't know, it felt better, I guess because it is closer to my work, and there were positive aspects, such as a lift." As you progress through your reasoning, you are trying to recover the factual elements that influenced the feelings that determined your choice.

This explanation relies on the idea that past choices contain valuable information that you used at the time of choice, but which stayed outside your conscious thoughts. Rationalising past choices can be a way to try to make sense of past actions to recover this information and help you make future decisions.

There are several reasons why past choices may contain information that is worth recovering. First, your memory may be limited. If you do not remember perfectly all the reasons that determined your choices in the past, you should take that into account in your present choices. Baliga and Ely (2011) used this idea to explain why we are often struck by a *sunk cost bias*. Imagine you wait for a bus at your regular bus stop. Suppose it does not arrive on time and you have to decide whether to wait further or to opt for an alternative solution, such as walking to a distant train station. Your decision should be based on your best assessment of the likely arrival time of the bus. Is the bus more likely to arrive as time passes (it was delayed in traffic) or less likely (there is a strike)? As you wonder whether to opt for the train or not, you may think along the line of "I have waited so long for this bus, it would be a pity to abandon now." But the time you have lost is a sunk cost that will be lost whatever decision you make. Your decision should therefore not depend on such costs. The evidence suggests, however, that we typically try to avoid sunk costs and tend to persist too long in costly ventures. While it sounds irrational, it makes sense if we have limited memory. At the time when deciding whether to abandon a costly venture, we may look at the initial choice of engaging in this venture as signalling good reasons that we may have forgotten. Perhaps, in the case of the bus, there are good reasons you have already waited so long. It may reflect your implicit assessment at the time of the likelihood that the bus would be here shortly. We may, as a result, be reluctant to abandon a costly venture too quickly.[6]

Cushman gives other reasons our past decisions can carry some information. When our decisions are driven by instinctive responses, evolution may have encoded in our genes behaviours that reflect a cost-benefit analysis. We may have a phobic reaction to a snake even if we have never seen one before. When asked about such a reaction, we may rationalise that the snake looked dangerous. This rationalisation recovers the underlying reason why our instinctive behaviour exists in the first place.

Situations where our decisions are driven by habits or customs present another case where costs and benefits may be recovered from our actions. Habits may emerge after we initially assessed what was the best behaviour to have. A habit can persist even after the original reasoning behind our decisions is lost. Customs may work like habits at the level of a group. A custom may reflect costs and benefits that were implicitly or explicitly assessed in the past, leading to culturally transmitted norms of behaviour. A good example is social norms about eating and cooking, which often reflect valid concerns towards pathogens (Curtis et al. 2011).

Because all the past (good) reasons for our choices are not always transparent to us, asking ourselves "Why did I do that?" may help us recover useful information that can help us make better decisions in the situations we face in the present. For that reason, rationalisation of choices after the fact may have a rational justification.

---

[6] Hirshleifer and Welch (2002) also show that the lack of memory for the reasons underlying past actions may lead people in some situations to display too much inertia (repeating past actions) and in some other situations to display too much impulsivity (only following recent information).

Warped Reasoning

While some rationalisation may be rational, the evidence on self-deception suggests that our reasoning is regularly biased in self-serving ways. This fact raises an important question: How do we engage in such biased reasoning, without being aware of the truth and how we deviate from it?

This question is natural: Isn't *reason* what helps us get more accurate beliefs about the world to make better decisions? Well, actually, this vision of our reasoning faculties is most likely an illusion. In a brilliant and insightful paper, Mercier and Sperber (2011) argue that our reasoning faculties have most certainly not been selected to help us learn the truth about the world. Instead, the main function of our reason is argumentative: it is to help us persuade others.

In other words, the reasoning ability of our ancestors was not selected because it could help them solve geometric problems or because it could help them to understand whether planets are gods or celestial objects moving far away from earth. Reason helped our ancestors successfully navigate the complexity of social interactions. Being successful usually requires convincing others to follow us, side with us, share with us. When trying to convince others to make a choice, arguing that this choice is good for them is a sensible strategy.[7] Reasoning can help the speaker to put convincing arguments together. For the listener, reasoning is also useful as a tool to exercise *epistemic vigilance*: tracking inconsistencies in others' arguments that may indicate an intent to misinform and deceive.

Mercier and Sperber show how this view of reason helps us understand many of the puzzles observed in human psychology. To start with, people's decisions often do not get better; instead, they get worse, when people are given time to think about it. In the example of a conflict between John and Jane above, one could think that inviting them to think carefully about the situation to find common ground would help. Unfortunately, the evidence suggests that thinking more about the situation may lead to more entrenched positions, because they would both find more reasons to back their current standpoints and grievances. The evidence also shows that people more knowledgeable of a problem tend to be more prone to motivated reasoning, possibly because they have better cognitive tools and an available array of evidence at their disposition to build a strong argument in favour of their position (Kahan et al. 2013; Guay and Johnston 2021).

So we may primarily use reason to put the best case forward to convince others that they should like us, trust us, welcome us. Even when nobody is around to listen to our stories, a lot of our reasoning can be seen as setting up arguments to be ready in case we are suddenly in need of justifying our

---

[7] In particular in hunter-gatherer societies that had a low degree of hierarchy and where typical members could not get others' support just because of their endowed authority.

positions or actions. In short, we may use reason more like lawyers than like scientists: to convince others, not to find the truth.

∴

Far from holding coherent and accurate beliefs, evidence abounds of humans forming systematically distorted beliefs about themselves and others. A particularly salient type of such bias is the existence of widespread overconfidence. These deviations are, it would seem, one of the major pieces of evidence against humans as being rational. But if humans hold distorted beliefs, it is not in a totally incoherent and nonsensical way. We were selected not for being right about the objective nature of the world but for being successful in convincing others in social interactions such as negotiations and competitions. For that reason, holding accurate beliefs may not be a requirement for success; instead, it may be an impediment. We likely have been selected by evolution to see the world in a way that serves our interest. And this bias explains the nature of a wide range of conflicts in social interactions.

PART IV

EPILOGUE

15

Rationality?

There are almost as many definitions of rationality as there are people who have written on the subject.

—Frank (1988, p. 2)

I have always been very uneasy about economists stating that they are producing a theory in which they assume that people are rational utility maximisers.... Let start with utility. I don't understand what it even means.

—Coase (1995)

No formal definition of rationality will be offered. I don't believe in the kind of Platonic ideal that rationalist philosophers seem to have in mind when they appeal to Immanuel Kant's notion of Practical Reason. I think that rationality principles are invented rather than discovered.

—Binmore (2008, p. 2)

Summary: The notion of rationality is at the heart of the economic approach to the study of behaviour. The homo economicus model is, in some areas, simply called the rational action theory. It is therefore surprising that this notion is rarely, if ever, discussed in depth in economic textbooks. When they define rationality, economic texts generally list principles of behaviour that characterise it. But why are these principles sufficient or necessary to characterise rationality? In this epilogue, I dive into the heart of this question: What is rationality? It may seem strange that a book on irrationality ends with a discussion on the definition of rationality. But as this epilogue shows, this definition is, actually, unclear among economists themselves.

This book is about rationality and irrationality. But the reader may have felt a sense of uneasiness as I never really defined rationality very precisely in the first place.[1] Indeed, in Chapter 1, I gave two definitions of rationality: "In everyday use, it typically means that somebody is sensible/reasonable. Economists define rationality according to a few principles of behaviour, like completeness and transitivity." You may note that, in giving these two definitions, I did not explain why rationality should be defined by the principles used by economists. In this epilogue, I would like to address this issue directly by delving into the definition of what rationality is. This concept has undoubtedly been one of the most important in economics. However, remarkably, the exact definition of the term has neither been simple nor unique.

An episode that took place at the start of my PhD illustrates the importance of the concept of rationality for economists, some time ago. As I started my doctoral studies, I was looking for a new topic of research. Having read sociological debates on the causes of inequality in education, I got the idea of translating in an economic framework the idea of a French sociologist, Pierre Bourdieu, about one of the causes of the lowest educational achievements of children from lower economic backgrounds. Bourdieu was a sociologist critical of how the educational system helps reproduce social inequality. He had proposed a theory where, through different mechanisms, children from lower economic backgrounds are penalised and end up reaching lower levels of achievement in school.[2] One of these mechanisms seemed, to me, amenable to analysis through economic modelling. Bourdieu suggested that economically disadvantaged children underestimate their chances of success at school and, for that reason, are less likely to opt for ambitious educational tracks, even if they have the required ability.

As a graduate student, uncertain about the quality/interest of potential topics, I presented this idea to a senior professor. His reaction was swift: "You want to assume that poorer children underestimate their chance of success? But why would they do so? It would be irrational." Damn! I had clearly done something wrong. My research proposal was visibly violating the rule of *rationality*. Unwilling to dare to venture on to dangerous grounds, I quickly followed his advice and went on to studying alternative explanations.

But, in truth, I would have been unable to state explicitly why my proposition was wrong. Undoubtedly, the suggestion that children from lower economic

---

[1] In this chapter, I will discuss the notion of rationality in the context of decisions. I will look at the answers to the question: "What is a rational decision?" In the recent book *Rationality*, Pinker (2021) presents an insightful discussion of rationality in what can seem a broader sense that encompasses the fact of grounding arguments on logically and factually correct elements. All reasoning is arguably, in the end, to make decisions, either between different actions or between different beliefs; the two are therefore linked.

[2] Bourdieu's theory had a Marxist flavour in its criticism of social institutions, and his theory on education (Bourdieu and Passeron 1977/1990) has a similar tone to the Marxist one produced by Bowles and Gintis (1976/2011).

backgrounds underestimate their chances of success implies miscalibrated beliefs. Skilled children who would opt out from university because they underestimate their chances would be making an *error*. But is the existence of an error enough to make a decision irrational? What if you are told something wrong by somebody whom you have good reasons to believe? Are the beliefs you form as a consequence irrational? And if you make a poor decision as a consequence, are you irrational?

Such a conclusion may not seem appropriate. If you made a wrong decision in a situation where you had good reason to believe something wrong, your decision may have been the right one at the time. We can extend this example to situations where whole groups of people get misleading informative signals. An example, for students from low economic backgrounds, could be self-fulfilling prophecies. If disadvantaged students don't see members of the previous generation going to university, they may form the belief that it is too hard. This belief may discourage them from going to university, and their decisions may, in turn, help shape the beliefs of the next generation of students from low economic backgrounds.

So was my proposed assumption "irrational"? What precise definition of rationality should we use to make such a judgement? In truth, there was never only one definition of rationality in economics, and economists' poised assurance about the importance of rationality masks the fact that it is not clear what we should consider as rational or not.

15.1 RATIONALITY AS MAXIMISATION

The word *rational* comes from the French *rationel*, which comes from the Latin *ratio*, reason. It is related to the word *reasonable*, which literally describes an action/idea for which a (good) reason can be given. A rational decision is therefore fundamentally a decision that can be *justified*.

To understand what is rational behaviour, let's think about the type of behaviour that would not be rational. One example of such behaviour could be a decision that is obviously wrong given the available information. This decision would not be justifiable. If, for instance, John wants to go from Paris to Rome and asks for a ticket to Madrid at the Paris train station, it is hard to think of it as a rational decision.

But that example may seem a bit too artificial. Is there any reason to think that John could ask a ticket for Madrid, if he wants to go to Rome? How often have you ever asked for a ticket to a wrong location when ordering at a train station ticket office? If this is what an irrational decision is, it seems a type of decision we are unlikely to make. You may therefore wonder whether any decision can be irrational. Isn't it the case that you always make choices that reflect what you want? You may have a few times in your lifetime been absent-minded and chosen an option you did not want to choose. But such situations would be very infrequent. So isn't it the case that, by this definition of rationality, we must be rational, most of the time?

This fundamental problem was already recognised in Plato's *Protagoras*, where Socrates states that "no one goes willingly towards the bad or what he believes to be bad." A person can act against his better interest only by ignorance of what is best. In our example, John could wrongly jump into the train heading to Madrid because somebody told him that it was the train going to Rome. That would be a mistake. However, it is not clear we would call it irrational. Indeed, at the time of the decision, John would have chosen the option he thought was best. He would have had a good reason to jump in that train.

Shortly after Plato, Aristotle articulated a view that gives a larger place to irrationality.[3] He argued that one can act against one's best judgment for two reasons: impetuosity or weakness. Each time, the deviation is driven by some emotions that lead people to act under the influence of passions, rather than reason.[4] We have seen how the existence of emotions can indeed constrain people's behaviour in ways that they may not be able to rationalise afterwards (Chapter 11). We have also seen that people's willpower is often too weak to resist present desires (Chapter 9). There is therefore credible room for irrational behaviour: in some cases, people may engage in actions they would not be able to justify with good reasons afterwards.

When people are following their best judgement, by making decisions that they can rationalise, they are making the choices that are good for them given their beliefs. Being rational can be considered equivalent to making good decisions. It seems to make sense. But trying to associate the notion of rationality with the quality of a decision leads to another question: What is a *good decision for the decision maker*? If we pause a moment and look at this question, we realise it is not a benign one. It is a profound question. To answer it, let's start with some conventional answers.

One obvious answer is that a good decision is what helps the decision maker get a good life. This answer is not entirely satisfying, though. It naturally leads to another question: What is a good life? A candidate answer could be that a good life is one where people experience *happiness*. But once again, this answer leads to another question: What is happiness? Is it merely joy and the feeling of satisfaction?

The view that a good life can be defined by the experience of subjective satisfaction has often be seen as wrong. In Plato's *Republic*, Socrates explains disparagingly how the pursuit of pleasures and the fear of pain characterises "children, women and slaves and the base rabble", while the best-born and

---

3 *Nicomachean Ethics*, VII, 340 BCE.
4 In Greek, the lack of willpower was labelled *akrasia*, while the ability to follow one's best judgement was *enkrateia*.

best-educated are characterised by "simple and moderate appetites" guided by "reason and right opinion".

Aristotle also addressed explicitly what a good life is, in the *Nicomachean Ethics*.[5] He differentiated it from the mere pursuit of pleasures, an aim he expressed clear disdain for: "most men, and men of the most vulgar type, seem (not without some ground) to identify the good, or happiness, with pleasure ... the mass of mankind are evidently quite slavish in their tastes, preferring a life suitable to beasts" (I.5). Instead, he states: "He is happy who lives in accordance with complete virtue and is sufficiently equipped with external goods, not for some chance period but throughout a complete life" (I.10). The ideal of a good life was later characterised as the pursuit of the highest good, or *summum bonum*, from Cicero[6] to the synthesis of Aristotelism and Christianity by Thomas Aquinas in his *Summa theologica*.[7] The notion of highest good could fit easily in the Christian doctrine, since the notion of a good different from pleasure can be linked with the requirement for virtuous behaviour requested by a higher being.

The idea that there is a hierarchy of goods and that the pursuit of pleasures is not at the top of it has certainly been present all throughout history. Even nowadays, it is common to think that, independently of the pleasure to the ear, there is something superior in an opera piece than in a piece of easy-listening music. This idea leads, however, to a tension: What about people who do not share this view of the highest good? Suppose Jane prefers easy-listening music, or some catchy hip-hop music, rather than, say, an opera piece. Is she wrong about what is really good for her? If we think she is wrong, what do we know better than her about what is good for her?

One of the contributions of utilitarianism has been to abandon such a hierarchical definition of what is good for people. In the *Rationale of Rewards*, Bentham (1825) made a provocative statement: "Prejudice apart, the game of push-pin is of equal value with the arts and sciences of music and poetry."[8] Bentham had been influenced on this question by Hobbes, who had rejected the idea of *summum bonum* in his *Leviathan*. Hobbes simply described man as a rational being pursuing his desires in the best way possible: "Felicity is a

---

[5] Aristotle (340 BCE).

[6] In *De finibus*, Cicero (45 BCE/1869) criticises both reduction of a good life to the pursuit of only physical pleasure or moral excellence: "the life we desire is one fully equipped with the virtues of mind and body; and such a life must constitute the supreme Good". Nonetheless, the excellence of the mind dominates the excellence of the body: "the most desirable of our faculties are those possessed of the highest intrinsic worth; so that the most desirable excellences are the excellences of the noblest parts of us, which are desirable for their own sake. The result will be that excellence of mind will be rated higher than excellence of body" (V).

[7] In this book, one of the most influential of its time, Aquinas (1265–1274/2015) states that "happiness is man's supreme good". But happiness is not the simple satisfaction of pleasures. It requires "wisdom, bodily health, and such like".

[8] Push-pin was a child game involving two players with a pin each trying to be the first to push it across the other player's pin.

continual progress of the desire from one object to another." And for Hobbes, reason is the instrument that allows man to reach this felicity.[9]

Building on these ideas, new thinkers conceived rationality as being about the maximisation of individuals' subjective satisfaction. Going from the individual to the society, Francis Hutcheson, the predecessor of Adam Smith at the University of Glasgow, defined the maximisation of happiness as the objective of economic policy: "That action is best, which procures the greatest happiness for the greatest numbers" (Hutcheson 1725).[10] Bentham later proposed systematising this idea and assessing whether an action is good by measuring whether it increased the amount of pleasure it is likely to generate (so-called *felicific calculus*). This approach describes not just what is good from the individual's point of view but also what the morally right way for an individual to behave in society is. He stated as a "fundamental axiom" that the "greatest happiness of the greatest number ... is the measure of right and wrong" (Bentham 1776). For Bentham, utility conceived as pleasure is something measurable. Its unit is the "faintest pleasure" that can be distinguished (Parekh 2016, p. 115).[11]

This *utilitarian* perspective was developed further by John Stuart Mill, who also saw the pursuit of happiness as the key driver of human behaviour.[12] While Mill was not reducing happiness to the pursuit of material well-being,[13] he restricted the domain of political economy to only a specific aspect of "man's nature": "It is concerned with him solely as a being who desires to possess wealth, and who is capable of judging the comparative efficacy of means for obtaining that end" (Mill 1836). Even though he never used the term itself, Mill is seen as the creator of the "homo economicus" (Persky 1995). The expression emerged first as the "economic man", used as a criticism for the view of humans as selfishly driven by self-interest.[14]

---

[9] Another influential thinker of that time, Locke, had reached a similar conclusion. He viewed man as driven by the pursuit of happiness: "Nature, I confess, has put into man a desire of happiness and an aversion to misery: these indeed are innate practical principles which (as practical principles ought) do continue constantly to operate and influence all our actions without ceasing" (Locke 1689, I. ii.3). Locke saw everything contributing to human happiness as good. "The most considerable under this head is ethics, which is the seeking out those rules and measures of human actions, which lead to happiness, and the means to practise them. The end of this is not bare speculation and the knowledge of truth; but right, and a conduct suitable to it" (I. iii.3).

[10] This view was also developed by the French encyclopedist Helvétius (1758), who joined virtue and interest: public good is the sum of individual goods.

[11] For a presentation of the early history of utilitarian thought, see Pribram (1983).

[12] "Happiness is the sole end of human action" (Mill 1861, chapter IV).

[13] Mill actually reintroduced a hierarchy with the notion of "higher pleasures", the pleasures of the intellect that he thought to be more desirable than other forms of pleasures (Mill 1861).

[14] The transition to the Latin version, homo economicus, came later (possibly from Pareto). In his review of the etymology of this term, Persky quotes an economist disparaging John Stuart Mill's political economy as an approach that "dealt not with real but with imaginary men – 'economic men' ... conceived as simply 'money-making animals'".

Towards the end of the nineteenth century, the marginalist revolution led economists like Jevons, Menger and Walras to lay the foundation of economic analysis on a conception of value derived from subjective utility. The marginalist revolution is often seen as the birth of modern economics. The classical economists like Adam Smith thought that a good's value is derived from the labour it requires. In contrast, the marginalist view is that a good's value derives from its utility, that is, from the satisfaction it gives to the consumer. More specifically, this value derives from the marginal (i.e., additional) utility it provides.

Marginalists were very much interested in the psychology of economic decisions, which in the end drove economic forces. In the line of Bentham and Mill, they perceived individuals as being driven by the pursuit of subjective satisfaction or utility.[15] They treated utility as something measurable. Jevons (1879, p. vii) defined economics as the "Calculus of Pleasure and Pain".[16]

The marginalists developed a quantitative approach to the discipline where individuals are seen as aiming to *maximise* their subjective satisfaction. In that endeavour, they conceived utility as a single dimension aggregating all the subjective satisfactions (e.g., pleasures) and dissatisfactions (e.g., pain) experienced. This point is important. Humans experience a wide range of satisfactions and dissatisfactions in different domains (e.g., sensory experience, social experience). The assumption that all these experiences can be converted into one measure of satisfaction is not trivial, but it makes it possible to think that every choice, even when it involves trade-offs between things, is driven by the maximisation of utility. Following Mill, these economists nonetheless limited the possible sources of satisfaction by considering individuals as economically self-interested.[17] So this maximisation of satisfaction could be roughly approximated by the pursuit of material well-being (e.g., consumption and wealth).

In that perspective, the notion of *rationality* was less central to describing behaviour than the notion of *maximisation*. Individuals pursue the highest level of utility (i.e., subjective satisfaction). This utility is assumed to be an actual quantity in principle measurable, even if not observable. Good decisions are therefore characterised by the maximisation of utility. Choices that maximise utility are straightforwardly rational, since the maximisation of utility is the goal of the individual.

---

[15] This summary brushes over the existence of differences in the perpectives of Jevons, Menger and Walras; see Moscati (2018).

[16] Later, Edgeworth (1881) called the science of the measurement of pleasure "hedonimetry".

[17] "Jevons describes his theory as 'the mechanics of utility and self-interest'; Edgeworth's 'economical calculus' begins with the famous declaration that 'The first principle of economics is that every agent is actuated only by self-interest'" (Bruni and Sugden 2007).

At the time, the properties later associated with economic rationality such as completeness and transitivity were not discussed as desirable as such, but they followed directly from the view of utility as a measurable quantity being maximised.

This view of economic rationality as the maximisation of utility was later superseded by the ordinalist revolution, which purported to remove psychological considerations from the foundations of economics as a science. However, the "maximisation of utility" view (or formally the cardinalist view) never disappeared fully from economics.[18]

15.2 RATIONALITY AS CONSISTENCY

At the start of the twentieth century, the marginalist view faced strong criticisms within economics. The assumption that utility is measurable seemed problematic, given that it is, in practice, not observable. At that time, the influence of positivism, the view that science should be based only on statements about observable facts, was rising.

Under the influence of Pareto, Hicks and, later on, Samuelson, economics progressively changed into a science whose core principles were based on observable actions (i.e., choices), not on unobservable mental states (e.g., satisfaction). In the process, the notion of utility itself changed. From a measure of subjective satisfaction, it became a simple index used to represent the order of preferences of individuals (ordinal utility). If people's preferences follow some principles of consistency, then their preferences can be represented with (utility) numbers allowing economists to use quantitative techniques to study human behaviour. The notion of utility, with this evolution, lost its psychological meaning. By talking of "utility", economists were no longer making assumptions about people's internal mental states.

---

[18] Moscati (2018) suggests that the instrumentalist approach proposed by Friedman played a key role in allowing the co-existence of the views of utility as either a psychological (cardinal) or a non-psychological (ordinal) notion. Friedman proposed seeing economic models as "as if" models without the need to have a position on whether they also reflect how things actually are:

> Consider the density of leaves around a tree. I suggest the hypothesis that the leaves are positioned as if each leaf deliberately sought to maximize the amount of sunlight it receives.... Is the hypothesis rendered unacceptable or invalid because, so far as we know, leaves do not "deliberate" or consciously "seek," have not been to school and learned the relevant laws of science or the mathematics required to calculate the "optimum" position, and cannot move from position to position? Clearly, none of these contradictions of the hypothesis is vitally relevant; the phenomena involved are not within the "class of phenomena the hypothesis is designed to explain"; the hypothesis does not assert that leaves do these things but only that their density is the same as if they did. (Friedman 1953, pp. 19–20)

A critical step in this process was the axiomatisation of utility functions: the process of finding simple principles of behaviour, which, if respected, would justify modelling behaviour as a maximisation of utility. These principles are typically labelled *axioms*. For choices between goods, major contributions to this axiomatisation were made by Samuelson, Houttaker and Afriat.[19] For choices between risky options, major contributions were made by von Neumann and Morgenstern first, and later Savage. These axiomatisations show that if a person's choices respect a few principles of consistency, then it is *as if* these choices are explained by a utility function whereby the person ascribes a utility number to each of the things (goods/risky options) considered and chooses the one with the highest utility.

In this as-if approach, no assumption is made about utility representing something about the psychology of the individual. The utility values do not explain the choices, they do not drive it. The possibility of using such values to reflect choices is simply a *consequence* of the consistency of choices. The utility values reflect only the order of the preferences, not some actual value as such. Given this focus on utility as reflecting an ordering of preferences, this movement became known as the ordinalist revolution.

Relative to the marginalist revolution, this new approach shifted the concern about rationality. For the marginalists, as for the utilitarians before them, rationality was reflected in the maximisation of a measurable thing, utility. The consistency of behaviour was a consequence of this maximising behaviour. For the economists who carried out the ordinalist revolution, the notion of rationality became attached to the consistency of behaviour itself. This consistency delivers a maximisation of utility that is convenient for analysis. But an individual's rationality is assessed by the respect of consistency in choices.

With the positivist turn, economists kept the consistency, which was a property of behaviour in the maximisation of cardinal utility, without having to assume that utility is an actual quantity of satisfaction. As we moved away from maximising something, the word *rationality* became associated with a characterisation of rules of behaviour.

But if we abandon the maximisation of utility as a primary explanation of human behaviour, why should principles of consistency be given pre-eminence under a label of "rationality"? Why should people follow these principles rather than others, now that these principles are not the by-product of a desirable maximisation of subjective utility?

To answer this question, let's look at the principles of consistency used by economists to characterise rationality. The choice of the term *axiom* is noteworthy. It comes from ancient Greek and describes a statement that is *self-evidently true*. So, calling these principles axioms suggests that they are

---

[19] It seems that the first axiomatisation of utility function was made my Alt (1936); see Moscati (2018, p. 107).

undoubtedly desirable properties of rational choices. A closer look at the key economic axioms of rationality shows, however, that they are not necessarily so evident.

Principles (Axioms) of Rationality

Completeness

Let's start with the axiom of completeness, which we already discussed in Chapter 8. It states that an agent is always able to rank two options in terms of preferences (or else be indifferent between the two). The completeness axiom rules out situations where individuals do not know which options they prefer. This axiom is often presented as benign, as if it "only" means that people should be able to make choices between options.

But this axiom is actually far from trivial. In many cases, we can get stuck when facing a decision and not be able to ascertain which option we really prefer. As stated in the most influential microeconomics textbook already cited in our earlier discussion of completeness: "Introspection quickly reveals how hard it is to evaluate alternatives that are far from the realm of common experience" (Mas-Colell et al. 1995). Indeed, we have good reasons to think that *preferences cannot be complete*, given the complexity of forming complete preferences. As pointed out by Bossaerts and Murawski (2017), even in mundane decision situations like going to the supermarket, "The number of choice sets available to the decision maker is effectively infinite." Given that attention is limited, decision makers may end up considering only a subset of the available alternatives, ignoring all others (Caplin et al. 2019). So, completeness seems like an unrealistic assumption.

One could ask an even more fundamental question: Should completeness be even seen as a *requirement* for rationality? Consider Jane having to choose between options with attractive features on different dimensions. She may hesitate between doing studies in classical literature, which is her passion (better choice for her personal self-fulfilment), and doing studies in business (better choice for her economic prospects). She may not know how to trade off these features to make the right choice between the two options (Sugden 1991). If we think that all different subjective considerations can be integrated into one single dimension, then Jane should be able to know how to trade off these different features. But assuming that this integration is possible would reintroduce a psychological vision of utility to justify the axiom. Instead, the modern economic approach is to propose the axiom as a first principle, which self-evidently characterises rationality. Without the assumption of a single dimension of utility it is difficult to say why Jane should necessarily feel that there is only one right way to make a decision in this difficult situation, in order to be rational.

Saying that the completeness axiom is a key principle of rationality implies that it is irrational to be conflicted about different considerations when facing a choice such that one is unsure about the best decision. In contrast to this idea, I suspect that many people would think that, in some cases, it is reasonable to be conflicted. It is perhaps not clear whether there is always a "better" choice.[20] Classical dilemmas of choice often feature situations where the decision maker is conflicted between choices associated with incommensurable outcomes such as loyalty and love (Shakespeare's *Romeo and Juliet*), honour and love (Corneille's *Le Cid*), material success and self-esteem (Balzac's *Père Goriot*).

Indeed, a criticism frequently addressed to economists is that they believe that everything can be traded off with everything else, in particular, with money. On many issues, people feel that there are dimensions that cannot be traded off with others. These limitations are called *taboo trade-offs* in psychology. For instance, most people think that it would be wrong to put a price on human organs, for them to be exchanged. The simple fact of considering this idea may feel morally repulsive.[21]

One solution would be to say that completeness must be a requirement for choices to be rational because people need to be able to make choices in the first place. If people are not able to make choices, there can't be rational choices, by definition. By saying this, we can restrict ourselves to analysing only the situations where choices are being made. We may concede that there is a wide range of choice situations where people are not sure how to make choices. These situations do not reflect necessarily an irrationality, but they lie outside the realm of rationality: you cannot reason about what does not exist. This redefinition heavily restricts the meaning and strength of the completeness axiom. It does not say anything about how much we can expect this axiom to apply to people's preferences. And it does not address the previous critique: What if people find it reasonable not to be able to make decisions in some cases? If we adopt this restricted role for the axiom of completeness, it may be a requirement for rational choices, but not for rationality as such.

Reflecting on these issues, Aumann (1962) stated: "Of all the axioms of utility theory, the completeness axiom is perhaps the most questionable. Like others of the axioms, it is inaccurate as a description of real-life; but unlike them, we find it hard to accept even from the normative viewpoint."[22]

---

[20] An extreme case is presented by the particularly cruel dilemma depicted in Styron's novel *Sophie's Choice* (1979), where Sophie, sent to the Auschwitz camp during World War II, is asked to choose one of her children to be saved.

[21] For a general discussion, see Fiske and Tetlock (1997). I discussed the implications of this notion in the specific setting of the COVID-19 epidemic (Page 2020).

[22] Aumann showed that a theory of expected utility can be developed without the completeness axiom. Something is lost along the way (the utility is not unique anymore). But many properties of the von Neumann and Morgenstern utility are retained, such as looking at choice problems as a maximisation of utility. Aumann remarked that the possibility of developing an expected utility theory without the completeness axiom was already suggested by von Neumann and Morgenstern (1944, p. 630). Aumann's work has been further developed by Dubra et al. (2004).

Transitivity

Transitivity is the second canonical axiom in the economic theory of decision. It states that, if John likes option A more than option B, and option B more than option C, then he should like option A more than option C. This axiom seems reasonable and is widely accepted as intuitively compelling. It has been described as a "hallmark of rationality" (Arrow 1951/1963, p. 22) and the "cornerstone of normative and descriptive decision theories" (Tversky 1969, p. 31).

Nonetheless, let's ask why we should adopt this principle as describing good decisions. It is obvious that, if John is maximising his subjective utility as a measurable quantity, then it must be the case that if his utility is greater for A than B, and greater for B than C, then it has to be greater for A than C. But if John is not maximising a quantity of utility, then *why* should transitivity be a primary principle of rationality?

The most influential argument in favour of transitivity was made by Davidson et al. (1955), in the form of the *money pump*: an individual with preferences violating transitivity could potentially be faced with a series of transactions leaving him with strictly less money without any change in his endowment in goods. The idea is the following: let's consider John, who has $100 and ten units of goods A, B and C each. Suppose John prefers good A to B, and good B to C, but also good C to A. His preferences thereby violates transitivity. You could take advantage of this intransitivity by proposing a series of exchanges to him. Take a look at the three exchanges below. John may accept them because each time he gets a unit of his preferred good for only a tiny additional cost of $1.

1. You'll give John one unit of good B, if he gives you one unit of good C, plus $1.
2. You'll give John one unit of good A, if he gives you back the unit of good B you just gave him, plus $1.
3. You'll give John one unit of good C, if he gives you back the unit of good A you just gave him, plus $1.

At the end of this series of exchanges, John would have the same quantities of goods A, B and C he had when he started, but he would have *less money*: $97! If you renew this cycle of transactions, you could progressively "pump" all the money out of John's pocket without changing his final endowment of goods. This money pump suggests that is it wrong to violate transitivity.

How compelling is this argument? There is, at the very least, a tension between the transitivity axiom, which characterises the preference of an individual at a given moment in time, and the money pump argument, which presents a series of choices made over time. One could, for instance, perfectly conceive John having preferences violating transitivity at any given moment in time. That could be observed when only one choice is elicited from time to time from him. But when faced with a money pump, John may realise he is simply losing money, and could then change his preferences in that situation. Changing his preferences when he realises he faces a money pump would not on principle prevent John from having intransitive preferences, when he is confident that no money pump is being implemented. Fishburn and LaValle (1988) summarise this argument: "Sensible people with cyclic preferences would simply refuse to get involved in the money pump game." The money pump argument is often used as suggesting that it would eliminate irrational intransitivity through a process similar to natural selection: intransitive decision makers would be taken advantage of and replaced by rational decision makers. But it is not clear that the money pump argument would necessarily back such a selection, given the possibility for decision makers to change their preferences over time.[23]

The stance that being safe from money pumps is a requirement for rationality raises another issue in the context of choices among risky prospects. This requirement imposes that decision makers must be *risk neutral*: they must choose the prospects that maximise expected value. Any decision maker who would deviate from maximising expected value – for instance, being risk averse as seen in the St Petersburg paradox (Chapter 6) – would be exposed to a *Dutch book*, a series of transactions that would lead to a loss of money (de Finetti 1931; Wakker 2010). Dutch books can then be used to create a money pump. This fact makes the avoidance of money pumps/Dutch books a very strong requirement that excludes preferences accepted as rational by economists. Reviewing the role of this argument in the theory of choice under risk, Yaari (1985) concludes that "as economists, we face the following dilemma: We must either take the extreme position that all agents are risk-neutral or else agree that agents would, in general, be vulnerable to Dutch Book. If nonrisk-neutral behavior is economically viable, then vulnerability to a Dutch Book must also be economically viable."[24]

Following these arguments and other ones, a number of thinkers have dissociated the notion of rationality from the principle of transitivity. Anand et al. (2009) describe the "modern view" on rationality as holding that "it is perfectly possible for rational agents to have intransitive preferences".

---

[23] It is also not clear that people would necessarily accept the money pump argument as a compelling one to make their choice transitive. In a fascinating interview that took place in 1968, Sarah Lichtenstein explained to a participant that his choices were inconsistent and could be used to create a money pump, even though the participant understood the problem. He stuck to his initially stated preferences (Lichtenstein and Slovic 2006, appendix 3). This interview was pointed out to me by Kirby Nielsen.

[24] See also Cubitt and Sugden's (2001) discussion of money pump arguments. They initially state: "how convincing money pump arguments are as a defence of consistency postulates is a matter of unresolved debate". After a formal discussion of the ability of money pump arguments to impose consistency in preferences, they conclude that "in relation to what we take to be their original objectives, money pump arguments are a failure."

Independence of Irrelevant Alternatives

In Chapter 8, we saw that economists think that choices between several options should be independent from the other options not considered (hence irrelevant). This principle, formally stated by Chernoff (1954) and Radner and Marschak (1954), is widely considered as an obvious principle for rational choice.[25] It is a direct consequence of the respect of completeness and transitivity (Wakker 1989, chapter 1). It imposes that your preferences between two options cannot depend on the menu of options they are presented in. Suppose you look at a restaurant menu proposing either (A) steak or (B) chicken. If you choose (A) steak you should not change your mind for (B) chicken if the waiter suddenly tells you that (C) fish is the special dish of the day. If you are not choosing fish, it is irrelevant. It should not change your preference between steak and chicken.

We have seen, in Chapter 8, that this principle is often violated by people making decisions as a function of the menu they face. How undesirable are such violations? One should appreciate that the principle of independence of irrelevant alternatives makes sense as a principle of rationality in situations where non-chosen alternatives are truly irrelevant to evaluating the alternatives being considered. It is the case when a decision-maker has complete information about the implications of each choice (e.g., how much the decision maker will enjoy the consequences of each decision afterwards). In that case, the choice between two options does not depend on the menu of choice they are inserted into. We have seen in Chapter 8 that decision makers often do not credibly have this level of information when making choices. In such cases, the menu of options can play a role by providing information to the decision maker about the options to consider. It is then not clear that the options not chosen are irrelevant.

A second criticism is that even if the decision maker has complete information about the options being chosen, it may not be the case for an observer. As a consequence, the observer may see what looks like violations of the independence of irrelevant alternatives while there are none really from the point of view of the decision maker. It is the case, for instance, when the menu available changes the value of the options due to social norms or signalling concerns. Sen (1993) gives the example of the choice between different slices of a cake. If you do not want to be seen as taking the largest slice available, you may opt for the second-largest slice, which will depend on the slices available. In such a situation, the decision maker is choosing not just between slices but

---

[25] Note that the term "independence of irrelevant alternatives" is used to characterise related but different principles. See Ray (1973) for a discussion of the different uses of this term. I will focus here on its use to characterise the rationality of individual decisions, following Radner and Marschak (1954). An earlier formal statement of a similar principle is by Nash (1950) in his discussion of good bargaining solutions. It has also been used to characterise a good property of social choice procedures, following Kenneth Arrow (1951/1963) in a way that can be retraced to eighteenth-century thinker de Condorcet (1788) discussing good rules to select winners in elections. See McLean (1995) for a discussion of the history of this principle.

between slices and the signals they convey. An observer who does not appreciate the actual domain of choice of the decision maker could wrongly conclude that the decision maker violates the independence of irrelevant alternatives. Unless an observer has perfect knowledge about the considerations used by a decision maker, it is not necessarily clear that apparent violations or the independence of irrelevant alternatives for the observer reflect actual violations for the decision maker. I revisit this point below.

Another type of criticism was leveraged by Sugden (1985). He points out that the evidence suggests that people experience *regret* when finding out what they get compared to what they would have got if their choice had been different. Regret is, by definition, dependent on the menu of options (I do not experience regret about the outcome of an option I would not have been able to choose). With his colleague Loomes, Sugden has proposed that people anticipate this possible regret and take it into account in their decision (Loomes and Sugden 1982). As a consequence, decision makers will violate the independence of irrelevant alternatives.[26] Sugden remarks that people commonly experience the feeling of regret and that it is therefore sensible for them to accommodate their choices to the prospect of this feeling in the future. We are faced with a situation of conflict between what economists call rational and what people are willing to do. In that case, it is not clear why the principle should be labelled rational: "It may be logically coherent to define 'rationality' so that certain sensations count as irrational, but if these feelings are common in the population, such a definition is hardly helpful" (Sugden 1985, p. 174).[27]

Independence Axiom
The axiom of independence, under its different versions, has been at the heart of expected utility theory (e.g., *strong independence axiom*; Samuelson 1952,

---

[26] Note that the discussion of this notion by Radner and Marschak (1954) was initiated by a criticism of the idea from Savage (1951) that people aim to minimise the maximum possible regret they could face.

[27] Note that there is also a very different sense in which the term "irrelevance of independent alternatives" is used. Since Luce (1958), it has also referred to how the *probability of choice* of an option should change as a function of the menu. We have seen, in Chapter 8, that choices seem to have a random aspect. When faced with two options A and B, a decision maker will sometimes choose A and sometimes B. We can consider the probability of choosing A as reflecting the preference of the decision maker for A relative to B. The hypothesis introduced by Luce is that, if another alternative is introduced, C, the ratio P(A)/P(B) should not change.

An example can make this principle easy to grasp. Suppose that when offered to choose between an orange and an apple, you choose the orange 2/3 of the time and the apple 1/3 of the time. If a pear is added to the basket of fruits you can choose from, you should still choose the orange twice as often as the apple. So, if you choose the pear 1/2 of the time, then you should choose the orange 2/6 of the time and the apple 1/6 of the time. This principle has been important in economics. Luce showed that it implies a specific type of a random utility model. And McFadden built on this to propose a specific random utility model respecting this principle, the *multinomial logit* (McFadden 1973, 2001). It has been a workhorse model to analyse individual choices between different alternatives in economics and other social sciences.

p. 672) and subjective expected utility theory (*sure thing principle*; Savage 1954, p. 218). This axiom, which should not be confused with the principle of independence of irrelevant alternatives,[28] has played a key role in the debate on economic rationality. As discussed in Chapter 7, the empirical rejection of the axiom of independence led to the development of non-expected utility theories where individuals weight probabilities (e.g., overweight small probabilities) when making decisions.

One of the fascinating aspects of this axiom is that it was not included in Von Neumann and Morgenstern's initial axiomatisation. Shortly after the publication of their book, several economists identified that an axiom was missing. Samuelson surmised that Von Neumann and Morgenstern had "implicitly added a hidden and unacceptable premise to their axioms" (Samuelson 1950).[29]

The axiom of independence means that there is no interdependence between different outcomes included in a lottery. I used as a metaphor, in Chapter 7,

However, it is well known that people do not respect this principle, and an important part of the research in econometrics of choice has been to develop models not imposing this constraint. It is also widely accepted that we should not expect rational decision makers to necessarily follow this principle. The classical criticism of this principle came from Debreu (1960), reviewing Luce's book one year after its publication. Debreu described what is now usually called the *red-bus/blue-bus problem*. Interestingly, Debreu used not buses in his argument but pieces of music from Debussy (Quartet) and Beethoven (Eighth Symphony with two different conductors). The earliest version of the bus example seems to be from Mayberry (1970). Here is the bus example: suppose a person takes the car 50% of the time and a blue bus 50% of the time. If a red bus is added to the line, the traveller, who may be indifferent to the bus' colour, may make the following choices: car 50%, blue bus 25%, red bus 25%. But these choices, which seem very reasonable, violate Luce's principle of independence of irrelevant alternatives since the ratio of car to blue bus is now 2 to 1!

[28] Since the principle contains the term "independence", it is useful to explain how it differs from the axiom of independence. The axiom of independence is used to characterise decisions between risky lotteries, but we can give an analogy in the case of decisions between goods to make the comparison with the independence of irrelevant alternatives intuitive. The axiom of independence says that you should not change your choice between two options if something common in the two options is changed for something else. In practice, if you are in a restaurant and you have the choice between (A) steak and mashed potatoes and (B) grilled chicken and mashed potatoes and you choose the steak, your choice should not change if the waiter tells you they ran out of mashed potatoes and your choice is actually between (A') steak and peas and (B') grilled chicken and peas. Note that it is not just an analogy; the axiom of independence is related to the notion of conjoint independence in consumer theory, which is the one used in the example (Fishburn and Wakker 1995). As I have pointed out already, this principle is not compelling in this situation. Mashed potatoes may combine better with steak and peas better with chicken. It is this possibility of interactions that was at the centre of the debate about the axiom of independence.

In comparison, the independence of irrelevant alternatives says that your choice between (A) steak and (B) grilled chicken does not depend on whether (C) fish is on the menu or not. In short, the axiom of independence is about the irrelevance of what options have in common when making a choice between them. The independence of irrelevant alternatives is about the irrelevance of options not chosen when choosing from a menu of options.

[29] This section takes a lot from the fascinating recollection of the early debates around the independence axioms described in Moscati (2016).

about the way objects weigh on balancing scales. If a banana and an orange are in perfect balance on scales, they will stay balanced if you add identical apples on each side. It does not matter that one apple is sitting with a banana on one side, and the other apple is sitting with an orange on the other side. There is no interaction between the weight of these objects; the weight of the apples is added on each side independently of what is besides the apple. This same principle underlies expected utility. If somebody is indifferent between two lotteries, changing identical elements in these lotteries with other elements, which are also identical, will leave the decision maker indifferent.[30]

At first, Samuelson was fiercely opposed to such an assumption as it imposes a sort of additivity of utility, which is a strong restriction. In the case of utility for goods, a similar assumption would imply that the value of each good in a basket does not depend on the other goods present in the basket. It is an assumption too strong in the case of a basket of goods. Suppose Jane is shopping and is indifferent between a basket with a jar of dipping sauce and a basket with a jar of chocolate spread. If you add a pack of corn chips in each of these baskets, it is reasonable to assume that she may prefer the basket with a jar of dipping sauce and the corn chips to the one with the chocolate spread and corn chips. It is because the values of these goods are not independent. The value of the jar of dipping sauce may be higher for Jane when associated with a bag of corn chips.

A series of exchanges took place around 1950 between Samuelson, on one side, and Friedman, Marschak and Savage, on the other. Marschak notably pointed out to Samuelson that, in the case of lotteries, the outcomes are never realised together. The assumption of independence is, therefore, more reasonable than in the case of baskets of goods. If a lottery says you have 50% chance of getting $100 and 50% chance of getting $50, you will, in the end get only either $100 or $50. Thus, it can be reasonable to assume that the utility of $100 in the lottery does not interact with the utility of $50.[31]

This argument contributed to convince Samuelson that the independence axiom was a reasonable principle, not imposing unrealistic constraints on behaviour. But Samuelson was also concerned with the normative nature of this axiom: he was not convinced that it should be included among the axioms defining rational behaviour (Moscati 2016, p. 229). Through a series of exchange of letters, Savage finally managed to convince Samuelson that a "sane

---

[30] See Fishburn and Wakker (1995) for a discussion of the different variants of the axiom and their relationship with the principle of independence in consumer theory and the principle of monotonicity.

[31] Marschak considered a man who is indifferent between beer and tea. Under the independence axiom, this man should also be indifferent between a lottery giving either beer or pretzels and another lottery giving either tea or pretzels. Marschak wrote: "I should not expect ... [the] man to tell me that the mere co-presence in the same lottery bag of tickets inscribes 'pretzels' with tickets inscribed 'tea' will contaminate (or enhance) the enjoyment of either the liquid or the solid that will be the subject's lot" (cited in Moscati 2016).

preferer" would respect the independence axiom. In a 1950 letter, Samuelson reluctantly, but firmly, accepted that the independence axiom should be part of the definition of rational behaviour. This agreement led to the adoption of the independence axiom and expected utility by Samuelson, Friedman, Savage and Marschak in the early 1950s, and expected utility theory took centre stage in economics.

One cannot help but noticing, however, that the independence axiom was anything but "self-evident". It took some time to emerge clearly from the discussions between these leading economists, and there were fundamental disagreements about its credibility as describing actual behaviour and about its requirement to characterise rationality. Given that three of the aforementioned economists were awarded Nobel Prizes, the fact that it took so long for them to agree is telling.

But another interesting aspect of this debate is how it was carried. How did these economists determine whether a principle should be considered rational or not? There was no rigorous methods such as formal logic to prove that an axiom characterises rationality or not. In practice, economists used examples and a call to the readers' intuitions. When introducing the sure-thing principle, a version of the axiom of independence, Friedman and Savage (1952) state: "We anticipate that if the reader considers this principle, in the light of the illustration that precedes and such others as he himself may invent, he will concede that *the principle is not one he would deliberately violate*" (p. 469, emphasis added). In this example, as in others, it is our intuition of what should be done that is called upon to adjudicate whether the principle should be considered as part of the definition of rationality or not.

As we have seen in Chapter 7, the independence axiom quickly faced serious challenges, with empirical data showing that it was very often not followed by people. Indeed, even Savage violated it, when Allais presented him with a series of choices in 1952. Today, whether or not the independence axiom should be considered as a normative principle is still debated.[32]

The empirical validity of the independence axiom also faces another problem: unlike Savage, many people who happen to violate the independence axiom do not change their choices, even after the axiom, and how it relates to their choice, is explained to them (Gilboa 2009, p. 140).[33]

---

[32] See McClennen (2009) for a critical presentation of the arguments in favour of the normative position.

[33] This observation was already made by MacCrimmon (1968) in one of the early experiments testing the validity of expected utility theory. In the case of the independence axiom, he found that a large proportion of subjects violated it in different choice situations. When interviewed by the experimenter and told about the normative justification of this axiom, 25% of participants still preferred not to follow this axiom in all choice situations. This fact was pointed out by Quiggin (1982) in his paper as a justification to propose his alternative theory to expected utility. For a recent study looking at the propensity of people to change (or not) their choices when confronted with their violation of the axiom of independence, see Nielsen and Rehbeck (2022).

This fact is a bit problematic for an axiom considered as a normative principle people should follow. If a substantial proportion of people reject this principle, even after they are told about the reason why this principle may be desirable, what is our ground to label their behaviour as "irrational"? To be able to apply such a label we would need an external rule that determines what is rational and what is not. But such a rule does not exist, and the way the discussions between Samuelson, Savage, Marschak and Friedman proceeded illustrates this fact: in the end, they and their intuitions on the matter were the final judges on whether the independence axiom reflects rational behaviour. So if some people's intuition stays in conflict with the independence axiom, even after a lengthy and clear exposition, what allows us to describe their behaviour as irrational?

If people are the judges of what they should do – as assumed by economists – it is rather inconvenient for the status of a decision theory if people do not want to follow it. Not only it is not an empirically relevant theory, but it is not clear either why it should have normative value. Reflecting on this issue, Gilboa (2009) concludes: "If ... people shrug their shoulders when we explain the logic of our axioms, or admit that these are nice axioms but argue that they are impractical, we should better refine the theories" (p. 141).

Bayesianism

Taken together, the axioms of Savage – completeness, transitivity, independence and a few others – imply that the rational way of choosing between different options is to act *as if* your belief about the possible outcomes of uncertain events takes the form of a *subjective probability*. When it is the case, the decision maker's belief about the plausibility of these outcomes respects the rules of consistency of a probability measure.

There is no restriction on these subjective probabilities. They could potentially be anything, providing that they respect the rules of a measure of probability. However, it is reasonable to assume that, for rational decision makers, these probabilities would reflect their information about the different possible events.[34] Moreover, Savage's axioms also imply that a decision maker would update these subjective probabilities using Bayes' rule to incorporate novel information. In that sense, Savage's theory really provides the foundation of a Bayesian theory of decision-making. In Bayesian terms, the initial distribution of beliefs of the decision maker is a *prior distribution of probability* (or "prior") and it becomes a *posterior distribution of probability* (or "posterior") once the decision maker receives new information and updates the prior distribution using Bayes' rule.

---

[34] Note that in the same way that the utility from ordinal theories does not require being seen as a subjective satisfaction, the probability measure in Savage's model does not require being seen as a subjective belief. Nonetheless, it is how it is most often interpreted.

Bayesianism is a very influential conceptual framework in statistics, and in many scientific disciplines, it is widely seen as the right way decisions should be made, including the decisions of scientists between hypotheses. It may, therefore, seem surprising to ask the question "Is it always rational to satisfy Savage's axioms" as Gilboa et al. (2009) did.

A key argument they put forward is that "in the absence of information, choosing a prior is arbitrary. If the prior is to have meaningful implications, it is more rational to admit one does not have sufficient information to generate a prior than to pretend that one does" (p. 285).[35] In practice, in the absence of information, one could think that an "ignorance prior"[36] can easily be identified. Such a prior is a distribution of probability that gives equal probability to all possibilities, reflecting our ignorance about the relative chances of the events. It is the principle of *insufficient reason*, initially stated by the French mathematician Laplace (1814). Suppose you watch a race between ten horses. If you know nothing about horse races, it may seem reasonable for you to give a priori a one in ten chance to win to each of them. This seemingly simple solution is deceptive, however: ignorant priors are typically not uniquely determined.

Imagine the following situation. Jane is considering going to a party. She is told that only one type of alcohol will be served: either wine or beer. Jane really dislikes beer and would like to make her decision whether to go or not on an assessment of the probability that wine will be served. But Jane has no idea about the preferences of the party's organisers. She has no idea about the type of alcohol that will most likely be served. In that case, the principle of insufficient reason could seem to suggest that the right ignorant prior is to consider wine and beer as equiprobable: 50%–50%. But that choice heavily depends on the binary division of the set of possibilities. Why not entertain other ways to divide the possibilities? Suppose that in Jane's country, there are ten varieties of beer being sold and twenty varieties of wine. Why not give the same probability to each variety of wine and beer? In that case, an ignorant prior would give a two thirds' chance that wine will be served at the party. There is no rule to decide which one of these ignorant priors is better than the other. And the choice of prior matters for Jane's choice. She may decide to go to the party if she believes that there are more than a 60% chance that wine will be served and opt not go if she believes there is less than a 60% chance. It is easy to realise that this problem does not stop at two priors. There may be many other reasonable ways to split the possible categories of alcohol: colour, sweetness/bitterness and so on. The choice of a prior will be arbitrary and it may seem strange for Jane to act on such a prior as if it were an informative belief (e.g., to choose to go because she used an ignorant prior on the varieties of wine and beer rather than on the overall categories of wine and beer).

---

[35] Even in the presence of information, a Bayesian prior, to be consistent, has to be a posterior belief given the available information. This posterior would use this evidence in a Bayesian way to update another prior. By going back in time, we can go back to a prior belief in a situation with no information.

[36] Often called a non-informative prior.

At the heart of this issue is that the choice of the labelling of the outcomes matters ("wine" or "Chardonnay, Shiraz, ..."). Does this problem go away when a labelling is provided to the decision maker? In Jane's situation, a friend may have provided a specific labelling of options by saying "wine or beer". Perhaps Jane should just take the labelling offered to her. It is easy to see that such a solution, if anything, leads to more problems. When considering a default labelling given to her, Jane should take into account the reasons why such a labelling was chosen to be provided rather than another one. Does this choice of labelling reflect some information from the person providing it? Is the person trying to influence her? If so, are the incentives of the person providing the labelling aligned with hers? Suppose that John is the person providing the labelling to Jane and that his aim is to convince Jane to come to the party. Suppose also that John is aware that Jane does not like beer. John may know that it is more likely that there will be beer (or perhaps he knows that there will be beer for sure). He may choose the seemingly neutral framing "wine or beer" as a way to artificially give an impression of balance in the chances of wine and beer.[37]

Fundamentally, at the root of this example is the fact that a default labelling of the possible categories of outcomes is frequently provided by agents with motives and beliefs of their own. There is no reason to consider these default labellings as uninformative. Instead, one would need some beliefs over these agents' motives and beliefs to form a view about the possible reasons behind the choices of a type of labelling rather than another one. It is reasonable to think that this is an even more difficult problem to resolve than determining a prior on unknown outcomes. In Gilboa et al.'s view, it means that in a situation of ignorance, it may simply be misleading to pick a prior and think that it makes the decision maker rational. Instead, "there may not be any decision that is perfectly rational" (p. 287). In that case, following some rules, like sticking to the status quo option, or aiming to minimise the worst-case scenario (e.g., the principle of precaution), may be "rational ... in the face of extreme uncertainty" (p. 288).

So, Bayesianism may not be rational when you do not know much about the different possible outcomes and when your choice would depend on an uninformed prior.[38] The problem of Bayesianism gets even deeper when you do not even know that there are things you do not know: when you are not aware of your ignorance. Savage's framework was designed for what he called

---

37 The term *paltering* can refer to the strategy of using carefully chosen true statements to mislead others (Schauer and Zeckhauser 2007).

38 Gelman and Yao (2020) discuss further limitations of Bayesianism as a statistical method. In particular, non-informative priors give too much weight to the available evidence, but subjective priors are incoherent since they imply that Bayesian updating has already occurred without the need for statistical models. They conclude, "As we have discussed elsewhere, 'in the popular and technical press, we have noticed that "Bayesian" is sometimes used as a catchall label for rational behavior'. But 'rationality' (both in the common-sense and statistical meanings of the word) is complex."

"small worlds": worlds where the decision maker knows all the possible events that can happen. An example of a small world is the throw of a die. There are six possible outcomes, one for each number. Knowing all these possible states, the decision maker can ascribe a subjective probability to each of them and update these probabilities when new information comes in. When introducing his framework, Savage pointed out that it would be "utterly ridiculous" to think that it could describe the actual process of decision making in the real world. It would require a decision maker to be able to consider all the actions possible and all the states of the world possible. In the words of Savage: "the task in making such a decision is not even remotely resembled by human possibility. It is even utterly beyond our power to plan a picnic or to play a game of chess in accordance with the principle, even when the world of states and the set of available acts to be envisaged are artificially reduced to the narrowest reasonable limits" (Savage 1972, chapter 2).

In a small world, there is no real *surprise* in the sense that a decision maker never observes an event they would never have anticipated could happen. As Binmore (2008) points out, the world we live in is not a small world, but a large world where "complete surprises" happen. A complete surprise is a situation where you observe an outcome that you would never have expected. For instance, things you think were true turn out to be false, and vice versa. Phenomena you'd never even consider just happen, like the 9/11 attacks, or the financial 2008 crisis driven by a collapse on the – usually very stable – housing market. When such surprises happen, one cannot be Bayesian. A classic example is the case of the black swan: a European believing that swans are all white would have put a zero probability on the chance of a swan being black (or another colour like pink or blue). But a direct implication of Bayesian updating is that a null belief cannot be updated to become a positive belief. Hence when seeing a surprising black swan, when arriving in Australia, the European would not be able to form a positive belief that black swans exist!

This view is clearly wrong. People happen to be truly surprised, and when that happens, they revise their beliefs. But what it means is that they cannot be Bayesians when doing so. In practice, Binmore suggests that people behave as if they have a model of the world that reflects what they believe about how the world works and about the events that can happen. When a surprise happens, the decision maker "throws away her old model and adopts a new model" (p. 152). But the process through which this change in beliefs happens is "a mystery".[39]

A normative model of decision-making should be able to say what should be done in real-world decision situations where, very often, there are "unknown

---

[39] It would be highly unconvincing to think that one solution to this problem would be to assume that the decision maker is able to put some (small) positive probability on all the possible models of the world. It would, for instance, mean that humans already had some small positive beliefs about the theory of relativity before it was proposed by Einstein.

unknowns", to take the now-famous expression of former US Secretary of Defense Donald Rumsfeld: there are things that we do not know that we do not know.[40] New economic models about decisions under unawareness (the fact of not being aware that some events are possible) try to tackle this question, departing from Savage's theory (Schipper 2014; Karni and Vierø 2017).

Why Consistency?

Beyond the validity of each axiom separately, Sen (1993) made a more fundamental critique: consistency in itself cannot be a criterion to define rationality. Consistency is a good property when it is the result of external goals that the agent pursues, such as the maximisation of utility or the respect of some norms. But without such things, which are external to the choices themselves, "there is no 'internal' way of determining whether a particular behavior pattern is or is not consistent".

One way of understanding Sen's critique is that observed choices between options do not uniquely determine what the decision maker is really choosing. For example, when Jane chooses one of the slices of a cake on a plate, is she simply considering the slices? If so, she should just pick the largest one if she is hungry. But what if she sees the choice of each slice as signalling something about her? In that case, the slices will have a hidden social payoff as well. Picking the largest slice may seem greedy. Picking the smallest one may suggest she is mindful of her diet. In that case, the set of choices will matter, and she may violate the independence of irrelevant alternatives as we discussed above.

Here is another example from Sen, already discussed in Chapter 8. Jane receives an invitation from John to have a drink at his place. Her choice is between accepting and refusing. Jane is going to accept the invitation when John adds the option to have some drug at his place. At that moment, Jane may change her mind and opt to decline John's invitation. If Jane is simply choosing between the options nothing, drink or drug, it is again a violation of the independence of irrelevant alternatives. The option of taking drugs is never chosen, but its addition in the set of options changed Jane's preference between accepting the invitation to drink and refusing it. This choice is perfectly understandable, if Jane is not choosing just a drink but also John as somebody

---

[40] The context where this judicious remark was made is worth mentioning. Asked about the absence of evidence for the existence of weapons of mass destruction in Iraq (note: none were found), Rumsfeld, who was supporting the military intervention in Iraq, stated: "Reports that say that something hasn't happened are always interesting to me, because as we know, there are known knowns; there are things we know we know. We also know there are known unknowns; that is to say we know there are some things we do not know. But there are also unknown unknowns – the ones we don't know we don't know. And if one looks throughout the history of our country and other free countries, it is the latter category that tend to be the difficult ones." It would not be a stretch to interpret his statement as suggesting that in the absence of evidence one needs to be extremely cautious and cater for the worst-case scenario (a solution, the principle of precaution, we just mentioned above).

to interact with. By suggesting the possibility to take a drug, John may signal traits that Jane finds undesirable in the prospect of interacting with him.

In these two examples, the observed choices do not uniquely constrain the motivation Jane may have when making these choices. What is really chosen (cake + social reputation or drink + prospect of interaction) is in Jane's head. It is unobservable. It is therefore impossible to qualify Jane's behaviour as rational or irrational based simply on the consistency of her observed choices, without knowing the motivations that drove these choices. A behaviour that may seem inconsistent at first sight may be consistent when understanding what people are trying to do: "We cannot determine whether the person is failing in any way without knowing what he is trying to do, that is, without knowing something external to the choice itself" (Sen 1993, pp. 498–501).

Let's sum up this discussion of rationality as consistency. For decades, mainstream economics has placed rationality as one of its pillars, either as a descriptive characterisation of behaviour or as a normative theory that should be followed. Rationality was characterised as consistency in preferences, and defined according to several key principles. Principles of rationality were, in practice, constraints on the types of theories of decision-making economists could propose. Innumerable economists, young and old, had ideas and papers rejected because they did not respect the admitted principles of rationality.

As we look at the evidence we just reviewed about the normative nature of these axioms, we get to appreciate the degree of arbitrariness these principles have.[41] For decades, students of economics were asked to accept these axioms as providing clear and obvious definitions of rationality, even though discussions about their validity were still taking place in the upper levels of the academic circles. This situation evokes Robinson's (1953) criticism about the teaching of non-trivial economic assumptions: students were asked to accept them and "before ever he does ask, he has become a professor, and so sloppy habits of thought are handed on from one generation to the next".[42]

That is not to say that we have not learned a lot from investigating rules of consistency in economic behaviour. We have. But it seems that the axioms that have been held as providing a straightforward minimal definition of rationality are not doing so.[43]

---

[41] This statement is not a criticism of economics as such. Taking some ideas for granted and not asking some questions is how a scientific paradigm works.

[42] Robinson's criticism was about macro-economic models, but I believe it is befitting to the way economics was taught with possibly too much certainty and not enough questions raised, until the economic student reached a PhD. At that point the student had often invested too much in the discipline to radically question its foundations.

[43] Another point touched on in Chapter 11 is that in many situations "rational" behaviour as defined in economics is self-defeating: people end up being worse off when following economic principles of rationality. It is another major concern when considering whether these principles have a normative value (i.e., they should be followed). See Sugden (1991) for the full development of this criticism.

On the Absence of Psychology in Ordinal Utility

The ordinal revolution was motivated by the desire to create a theory of economic decisions on observable facts and choices, not on unobservable ones like states of mind. The success of this approach was to show that, under some principles of behaviour, it was *as if* a decision maker was choosing options by ascribing a utility to them and selecting the one with the higher number. What could be behind the utility number was left for considerations outside economics. Psychologists and sociologists could investigate what people like and why. Economists would investigate how people make decisions given what their observed preferences are.

In this ordinalist perspective, we don't need to make any assumption about utility as a measure; we just need people to respect observable rules when making decisions, to say that a number, utility, can be ascribed to the options being chosen. This view seems strange, however. It is useful to compare it to the modern theory of measurement that, starting in the early twentieth century, showed that a measure like weight can be represented by observable comparisons being objects. Theorists like Hölder and Nagel showed that a few axioms about observable comparisons can characterise the notion of weight (Michell 1993). But even if weight as a measure can be represented with axioms, it would seem strange to use this fact to argue that weight is only an "as if" concept that does not refer to some intrinsic property of the objects.[44]

The non-intuitive nature of the ordinalist approach is apparent in how economists themselves discuss the notion of utility. Statements about utility being an as-if quantity without psychological meaning are typically more frequent in discussions about the principles of the discipline. But a careful listener will notice that economists very often seem to discuss utility as related to satisfaction. Economists will say that a decision maker "derives utility" from consumption and "experiences disutility" from effort. They frequently assume that consumption is associated with "decreasing marginal utility": the last unit consumed has less utility than the previous one. In all these expressions, the word *utility* could easily be replaced by *satisfaction*. In addition, economists often suggest that the maximisation of utility is what *drives* behaviour instead of utility being a *reflection* of the rationality of behaviour.[45]

Listening to economists discussing the absence of psychology in the notion of utility, one may be tempted to refer to the duck test: "If it looks like a duck, swims like a duck, and quacks like a duck, then it probably is a duck." Similarly, if utility helps in choosing between options like a subjective satisfaction, is mentioned in economic discussions like a subjective satisfaction, and is a

---

[44] The weight of an object on earth is determined by the mass of its constitutive atoms and the earth's gravity.

[45] Indeed, it is the way I discussed the homo economicus in Chapter 1, stating that agents aim to get the "highest expected subjective satisfaction".

measure of something like a level of satisfaction, then economists probably really use it as if it was a subjective satisfaction.

15.3 RATIONALITY AFTER THE BEHAVIOURAL REVOLUTION

Behavioural economics' criticism of the homo economicus model is commonly interpreted as showing that people are not rational because they violate key principles of rationality. The previous section points to a somewhat more fundamental criticism. There are serious questions about whether the central axioms of economic behaviour adequately define the notion of rationality itself. If we abandon these economic axioms and, perhaps with them, the notion of consistency as defining rationality, what should we do with the notion of rationality?

Back to Subjective Satisfaction

One option would be to go back to the notion of subjective satisfaction. The unobservability of utility motivated economists to abandon a subjective and psychological definition of utility. Modern advances in neuroscience create the prospect of resolving this problem by making utility observable. Studies have found that the subjective perception of the value of options is tightly associated with the firing rate of dopaminergic neurons.[46] This firing rate can be observed through the BOLD signals they give in fMRI scanners.[47] Summarising the research on this question, Glimcher (2011, pp. 354–355) states that "there exists in the human brain a central representation of subjective value ... it is now clear that if one wants to measure expected subjective values, one can do so using a brain scanner or an electrode in these general areas."

Clearly, as evolution pushes animals towards the evolution of the maximisation of fitness, it could make sense for it to design organisms to form something like a utility scale lined up with the impact on fitness of the different choices it faces. John Maynard Smith made this point very clearly: "The theory requires, that the values of different outcomes (for example, financial rewards, the risks of death and the pleasures of a clear conscience) be measured on a single scale" (Maynard Smith 1982, p. vii).

The idea of defining rationality as the maximisation of subjective satisfaction would come back to the utilitarian origin of modern economics. This option faces some problems, however. First, assuming that our subjective satisfaction tracks fitness, it was designed to track it in a very different type of environment than the one we are facing now. Modern urban societies are very new on an evolutionary time scale, and natural selection has not had time to fine-tune our

---

[46] Which release dopamine, the neurotransmitter associated with rewards and learning.
[47] BOLD (blood oxygen level–dependent) signals are measurements provided by fMRI scanners indicative of the neurons' release of oxygen associated with their firing rate.

subjective rewards system to this new environment. As a consequence, we face an evolutionary mismatch in many circumstances, and our subjective rewards may be triggered in ways that are not conducive to our proper interest. Our taste for food rich in energy (e.g., sugar) is the classic example. While useful when energy-rich food was scarce, it leads to issues in our modern environment. For a large proportion of the population, it can lead to different degrees of obesity. Another radically different example is the case of addictive drugs, which are products triggering our subjective reward system, even though they likely have, in many cases, a negative effect on our expected fitness. Natural selection has not had time to select for a distaste of these new chemical products. For these reasons, it is not clear that the pursuit of maximal subjective satisfaction is the way to define a rational behaviour.[48]

People may not even agree that maximising their subjective satisfaction should be their goal. A thought experiment proposed by the philosopher Robert Nozick (1974) illustrates this fact:

Suppose there were an experience machine that would give you any experience you desired. Superduper neuropsychologists could simulate your brain so that you would think and feel you were writing a great novel, or making a friend, or reading an interesting book. All the time you would be floating in a tank, with electrodes attached to your brain. Should you plug into this machine for life, preprogramming your life's experiences? (p. 42)

Confronted with such a scenario, most people reject the idea that it would be a desirable life.[49] The experience of satisfaction itself is not our unique goal. In the case of the experience machine, there is an aversion to the inauthenticity of the experience proposed.[50]

Another observation is that people frequently choose to pursue courses of action that are challenging and frustrating. Many people go through painful physical activities to improve their body shape. Professional athletes often endure privations and hardship all year long to participate in top competitions.

---

[48] Note that the uneasiness of many thinkers with the idea of simply pursuing satisfaction may somehow be driven by an intuitive understanding that it would not be suitable to actually reach a happy life in the long run in an urban society (even if it was Athens in 400 BCE). It is a possibility that temperance and the need to rein in short-term desires ("passions") may have contributed to the intuitions of thinkers like Aristotle and J. S. Mill.

[49] In an international survey of 1,642 philosophers, 77% said they would opt not to enter the machine. Only 13% said they would (Bourget and Chalmers 2020).

[50] *The Matrix* movie provides an illustration of this choice, when Cypher has the choice to opt for a fictitious and pleasing life experience or to stay in the harsh reality. His choice to opt for the fictitious reality is a betrayal of his friends, but it also seems wrong in itself. We may wonder how we can feel that it is wrong, given that our hedonic system is what determines the value of our choices. One possibility is that we are aware that this hedonic system may backfire. Some actions can make us feel happy in the present, but make us worse off eventually (e.g., drinking too much alcohol one night). Nozick's experience machine and the *Matrix* scenario may raise our awareness that something is off with giving away our real life simply for an experience of subjective pleasure, which is not associated with things objectively happening to us.

These hardships are the result of self-imposed, ambitious goals. In the quest for achieving such ambitious goals, many people seem to be willing forgo their subjective satisfaction.

Having lower aspirations would be an easy way to reach satisfaction by learning to like what one has. Accepting not to aspire to more is one of the simplest routes to happiness. It is a point that has long been recognised. Writing around 400 BCE in China, Lao Tzu recommended "Be content with what you have; rejoice in the way things are"(*Tao Te Ching*, chapter 44). Several centuries later, around 108 CE, the Greek stoic Epictetus made a similar recommendation: "Rejoice in that which is present" (*The Discourses*, IV.4). But abandoning hopes and ambition may seem unappealing to many of us, even if working towards these hopes and ambitions comes at a cost. Indeed, many modern self-help books have become bestsellers by telling people to shoot for the stars and not to abandon their dreams.

There is a likely more damning reason why the maximisation of subjective satisfaction may not constitute a credible goal. I said that our subjective reward system, which triggers our feelings of satisfaction, must have been designed by evolution to maximise our fitness.[51] But this statement does not mean that we are endowed with a reward system that generates subjective satisfaction as a measure, even just approximate, of the fitness of the different options we face. We have seen, in Chapters 6 and 8, that, due to constraints faced by our reward system, it is characterised by value signals that help us make the right choices but that do not reflect the levels of fitness associated with the different options we face. For a start, our subjective satisfaction is reference-dependent and not absolute, as stressed by Glimcher (2011). This feature may be present right at the level of our perceptual sensors, meaning that *no absolute information* is carried to our brain where our decisions are made. One of the consequences of this reference-dependence is the phenomenon of habituation: as we get more of something, we get used to it and we eventually stop feeling good about what we have.

In short, while our reward system has been designed to maximise our fitness, this reward system has not been designed to provide a measure of satisfaction that can be pursued and reached. Said otherwise, *we have not been designed to maximise our happiness*. Instead, frustration with what we do not have and the hope of reaching happiness by getting more are the incentives evolution has given us to make us try to strive as much as possible. The pursuit of long-lasting satisfaction is, in that sense, doomed. It is like aiming to reach the horizon: as you move forward, the horizon also moves ahead. This idea is well described by the term "hedonic treadmill" coined by Brickman (1971).

A further damning problem is that we are often oblivious to how we will habituate to favourable circumstances in the future. The "focusing illusion", discussed in Chapter 8, describes how we tend to believe that the next positive

[51] Or at least evolution must have pushed *towards* maximisation.

change or achievement within reach is going to make us happier than it actually will. This belief motivates us to work hard for these achievements. A professional athlete aiming to get a medal in a competition, or an employee aiming to get a promotion in an organisation, can make great sacrifices in the hope that the achievement ahead will be worth it and deliver great satisfaction. However, studies reveal that people adjust a lot to changes in outcomes and that, a few months after reaching the desired achievement, they do not feel as happy as they expected they would.

These different elements suggest that the maximisation of subjective satisfaction is, in the end, an unlikely candidate to redefine rationality.

Maximising Fitness

Another possibility could then be to aim to maximise fitness directly. If satisfaction does not track fitness well enough because of evolutionary mismatches, should we not just think that it is rational to maximise fitness?

A quick consideration reveals that this idea is unlikely to work either. The reason is simple. We have not been designed to maximise fitness directly. On that point, the evolutionary psychologists Tooby and Cosmides (1990) stressed that it is an error to think that "evolution's 'goal' is the goal of organisms; that because evolution fitness-maximizes, organisms are goal-seeking fitness-maximizers".

We are endowed with a reward system that, under past circumstances, was helping us maximise fitness. This reward system defines what we want. When what we want conflicts with maximising fitness, what higher principle would compel us to maximise fitness instead of just doing what we want? If this argument seems a bit abstract, a simple thought experiment shows that almost nobody would want to adopt the maximisation of fitness as a normative principle.

Let's imagine the life of John and Jane, who have adopted the doctrine that rational behaviour is maximising fitness (they consequently aim to do so). John does not behave like most men on the planet. He does not want a lifelong partner; instead, he dedicates all his energy to give his gametes to as many sperm banks as possible. He also contributes to the black market for sperm donation and spends his time and money connecting with as many women as possible looking for a sperm donor. Doing so, John is able to dwarf the fitness of most men on earth and may have, literally, hundreds of children.[52] Jane cannot hope to have so many children. But nonetheless, starting early and focussing only on child-rearing, she would be able to reach eight or more children in a developed

---

[52] In 2018, *The Guardian* reported the case of a Dutchman who had, that way, fathered 200 children. His efforts were apparently dwarfed, however, by an Englishman who gave his sperm once a week for sixteen years and estimated, according to the *BBC*, to have given birth to 800 children in 2016. His goal was to reach 1,000.

country characterised by a good health care system.[53] Such an effort would be tremendously costly in resources, time and also certainly for her health. But Jane, having decided to focus on her fitness, is willing to make all these sacrifices to reach the highest fitness as possible.[54]

There is no ambiguity that John and Jane would have a much larger number of offspring than most people on the planet. But I would venture that only a tiny minority of people would want to adopt their focus on fitness as a normative principle for their lives. Unlike John, men may want to form a family with a long-term partner and children to raise. Unlike Jane, women may want to have a life with leisure and a professional career, besides being a mother. Our reluctance to follow the model of John and Jane simply reflects that our reward system has not been designed to track the modern possibilities in terms of fitness. And that is all there is to it. Consider Sam and Sally, who do not follow John and Jane's quest for offspring. They form a couple, in their early thirties without children. They are young professionals, living in a great city with an entertaining nightlife. They travel around the world and enjoy their lifestyle greatly. They are thinking of (possibly) having a child, or perhaps two. But they have not set their mind about it yet. Who could say that Sam and Sally are wrong and that maximising their fitness should be their goal instead? The simple answer is: nobody.

The fact is that evolution designed our subjective reward system for us to maximise fitness in an ancestral environment. We are no longer in this ancestral environment, and we can get these rewards without having to chase the maximisation of our fitness.

In Chapter 5, I described the work of evolution as similar to what we would do when creating robots we send to a far-away planet. We would equip these robots with a reward system for them to make the best decisions given the conditions on the planet. Our situation is similar to the situation of robots who landed on a planet where some conditions were not fully anticipated by their designers. We can enjoy life without maximising fitness, as our reward system is not finely adapted to the circumstances we face. Should we readjust our tastes to learn to like what is good for our fitness, even though we were not designed to do so? It would seem a very strange proposition: on a positive point of view,

---

53 Stated records of number of children by a woman can go much higher. A Russian couple in the eighteenth century is credited of having had sixty-nine children. More recent – and more reliable – records still give incredibly large numbers by modern standards. Moddie Oliver (USA), Maria Addolorata Casalini (Italy) and Maria Benita Olivera (Argentina) are all credited with having had thirty-two children in the twentieth century.

54 One may wonder about the possible cost of having too many children on the fitness of these children. There is potentially a trade-off between the number of children and the reproductive success of these children. Nonetheless, in modern societies such a trade-off does not seem to be very significant: Kaplan et al. (1995) found a near-linear relationship between the number of children and number of grandchildren in New Mexico, and Zietsch et al. (2014) found that the genetic influences on the number of offspring and number of grand-offspring are identical (Swedish data).

if we do not have a direct taste for fitness, what would motivate us to acquire such a taste? On a normative point of view, why should we aim to do that? Surely we do not owe anything to evolution, which shaped us to maximise fitness. Evolution is just an impersonal and random process. If its design is now mismatched with modern circumstances, humans are not under any duty to pursue the maximisation of their fitness instead of just benefitting from some of these mismatches.

A More Modest Place for Rationality

Rationality has not always been a core principle in economics. Before the ordinalist revolution, it was, rather, a natural description of acting in a way maximising utility. The rise to pre-eminence of the concept of rationality came with the substitution of a psychological notion of utility with principles of consistency. I have shown in this epilogue that this redefinition of the notion of rationality is much more problematic than economists have assumed and claimed. At the same time, there is no easy way to redefine this notion in a cogent way, compatible with the evidence about how people actually behave and how they want to behave.

Simply abandoning the notion would likely be too strong an option. *Rationality* is a word perceived as meaningful by people. It is used to somehow characterise good decisions. Economics is about how to make good decisions, and not being able to use and/or define this word would be somewhat strange. Perhaps the solution is simply to redefine rationality in a more modest way. Gilboa (2009) has proposed doing just that, by redefining rationality from the strict perspective of the decision maker. He starts by defining irrationality in the following way: "A mode of behavior is irrational for a given decision maker, if, when the decision maker behaves in this mode and is then exposed to the analysis of her behavior, she feels embarrassed" (p. 139). The definition of rationality follows: "All that is not irrational is rational."

As pointed out by Gilboa, the same mode of behaviour can be irrational for some people and rational for other people. Furthermore, people with less knowledge or intelligence may be more rational than others because they are less able to recognise logical inconsistencies in their behaviour.

This aspect of Gilboa's definition may seem frustrating, but it is likely the price to pay not to have a definition based on an external imposition of normative principles that act as *skyhooks* to make the theory artificially hold together.[55] To this definition of a subjective rationality, Gilboa, however, proposes to add an objective notion of rationality that relies on the agreement of other people too: "A decision is objectively rational if the decision maker can convince others that she is right in making it" (p. 140). This redefinition of

---

[55] I take this use of the word *skyhook* from Dennett (1996), and its use later by Binmore (2005b).

rationality somewhat comes back to the origin of the word: an action is rational for which the decision maker can give reasons for it.[56]

This redefinition of rationality based only on the view of the decision maker echoes Rawls' (1971) redefinition of ethical principles based on what people would want to do themselves. Here too, Rawls substituted the call to external principles acting as skyhooks with the agreement of the people.[57] In the process, Rawls proposes the notion of *reflective equilibrium* as a way for somebody to form consistent views between preferences in particular situations and general principles of behaviour. To work towards a reflective equilibrium you can test your preferences in specific situations and compare how they match the general principles you want to follow. When a conflict appears, you have a choice. You can change your preferences in specific situations (as Savage did when violating the axiom of independence), or you can change the principles you held because you feel they do not reflect your preferences well enough. Reaching a reflective equilibrium is a way to avoid being "embarrassed" about one's choices and being irrational in the sense given by Gilboa.[58]

Gilboa's definition has the merit of being sustainable because it no longer relies on the quest for objective principles of rationality, somehow written somewhere. But being a much more modest definition, it loses the strength of the notion of rationality held previously by economists. If decisions can be rational when people simply are happy not to change their mind, the concept of rationality does not have much bite to explain actual behaviour. It is not clear that the concept has much normative content either: any mode of behaviour can be subjectively rational if people are happy with it. As indicated by Gilboa (2009):

According to this view, rationality is not a medal of honor bestowed on selected decision makers by the theorist. Rather, "irrational" means "is likely to change his mind" whereas "rational" means "is likely to insist on her behavior". The terms are used to facilitate discussion, while the decision maker remains the ultimate judge of the choices that are rational for her. (p. 141)

---

[56] Even if this reason is simply "that's what I want".

[57] There is something fundamentally positivist in the fact of renouncing the metaphysical claim that some "objective" principles exist that tell us what we *should* do. Rawls and Gilboa redefine these normative principles based on the only thing we can observe: the views of the very same people who are making the decisions. In the words of Dennett (1996, p. 75), such an approach replaces skyhooks with *cranes*: "Cranes can do the lifting work our imaginary skyhooks might do, and they do it in an honest, non-question-begging fashion. They are expensive, however. They have to be designed and built, from everyday parts already on hand, and they have to be located on a firm base of existing ground."

[58] Rawls adapted the notion of reflective equilibrium from a process described by the philosopher Nelson Goodman to make judgements about specific inferences and general principles consistent with each other: "A rule is amended if it yields an inference we are unwilling to accept; an inference is rejected if it violates a rule we are unwilling to amend" (Goodman 1965, p. 67).

Such a definition of rationality would certainly play a more modest role in economics compared to the stronger notion of rationality used previously. But it would credibly retain some use for situations where we have a reasonable understanding of what people want. For instance, when studying investment decisions it is reasonable to think that a decision maker is motivated by financial returns. Decisions that lead to lower financial returns would then reasonably be considered by the decision maker as irrational. And if, nonetheless, some seemingly irrational behaviour is observed, the assumptions about the decision makers' preferences should be questioned, to ensure there are no good reasons that actually make the observed behaviour rational, from their point of view.

In any case, whether such a weaker definition of rationality is adopted or not, the old notion of rationality is already on the wane. In the aftermath of the behavioural revolution and the empirical turn in economics,[59] new generations of economists have less interest in the question of whether people are rational or not. Instead, they simply study how they behave in practice.[60]

∴

To the new generations of economists who are reading this book, the advice to take from it would be to go beyond the piecemeal descriptions of behaviour across different situations and the study of deviations of the standard model of economic rationality. Documenting specific behaviours in a range of different settings and labelling these behaviours as deviations from a standard of rationality cannot be the end of a behavioural science. Science aims for general unifying principles behind (sometimes complex) observed phenomena. While people are not homo economicus as thought by economists a short time ago, they are not nonsensical either. What economists should aim for is to understand why people behave the way they do and to look for the good reasons behind people's behaviour. As I hope I have shown here, economics can provide very compelling explanations of seemingly puzzling behaviours, when we enrich economic models to reflect the evolutionary origin of our preferences, the constraints we face when trying to make decisions, the type of uncertainty we face in the real world and the complex social interactions in which we engage.

---

[59] Economists have become more focused on the study of real behaviour through empirical studies than on the building of theoretical models of behaviour.

[60] Kuhn noted that "when paradigms change, there are usually significant shifts in the criteria determining the legitimacy both of problems and of proposed solutions" (Kuhn 1962/2012, p. 109).

Bibliography

Abbink, Klaus and Donna Harris (2019) "In-group favouritism and out-group discrimination in naturally occurring groups," *PLoS ONE*, Vol. 14, No. 9, p. e0221616.

Adida, Claire L., David D. Laitin and Marie-Anne Valfort (2014) "Muslims in France: Identifying a discriminatory equilibrium," *Journal of Population Economics*, Vol. 27, No. 4, pp. 1039–1086.

Agassi, Andre (2010) Open: An Autobiography. HarperCollins

Ainslie, George (1975) "Specious reward: A behavioral theory of impulsiveness and impulse control," *Psychological Bulletin*, Vol. 82, No. 4, p. 463.

Akerlof, George A. and Rachel Kranton (2010) "Identity economics," *The Economists' Voice*, Vol. 7, No. 2.

Alchian, Armen A (1950) "Uncertainty, evolution, and economic theory," *Journal of Political Economy*, Vol. 58, No. 3, pp. 211–221.

Alexander, Richard D. (1987) *The biology of moral systems*. Transaction Publishers.

Alger, Ingela and Jörgen W. Weibull (2013) "Homo moralis–Preference evolution under incomplete information and assortative matching," *Econometrica*, Vol. 81, No. 6, pp. 2269–2302.

Allais, Maurice (1953) "Le comportement de l'homme rationnel devant le risque: Critique des postulats et axiomes de l'école américaine," *Econometrica*, pp. 503–546.

Allais, Maurice and G. M. Hagen (1979) *Expected utility hypotheses and the Allais paradox*. Springer.

Allen, Eric J., Patricia M. Dechow, Devin G. Pope and George Wu (2017) "Reference-dependent preferences: Evidence from marathon runners," *Management Science*, Vol. 63, No. 6, pp. 1657–1672.

Allen, M. W. and T. L. Jones, eds. (2016) *Violence and warfare among hunter-gatherers*. Routledge.

Alt, Franz (1936) "Über die messbarkeit des nutzens," *Zeitschrift für Nationalökonomie/Journal of Economics*, Vol. 7, No. 2, pp. 161–169.

Ammer, Christine (2013) *The American heritage dictionary of idioms: American English idiomatic expressions & phrases*. HMH.

Anand, Paul, Prasanta Pattanaik and Clemens Puppe (2009) *The handbook of rational and social choice*. Oxford University Press.

Anderson, Ashton and Etan A. Green (2018) "Personal bests as reference points," *Proceedings of the National Academy of Sciences*, Vol. 115, No. 8, pp. 1772–1776.

Anderson, John Robert (1990) *The adaptive character of thought*. Psychology Press.

Angilletta, Michael J., Jr., Gregory Kubitz and Robbie S. Wilson (2019) "Self-deception in nonhuman animals: Weak crayfish escalated aggression as if they were strong," *Behavioral Ecology*, Vol. 30, No. 5, pp. 1469–1476.

Angner, Erik (2019) "We're all behavioral economists now," *Journal of Economic Methodology*, Vol. 26, No. 3, pp. 195–207.

Aquinas, T., (1265–1274/2015). *Summa theologica*. Xist Publishing.

Arendt, Hannah (1963/2006) *Eichmann in Jerusalem: A Report on the Banality of Evil*. Penguin.

Ariely, Dan and Klaus Wertenbroch (2002) "Procrastination, deadlines, and performance: Self-control by precommitment," *Psychological Science*, Vol. 13, No. 3, pp. 219–224.

Aristotle (340 BCE). *Nicomachean ethics*.

    (350 BCE) *On the heavens*.

Arrow, Kenneth J. (1951/1963) *Social choice and individual values*. Yale University Press.

    (1972) "Some mathematical models of race discrimination in the labor market," in Anthony Pascal, ed., *Racial discrimination in economic life*. Lexington, MA: Lexington Books, pp. 187–204.

Ashar, Jayen, Jaiden Ashmore, Brad Hall, Sean Harris, Bernhard Hengst, Roger Liu, Zijie Mei, Maurice Pagnucco, Ritwik Roy, Claude Sammut, Oleg Sushkov, Belinda Teh and Luke Tsekouras (2015) "RoboCup SPL 2014 champion team paper," in R. A. Bianchi, H. L. Akin, S. Ramamoorthy, and K. Sugiura, eds., *RoboCup 2014: Robot World Cup XVIII* (Vol. 8992). Springer, pp. 70–81.

Aumann, Robert J. (1960) "Acceptable points in games of perfect information," *Pacific Journal of Mathematics*, Vol. 10, No. 2, pp. 381–417.

Aumann, Robert J. (1962) "Utility theory without the completeness axiom," *Econometrica*, Vol. 30, No. 3, pp. 445–462.

    (2019) "A synthesis of behavioural and mainstream economics," *Nature Human Behaviour*, Vol. 3, No. 7, pp. 666–670.

Axelrod, Robert (1980a) "Effective choice in the prisoner's dilemma," *Journal of Conflict Resolution*, Vol. 24, No. 1, pp. 3–25.

    (1980b) "More effective choice in the prisoner's dilemma," *Journal of Conflict Resolution*, Vol. 24, No. 3, pp. 379–403.

Babcock, Linda and George Loewenstein (1997) "Explaining bargaining impasse: The role of self-serving biases," *Journal of Economic Perspectives*, Vol. 11, No. 1, pp. 109–126.

Bacharach, Michael (1999) "Interactive team reasoning: A contribution to the theory of co-operation," *Research in Economics*, Vol. 53, No. 2, pp. 117–147.

    (2006) *Beyond individual choice: Teams and frames in game theory*. Princeton University Press.

Baliga, Sandeep and Jeffrey C. Ely (2011) "Mnemonomics: The sunk cost fallacy as a memory kludge," *American Economic Journal: Microeconomics*, Vol. 3, No. 4, pp. 35–67.

Balliet, Daniel, Junhui Wu and Carsten K. W. De Dreu (2014) "Ingroup favoritism in cooperation: A meta-analysis," *Psychological Bulletin*, Vol. 140, No. 6, p. 1556.

Barber, Brad M. and Terrance Odean (2001) "Boys will be boys: Gender, overconfidence, and common stock investment," *The Quarterly Journal of Economics*, Vol. 116, No. 1, pp. 261–292.

Barber, Benjamin S., IV and William English (2019) "The origin of wealth matters: Equity norms trump equality norms in the ultimatum game with earned endowments," *Journal of Economic Behavior & Organization*, Vol. 158, pp. 33–43.

Barrett, Justin L (2000) "Exploring the natural foundations of religion," *Trends in Cognitive Sciences*, Vol. 4, No. 1, pp. 29–34.

Baumard, Nicolas, Jean-Baptiste André and Dan Sperber (2013) "A mutualistic approach to morality: The evolution of fairness by partner choice," *Behavioral and Brain Sciences*, Vol. 36, No. 1, pp. 59–78.

Beaufils, Bruno, Jean-Paul Delahaye and Philippe Mathieu (1997) "Our meeting with gradual, a good strategy for the iterated prisoner's dilemma," in *Proceedings of the Fifth International Workshop on the Synthesis and Simulation of Living Systems*. MIT Press, pp. 202–209.

Bechara, Antoine, Antonio R. Damasio, Hanna Damasio, Steven W. Anderson et al. (1994) "Insensitivity to future consequences following damage to human prefrontal cortex," *Cognition*, Vol. 50, pp. 1–3.

Becker, Gary S. (1957) *The economics of discrimination*. University of Chicago press.

(1976) "Altruism, egoism, and genetic fitness: Economics and sociobiology," *Journal of Economic Literature*, Vol. 14, No. 3, pp. 817–826.

(1981) "Altruism in the family and selfishness in the market place," *Economica*, Vol. 48, No. 189, pp. 1–15.

Bénabou, Roland and Jean Tirole (2002) "Self-confidence and personal motivation," *The Quarterly Journal of Economics*, Vol. 117, No. 3, pp. 871–915.

Benson, K. E. and D. W. Stephens (1996) "Interruptions, tradeoffs, and temporal discounting," *American Zoologist*, Vol. 36, No. 4, pp. 506–517.

Bentham, Jeremy (1776) *A fragment on government*.

(1825) *The rationale of reward*: John and H. L. Hunt.

(1832/1998) "Anarchical fallacies," *Headline Series*, No. 318, p. 56.

Berns, G.S., Laibson, D. and Loewenstein, G., 2007. Intertemporal choice–toward an integrative framework. *Trends in cognitive sciences*, 11(11), pp.482–488.

Bhui, Rahul and Yang Xiang (2021) "A rational account of the repulsion effect." https://psyarxiv.com/hxjqv/.

Bicchieri, Cristina (2005) *The grammar of society: The nature and dynamics of social norms*. Cambridge University Press.

Binmore, Ken (1987) "Modeling rational players: Part I," *Economics & Philosophy*, Vol. 3, No. 2, pp. 179–214.

(1988) "Modeling rational players: Part II," *Economics & Philosophy*, Vol. 4, No. 1, pp. 9–55.

(1994b) *Game theory and the social contract, vol. 1: Playing fair*. MIT Press.

(2005a) "Economic man—Or straw man?" *Behavioral and Brain Sciences*, Vol. 28, No. 6, pp. 817–818.

(2005b) *Natural justice*. Oxford University Press.

(2007) *Game theory: A very short introduction*. Oxford University Press.

(2008) *Rational decisions*. Princeton University Press.

(2012) "Kitcher on natural morality," *Analyse & Kritik*, Vol. 34, No. 1, pp. 129–140.

Binmore, Kenneth (1994a) *Game theory and the social contract, vol. 2: Just playing.* MIT Press.

Birger, Jon (2015) *Date-Onomics: How dating became a lopsided numbers game.* Workman Publishing.

Blanchflower, David G., Bert Van Landeghem and Andrew J. Oswald (2009) "Imitative obesity and relative utility," *Journal of the European Economic Association*, Vol. 7, Nos. 2–3, pp. 528–538.

Bogacz, Rafal, Eric Brown, Jeff Moehlis, Philip Holmes and Jonathan D. Cohen (2006) "The physics of optimal decision making: A formal analysis of models of performance in two-alternative forced-choice tasks," *Psychological review*, Vol. 113, No. 4, p. 700.

Bohren, J. Aislinn, Kareem Haggag, Alex Imas and Devin G. Pope (2019) "Inaccurate statistical discrimination," Technical report, National Bureau of Economic Research.

Bond, Charles F. and Bella M. DePaulo (2006) "Accuracy of deception judgments," *Personality and Social Psychology Review*, Vol. 10, No. 3, pp. 214–234.

Bossaerts, Peter and Carsten Murawski (2017) "Computational complexity and human decision-making," *Trends in Cognitive Sciences*, Vol. 21, No. 12, pp. 917–929.

Bourdieu, Pierre and Jean-Claude Passeron (1977/1990) *Reproduction in education, society and culture*, vol. 4. Sage.

Bourget, D. and D. J. Chalmers (2020) "Philosophers on philosophy: The PhilPapers 2020 Survey." https://philpapers.org/rec/BOUPOP-3.

Bowles, Samuel and Herbert Gintis (1976/2011) *Schooling in capitalist America: Educational reform and the contradictions of economic life.* Haymarket Books.

(2013) *A cooperative species: Human reciprocity and its evolution.* Princeton University Press.

Boyer, Pascal (2008) *Religion explained.* Random House.

Brickman, Philip (1971) "Hedonic relativism and planning the good society," in M. H. Appley, ed., *Adaptation level theory.* New York: Academic Press, pp. 287–301.

Brosnan, Sarah F., Owen D. Jones, Susan P. Lambeth, Mary Catherine Mareno, Amanda S. Richardson and Steven J. Schapiro (2007) "Endowment effects in chimpanzees," *Current Biology*, Vol. 17, No. 19, pp. 1704–1707.

Brown, Zachariah C., Eric M. Anicich and Adam D. Galinsky (2020) "Compensatory conspicuous communication: Low status increases jargon use," *Organizational Behavior and Human Decision Processes*, Vol. 161, pp. 274–290.

Bruni, Luigino and Robert Sugden (2007) "The road not taken: How psychology was removed from economics, and how it might be brought back," *The Economic Journal*, Vol. 117, No. 516, pp. 146–173.

Buggle, Johannes C. (2020) "Growing collectivism: Irrigation, group conformity and technological divergence," *Journal of Economic Growth*, Vol. 25, No. 2, pp. 147–193.

Bursztyn, Leonardo, Bruno Ferman, Stefano Fiorin, Martin Kanz and Gautam Rao (2018) "Status goods: Experimental evidence from platinum credit cards," *The Quarterly Journal of Economics*, Vol. 133, No. 3, pp. 1561–1595.

Buss, David M. (1988) "Love acts: The evolutionary biology of love," in R. J. Sternberg and M. L. Barnes, eds., *Psychology of love.* Yale University Press, 100–118.

(2003) *The evolution of desire: Strategies of human mating.* Basic Books.

(2006) "The evolution of love," in Robert J. Sternberg and Karin Sternberg, eds., *The new psychology of love*. Yale University Press, pp. 65–86.

(2019) Evolutionary psychology: *The new science of the mind*. Routledge.

Camerer, Colin, Linda Babcock, George Loewenstein and Richard Thaler (1997) "Labor supply of New York City cabdrivers: One day at a time," *The Quarterly Journal of Economics*, Vol. 112, No. 2, pp. 407–441.

Camerer, Colin F. (2011) *Behavioral game theory: Experiments in strategic interaction*. Princeton University Press.

Cameron, J. J. and E. Curry (2020) "Gender roles and date context in hypothetical scripts for a woman and a man on a first date in the twenty-first century." *Sex Roles*, Vol. 82, No. 5, pp. 345–362.

Caplin, Andrew, Mark Dean and John Leahy (2019) "Rational inattention, optimal consideration sets, and stochastic choice," *The Review of Economic Studies*, Vol. 86, No. 3, pp. 1061–1094.

Carlin, John (2008) *Playing the enemy: Nelson Mandela and the game that made a nation*. Penguin.

Carmichael, H. Lorne and W. Bentley MacLeod (1997) "Gift giving and the evolution of cooperation," *International Economic Review*, Vol. 38, No. 3, pp. 485–509.

Carmon, Ziv and Dan Ariely (2000) "Focusing on the forgone: How value can appear so different to buyers and sellers," *Journal of Consumer Research*, Vol. 27, No. 3, pp. 360–370.

Casey, B. J., Leah H. Somerville, Ian H. Gotlib, Ozlem Ayduk, Nicholas T. Franklin, Mary K. Askren, John Jonides, Marc G. Berman, Nicole L. Wilson, Theresa Teslovich et al. (2011) "Behavioral and neural correlates of delay of gratification 40 years later," *Proceedings of the National Academy of Sciences*, Vol. 108, No. 36, pp. 14998–15003.

Chagnon, Napoleon A. (1988) "Life histories, blood revenge, and warfare in a tribal population," *Science*, Vol. 239, No. 4843, pp. 985–992.

Charness, Gary and Yan Chen (2020) "Social identity, group behavior, and teams," *Annual Review of Economics*, Vol. 12.

Charness, Gary and Matthew Rabin (2002) "Understanding social preferences with simple tests," *The Quarterly Journal of Economics*, Vol. 117, No. 3, pp. 817–869.

Chernoff, Herman (1954) "Rational selection of decision functions," *Econometrica*, pp. 422–443.

Choi, Jung-Kyoo and Samuel Bowles (2007) "The coevolution of parochial altruism and war," *Science*, Vol. 318, No. 5850, pp. 636–640.

Cicero, Marcus Tullius (45 BCE/1869) *De finibus bonorum et malorum*. Imprensis Librariae Glydendalianae (Frederici Hegel).

Clark, Andrew E. (2016) "Happiness, habits, and high rank," in S. Bartolini, E. Bilancini, L. Bruni and P. L. Porta, eds., *Policies for happiness*. Oxford University Press, p. 62.

Clark, Andrew E., Paul Frijters and Michael A. Shields (2008) "Relative income, happiness, and utility: An explanation for the Easterlin paradox and other puzzles," *Journal of Economic Literature*, Vol. 46, No. 1, pp. 95–144.

Clark, Andrew E. and Andrew J. Oswald (1996) "Satisfaction and comparison income," *Journal of Public Economics*, Vol. 61, No. 3, pp. 359–381.

Coase, R. (1995) "Interview with Gary Becker-Consumer Behavior." YouTube video, available at www.youtube.com/watch?v=edOr4RZ7_Ys.

Coate, Stephen and Michael Conlin (2004) "A group rule-utilitarian approach to voter turnout: Theory and evidence," *American Economic Review*, Vol. 94, No. 5, pp. 1476–1504.

Coates, Ta-Nehisi (2016) "'It's what we do more than what we say': Obama on race, identity, and the way forward," *The Atlantic*, December, No. 22.

Cohen, Jonathan D., Samuel M. McClure and Angela J. Yu (2007) "Should I stay or should I go? How the human brain manages the trade-off between exploitation and exploration," *Philosophical Transactions of the Royal Society B: Biological Sciences*, Vol. 362, No. 1481, pp. 933–942.

Constantinople, Christine M., Alex T. Piet and Carlos D. Brody (2019) "An analysis of decision under risk in rats," *Current Biology*, Vol. 29, No. 12, pp. 2066–2074.

Conte, Anna, John D. Hey and Peter G. Moffatt (2011) "Mixture models of choice under risk," *Journal of Econometrics*, Vol. 162, No. 1, pp. 79–88.

Cooper, W. S. (1989) "How evolutionary biology challenges the classical theory of rational choice," *Biology and Philosophy*, Vol. 4, No. 4, pp. 457–481.

Cornell, Bradford and Ivo Welch (1996) "Culture, information, and screening discrimination," *Journal of Political Economy*, Vol. 104, No. 3, pp. 542–571.

Cox, James C., Daniel Friedman and Vjollca Sadiraj (2008) "Revealed altruism 1," *Econometrica*, Vol. 76, No. 1, pp. 31–69.

Cross, K. Patricia (1977) "Not can, but will college teaching be improved?" *New Directions for Higher Education*, Vol. 1977, No. 17, pp. 1–15.

Cubitt, Robin P. and Robert Sugden (2001) "On money pumps," *Games and Economic Behavior*, Vol. 37, No. 1, pp. 121–160.

Curtis, Valerie, Micheal de Barra and Robert Aunger (2011) "Disgust as an adaptive system for disease avoidance behaviour," *Philosophical Transactions of the Royal Society B: Biological Sciences*, Vol. 366, No. 1563, pp. 389–401.

Cushman, Fiery (2020) "Rationalization is rational," *Behavioral and Brain Sciences*, Vol. 43, pp. 1–59.

Damasio, Antonio R. (2006) *Descartes' error*. Random House.

Darwin, Charles (1859) *The origin of species*. London: John Murray.

(1871/1981) *The descent of man, and selection in relation to sex*. Princeton University Press.

Darwin, Charles (1897) *The expression of the emotions in man and animals*. D. Appleton and Company.

Dasgupta, Partha and Eric Maskin (2005) "Uncertainty and hyperbolic discounting," *American Economic Review*, Vol. 95, No. 4, pp. 1290–1299.

Davidson, Donald, John Charles Chenoweth McKinsey and Patrick Suppes (1955) "Outlines of a formal theory of value, I," *Philosophy of Science*, Vol. 22, No. 2, pp. 140–160.

Dawes, Robyn M. and Richard H. Thaler (1988) "Anomalies: Cooperation," *Journal of Economic Perspectives*, Vol. 2, No. 3, pp. 187–197.

Dawkins, Richard (1976) *The selfish gene*. Oxford University Press.

(1997) *Climbing mount improbable*. W. W. Norton.

(2008) *River out of Eden: A Darwinian view of life*. Basic Books.

De Freitas, Julian, Kyle Thomas, Peter DeScioli and Steven Pinker (2019) "Common knowledge, coordination, and strategic mentalizing in human social life," *Proceedings of the National Academy of Sciences*, Vol. 116, No. 28, pp. 13751–13758.

De Vignemont, Frederique and Tania Singer (2006) "The empathic brain: How, when and why?" *Trends in Cognitive Sciences*, Vol. 10, No. 10, pp. 435–441.

de Finetti, Bruno (1931) "Sul significato soggettivo della probabilità," ñ*Fundamenta Mathematicae*, Vol. 17, pp. 298–329.

de Condorcet, Jean Antoine Nicolas (1788) *Essai sur la constitution et les fonctions des assemblées provinciales.*

Debreu, Gerard (1960) "Review of RD Luce, *Individual choice behavior: A theoretical analysis*," *American Economic Review*, Vol. 50, No. 1, pp. 186–188.

Dekel, Eddie and Marciano Siniscalchi (2015) "Epistemic game theory," in H. P. Young and S. Zamir, eds., *Handbook of game theory with economic applications*, vol. 4. Elsevier, pp. 619–702.

DellaVigna, Stefano and Ulrike Malmendier (2006) "Paying not to go to the gym," *American Economic Review*, Vol. 96, No. 3, pp. 694–719.

Dennett, Daniel (1996) *Darwin's dangerous idea: Evolution and the meaning of life.* Simon and Schuster.

Dennett, Daniel Clement (1987) *The intentional stance.* MIT Press.

Descamps, Ambroise, Sebastien Massoni, Lionel Page et al. (2019) "Learning to hesitate," Technical report.

Dobzhansky, Theodosius (1973) "Nothing in biology makes sense except in the light of evolution," *The American Biology Teacher*, Vol. 35, No. 3, pp. 125–129.

Doleac, Jennifer L. and Luke C. D. Stein (2013) "The visible hand: Race and online market outcomes," *The Economic Journal*, Vol. 123, No. 572, pp. F469–F492.

Donihue, Colin M., Alex M. Kowaleski, Jonathan B. Losos, Adam C. Algar, Simon Baeckens, Robert W. Buchkowski, Anne-Claire Fabre, Hannah K. Frank, Anthony J. Geneva, R. Graham Reynolds et al. (2020) "Hurricane effects on neotropical lizards span geographic and phylogenetic scales," *Proceedings of the National Academy of Sciences*, Vol. 117, No. 19, pp. 10429–10434.

Douglas, Karen M. and Ana C. Leite (2017) "Suspicion in the workplace: Organizational conspiracy theories and work-related outcomes," *British Journal of Psychology*, Vol. 108, No. 3, pp. 486–506.

Drayton, Lindsey A., Sarah F. Brosnan, Jodi Carrigan and Tara S. Stoinski (2013) "Endowment effects in gorillas (*Gorilla gorilla*)," *Journal of Comparative Psychology*, Vol. 127, No. 4, p. 365.

Dressler, Joshua (1982) "Rethinking heat of passion: A defense in search of a rationale," *J. Crim. L. & Criminology*, Vol. 73, p. 421.

Dubra, Juan, Fabio Maccheroni and Efe A. Ok (2004) "Expected utility theory without the completeness axiom," *Journal of Economic Theory*, Vol. 115, No. 1, pp. 118–133.

Dufwenberg, Martin and Georg Kirchsteiger (2004) "A theory of sequential reciprocity," *Games and Economic Behavior*, Vol. 47, No. 2, pp. 268–298.

Dunbar, Robin I. M. (2004) "Gossip in evolutionary perspective," *Review of General Psychology*, Vol. 8, No. 2, pp. 100–110.

Eagleman, David (2011) *Incognito: The secret lives of the brain.* Pantheon Books.

Easterlin, Richard A. (1974) "Does economic growth improve the human lot? Some empirical evidence," in P. A. David and M. W. Reder, eds., *Nations and households in economic growth: Essays in honor of Moses Abramovitz.* Elsevier, pp. 89–125.

Edgeworth, Francis Ysidro (1881) *Mathematical psychics: An essay on the application of mathematics to the moral sciences.* Kegan Paul.

Edwards, Ward (1954) "The theory of decision making," *Psychological Bulletin*, Vol. 51, No. 4, p. 380.

Ely, Jeffrey C. (2011) "Kludged," *American Economic Journal: Microeconomics*, Vol. 3, No. 3, pp. 210–231.

Engelmann, Jan M. and Michael Tomasello (2019) "Children's sense of fairness as equal respect," *Trends in Cognitive Sciences*, Vol. 23, No. 6, pp. 454–463.

Engler, Yola, Rudolf Kerschbamer and Lionel Page (2018) "Why did he do that? Using counterfactuals to study the effect of intentions in extensive form games," *Experimental Economics*, Vol. 21, No. 1, pp. 1–26.

Enke, Benjamin and Thomas Graeber (2019) "Cognitive uncertainty," National Bureau of Economic Research, No. 26518.

Epley, Nicholas and Erin Whitchurch (2008) "Mirror, mirror on the wall: Enhancement in self-recognition," *Personality and Social Psychology Bulletin*, Vol. 34, No. 9, pp. 1159–1170.

Epper, Thomas and Helga Fehr-Duda (2012) "The missing link: Unifying risk taking and time discounting," University of Zurich Department of Economics Working Paper, No. 96.

Erev, Ido, Thomas S. Wallsten and David V. Budescu (1994) "Simultaneous over and underconfidence: The role of error in judgment processes," *Psychological Review*, Vol. 101, No. 3, p. 519.

Ericson, Keith Marzilli and David Laibson (2018) "Intertemporal choice," Technical report, National Bureau of Economic Research.

Erikson, Erik H. (1968) *Identity: Youth and crisis*. W. W. Norton.

Eysenck, Hans J. (1985) *Decline and fall of the Freudian empire*. Pelican.

Falk, Armin, Ernst Fehr and Urs Fischbacher (2003) "On the nature of fair behavior," *Economic Inquiry*, Vol. 41, No. 1, pp. 20–26.

Fardouly, Jasmine, Phillippa C. Diedrichs, Lenny R. Vartanian and Emma Halliwell (2015) "Social comparisons on social media: The impact of Facebook on young women's body image concerns and mood," *Body Image*, Vol. 13, pp. 38–45.

Feddersen, Timothy J. (2004) "Rational choice theory and the paradox of not voting," *Journal of Economic Perspectives*, Vol. 18, No. 1, pp. 99–112.

Feddersen, Timothy and Alvaro Sandroni (2006) "A theory of participation in elections," *American Economic Review*, Vol. 96, No. 4, pp. 1271–1282.

Feltovich, Nick, Richmond Harbaugh and Ted To (2002) "Too cool for school? Signalling and countersignalling," *RAND Journal of Economics*, pp. 630–649.

Fessler, Daniel M. T., Serena J. Eng and C. David Navarrete (2005) "Elevated disgust sensitivity in the first trimester of pregnancy: Evidence supporting the compensatory prophylaxis hypothesis," *Evolution and Human Behavior*, Vol. 26, No. 4, pp. 344–351.

Fink, Philip W., Patrick S. Foo, and William H. Warren (2009) "Catching fly balls in virtual reality: A critical test of the outfielder problem," *Journal of Vision*, Vol. 9, No. 13, pp. 1–8.

Fischbacher, Urs and Simon Gachter (2010) "Social preferences, beliefs, and the dynamics of free riding in public goods experiments," *American Economic Review*, Vol. 100, No. 1, pp. 541–556.

Fishburn, Peter C. and Irving H. LaValle (1988) "Context-dependent choice with nonlinear and nontransitive preferences," *Econometrica*, pp. 1221–1239.

Fishburn, Peter and Peter Wakker (1995) "The invention of the independence condition for preferences," *Management Science*, Vol. 41, No. 7, pp. 1130–1144.

Fiske, Alan Page and Philip E. Tetlock (1997) "Taboo trade-offs: Reactions to transactions that transgress the spheres of justice," *Political Psychology*, Vol. 18, No. 2, pp. 255–297.

Fiske, Susan T. (2015) "Intergroup biases: A focus on stereotype content," *Current Opinion in Behavioral Sciences*, Vol. 3, pp. 45–50.

Fiske, Susan T. and Shelley E. Taylor (1991) *Social Cognition*. McGraw-Hill Book Company.

Flood, Merrill M. (1958) "Some experimental games," *Management Science*, Vol. 5, No. 1, pp. 5–26.

Fourcade, Marion, Etienne Ollion and Yann Algan (2015) "The superiority of economists," *Journal of Economic Perspectives*, Vol. 29, No. 1, pp. 89–114.

Frank, Robert H. (1985) *Choosing the right pond: Human behavior and the quest for status*. Oxford University Press.

(1987) "Shrewdly irrational," *Sociological Forum*, Vol. 2, pp. 21–41.

(1988) *Passions within reason: The strategic role of the emotions*. W. W. Norton.

Frank, Robert H., Thomas Gilovich and Dennis T. Regan (1993) "The evolution of one-shot cooperation: An experiment," *Ethology and Sociobiology*, Vol. 14, No. 4, pp. 247–256.

Frederick, Shane (2005) "Cognitive reflection and decision making," *Journal of Economic Perspectives*, Vol. 19, No. 4, pp. 25–42.

Frederick, Shane, George Loewenstein and Ted O'Donoghue (2002) "Time discounting and time preference: A critical review," *Journal of Economic Literature*, Vol. 40, No. 2, pp. 351–401.

Freud, Sigmund (1916–1917/1977) *Introductory lectures on psychoanalysis*, translated by J. Strachey. W. W. Norton.

Friedman, James W. (2000) "A guided tour of the Folk Theorem," in George Norman and Jean Francois Thisse The eds., *Market structure and competition policy*. Cambridge University Press, pp. 51–69.

Friedman, Milton (1953) *Essays in positive economics*. University of Chicago Press.

Friedman, Milton and Leonard J. Savage (1948) "The utility analysis of choices involving risk," *Journal of Political Economy*, Vol. 56, No. 4, pp. 279–304.

(1952) "The expected-utility hypothesis and the measurability of utility," *Journal of Political Economy*, Vol. 60, No. 6, pp. 463–474.

Frymer-Kensky, Tikva (1980) "Tit for tat: The principle of equal retribution in Near Eastern and Biblical law," *The Biblical Archaeologist*, Vol. 43, No. 4, pp. 230–234.

Fudenberg, Drew, Philipp Strack and Tomasz Strzalecki (2017) "Stochastic choice and optimal sequential sampling." https://arxiv.org/abs/1505.03342.

Gabaix, Xavier and David Laibson (2017) "Myopia and discounting," Technical report, National Bureau of Economic Research.

Gabriel, Marsha T., Joseph W. Critelli, and Jullana S. Ee (1994) "Narcissistic illusions in self-evaluations of intelligence and attractiveness," *Journal of Personality*, Vol. 62, No. 1, pp. 143–155.

Gambetta, Diego (2011) *Codes of the underworld: How criminals communicate*. Princeton University Press.

Gandolfi, Anna Sachko (2002/2018) *Economics as an evolutionary science: From utility to fitness*. Routledge.

Gelman, Andrew and Yuling Yao (2020) "Holes in Bayesian statistics," arXivpreprintarXiv:2002.06467.

Georgescu-Roegen, Nicholas (1936) "The pure theory of consumers behavior," *The Quarterly Journal of Economics*, Vol. 50, No. 4, pp. 545–593.

Gershman, Samuel J. and Rahul Bhui (2020) "Rationally inattentive intertemporal choice," *Nature Communications*, Vol. 11, No. 1, pp. 1–8.

Gigerenzer, Gerd (2000) *Adaptive thinking: Rationality in the real world.* Oxford University Press.

  (2007) *Gut feelings: The intelligence of the unconscious.* Penguin.

  (2018) "The bias bias in behavioral economics," *Review of Behavioral Economics*, Vol. 5, Nos. 3–4, pp. 303–336.

Gigerenzer, Gerd and Henry Brighton (2009) "Homo heuristicus: Why biased minds make better inferences," *Topics in Cognitive Science*, Vol. 1, No. 1, pp. 107–143.

Gigerenzer, Gerd and Daniel G. Goldstein (1996) "Reasoning the fast and frugal way: Models of bounded rationality," *Psychological Review*, Vol. 103, No. 4, p. 650.

Gigerenzer, Gerd and Ulrich Hoffrage (1995) "How to improve Bayesian reasoning without instruction: Frequency formats," *Psychological Review*, Vol. 102, No. 4, p. 684.

Gilboa, Itzhak (2009) *Theory of decision under uncertainty.* Cambridge University Press.

Gilboa, Itzhak, Andrew Postlewaite and David Schmeidler (2009) "Is it always rational to satisfy Savage's axioms?," *Economics & Philosophy*, Vol. 25, No. 3, pp. 285–296.

Gilliver, K. M. (2004) *Caesar's Gallic Wars 58–50 BC.* Routledge.

Gilovich, Thomas and Dale Griffin (2002) "Introduction-heuristics and biases: Then and now," in T. Gilovich, D. Griffin and D. Kahneman, eds., *Heuristics and biases: The psychology of intuitive judgment.* Cambridge University Press, pp. 1–18.

Gilovich, Thomas, Robert Vallone and Amos Tversky (1985) "The hot hand in basketball: On the misperception of random sequences," *Cognitive Psychology*, Vol. 17, No. 3, pp. 295–314.

Gintis, Herbert (2007) "A framework for the unification of the behavioral sciences," *Behavioral and Brain Sciences*, Vol. 30, No. 1, pp. 1–16.

Glimcher, Paul W. (2011) *Foundations of neuroeconomic analysis.* Oxford University Press.

Goethals, George R. and John M. Darley (1977) "Social comparison theory: An attributional approach," in J. M. Suls and R. L. Miller, eds., *Social comparison processes: Theoretical and empirical perspectives.* Hemisphere, pp. 259–278.

Goffman, Erving (1959) *The presentation of self in everyday life.* Anchor Books.

  (1971) *Relations in public.* Basic Books.

Gold, Joshua I. and Michael N. Shadlen (2002) "Banburismus and the brain: Decoding the relationship between sensory stimuli, decisions, and reward," *Neuron*, Vol. 36, No. 2, pp. 299–308.

Goodman, Nelson (1965) *Fact, fiction, and forecast.* Bobbs-Merrill.

Gould, Stephen Jay and Richard C. Lewontin (1979) "The spandrels of San Marco and the Panglossian paradigm: A critique of the adaptationist programme," *Proceedings of the Royal Society of London. Series B. Biological Sciences*, Vol. 205, No. 1161, pp. 581–598.

Green, Brett and Jeffrey Zwiebel (2018) "The hot-hand fallacy: Cognitive mistakes or equilibrium adjustments? Evidence from major league baseball," *Management Science*, Vol. 64, No. 11, pp. 5315–5348.

Green, Elliott (2021) "The politics of ethnic identity in sub-Saharan Africa," *Comparative Political Studies*, Vol. 54, No. 7, pp. 1197–1226.

Green, Leonard and Joel Myerson (1996) "Exponential versus hyperbolic discounting of delayed outcomes: Risk and waiting time," *American Zoologist*, Vol. 36, No. 4, pp. 496–505.

Grether, David M. and Charles R. Plott (1979) "Economic theory of choice and the preference reversal phenomenon," *The American Economic Review*, Vol. 69, No. 4, pp. 623–638.

Grotius, Hugo (1625) *De jure belli ac pacis*. French National Library.

Guay, Brian and Christopher Johnston (2021) "Ideological asymmetries and the determinants of politically motivated reasoning," *American Journal of Political Science*, Vol. 66, No. 2, pp. 285–301.

Gurdal, Mehmet Y., Joshua B. Miller and Aldo Rustichini (2013) "Why blame?" *Journal of Political Economy*, Vol. 121, No. 6, pp. 1205–1247.

Güth, Werner, Rolf Schmittberger and Bernd Schwarze (1982) "An experimental analysis of ultimatum bargaining," *Journal of Economic Behavior & Organization*, Vol. 3, No. 4, pp. 367–388.

Haidt, Jonathan (2006) *The happiness hypothesis: Putting ancient wisdom and philosophy to the test of modern science*. Random House.

Haldeman, Harry R. and Joseph DiMona (1978) *The ends of power*. Dell Publishing Company.

Halevy, Yoram (2008) "Strotz meets Allais: Diminishing impatience and the certainty effect," *American Economic Review*, Vol. 98, No. 3, pp. 1145–1162.

(2015) "Time consistency: Stationarity and time invariance," *Econometrica*, Vol. 83, No. 1, pp. 335–352.

Hamilton, William D. (1963) "The evolution of altruistic behavior," *The American Naturalist*, Vol. 97, No. 896, pp. 354–356.

(1964) "The genetical evolution of social behaviour. II," *Journal of Theoretical Biology*, Vol. 7, No. 1, pp. 17–52.

Hamlin, Robert P. (2017) ""The gaze heuristic:" Biography of an adaptively rational decision process," *Topics in Cognitive Science*, Vol. 9, No. 2, pp. 264–288.

Hammerstein, Peter and Edward H. Hagen (2005) "The second wave of evolutionary economics in biology," *Trends in Ecology & Evolution*, Vol. 20, No. 11, pp. 604–609.

Handa, Jagdish (1977) "Risk, probabilities, and a new theory of cardinal utility," *Journal of Political Economy*, Vol. 85, No. 1, pp. 97–122.

Harbaugh, Richmond and Theodore To (2020) "False modesty: When disclosing good news looks bad," *Journal of Mathematical Economics*, Vol. 87, pp. 43–55.

Harsanyi, John C. (1982) "Rule utilitarianism, rights, obligations and the theory of rational behavior," in *Papers in game theory*. Springer, pp. 235–253.

Haselton, Martie G., Gregory A. Bryant, Andreas Wilke, David A. Frederick, Andrew Galperin, Willem E. Frankenhuis and Tyler Moore (2009) "Adaptive rationality: An evolutionary perspective on cognitive bias," *Social Cognition*, Vol. 27, No. 5, pp. 733–763.

Haselton, Martie G. and David M. Buss (2000) "Error management theory: A new perspective on biases in cross-sex mind reading," *Journal of Personality and Social Psychology*, Vol. 78, No. 1, p. 81.

Haslam, S. Alexander, Stephen D. Reicher and Michael J. Platow (2010) *The new psychology of leadership: Identity, influence and power*. Psychology Press.

Hayden, Benjamin Y. (2016) "Time discounting and time preference in animals: A critical review," *Psychonomic Bulletin & Review*, Vol. 23, No. 1, pp. 39–53.

Heath, Chip, Richard P. Larrick and George Wu (1999) "Goals as reference points," *Cognitive Psychology*, Vol. 38, No. 1, pp. 79–109.

Heifetz, Aviad, Chris Shannon and Yossi Spiegel (2007a) "What to maximize if you must," *Journal of Economic Theory*, Vol. 133, No. 1, pp. 31–57.

(2007b) "The dynamic evolution of preferences," *Economic Theory*, Vol. 32, No. 2, pp. 251–286.

Helvétius, Claude Adrien (1758) *De l'esprit*. Durand.

Henrich, Joseph (2004) "Cultural group selection, coevolutionary processes and large-scale cooperation," *Journal of Economic Behavior & Organization*, Vol. 53, No. 1, pp. 3–35.

Henrich, Joseph, Robert Boyd, Samuel Bowles, Colin Camerer, Ernst Fehr, Herbert Gintis, Richard McElreath, Michael Alvard, Abigail Barr, Jean Ensminger et al. (2005) "'Economic man' in cross-cultural perspective: Behavioral experiments in 15 small-scale societies," *Behavioral and Brain Sciences*, Vol. 28, No. 6, pp. 795–815.

Herold, Florian and Nick Netzer (2010) "Probability weighting as evolutionary second-best," Technical report, working paper.

Hertwig, Ralph and Gerd Gigerenzer (1999) "The 'conjunction fallacy' revisited: How intelligent inferences look like reasoning errors," *Journal of Behavioral Decision Making*, Vol. 12, No. 4, pp. 275–305.

Hilton, Denis J (1995) "The social context of reasoning: Conversational inference and rational judgment," *Psychological Bulletin*, Vol. 118, No. 2, p. 248.

Hintze, Arend, Randal S Olson, Christoph Adami and Ralph Hertwig (2015) "Risk sensitivity as an evolutionary adaptation," *Scientific Reports*, Vol. 5, p. 8242.

Hirshleifer, David and Ivo Welch (2002) "An economic approach to the psychology of change: Amnesia, inertia, and impulsiveness," *Journal of Economics & Management Strategy*, Vol. 11, No. 3, pp. 379–421.

Hirshleifer, Jack (1977) "Economics from a biological viewpoint," *The Journal of Law and Economics*, Vol. 20, No. 1, pp. 1–52.

(1985) "The expanding domain of economics," *The American Economic Review*, Vol. 75, No. 6, pp. 53–68.

(1987) "On the emotions as guarantors of threats and promises," in J. E. Dupré, ed., *The latest on the best: Essays on evolution and optimality*. MIT Press, pp. 307–26.

Ho, Benjamin (2021) *Why Trust Matters: An Economist's Guide to the Ties That Bind Us*. Columbia University Press.

Hobbes, Thomas (1651) *Leviathan*.

Hoffman, Elizabeth, Kevin McCabe, Keith Shachat and Vernon Smith (1994) "Preferences, property rights, and anonymity in bargaining games," *Games and Economic Behavior*, Vol. 7, No. 3, pp. 346–380.

Hoffman, Elizabeth, Kevin McCabe and Vernon L Smith (1996) "Social distance and other-regarding behavior in dictator games," *The American Economic Review*, Vol. 86, No. 3, pp. 653–660.

Hoffman, Moshe, Christian Hilbe and Martin A. Nowak (2018) "The signal-burying game can explain why we obscure positive traits and good deeds," *Nature Human Behaviour*, Vol. 2, No. 6, p. 397.

Hoffman, Moshe, Erez Yoeli and Martin A. Nowak (2015) "Cooperate without looking: Why we care what people think and not just what they do," *Proceedings of the National Academy of Sciences*, Vol. 112, No. 6, pp. 1727–1732.

Hofstadter, Douglas R. (1983) "The prisoner's dilemma computer tournaments and the evolution of cooperation," *Scientific American*, Vol. 248, No. 5, pp. 14–20.

Hornsey, Matthew J. and Sarah Esposo (2009) "Resistance to group criticism and recommendations for change: Lessons from the intergroup sensitivity effect," *Social and Personality Psychology Compass*, Vol. 3, No. 3, pp. 275–291.

Huber, Joel, John W. Payne and Christopher Puto (1982) "Adding asymmetrically dominated alternatives: Violations of regularity and the similarity hypothesis," *Journal of Consumer Research*, Vol. 9, No. 1, pp. 90–98.

Hume, David (1739/2003) *A treatise of human nature.* Courier Corporation.

Hutcheson, Francis (1725) *Inquiry into the original of our ideas of beauty and virtue.*

Huttegger, Simon M. and Kevin J. S. Zollman (2012) "Evolution, dynamics, and rationality: The limits of ESS methodology," in Samir Okasha and Ken Binmore, eds., *Evolution and rationality.* Cambridge University Press, pp. 67–83.

Iredale, Wendy and Mark van Vugt (2012) "Altruism as showing off: A signalling perspective on promoting green behaviour and acts of kindness," in Craig Roberts, ed., *Applied evolutionary psychology.* Oxford University Press, pp. 173–185.

Jean, Roger V. (2009) *Phyllotaxis: A systemic study in plant morphogenesis.* Cambridge University Press.

Jevons, William Stanley (1879) *The theory of political economy.* Macmillan and Company.

Johnson, Dominic and Jesse Bering (2006) "Hand of God, mind of man: Punishment and cognition in the evolution of cooperation," *Evolutionary Psychology*, Vol. 4, No. 1, pp. 219–233.

Johnson, Dominic D. P. and James H. Fowler (2011) "The evolution of overconfidence," *Nature*, Vol. 477, No. 7364, p. 317.

Jones, Adam G. and Nicholas L. Ratterman (2009) "Mate choice and sexual selection: What have we learned since Darwin?," *Proceedings of the National Academy of Sciences*, Vol. 106, Supplement No. 1, pp. 10001–10008.

Jones, Owen D. (2000) "Time-shifted rationality and the law of law's leverage: Behavioral economics meets behavioral biology," *Northwestern University Law Review*, Vol. 95, p. 1141.

Jussim, Lee, Thomas R. Cain, Jarret T. Crawford, Kent Harber and Florette Cohen (2009) "The unbearable accuracy of stereotypes," in *Handbook of Prejudice, Stereotyping, and Discrimination*, Vol. 199, p. 227.

Kagel, John H., Leonard Green and Thomas Caraco (1986) "When foragers discount the future: Constraint or adaptation?," *Animal Behaviour*, Vol. 34, pp. 271–283.

Kahan, Dan M., Ellen Peters, Erica Dawson and Paul Slovic (2013) "Motivated numeracy and enlightened self-government," *Behavioural Public Policy*, Vol. 1, pp. 54–86.

Kahneman, Daniel (2003) "A perspective on judgment and choice: Mapping bounded rationality," *American Psychologist*, Vol. 58, No. 9, p. 697.

(2011) *Thinking, fast and slow.* Macmillan.

Kahneman, Daniel, Jack L. Knetsch and Richard Thaler (1986) "Fairness as a constraint on profit seeking: Entitlements in the market," *The American Economic Review*, pp. 728–741.

Kahneman, Daniel and Amos Tversky (1979) "Prospect theory: An analysis of decision under risk," *Econometrica*, Vol. 47, No. 2, pp. 263–292.

Kamenica, Emir (2008) "Contextual inference in markets: On the informational content of product lines," *American Economic Review*, Vol. 98, No. 5, pp. 2127–2149.

Kaplan, Hillard S., Jane B. Lancaster, Sara E. Johnson and John A. Bock (1995) "Does observed fertility maximize fitness among New Mexican men?," *Human Nature*, Vol. 6, No. 4, pp. 325–360.

Karlan, Dean and Margaret A. McConnell (2014) "Hey look at me: The effect of giving circles on giving," *Journal of Economic Behavior & Organization*, Vol. 106, pp. 402–412.

Karni, Edi and Marie-Louise Vierø (2017) "Awareness of unawareness: A theory of decision making in the face of ignorance," *Journal of Economic Theory*, Vol. 168, pp. 301–328.

Keeley, Lawrence H., 1996. War before civilization. OUP USA.

Keren, Gideon and Peter Roelofsma (1995) "Immediacy and certainty in intertemporal choice," *Organizational Behavior and Human Decision Processes*, Vol. 63, No. 3, pp. 287–297.

Knight, Frank H. (1921) *Risk, uncertainty and profit*. Harper & Row.

Knill, David C. and Alexandre Pouget (2004) "The Bayesian brain: The role of uncertainty in neural coding and computation," *Trends in Neurosciences*, Vol. 27, No. 12, pp. 712–719.

Kolmogorov, Andreĭ Nikolaevich and Albert T. Bharucha-Reid (1933/2018) *Foundations of the theory of probability*, 2nd English edition. Courier Dover Publications.

Koopmans, Tjalling C. (1960) "Stationary ordinal utility and impatience," *Econometrica*, pp. 287–309.

Köszegi, Botond and Matthew Rabin (2006) "A model of reference-dependent preferences," *The Quarterly Journal of Economics*, Vol. 121, No. 4, pp. 1133–1165.

Krasnova, Hanna, Helena Wenninger, Thomas Widjaja and Peter Buxmann (2013) "Envy on Facebook: A hidden threat to users' life satisfaction?", in *Proceedings of the 11th International Conference on Wirtschaftsinformatik (WI2013)*, Universität Leipzig, Germany, 27 February–3 January 2013.

Kuhn, Thomas S. (1962/2012) *The structure of scientific revolutions*. University of Chicago Press.

Kühne, Thomas (2011) "The pleasure of terror: Belonging through genocide," in *Pleasure and power in Nazi Germany*. Springer, pp. 234–255.

Kunda, Ziva (1987) "Motivated inference: Self-serving generation and evaluation of causal theories," *Journal of Personality and Social Psychology*, Vol. 53, No. 4, p. 636.

Laibson, David (1997) "Golden eggs and hyperbolic discounting," *The Quarterly Journal of Economics*, Vol. 112, No. 2, pp. 443–478.

Lakshminaryanan, Venkat, M. Keith Chen and Laurie R. Santos (2008) "Endowment effect in capuchin monkeys," *Philosophical Transactions of the Royal Society B: Biological Sciences*, Vol. 363, No. 1511, pp. 3837–3844.

Laplace, Pierre-Simon (1814) *Essai philosophique sur les probabilités*. Paris: Mme Ve Courcier.

Laughlin, Simon (1981) "A simple coding procedure enhances a neuron's information capacity," *Zeitschrift für Naturforschung C*, Vol. 36, Nos. 9–10, pp. 910–912.

Lazear, Edward P. (2000) "Economic imperialism," *The Quarterly Journal of Economics*, Vol. 115, No. 1, pp. 99–146.

Lendon, Jon E. (2005) *Soldiers and ghosts: A history of battle in classical antiquity.* Yale University Press.

Levine, David K. (1998) "Modeling altruism and spitefulness in experiments," *Review of Economic Dynamics*, Vol. 1, No. 3, pp. 593–622.

Levitt, Steven D. and Stephen J. Dubner (2005) *Freakonomics.* William Morrow.

Li, Shengwu and Ning Neil Yu (2018) "Context-dependent choice as explained by foraging theory," *Journal of Economic Theory*, Vol. 175, pp. 159–177.

Lichtenstein, Sarah and Paul Slovic (1971) "Reversals of preference between bids and choices in gambling decisions," *Journal of Experimental Psychology*, Vol. 89, No. 1, p. 46.

(2006) *The construction of preference.* Cambridge University Press.

Lieder, Falk and Thomas L. Griffiths (2020) "Resource-rational analysis: Understanding human cognition as the optimal use of limited computational resources," *Behavioral and Brain Sciences*, Vol. 43.

Lieder, Falk, Thomas L. Griffiths and Ming Hsu (2018) "Overrepresentation of extreme events in decision making reflects rational use of cognitive resources," *Psychological Review*, Vol. 125, No. 1, p. 1.

Locke, John (1689) *An essay concerning human understanding.*

Loomes, Graham and Robert Sugden (1982) "Regret theory: An alternative theory of rational choice under uncertainty," *The Economic Journal*, Vol. 92, No. 368, pp. 805–824.

Loury, Glenn C. (1994) "Self-censorship in public discourse: A theory of 'political correctness' and related phenomena," *Rationality and Society*, Vol. 6, No. 4, pp. 428–461.

Luce, R. Duncan (1958) *Individual choice behavior: A theoretical analysis.* John Wiley.

Luce, R. Duncan and Howard Raiffa (1957) *Games and decisions.* John Wiley & Sons.

Luce, R. Duncan et al. (1986) *Response times: Their role in inferring elementary mental organization.* Oxford University Press.

MacCrimmon, Kenneth R. (1968) "Descriptive and normative implications of the decision-theory postulates," in *Risk and uncertainty.* Springer, pp. 3–32.

Malmendier, Ulrike and Geoffrey Tate (2005) "Does overconfidence affect corporate investment? CEO overconfidence measures revisited," *European Financial Management*, Vol. 11, No. 5, pp. 649–659.

Mann, Michael (1986) *The sources of social power, vol. 1: A history of power from the beginning to AD 1760.* Cambridge University Press.

Marcus, Gary (2009) *Kluge: The haphazard evolution of the human mind.* Houghton Mifflin Harcourt.

Markowitz, Harry (1952) "The utility of wealth," *Journal of Political Economy*, Vol. 60, No. 2, pp. 151–158.

Marschak, Jacob (1950) "Rational behavior, uncertain prospects, and measurable utility," *Econometrica*, pp. 111–141.

Mas-Colell, Andreu, Michael Dennis Whinston, Jerry R. Green et al. (1995) *Microeconomic theory*, vol. 1. Oxford University Press.

Mauss, Marcel (1990) *The gift: The form and reason for exchange in archaic societies.* Routledge.

Mayberry, John P. (1970) "Structural requirements for abstract-mode models of passenger transportation," in R. E. Quandt, ed., *The demand for travel: Theory and measurement.*

Maynard Smith, John (1982) *Evolution and the theory of games.* Cambridge University Press.

McBeath, Michael K., Dennis M Shaffer and Mary K. Kaiser (1995) "How baseball outfielders determine where to run to catch fly balls," *Science*, Vol. 268, No. 5210, pp. 569–573.

McClennen, Edward (2009) "The Normative Status of the Independence Principle," in Paul Anand, Prasanta Pattanaik and Clemens Puppe, eds., *The handbook of rational and social choice.* Oxford University Press, pp. 140–155.

McFadden, Daniel (1973) "Conditional logit analysis of qualitative choice behavior," in P. Zarembka, ed., *Frontiers in econometrics.* New York: Academic Press, pp. 105–142.

(2001) "Economic choices," *American Economic Review*, Vol. 91, No. 3, pp. 351–378.

McLean, Iain (1995) "Independence of irrelevant alternatives before Arrow," *Mathematical Social Sciences*, Vol. 30, No. 2, pp. 107–126.

McNamara, John M. and Alasdair I. Houston (1987) "Starvation and predation as factors limiting population size," *Ecology*, Vol. 68, No. 5, pp. 1515–1519.

Meijaard, Jaap P., Jim M. Papadopoulos, Andy Ruina and Arend L. Schwab (2007) "Linearized dynamics equations for the balance and steer of a bicycle: A benchmark and review," *Proceedings of the Royal Society A: Mathematical, Physical and Engineering Sciences*, Vol. 463, No. 2084, pp. 1955–1982.

Mellers, Barbara, Ralph Hertwig and Daniel Kahneman (2001) "Do frequency representations eliminate conjunction effects? An exercise in adversarial collaboration," *Psychological Science*, Vol. 12, No. 4, pp. 269–275.

Mély, David A., Drew Linsley and Thomas Serre (2018) "Complementary surrounds explain diverse contextual phenomena across visual modalities," *Psychological Review*, Vol. 125, No. 5, p. 769.

Mercier, Hugo and Dan Sperber (2011) "Why do humans reason? Arguments for an argumentative theory," *Behavioral and Brain Sciences*, Vol. 34, No. 2, pp. 57–74.

Mertens, Jean-Francois and Shmuel Zamir (1985) "Formulation of Bayesian analysis for games with incomplete information," *International Journal of Game Theory*, Vol. 14, No. 1, pp. 1–29.

Metz, J. A. J., S. D. Mylius and O. Diekmann (2008) "When does evolution optimize?," *Evolutionary Ecology Research*, Vol. 10, pp. 629–654.

Michell, Joel (1993) "The origins of the representational theory of measurement: Helmholtz, Hölder, and Russell," *Studies in History and Philosophy of Science Part A*, Vol. 24, No. 2, pp. 185–206.

Milkman, Katherine L., Todd Rogers and Max H. Bazerman (2009) "Highbrow films gather dust: Time-inconsistent preferences and online DVD rentals," *Management Science*, Vol. 55, No. 6, pp. 1047–1059.

Mill, John Stuart (1836) "On the definition of political economy; and on the method of investigation proper to it."

(1861) *Utilitarianism.*

Miller, Joshua B. and Adam Sanjurjo (2014) A cold shower for the hot hand fallacy (No. 518). IGIER working paper.

(2018) "Surprised by the hot hand fallacy? A truth in the law of small numbers," *Econometrica*, Vol. 86, No. 6, pp. 2019–2047.

Mischel, Walter and Ebbe B. Ebbesen (1970) "Attention in delay of gratification," *Journal of Personality and Social Psychology*, Vol. 16, No. 2, p. 329.

Mischel, Walter, Ebbe B. Ebbesen and Antonette Raskoff Zeiss (1972) "Cognitive and attentional mechanisms in delay of gratification," *Journal of Personality and Social Psychology*, Vol. 21, No. 2, p. 204.

Mitchell, Kevin J. (2020) *Innate: How the wiring of our brains shapes who we are.* Princeton University Press.

Mobbs, Dean, Pete C. Trimmer, Daniel T. Blumstein and Peter Dayan (2018) "Foraging for foundations in decision neuroscience: Insights from ethology," *Nature Reviews Neuroscience*, Vol. 19, No. 7, pp. 419–427.

Modelling Animal Decisions Group, Tim W. Fawcett, Benja Fallenstein, Andrew D. Higginson, Alasdair I. Houston, Dave E. W. Mallpress, Pete C. Trimmer and John M. McNamara (2014) "The evolution of decision rules in complex environments," *Trends in Cognitive Sciences*, Vol. 18, No. 3, pp. 153–161.

Monger, G. (2004) *Marriage customs of the world: From henna to honeymoons.* Abc-clio.

Montague, Read (2006) *Why choose this book? How we make decisions.* E. P. Dutton.

Morris, Stephen (2001) "Political correctness," *Journal of Political Economy*, Vol. 109, No. 2, pp. 231–265.

Moscati, Ivan (2016) "Retrospectives: How economists came to accept expected utility theory: The case of Samuelson and Savage," *Journal of Economic Perspectives*, Vol. 30, No. 2, pp. 219–236.

(2018) *Measuring utility: From the marginal revolution to behavioral economics.* Oxford University Press.

Mosteller, Frederick and Philip Nogee (1951) "An experimental measurement of utility," *Journal of Political Economy*, Vol. 59, No. 5, pp. 371–404.

Mullen, Brian and Li-tze Hu (1989) "Perceptions of ingroup and outgroup variability: A meta-analytic integration," *Basic and Applied Social Psychology*, Vol. 10, No. 3, pp. 233–252.

Naimark, Norman M. (2017) *Genocide: A world history.* Oxford University Press.

Nash, John F. (1950) "The bargaining problem," *Econometrica*, Vol. 18, No. 2, pp. 155–162.

Nesse, R. M. (2001) "The smoke detector principle: Natural selection and the regulation of defensive responses," *Annals of the New York Academy of Sciences*, Vol. 935, pp. 75–85.

Netzer, Nick (2009) "Evolution of time preferences and attitudes toward risk," *American Economic Review*, Vol. 99, No. 3, pp. 937–955.

Neuberg, Steven L., Douglas T. Kenrick and Mark Schaller (2011) "Human threat management systems: Self-protection and disease avoidance," *Neuroscience & Biobehavioral Reviews*, Vol. 35, No. 4, pp. 1042–1051.

Newton, Isaac (1687/1999) *The Principia: Mathematical principles of natural philosophy.* University of California Press.

Nielsen, K. and Rehbeck, J., 2022. When Choices are mistakes. American Economic Review, 112(7), pp. 2237–68.

Nietzsche, Friedrich Wilhelm (1882/2001) *The gay science*. Cambridge University Press.

Nisbett, Richard E. and Dov Cohen (1996) *Culture of honor: The psychology of violence in the south*. Westview Press.

Norenzayan, Ara and Azim F. Shariff (2008) "The origin and evolution of religious prosociality," *Science*, Vol. 322, No. 5898, pp. 58–62.

Nowak, Martin and Karl Sigmund (1993) "A strategy of win-stay, lose-shift that out-performs tit-for-tat in the Prisoner's Dilemma game," *Nature*, Vol. 364, No. 6432, p. 56.

Nowak, Martin A. and Karl Sigmund (2005) "Evolution of indirect reciprocity," *Nature*, Vol. 437, No. 7063, pp. 1291–1298.

Nozick, Robert (1974) *Anarchy, state, and utopia*. Basic Books.

O'Donoghue, Ted and Charles Sprenger (2018) "Reference-dependent preferences," in K. M. Ericson, D. Laibson, B. D. Bernheim and D. Stefano, eds., *Handbook of behavioral economics: Foundations and applications*, Vol. 1, p. 1.

Oesch, Daniel (2008) "Explaining workers' support for right-wing populist parties in Western Europe: Evidence from Austria, Belgium, France, Norway, and Switzer-land," *International Political Science Review*, Vol. 29, No. 3, pp. 349–373.

Okabe, Takuya (2015) "Biophysical optimality of the golden angle in phyllotaxis," *Scientific Reports*, Vol. 5, p. 15358.

Okabe, Takuya, Atsushi Ishida and Jin Yoshimura (2019) "The unified rule of phyl-lotaxis explaining both spiral and non-spiral arrangements," *Journal of the Royal Society Interface*, Vol. 16, No. 151, pp. 1–7.

Okasha, Samir (2018) *Agents and goals in evolution*. Oxford University Press.

Okasha, Samir and Ken Binmore (2012) *Evolution and rationality: Decisions, co-operation and strategic behaviour*. Cambridge University Press.

Olberg, R. M., A. H. Worthington, and K. R. Venator (2000) "Prey pursuit and interception in dragonflies," *Journal of Comparative Physiology A*, Vol. 186, No. 2, pp. 155–162.

Oliver, J. Eric and Thomas Wood (2014) "Medical conspiracy theories and health behaviors in the United States," *JAMA Internal Medicine*, Vol. 174, No. 5, pp. 817–818.

Orr, H. Allen (2009) "Fitness and its role in evolutionary genetics," *Nature Reviews Genetics*, Vol. 10, No. 8, pp. 531–539.

Osborne, Martin J. and Ariel Rubinstein (1994) *A course in game theory*. MIT Press.

Page, Lionel (2020) "The ethics of social choices and the role of economists in a pandemic," *Journal of Behavioral Economics for Policy*, Vol. 4, No. S, pp. 17–22.

Parekh, Bhikhu (2016) *Bentham's political thought*. Routledge.

Pareto, Vilfredo (1906/2014) *Manual of political economy: A critical and variorum edition*. Oxford University Press.

Persky, Joseph (1995) "The ethology of homo economicus," *Journal of Economic Perspectives*, Vol. 9, No. 2, pp. 221–231.

Phelps, Edmund S. (1972) "The statistical theory of racism and sexism," *The American Economic Review*, Vol. 62, No. 4, pp. 659–661.

Phillips, Lawrence D. and Detlof von Winterfeldt (2007) "5 reflections on the contri-butions of Ward Edwards to decision analysis and behavioral research," in Ward Edwards, Ralph F. Miles Jr., Detlof von Winterfeldt, eds., *Advances in decision analysis: From foundations to applications*. Cambridge University Press, p. 71.

Pinker, Steven (2011a) *The better angels of our nature: The decline of violence in history and its causes*. Penguin UK.

(2011b) "Representations and decision rules in the theory of self-deception," *Behavioral and Brain Sciences*, Vol. 34, No. 1, pp. 35–37.

(2021) *Rationality: What it is, why it seems scarce, why it matters*. Penguin UK.

Pinker, Steven, Martin A. Nowak, and James J. Lee (2008) "The logic of indirect speech," *Proceedings of the National Academy of Sciences*, Vol. 105, No. 3, pp. 833–838.

Planck, Max (1950) *Scientific autobiography and other papers*. Williams and Northgate.

Plato (375 BC) *The Republic*.

(490–420 BCE) *Protagoras*.

Poddiakov, Alexander N. (2013) "Catching a a flying ball: Is that really that easy? A contributionv to the critique of G. Gigerenzer's approach," in A. G. Egorov and V. V. Selivanov, eds., *Psychologia Kognitivnykh Processov: Materialy*. Smolensk: Smolensk State University, pp. 83–86.

Poon, Kai-Tak and Wing-Yan Wong (2018) "Stuck on the train of ruminative thoughts: The effect of aggressive fantasy on subjective well-being," *Journal of Interpersonal Violence*, Vol. 36, Nos. 11–12, pp. NP6390–NP6410.

Popper, Karl (1945/2005) *The logic of scientific discovery*. Routledge.

(1948) *Objective knowledge: An evolutionary approach*. Clarendon Press.

Poundstone, William (1993) *Prisoner's Dilemma: John von Neumann, game theory and the puzzle of the bomb*. Anchor.

Preston, Malcolm G. and Philip Baratta (1948) "An experimental study of the auction-value of an uncertain outcome," *The American Journal of Psychology*, Vol. 61, No. 2, pp. 183–193.

Pribram, Karl (1983) *A history of economic reasoning*. Johns Hopkins University Press.

Price, Michael Holton and James Holland Jones (2020) "Fitness-maximizers employ pessimistic probability weighting for decisions under risk," *Evolutionary Human Sciences*, Vol. 2, pp. 1–32.

Prusinkiewicz, Przemyslaw and Aristid Lindenmayer (2012) *The algorithmic beauty of plants*. Springer Science + Business Media.

Quiggin, John (1982) "A theory of anticipated utility," *Journal of Economic Behavior & Organization*, Vol. 3, No. 4, pp. 323–343.

Quine, Willard V. (1969) "Natural kinds," in Nicholas Rescher, ed., *Essays in honor of Carl G. Hempel*. Springer, pp. 5–23.

Rabin, Matthew (1993) "Incorporating fairness into game theory and economics," *The American Economic Review*, Vol. 83, No. 5, pp. 1281–1302.

Radner, Roy and Jacob Marschak (1954) "Note on some proposed decision criteria," in R. M. Thrall, C. H. Coombs and R. L. Davis, eds., *Decision process*. Wiley.

Ramsey, Frank Plumpton (1928) "A mathematical theory of saving," *The Economic Journal*, Vol. 38, No. 152, pp. 543–559.

Ransford, H. Chris (2015) "The 8 most complex object in the known universe," in *The far horizons of time*. Sciendo Migration, pp. 32–35.

Rawls, John (1971) *A theory of justice*. Belknap.

Ray, Paramesh (1973) "Independence of irrelevant alternatives," *Econometrica*, pp. 987–991.

Rayo, Luis and Gary S. Becker (2007) "Evolutionary efficiency and happiness," *Journal of Political Economy*, Vol. 115, No. 2, pp. 302–337.

Redelmeier, Donald A. and Amos Tversky (1992) "On the framing of multiple prospects," *Psychological Science*, Vol. 3, No. 3, pp. 191–193.

Ridley, J. N. (1982) "Packing efficiency in sunflower heads," *Mathematical Biosciences*, Vol. 58, No. 1, pp. 129–139.

Rieskamp, Jörg, Jerome R. Busemeyer and Barbara A. Mellers (2006) "Extending the bounds of rationality: Evidence and theories of preferential choice," *Journal of Economic Literature*, Vol. 44, No. 3, pp. 631–661.

Robbins, Lionel (2007) *An essay on the nature and significance of economic science.* Ludwig von Mises Institute.

Robinson, Joan (1953) "The production function and the theory of capital," *The Review of Economic Studies*, Vol. 21, No. 2, pp. 81–106.

Robson, Arthur and Larry Samuelson (2011) "The evolution of decision and experienced utilities," *Theoretical Economics*, Vol. 6, No. 3, pp. 311–339.

Robson, Arthur J. (2001) "The biological basis of economic behavior," *Journal of Economic Literature*, Vol. 39, No. 1, pp. 11–33.

Robson, Arthur J. and Larry Samuelson (2007) "The evolution of intertemporal preferences," *American Economic Review*, Vol. 97, No. 2, pp. 496–500.

(2009) "The evolution of time preference with aggregate uncertainty," *American Economic Review*, Vol. 99, No. 5, pp. 1925–1953.

Robson, A. J., L. A. Whitehead and N. Robalino (2018) Adaptive hedonic utility. Working paper.

Roller, Steve (2012) "Let's write a swimming pool," *American Writers and Artists Inc.*, www.awai.com/2012/02/lets-write-a-swimming-pool/.

Rose, Arnold M. (1957) "A study of irrational judgments," *Journal of Political Economy*, Vol. 65, No. 5, pp. 394–402.

Ross, Michael and Fiore Sicoly (1979) "Egocentric biases in availability and attribution," *Journal of Personality and Social Psychology*, Vol. 37, No. 3, p. 322.

Rousseau, Jean-Jacques (1755/1999) *Discourse on the origin of inequality.* Oxford University Press.

Roymans, Nico (2017) "A Roman massacre in the far north: Caesar's annihilation of the Tencteri and Usipetes in the Dutch river area," in M. Fernández-Götz and N. Roymans, eds., *Conflict archaeology: Materialities of collective violence from prehistory to Late Antiquity.* Routledge, pp. 167–181.

Rubin, Paul H. and Chris W. Paul (1979) "An evolutionary model of taste for risk," *Economic Inquiry*, Vol. 17, No. 4, pp. 585–596.

Rubinstein, Ariel (1989) "The Electronic Mail Game: Strategic Behavior under 'almost common knowledge'," *The American Economic Review* Vol. 79, No. 3, pp. 385–391.

Saleh, Mohamed (2018) "On the road to heaven: Taxation, conversions, and the Coptic-Muslim socioeconomic gap in medieval Egypt," *The Journal of Economic History*, Vol. 78, No. 2, pp. 394–434.

Sally, David (2005) "Can I say 'bobobo' and mean 'There's no such thing as cheap talk'?" *Journal of Economic Behavior & Organization*, Vol. 57, No. 3, pp. 245–266.

Samuels, Richard, Stephen Stich and Michael Bishop (2002) "Ending the rationality wars: How to make disputes about human rationality disappear," in Renee Elio, ed., *Common sense, reasoning and rationality.* Oxford University Press.

Samuelson, Larry (2004) "Information-based relative consumption effects," *Econometrica*, Vol. 72, No. 1, pp. 93–118.

Samuelson, Larry and Jeroen M. Swinkels (2006) "Information, evolution and utility," *Theoretical Economics*, Vol. 1, No. 1, pp. 119–142.

Samuelson, Paul A (1937) "A. note on measurement of utility," *The Review of Economic Studies*, Vol. 4, No. 2, pp. 155–161.

——— (1950) "Probability and the attempts to measure utility," *Economic Review (Japanese)*, Vol. 1, No. 3, pp. 167–173.

——— (1952) "Probability, utility, and the independence axiom," *Econometrica*, Vol. 20, No. 4, pp. 670–678.

Savage, L. J. (1954). *The foundations of statistics*. Wiley.

Savage, Leonard J. (1951) "The theory of statistical decision," *Journal of the American Statistical Association*, Vol. 46, No. 253, pp. 55–67.

——— (1972) *The foundations of statistics*. Courier Corporation.

Sayer, Andrew (1997) "Essentialism, social constructionism, and beyond," *The Sociological Review*, Vol. 45, No. 3, pp. 453–487.

Schauer, Frederick and Richard J. Zeckhauser (2007) "Paltering," SSRN working paper, http://ssrn.com/abstract=832634.

Schelling, Thomas C. (1960/1980) *The strategy of conflict*. Harvard University Press.

Schipper, Burkhard C. (2014) "Unawareness: A gentle introduction to both the literature and the special issue," *Mathematical Social Sciences*, Vol. 70, pp. 1–9.

Schkade, David A. and Daniel Kahneman (1998) "Does living in California make people happy? A focusing illusion in judgments of life satisfaction," *Psychological Science*, Vol. 9, No. 5, pp. 340–346.

Schmeidler, David (1989) "Subjective probability and expected utility without additivity," *Econometrica*, pp. 571–587.

Schroeder, Juliana, Eugene M. Caruso and Nicholas Epley (2016) "Many hands make overlooked work: Over-claiming of responsibility increases with group size," *Journal of Experimental Psychology: Applied*, Vol. 22, No. 2, p. 238.

Schultz, Wolfram (2007) "Behavioral dopamine signals," *Trends in Neurosciences*, Vol. 30, No. 5, pp. 203–210.

Schwardmann, Peter and Joel Van der Weele (2019) "Deception and self-deception," Nature Human Behaviour, Vol. 3, No. 10, pp. 1055–1061.

Schwarz, Norbert, Fritz Strack, Denis Hilton and Gabi Naderer (1991) "Base rates, representativeness, and the logic of conversation: The contextual relevance of 'irrelevant' information," *Social Cognition*, Vol. 9, No. 1, pp. 67–84.

Seabright, Paul (2010) *The company of strangers: A natural history of economic life, revised edition*. Princeton University Press.

Sell, Aaron, John Tooby and Leda Cosmides (2009) "Formidability and the logic of human anger," *Proceedings of the National Academy of Sciences*, Vol. 106, No. 35, pp. 15073–15078.

Sen, Amartya (1993) "Internal consistency of choice," *Econometrica*, Vol. 61, No. 3, pp. 495–521.

Shackle, G. L. S. (1941) "A means of promoting investment," *The Economic Journal*, Vol. 51, Nos. 202–203, pp. 249–260.

Shaffer, Dennis M., Scott M. Krauchunas, Marianna Eddy and Michael K. McBeath (2004) "How dogs navigate to catch Frisbees," *Psychological Science*, Vol. 15, No. 7, pp. 437–441.

Sharot, Tali, Cristina M. Velasquez and Raymond J. Dolan (2010) "Do decisions shape preference? Evidence from blind choice," *Psychological Science*, Vol. 21, No. 9, pp. 1231–1235.

Shayo, Moses (2009) "A model of social identity with an application to political economy: Nation, class, and redistribution," *American Political Science Review*, Vol. 103, No. 2, pp. 147–174.

(2020) "Social identity and economic policy," *Annual Review of Economics*, Vol. 12, pp. 355–389.

Shoda, Yuichi, Walter Mischel and Philip K. Peake (1990) "Predicting adolescent cognitive and self-regulatory competencies from preschool delay of gratification: Identifying diagnostic conditions.," *Developmental Psychology*, Vol. 26, No. 6, p. 978.

Shubik, Martin (1959) *Strategy and market structure: Competition, oligopoly, and the theory of games*. Wiley.

Simon, Herbert A. (1957) *Administrative behavior: A study of decision-making processes in administrative organization*. Macmillan.

Singer, Tania, Ben Seymour, John O'Doherty, Holger Kaube, Raymond J. Dolan and Chris D. Frith (2004) "Empathy for pain involves the affective but not sensory components of pain," *Science*, Vol. 303, No. 5661, pp. 1157–1162.

Skyrms, Brian (2001) "The stag hunt," in *Proceedings and Addresses of the American Philosophical Association*, Vol. 75, pp. 31–41. JSTOR.

Smith, Adam (1759/2010) *The theory of moral sentiments*. Penguin.

(1776/2019) *The wealth of nations*. Courier Dover Publications.

Smith, Megan K., Robert Trivers and William von Hippel (2017) "Self-deception facilitates interpersonal persuasion," *Journal of Economic Psychology*, Vol. 63, pp. 93–101.

Solda, Alice, Changxia Ke, Bill von Hippel and Lionel Page (2020) "Absolute vs. relative success: Why overconfidence is an inefficient equilibrium." Mimeo.

Solda, Alice, Changxia Ke, Lionel Page and Bill von Hippel (2019) "Strategically delusional," working paper, *GATE Lyon Saint-Etienne*.

Solnick, Sara J. and David Hemenway (1998) "Is more always better? A survey on positional concerns," *Journal of Economic Behavior & Organization*, Vol. 37, No. 3, pp. 373–383.

Soman, Dilip (2015) *The last mile: Creating social and economic value from behavioral insights*. University of Toronto Press.

Sozou, Peter D. (1998) "On hyperbolic discounting and uncertain hazard rates," *Proceedings of the Royal Society of London. Series B: Biological Sciences*, Vol. 265, No. 1409, pp. 2015–2020.

Sozou, Peter D. and Robert M. Seymour (2005) "Costly but worthless gifts facilitate courtship," *Proceedings of the Royal Society B: Biological Sciences*, Vol. 272, No. 1575, pp. 1877–1884.

Spencer, Herbert (1864) *The principles of biology*. Appleton.

Sperber, Dan (1994) "The modularity of thought and the epidemiology of representations," in J. Tooby, A. M. Leslie, D. Sperber, A. Caramazza, A. E. Hillis, E. C. Leek, M. Miozzo and L. Cosmides, eds., *Mapping the mind: Domain specificity in cognition and culture*. Cambridge University Press, pp. 39–67.

Spiegler, Rani (2019) "Behavioral economics and the atheoretical style," American Economic Journal: Microeconomics, Vol. 11, No. 2, pp. 173–194.

Spinoza, Benedict (1670/1958) *The political works*, ed. and trans. A. G. Wernham. Clarendon Press.

Stanford, P. Kyle (2018) "The difference between ice cream and Nazis: Moral external-ization and the evolution of human cooperation," *Behavioral and Brain Sciences*, Vol. 41, pp. 1–49.

Stanovich, Keith E. and Richard F. West (2000) "Individual differences in reasoning: Implications for the rationality debate?," *Behavioral and Brain Sciences*, Vol. 23, No. 5, pp. 645–665.

Steiner, Jakub and Colin Stewart (2016) "Perceiving prospects properly," *American Economic Review*, Vol. 106, No. 7, pp. 1601–1631.

Stewart-Williams, Steve (2018) *The ape that understood the universe: How the mind and culture evolve*. Cambridge University Press.

Stigler, George (1981) "Economics or ethics?," in Sterling M. McMurrin, ed., *The Tanner lectures on human values*, Vol. 2. University of Utah Press, pp. 143–191.

Stigler, George J. and Gary S. Becker (1977) "De gustibus non est disputandum," *The American Economic Review*, Vol. 67, No. 2, pp. 76–90.

Straub, Paul G. and J. Keith Murnighan (1995) "An experimental investigation of ulti-matum games: Information, fairness, expectations, and lowest acceptable offers," *Journal of Economic Behavior & Organization*, Vol. 27, No. 3, pp. 345–364.

Strotz, Robert Henry (1955) "Myopia and inconsistency in dynamic utility maximiza-tion," *The Review of Economic Studies*, Vol. 23, No. 3, pp. 165–180.

Sugden, Robert (1985) "Why be consistent? A critical analysis of consistency require-ments in choice theory," *Economica*, Vol. 52, No. 206, pp. 167–183.

(1991) "Rational choice: A survey of contributions from economics and philosophy," *The Economic Journal*, Vol. 101, No. 407, pp. 751–785.

(2003) "The logic of team reasoning," *Philosophical Explorations*, Vol. 6, No. 3, pp. 165–181.

Sunstein, Cass R. and Adrian Vermeule (2009) "Conspiracy theories: Causes and cures," *Journal of Political Philosophy*, Vol. 17, No. 2, pp. 202–227.

Svenson, Ola (1981) "Are we all less risky and more skillful than our fellow drivers?" *Acta psychologica*, Vol. 47, No. 2, pp. 143–148.

Sznycer, Daniel and Aaron W. Lukaszewski (2019) "The emotion–valuation constella-tion: Multiple emotions are governed by a common grammar of social valuation," *Evolution and Human Behavior*, Vol. 40, No. 4, pp. 395–404.

Tajfel, Henri (1970) "Experiments in intergroup discrimination," *Scientific American*, Vol. 223, No. 5, pp. 96–103.

(1974) "Social identity and intergroup behaviour," *Information (International Social Science Council)*, Vol. 13, No. 2, pp. 65–93.

Tajfel, Henri, John C. Turner, William G. Austin and Stephen Worchel (2004) "An integrative theory of intergroup conflict," in M. J. Hatch and M. Schultz, eds., Oxford. *Organizational identity: A reader*. Oxford University Press, p. 65.

Tanner-Smith, E. E., S. J. Wilson and M. W. Lipsey (2013) "Risk factors and crime," in The Oxford handbook of criminological theory. Oxford University Press, pp. 89–111.

Taylor, Shelley E. and Jonathon D. Brown (1988) "Illusion and well-being: A social psychological perspective on mental health," *Psychological Bulletin*, Vol. 103, No. 2, p. 193.

Tenenbaum, Joshua B., Thomas L. Griffiths et al. (2001) "The rational basis of representativeness," in *Proceedings of the 23rd annual conference of the Cognitive Science Society*. Erlbaum, pp. 1036–1041.

Teoh, Siew Hong and Chuan Yang Hwang (1991) "Nondisclosure and adverse disclosure as signals of firm value," *The Review of Financial Studies*, Vol. 4, No. 2, pp. 283–313.

Thaler, Richard H. (2015) *Misbehaving: The making of behavioral economics*. W. W. Norton.

(2016) "Behavioral economics: Past, present, and future," *American Economic Review*, Vol. 106, No. 7, pp. 1577–1600.

Tooby, John and Leda Cosmides (1990) "The past explains the present: Emotional adaptations and the structure of ancestral environments," *Ethology and Sociobiology*, Vol. 11, Nos. 4–5, pp. 375–424.

Train, Kenneth E. (2009) *Discrete choice methods with simulation*. Cambridge University Press.

Trivers, R. L. (1976) "Foreword," in R. Dawkins, *The selfish gene*. Oxford University Press, pp. xiv–xx.

Trivers, Robert (1972) "Parental investment and sexual selection," in *Sexual Selection and the descent of man*. Aldine de Gruyter, pp. 136–179.

Trivers, Robert L. (1971) "The evolution of reciprocal altruism," *The Quarterly Review of Biology*, Vol. 46, No. 1, pp. 35–57.

Tung, Ka-Kit (2007) *Topics in mathematical modeling*. Princeton University Press.

Turmunkh, Uyanga, Martijn J. van den Assem and Dennie Van Dolder (2019) "Malleable lies: Communication and cooperation in a high stakes TV game show," *Management Science*, Vol. 65, No. 10, pp. 4795–4812.

Turner, John C. (1996) "Henri Tajfel: An introduction," in W. P. Robinson and H. Tajfel, H. eds., *Social groups and identities: Developing the legacy of Henri Tajfel*. Psychology Press, p. 23.

Tversky, A. and D. Kahneman (1982) "Judgments of and by representativeness (No. TR-3)," in D. Kahneman, P. Slovic and A. Tversky, eds., *Judgment under uncertainty: Heuristics and biases*. Cambridge University Press.

Tversky, Amos (1969) "Intransitivity of preferences," *Psychological Review*, Vol. 76, No. 1, p. 31.

Tversky, Amos and Daniel Kahneman (1974) "Judgment under uncertainty: Heuristics and biases," *Science*, Vol. 185, No. 4157, pp. 1124–1131.

(1992) "Advances in prospect theory: Cumulative representation of uncertainty," *Journal of Risk and Uncertainty*, Vol. 5, No. 4, pp. 297–323.

Tversky, Amos and Itamar Simonson (1993) "Context-dependent preferences," *Management Science*, Vol. 39, No. 10, pp. 1179–1189.

Van den Steen, Eric (2004) "Rational overoptimism (and other biases)," *American Economic Review*, Vol. 94, No. 4, pp. 1141–1151.

van Prooijen, Jan-Willem and Mark van Vugt (2018) "Conspiracy theories: Evolved functions and psychological mechanisms," *Perspectives on Psychological Science*, Vol. 13, No. 6, pp. 770–788.

Veblen, Thorstein (1899/2017) *The theory of the leisure class*. Routledge.

von Böhm-Bawerk, Eugen (1891) *The positive theory of capital*. G. E. Stechert.

von Hippel, William (2018) *The social leap*. HarperCollins.

von Hippel, William, Ernest Baker, Robbie Wilson, Loic Brin and Lionel Page (2016) "Detecting deceptive behaviour after the fact," *British Journal of Social Psychology*, Vol. 55, No. 2, pp. 195–205.

Von Hippel, William and Robert Trivers (2011) "The evolution and psychology of self-deception," *Behavioral and Brain Sciences*, Vol. 34, No. 1, p. 1.

von Neumann, John and Oskar Morgenstern (1944) *Theory of games and economic behavior*. Princeton University Press.

Vorzimmer, Peter (1969) "Darwin, Malthus, and the theory of natural selection," *Journal of the History of Ideas*, Vol. 30, No. 4, pp. 527–542.

Wakker, Peter P. (1989) *Additive representations of preferences: A new foundation of decision analysis*, Vol. 4. Springer Science + Business Media.

(2010) *Prospect theory: For risk and ambiguity*: Cambridge University Press.

Wald, Abraham (1945) "Sequential tests of statistical hypotheses," *The Annals of Mathematical Statistics*, Vol. 16, No. 2, pp. 117–186.

Wald, Abraham and Jacob Wolfowitz (1948) "Optimum character of the sequential probability ratio test," *The Annals of Mathematical Statistics*, Vol. 19, No. 3, pp. 326–339.

Watts, Tyler W., Greg J. Duncan and Haonan Quan (2018) "Revisiting the marshmallow test: A conceptual replication investigating links between early delay of gratification and later outcomes," *Psychological Science*, Vol. 29, No. 7, pp. 1159–1177.

Webb, Ryan (2018) "The (neural) dynamics of stochastic choice," *Management Science*, Vol. 65, No. 1, pp. 230–255.

Weber, Max (1915/1953) *The religion of China. Confucianism and Taoism*. Free Press.

Weinstein, Neil D. (1980) "Unrealistic optimism about future life events," *Journal of Personality and Social Psychology*, Vol. 39, No. 5, p. 806.

Weiss, Yair, Eero P. Simoncelli and Edward H. Adelson (2002) "Motion illusions as optimal percepts," *Nature Neuroscience*, Vol. 5, No. 6, pp. 598–604.

Wernerfelt, Birger (1995) "A rational reconstruction of the compromise effect: Using market data to infer utilities," *Journal of Consumer Research*, Vol. 21, No. 4, pp. 627–633.

White, Matthew (2011) *The great big book of horrible things*. Norton.

Wilcox, Nathaniel T. (2008) "Stochastic models for binary discrete choice under risk: A critical primer and econometric comparison," in *Risk aversion in experiments*, pp. 197–292, Emerald Group..

Wilson, David Sloan and Elliott Sober (1994) "Reintroducing group selection to the human behavioral sciences," *Behavioral and Brain Sciences*, Vol. 17, No. 4, pp. 585–607.

Winter, Eyal (2014) *Feeling smart: Why our emotions are more rational than we think*. PublicAffairs.

Woodford, Michael (2012a) "Inattentive valuation and reference-dependent choice." Report, Columbia Academic Commons, https://academiccommons.columbia.edu/doi/10.7916/D8VD6XVK.

(2012b) "Prospect theory as efficient perceptual distortion," *American Economic Review*, Vol. 102, No. 3, pp. 41–46.

World Health Organization (2018) *Global status report on road safety 2015*. World Health Organization.

Yaari, M. E. (1985) "On the role of 'Dutch books' in the theory of choice under risk." Nancy L. Schwartz Memorial Lecture, J. L. Kellogg Graduate School of Management, Northwestern University.

Yaari, Menahem E. (1987) "The dual theory of choice under risk," *Econometrica*, pp. 95–115.

Yamagishi, Toshio, Yutaka Horita, Nobuhiro Mifune, Hirofumi Hashimoto, Yang Li, Mizuho Shinada, Arisa Miura, Keigo Inukai, Haruto Takagishi and Dora Simunovic (2012) "Rejection of unfair offers in the ultimatum game is no evidence of strong reciprocity," *Proceedings of the National Academy of Sciences*, Vol. 109, No. 50, pp. 20364–20368.

Yamagishi, Toshio and Nobuhiro Mifune (2016) "Parochial altruism: Does it explain modern human group psychology?," *Current Opinion in Psychology*, Vol. 7, pp. 39–43.

Yzerbyt, Vincent (2016) "Intergroup stereotyping," *Current Opinion in Psychology*, Vol. 11, pp. 90–95.

Zahavi, Amotz (1975) "Mate selection: A selection for a handicap," *Journal of Theoretical Biology*, Vol. 53, No. 1, pp. 205–214.

Zietsch, Brendan P., Ralf Kuja-Halkola, Hasse Walum and Karin J. H. Verweij (2014) "Perfect genetic correlation between number of offspring and grandoffspring in an industrialized human population," *Proceedings of the National Academy of Sciences*, Vol. 111, No. 3, pp. 1032–1036.

Zimring, Franklin E. and Gordon Hawkins (1999) *Crime is not the problem: Lethal violence in America.* Oxford University Press.

Zizzo, Daniel John and Andrew J. Oswald (2001) "Are people willing to pay to reduce others' incomes?," *Annales d'Economie et de Statistique*, Nos. 63–64, pp. 39–65.

Made in United States
Orlando, FL
30 August 2024